MILITANT TRICKS

MILITANT TRICKS

BATTLEFIELD RUSES OF THE ISLAMIC INSURGENT

ILLUSTRATED

H. JOHN POOLE

FOREWORD BY

MAJ.GEN. RAY L. SMITH USMC (RET.)

POSTERITY
PRESS

Published by Posterity Press
P.O. Box 5360, Emerald Isle, NC 28594
(www.posteritypress.org)

Cataloging-in-Publication Data
Poole, H. John, 1943-
Militant Tricks.
    Includes bibliography and index.
    1. Infantry drill and tactics.
    2. Military art and science.
    3. Military history.
I. Title.   ISBN-10: 0-9638695-8-2   2005   355'.42
             ISBN-13: 978-0-9638695-8-6
Library of Congress Control Number: 2005904238

Cover art © 2005 by Michael Leahy
Edited by Dr. Mary Beth Poole
Proofread by William E. Harris

Third printing, United States of America, January 2007

To all the U.S. service personnel who have already made the ultimate sacrifice in the "War on Terror."

Lure the tiger off the mountain.
—Third Stratagem for Attack

(Source: *DA PAM 550-175* (September, 1988), p. 43)

Contents

Illustrations

Maps

Figures

Foreword

John Poole's new book, *Militant Tricks,* provides a detailed "blueprint for victory" in not only Iraq, but also Afghanistan. Over the last year, many war veterans (myself included) have become quite concerned with our new enemy's degree of resilience. While U.S. fighting men have continued to show great resolve on the battlefield, the Muslim militants' method involves more than just ground combat. It sadly qualifies as 4th-Generation Warfare (4GW)—that which is fought in the arenas of politics/media, religion/psychology, and economics/infrastructure as well. To beat it, we must excel in all areas at once. Compounding the problem is the terrorist overseer's apparent mastery of all forms of deception. In *Militant Tricks,* Poole cuts through that deception to reveal the overseer's true face and actual plan. While fleeing superior firepower, his insurgent proxies have nonetheless created enough of a diversion to facilitate other 4GW gains. To facilitate an answer, Poole enumerates those gains.

The most strategically important ground in either theater of war is the cities. They must be captured and held—not in the old-fashioned way of mechanized assault and protective barbed wire, but in the new way of community involvement. U.S. forces must replace the vehicular patrolling of urban zones with joint (U.S./ Iraqi police and army) garrisons in every tiny neighborhood. This will give the insurgents vastly fewer IED targets. It will halve the Coalition's fuel needs. It will displace the radical elements who currently control those neighborhoods. And, most importantly, it will help their citizens to restore local infrastructure and basic services.

So wide a distribution of U.S. forces may sound dangerous, but it really isn't. The urban defense is the strongest of all tactical mediums. Poole's Chapter 13 provides a state-of-the-art defensive maneuver. His Chapter 15 shows how every American soldier and

Marine, whether infantry or combat-service support, could be quickly prepared for such a mission. Within his scheme is even a way to quell the recently reported subversion of Iraqi police and army units. Once the people in each neighborhood see that the local momentum has shifted, they will provide more real-time human intelligence to their liberators and band together to rid themselves of any radical element.

As commander of the first replacement battalion into Beirut after the 1983 Marine Barracks bombing, I had a feeling I would see that particular enemy again. According to Poole, he and his hidden sponsor are behind much of the trouble in Iraq and Afghanistan today. For all Americans who want to see his so-far-successful method defeated, I can't recommend this book highly enough.

M.GEN. RAY L. SMITH USMC (RET.)

Preface

After 9/11, the word *"al-Qaeda"* became irreversibly lodged in every American's mind. The United States was again under attack, but by whom? *Al-Qaeda* was more of a movement than it was an organization. Its methods were neither new nor particularly sophisticated. They were simply the product of a century-old Asian search for what the West would consider to be "asymmetric" warfare. To counter those methods, one has only to think like an Asian. But thinking like an Asian is not something that comes easily to American soldiers or Marines. That's why—in Vietnam—they diligently prepared for human-wave assaults, while lone sappers repeatedly destroyed their strategic assets.[1] In the Orient, negotiation is not the antithesis of battle, it is an extension. The United States should have learned that at Pearl Harbor. Yet—to this day—it cooperates with avowed enemies of Western culture. Deception is the hallmark of the Eastern style of war. To succeed in Iraq and Afghanistan, America must become more familiar with the particulars of that deception. Then, it must counter the militants' tricks without compromising its own integrity.

Literally translated, *al-Qaeda* means "the base." The word "base" plays a dual-role in Communist writing. When capitalized, it applies to a huge guerrilla region. When uncapitalized, it means the hidden (often subterranean) headquarters of an individual cell.[2] Thus, one suspects a word game with *"al-Qaeda."* If *al-Qaeda* were simply a "front" or "umbrella" for the actual dispensers of terror, then the United States would have less chance of finding them. That explains why *al-Qaeda* takes credit for everything that happens. By providing strategic guidance and tactical technique, *al-Qaeda* does function as a pseudo-headquarters for any aspiring cell to visit its websites. To those who ask, it will sometimes dispatch money, advisers/instructors, and equipment. But *al-Qaeda* is not an army by any stretch of the imagination. It is the self-professed leader of a fringe-element alliance formed in 1998—the International Islamic

Front for the Jihad against Jews and Crusaders (IIFJ). Most of its heavy work is done by movements, agencies, and nations (several Shiite) that—through *al-Qaeda's* umbrella—manage to remain anonymous. Among IIFJ's acknowledged members are Egypt's *Jamaat al-Islamia* and *al-Jihad,* Lebanon's *Hezbollah*, Palestine's *Hamas*, and Pakistan's *Harakat ul-Mujahideen (HUM)* and *Lashkar e-Ansar.*[3] *HUM's* parent is the *Jamaat-e-Ulema-e-Islami Fazlur Rehman (JUI/F)* party.[4] *Lashkar e-Ansar* may have been a short-lived alias for *Lashkar e-Toiba (LET)*. If so, its parent is Pakistan's *Markaz-ud-Dawa-wal-Irshad (MDI)* group. Or it could have been an alias for *Lashkar-e-Jhangvi (LJ)*. Then, its parent is the *Sipah-i-Sahaba Pakistan (SSP)* group.[5] One reference shows both *LET* and *LJ* in the IIFJ.[6] Many of the so-called *al-Qaeda* training camps were nothing more than religious-party facilities with an *al-Qaeda* presence. These groups and parties are dangerous, but all work for larger entities.

To win the "War on Terror," America must go after those larger entities. They are the ones with infrastructure and substance. By never centralizing control, al-*Qaeda* has virtually guaranteed its own limited role. Its media blitz would continue if bin Laden and al-Zawahiri were both killed on the same day. For what happens on the ground in Iraq and Afghanistan, *al-Qaeda* depends on the larger, movements, agencies, and nations beneath its umbrella. Its own disjointed, "bottom-up" structure makes it all but immune to attack. Its core cadre of advisers/recruiters/trainers can quickly mend whichever relationship gets damaged. *Al-Qaeda* has now evolved into the Eastern equivalent of a "dummy headquarters." Its way of operating confuses the Western, "top-down" thinker.

"Al-Qaeda's training program is designed to create self-contained cells that operate independently of a central command."[7] The job of those cells is to draw the attention of America and its Coalition partners away from the larger entities beneath the umbrella. As the cells create horrific headlines, their spokesmen promise an end to the violence as soon as Western occupiers leave Muslim lands. Within every peace initiative resides a veiled threat.

> To the people of the crusader coalition . . . Sheikh Osama has offered you a truce so that you leave Muslim land. As he said you will not dream of security until we live it as a reality in Palestine.[8]
> — *Al-Qaeda's* al-Zawahiri after London bombings

What *al-Qaeda* really wants is an end to all Western influence in South Asia, the Middle East, and North Africa. This would give the larger, unseen entities beneath its umbrella free rein to reestablish the old Muslim empire. These fall into four categories: (1) expansionist nations, (2) rogue agencies, (3) fundamentalist movements, and (4) armed militias. It is they that must be dealt with abroad to stop the violence at home. Unfortunately, many have become more skilled at political hardball (to include vote rigging) than they are at battlefield maneuvers. As those larger entities are beaten at their own game, their fearsome umbrella will lose its imaginary power.

The U.S. military may be killing more people than it is losing in Iraq and Afghanistan, but—in a guerrilla war—that does not ensure victory. In it, more depends on whether basic services and infrastructure can be restored. From June 2004 to June 2005 in Iraq (after 7.9 billion dollars in relief and reconstruction aid), there was little improvement in security. Over the same period, oil production was down 95,000 barrels, oil revenue off $0.67 billion, electricity less by 258 megawatts, and inflation up 10.8 percent.[9] One year after the return of sovereignty to the Iraqis, 40% had enough water and 25% had reliable electricity.[10] Thus, while U.S. troops have been displaying plenty of courage and determination, their commanders must keep looking for a viable strategy. This book provides some very promising tactical alternatives.

If all human interactions are based on perceptions, then one must learn the perceptions of his enemy. To satisfactorily conclude the wars in Iraq and Afghanistan, many U.S. military leaders must change how they view the world. First, they must acknowledge the greater role that morality plays in the waging of a 21st-Century war. Then, they must realize that their straightforward, "big-picture" approach to problem solving is not shared by the enemy. This book has been written to help all U.S. soldiers and Marines to decipher—from the standpoint of Eastern deception—what the Muslim militant has, or has not, accomplished between September 2004 and September 2005.

The Morality Factor

Wars are dangerous. Though sometimes required to stop a determined aggressor, they can still lead to moral error. While initially meeting all four of the Christian "just-war" prerequisites,[11] they can subsequently stray in their prosecution. The armed resistance in Iraq and Afghanistan may seem amateurish and barbaric, but it sadly qualifies as "fourth-generation warfare (4GW)"—that which spills over into the arenas of religion/psychology, politics/media, and economics/infrastructure. To achieve a final victory in this type of war, U.S. commanders must strictly follow a moral compass. Without it, their overall mission (of restoring peace) may be in as much jeopardy as their spiritual health. They will be tempted to do three things: (1) distort the truth, (2) intensify the violence, and (3) overprotect the infantrymen.

Truth is generally acknowledged to be the first casualty of war. Commanders are tempted to downplay any battlefield setback so as not to demoralize their personnel, give comfort to the enemy, or disclose some unit deficiency. If they downplay often enough, their parent organization may never realize the need for corrective action.

To curtail the bloodshed, commanders are next tempted to increase the level of violence. Fortunately, wars are not won by killing. They are won by destroying the enemy's strategic assets. With a nondeceptive foe and accurate intelligence, one might do that with precision munitions. But a satellite cannot tell whether a suspected safe house has filled with enemy fighters or orphaned children. Only a nearby ground observer can do that. Thus, in populated areas, battles are most morally waged by dismounted infantrymen. The frontline soldier can exercise last-second mercy, whereas an aircraft-launched "smart" bomb cannot.

To take fewer casualties, commanders are finally tempted to bombard everything in their path. As this can kill many civilians, they face a moral quandary. What makes the life of the liberator more valuable than the life of the person being liberated? It isn't the local housewife's fault that she cannot control some of her countrymen. To comply with the "morality of battle," one needs infantrymen with enough skill to safely maneuver without preliminary bombardment. Just as policemen cannot destroy a hostage-taker's building, peacekeepers cannot level a terrorist-occupied tenement.

In essence, "just" wars must be waged in a Christian manner. Otherwise, they can cause more problems than they solve. In *Crossing the Threshold of Hope,* Pope John Paul II explains the paradox.

[T]he hypothesis of legitimate defense, which never concerns

an innocent but always and only an unjust aggressor, must respect the principle that moralists call the *principium inculpatae tutelae* (the principle of nonculpable defense). In order to be legitimate, the "defense" must be carried out in a way that causes the least damage and, if possible, saves the life of the aggressor.[12]
— His Holiness John Paul II, 1995

Implicit in the Pope's edict is the concurrent protection of noncombatants. Whether precision weaponry can succeed in this regard depends on the accuracy of intelligence, dynamics of blast, and proximity of bystanders. Electronic imaging can't distinguish man from woman, rifle from rake, or survival instinct from criminal intent; ground troops can. America will need squads with enough skill and authority to single-handedly police a small neighborhood. U.S. commanders can make this possible by better educating their junior enlisted personnel on Christian principles, Islamic culture, militant tactics, obscure movement, and minimal force. This is a new kind of war—one in which the body of knowledge must shape the political agenda instead of the other way around. U.S. soldiers and Marines cannot afford the luxury of political correctness. To have the best chance of defeating a determined foe, they must deal strictly with facts. To help those soldiers and Marines arrive at those facts, this book offers an alternative perspective on events in Iraq and Afghanistan. The enemy there is highly deceptive. He routinely works through the news media to further his cause. Thus, much of what he admits to may be a ruse. It is not the intent of this book to discredit the popular perception of the situation, but rather to enhance it.

The Indirect, "Little-Picture" Approach to Warfare

Iraq is in Asia Minor. Asians are indirect, "little-picture" thinkers. Instead of earth-moving equipment, they used thousands of coolies to build a 600-mile road through almost impenetrable jungle in 1954. In just three months, they linked their Chinese supply depot with Dien Bien Phu.[13] To hide their road from the French, they pulled the tree branches together.

Like it or not, America's approach to governmental bureaucracy is of "top-down" French and British origin. Thus, U.S. military leaders are (for the most part) direct, "big-picture" thinkers. For the last 100 years, they have taken the most direct approach to war—overwhelming the opposition with firepower. In response, their perennial adversaries have come up with an obscure way to fight. It consists of a thousand tiny cuts, none of which a "big-picture" thinker deems worthy of his attention. For certain victory, the Easterner throws in ruses. To see how effective the dual strategy can be, one must analyze a long string of minor events.

The Research Method

The military heritage of Asia Minor is quite different from that of France, Britain, and America. In Asia Minor, loose encirclements and tiny probes are more common than mass assaults. There, one can often win while running away. Such paradoxical tactics come from the Mongols. They controlled what is now Iran, Iraq, and Afghanistan for over 200 years. When Genghis Khan became the emperor of China in 1227 A.D.,[14] his armies learned of the *36 Stratagems of Deception*. Dating back to 200 B.C.,[15] most are based on the *yin-yang* antitheses of the *I Ching* (Book of Changes). Like the Chinese, southwest Asian insurgents practice the "False Face and Art of Delay." First, they show the Westerner what they want him to see. Then, they wait for him to make the first, incorrect move. Finally, they secretly launch a maneuver that he would not choose under similar circumstances. To fight people like this, Western soldiers must learn which feints precede what secret maneuvers. Part One sets the stage for the investigation with the latest news from Iraq and Afghanistan. Part Two works through the famous *36 Stratagems* to uncover enemy ruses. Part Three shows how to counteract those ruses.

Some may find such an approach too farfetched. They are reminded that *al-Qaeda*, Lebanese *Hezbollah*, Palestinian *Hamas*, and Iranian Revolutionary Guard leaders have regularly met in Sudan since the early 1990's, and that upwards of 4000 Chinese military personnel have been stationed in Sudan since the year 2000. They are further reminded that Iran regularly sends its Revolutionary Guard leaders to North Korea for psychological warfare training.[16]

The Book's Utility

Parts of this book are heavily detailed. It takes that much detail to see beyond the Muslim militant's "false face." Until Western military strategists acknowledge the obscure particulars of his so-far-successful method, they will be unable to do much about it. As America's frontline fighters better understand his ruses, they should be able to slow his momentum. If the U.S. Marine Corps and U.S. Army were further willing to shift from a headquarters-driven (standardized) way of training their infantry squads to a unit-generated (experimental) approach, they could still win both wars.

For those deeply committed to defeating the Iraqi and Afghan insurgencies, this book will be spellbinding. For everyone else, it should be treated as an intelligence reference manual—to be read a few paragraphs at a time. Specifically, it covers what the world media and regional literature have discovered about the enemy. *Militant Tricks* is not intended as a literary offering, but rather as a tool with which America's finest can more quickly prevail.

H. JOHN POOLE

Acknowledgments

Once again, most of the credit for this work goes to a free society and loving God. While that God may not totally agree with America's approach to the "War on Terror," He most certainly wants it concluded. It is different from other wars in that its outcome depends more upon civilian perceptions than upon military power. That is why its political, economic, and religious aspects are so important.

The overseers of worldwide terrorism are masters of deception. They will stop at nothing to maintain plausible deniability. To study them, one must abandon preconceived notions, delve into Eastern culture, and shuffle details. This book attempts to extract—from international literature—the overseers' trail of evidence. That trail necessarily includes pieces of partially verified information. A picture emerges that is strikingly different from the official viewpoint. The whole truth must lie somewhere in between. Thus, there is no insinuation of U.S. cover-up or collusion, merely of misinterpreted intelligence and bureaucratic inertia.

It has been said that God withholds from each of His children the whole picture on any given subject so that all will know their place. To unravel a mystery as convoluted as the one in Southwest Asia, one needs collective insight. Many people of every description therefore helped with this work. It is hoped that their combined viewpoint has been accurately portrayed.

Part One

The Ongoing War on Terror

"Our policy, strategy, tactics, et cetera, are still screwed up."
— Gen. Anthony C. Zinni USMC (Ret.)
former CENTCOM commander, 2004

(Source: "For Zinni, a War That Ignores the Facts," by Thomas E. Ricks, *The Washington Post,* nat. weekly ed., 12-18 January 2004, p. 9)

1 The Deteriorating Situation in Iraq

- *In which ways have the insurgents succeeded?*
- *Have U.S. forces adapted quickly enough?*

THE BATTLE FOR THE "GREEN ZONE"

(Source: Courtesy of Sorman Info. & Media, illustration by Wolfgang Bartsch, from *SoldF: Soldaten i falt,* © 2001 Forsvarsmakten, Stockholm, p. 293)

Appearances Can Be Deceiving in Southwest Asia Too

While ostensibly crude, the Muslim militant's method has never been defeated. Through multiple deception and continual mutation, it has so far bested Russia in Afghanistan and Chechnya, Israel in Southern Lebanon and Gaza, and the United States in Beirut and Mogadishu. To finally defeat that method, every deployed (or about-to-be-deployed) GI must become thoroughly familiar with its latest configuration. That will take a good, hard look at all that has happened over the last year.

In Iraq, U.S. forces have won every firefight and killed thou-

3

sands of Islamic fighters. (See Map 1.1.) Unfortunately, wars are not won by occupying nonstrategic ground or killing opposition soldiers. They are won by destroying the enemy's "strategic assets." Eastern insurgents don't have many strategic assets. Whatever they need, they can generally take from a well-supplied adversary. To make matters worse, they have the edge in a 4th-generation-

Map 1.1: Iraqi Provinces

(Source: Courtesy of General Libraries, University of Texas at Austin, from their website for map designator "iraq_pol99.pdf")

warfare (4GW) environment—one in which combat/tactics, religion/ psychology, politics/media, and economics/infrastructure all come into play. In a densely populated area, they are virtually immune to electronic surveillance and precision bombardment. Every time their pursuer overreacts, he damages local infrastructure and loses popular support. As such, Eastern insurgents develop a full portfolio of battlefield feints.

What has, or has not, occurred in Iraq deserves a closer look from this perspective. Marco Polo did, after all, warn of the diabolical mysteries of Upper Persia. Could U.S. forces have "won" every firefight in Iraq and still be losing the war? They were equally lethal and never driven from the field in Vietnam.

Within the context of Eastern intrigue, Iraq's future looks far less certain than one might think. The U.S. military has had trouble countering its new foe's propensity for chaos and deception. To do so now, it must identify, analyze, and compare every one of his strategic initiatives between September 2004 to September 2005. For many, there was a hidden objective, subtle diversion, and secret maneuver.

The Muslim Militants' So-Far-Successful Equation

The Iraqi "insurgency" is not the first regional *jihad* against a "high-tech" invader. Its architects have drawn on the lessons of Southern Lebanon, Afghanistan, and Chechnya. Their initial strategy is the same as it was there—to create chaos. By so doing, they hope to bankrupt the occupier, discredit the government, and manipulate the people. Since the U.S. invasion of Iraq, the opposition has done whatever it could to disrupt the everyday workings of that country. It has crippled the infrastructure, discouraged foreign aid, and terrorized the population. All the while, it has managed to create the impression that someone else was to blame. For the U.S. to succeed in Iraq, it must first discover how this "projection" of complicity has been accomplished. Below are the first two of this chapter's many examples.

When the Iraqi militants blew up five Christian churches on 16 October 2004, they managed to turn many parishioners against the Americans. Those parishioners blamed U.S. forces for not being able to provide security. Some went so far as to say that America needed chaos as a reason to stay in Iraq.[1]

Three days later, longtime CARE (Cooperative for Assistance and Relief Everywhere) representative Margaret Hassan was kidnapped. Threatened with beheading, she pled for the release of female prisoners and the removal of British forces.[2] Again, she was portrayed as the villain.

While the Iraqi insurgency has any number of diverse participants, it still appears to be following a master plan of deception. To unravel that plan, one must turn back the clock to the spring of 2004.

At First, the Shiites and Sunnis Appeared to Be Taking Turns

Things first started to heat up when four U.S. contractors were butchered at Sunni-dominated Fallujah in late March 2004. Then, al-Sadr launched a Shiite rebellion at Baqubah, East Baghdad, Muqdadiyah, Al Kut, Najaf, Kufah, Karbala, Nasiriyah, and Al'Amarah. (See Map 1.2.) When soldiers of the former regime promised to restore order to Fallujah, U.S. forces suspended their initial assault on that city. In May, they began to take back the government facilities that had been captured by al-Sadr's "Mahdi Army" in other cities. Though al-Sadr quickly agreed to vacate those facilities, his men violated the cease fire on 10 June by attacking a Najaf police station.[3]

In compliance with U.N. Security Council resolution, "full sovereignty" was passed from the Coalition Provisional Authority (CPA) to the new Iraqi government on 28 June. Al-Sadr announced support for the new government, but his actions spoke otherwise. On 29 June, his forces captured and released 25 policemen in Najaf.[4] Two days later, they were contesting the Al'Amarah police.[5] On 4 July, al-Sadr declared the new regime illegitimate and vowed to keep fighting. He also spoke of turning his movement into a political party.[6]

Under Coalition attack at Najaf in early August, al-Sadr's forces went on the offensive elsewhere. True to form, he agreed to a peace plan on 18 August and then allowed his people to keep fighting. While stalling for time in Najaf, they blew up oil pipelines near Al'Amarah on 20 August and Basra on the 21st.[7] Then, five days later, Grand Ayatollah al-Sistani brokered a deal and brought in pilgrims.[8] His "deal" had all the earmarks of a delaying and replacement operation. It coincided with 20 oil pipelines being simultaneously attacked in southern Iraq, effectively shutting off that country's export of oil.[9] On the 30th of August, Mahdi Army fighters bragged about having recruited 3,000 suicide bombers during the Najaf standoff.[10]

Two months earlier (a week before the turnover of power), there had been a series of car-bomb and rocket-propelled-grenade attacks

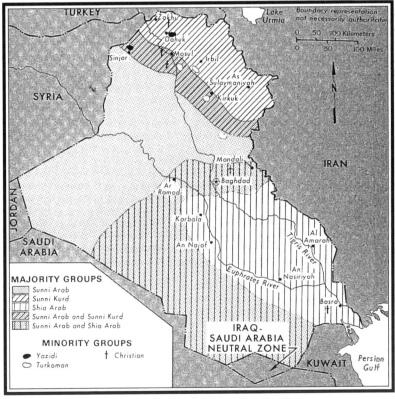

Map 1.2: Iraq's Ethnic Distribution

(Source: *DA PAM 550-31* (May, 1988). fig. 7, p. 82)

across the northern half of Iraq for which al-Zarqawi's *"Tawhid and Jihad"* movement took all the credit. U.S. forces became convinced that al-Zarqawi's headquarters was in Fallujah and resumed the bombing of that city. About this time, al-Sadr agreed to the cease fire in the southern holy cities. It would appear that the *Tawhid and Jihad* had shifted the Coalition's attention away from al-Sadr's militia.

Possibly happening was the mobilization of Iraqi Sunnis by *al-Qaeda* and Iraqi Shiites by *Hezbollah*. One got the distinct impression that the two had been taking turns causing the trouble—*al-Qaeda* in Sunni Triangle and North, *Hezbollah* in East Baghdad and South. Even more disturbing was the fact that both were now after the same targets: (1) police facilities, (2) hostages, and (3) oil lines.

The Negotiation That Ended the Second Sadr Rebellion

On 8 October 2004, al-Sadr agreed to a cease fire in East Baghdad. In exchange for the release of prisoners and cessation of all U.S. ground and air operations in Sadr City, he agreed to a cash-for-heavy-weapons swap.[11] The swap was to last five days, and each weapon was to bring $1000. On the first day, most of the rocket-propelled-grenade launchers (RPGs), machineguns, and mortars were old or rusted.[12] By the end of the second day, only 400 weapons had been exchanged. By 20 October, the deal had also produced about 700 aging mortar rounds and another 400 aging RPG rounds.[13] Al-Sadr had done something for which his Iranian sponsors are famous—saying anything to further a strategic objective. While not part of American culture, this way of negotiating is common throughout Asia. It is not based on a lack of integrity per se, but rather a broader tradition of battlefield deception. Those who would war against, or negotiate with, Asians must come to realize that.

Al-Zarqawi's "Not-So-Certain" Role in the Proceedings

Alternately in the news throughout 2004 were Muqtada al-Sadr and Abu Mussab al-Zarqawi. Every time al-Sadr's Shiites would get beaten in one part of the country, al-Zarqawi's Sunnis would attack in another. While constantly billed as one of Osama bin

Laden's top lieutenants, al-Zarqawi may never have been a member of *al-Qaeda*. This erstwhile Jordanian was behaving more like a limelight-seeking sociopath than a dedicated *jihadist*. One wonders what other movement may have benefitted from his willingness to take the blame for every terrorist act in Northern Iraq. A closer look at al-Zarqawi's past reveals some interesting clues. He had been a rival of bin Laden. Initially rejected by *al-Qaeda*, al-Zarqawi had started up his own terrorist school in Herat. He went from there to Iran, and then to Iraq.[14]

> [B]y the time he got there [from Jordan to Afghanistan], the war was over. . . . Then [in 1999] he returned to Afghanistan, but was apparently rejected by al-Qaeda, instead running his own training camp in Herat. . . .
> Before the war in Iraq, U.S. officials touted Zarqawi as evidence of a link between Osama bin Laden and Saddam Hussein. Washington claimed Zarqawi had been treated in a Baghdad hospital after losing a leg in a U.S. airstrike in Afghanistan. But that is now dubbed "disinformation" by U.S. intelligence officials, who say he actually has both legs. And the available evidence is that as recently as last winter, Zarqawi had only tenuous connections to Osama bin Laden. In a letter Zarqawi wrote to the al-Qaeda leader at the time . . . he practically begged for bin Laden's patronage. . . . The letter, which U.S. intelligence regards as genuine, ended on a note of humility: "We do not see ourselves as fit to challenge you."[15]
> — *Newsweek,* 1 November 2004

A top *al-Qaeda* official would not talk like that. Herat is near the Iranian border, and its residents are heavily influenced by that country. "Since the collapse of the Taliban, Iran has helped [to] smuggle . . . Abu Musab al-Zarqawi [and others] out of Afghanistan and into Lebanon where they are linking up with *Hezbollah.*"[16] It is al-Sadr's sponsors—Lebanese *Hezbollah* and the Iranian Revolutionary Guard *(Sepah)*—that would most benefit from al-Zarqawi's claims of all the mischief. Is he an unsuspecting pawn or a willing scapegoat? Some 12 insurgent groups claim that he was killed by U.S. bombs in 2003.[17] U.S. voice recognition experts say the same person committed most of the videotaped beheadings, but they fail to say how they know it is al-Zarqawi.

Because al-Zarqawi is Salafy Sunni and guilty of anti-Shiite rhetoric,[18] many automatically assume that he would not help fundamentalist Shiites with a similar agenda. In a style of war that embraces chaos, this is not a valid assumption. In the fall of 2004, al-Zarqawi assumed a different role. As late as 16 October, Fallujah clerics insisted he was not in that city.[19] By convincing the Coalition that he was, the opposition built up its popular support. By the end of summer, U.S. planes had been routinely bombing Fallujah neighborhoods.[20] Many Fallujans came to see Americans more as destroyers than liberators.[21] As news of the aerial bombing reached other Iraqis, many were reminded of their Islamic duty to expel invaders and revenge the death of family and friends.

On 16 December, Iraqi Defense Minister Hazem Shaalan "accused Iran . . . of cooperating with Abu Musab al-Zarqawi."[22] One of two things was happening. Either *Sepah/Hezbollah* and *al-Qaeda* were closely coordinating battlefield operations or al-Zarqawi was helping the Iranians. Al-Zarqawi may even be an Iranian operative.

> Though intelligence analysts differ over Zarqawi's exact relationship to Osama bin Laden, they agree . . . he has . . . links . . . with . . . Lebanese Hezbollah. . . .
> American intelligence officials have said they tracked Zarqawi to a meeting in south Lebanon in August 2002 with Hezbollah leaders.[23]
> — *Christian Science Monitor,* 23 January 2004

After reaching out to Osama for months, al-Zarqawi was finally endorsed by the *al-Qaeda* leader on 27 December 2004. In a statement released to al-Jazeera TV, Osama indicated that al-Zarqawi had taken "great steps toward unifying the efforts of the *mujahideen.*"[24] That does not sound like what a top boss would say to a longtime department head. Which *mujahideen* had al-Zarqawi unified, the Sunnis and the Shiites? If al-Zarqawi had always been Osama's right-hand man in Iraq, why then in late 2004, did he feel obligated to change his organizational name from *"Tawhid and Jihad"* to *"Al-Qaeda in Iraq"* and pledge allegiance to the *al-Qaeda* network?[25] In July of that year, it was *Hezbollah* supporting al-Zarqawi.[26]

As late as 21 December, al-Zarqawi's very existence was still in doubt. "Most Iraqis swear that he does not exist and was invented by the Americans to justify their bombing campaigns." It is more likely that the Iranians enlarged his reputation. Even Sadi Ahmed Pire, the head of PUK security in Mosul, doubts his existence.[27] If alive, al-Zarqawi is far less important to the insurgency than has been portrayed.

[H]e [Toby Dodge, Iraq expert at the University of London] warns that the insurgency itself is made up of 60 different, mostly autonomous, groups, and that Mr. Zarqawi—with just 200 loyalists, who have claimed some of the worst atrocities in Iraq in the past year—is a "fringe player."[28]
— *Christian Science Monitor*, 1 February 2004

Fallujah Had Some Non-Sunni Defenders

In October and November of 2004, there was evidence that Iran (though Shiite) had been contributing personnel to the Fallujah fight. Brig. Sarkout Hassan Jalal, Sulaimanyah's security director, said that the insurgents "are smuggling recruits into Iraq from Iran . . . (and) then take them to Fallujah."[29]

After the fighting stopped in Najaf, many of the Lebanese "recruits" from the Bekaa Valley volunteered for service against the Americans in Fallujah. Before making the trip, they received ten days of training, a green uniform, and a new AK-47 from the Mahdi Army.[30] Ten Iranians, a Saudi, a Sudanese, an Egyptian, and a Jordanian were later captured in Fallujah.[31]

Syria is governed by Baathists but also hosts *Hezbollah* and *Hamas* training camps.[32] Before the U.S. assault on Fallujah, an unusually high number of so-called "Syrians" were controlling the city.[33] While some of the foot soldiers may have been Lebanese Sunnis, their leaders could still have been Lebanese Shiites.

[V]isitors to Fallujah . . . say that masked fighters with Syrian accents are everywhere. They are especially noticeable at checkpoints run by the most hard-line groups—the ones that take hostages and let off [detonate] bombs in crowded streets. . . .

Syria . . . is making a great show trying to put a stop to
jihadi recruitment in Lebanon.[34]

How the Coalition's Attention Was Shifted from Fallujah

The Fallujah diversion may have started as early as 24 October
2004 when 50 fledgling Iraqi National Guardsmen were massacred
on a road near the Iranian border.[35]

Then, as U.S. troops prepared to storm Fallujah in early November, their "model" city of Samarra showed signs of weakening.
It was there that guerrillas stormed police stations, mortared government buildings, car-bombed the mayor's office, and killed the
local National Guard commander on 6 November. Such a counterattack should have come as no surprise, because Samarra had once
served as the capital of the Muslim Empire.[36]

Shortly after the 7 November U.S. assault on Fallujah, police
and government facilities were attacked in Baqubah.[37] Then, four
days later, rebels attacked nine police stations and executed National Guardsmen in Mosul, Iraq's third largest city.[38] In response
to insurgent bands openly roaming the streets,[39] the U.S. resorted
to airstrikes.[40] On 14 November—with Coalition reinforcements
now present—the insurgents overran two more police stations.[41] As
of 17 November, the fallen police station count was up to "a dozen or
so."[42]

There had also been increased guerrilla activity in Samarra,
Baqubah, Ramadi, Baghdad, Hit,[43] Taji,[44] Tal Afar,[45] Qaim,[46] Beiji,[47]
Rutba,[48] Suwayrah,[49] Buhriz,[50] Latifiyah,[51] and Haditha.[52]

Targeted once again in Baqubah,[53] Ramadi,[54] Baghdad,[55] Rutba,[56]
Suwayrah,[57] Haditha,[58] and Latifiyah,[59] were government, police, or
National Guard facilities and convoys. Concurrently, the militants
pursued the other parts of their triple strategy—hostages and oil.[60]

Rebuilding Fallujah's Image

After employing non-Sunni defenders and blatant diversions,
the Coalition's principal adversary badly needed to affirm that
Fallujah had been at the heart of a Sunni insurgency. It came up
with something so obviously invented as to be almost insulting.

According to [Cable News Network] CNN's footage, the suspected al-Zarqawi command center was in an imposing house with concrete columns and a large sign in Arabic reading "Al-Qaeda Organization."[61]
— Associated Press, 19 November 2004

This great a security breach can only be a decoy. It is either to divert bombs or to spread disinformation. *Hezbollah* played a bigger role in the defense of Fallujah than did *al-Qaeda*. What better way to make a "headquarters-oriented" occupier think that he had crippled a Sunni insurgency. In fact, neither *al-Qaeda* nor *Hezbollah* has much organizational structure. Their job is to recruit and train people for the active militias.

While the fight for Fallujah was in progress, trouble broke out at other places inside the Sunni Triangle. Not all of that trouble subsided after U.S./Coalition counterstroke. Was it possible that the insurgents were trying to hold ground (one of the stages in Maoist guerrilla warfare)?

Trouble Persists at Other Locations

After 1,200 U.S. troops launched an offensive to reclaim the Mosul police stations on 16 November 2004,[62] rebel attacks on that city persisted. By the next day, only 20% of the city's 5,000 policemen had returned to work.[63] On 22 November, the insurgents stormed two more police stations.[64] The same day, U.S. forces found the executed remains of nine Iraqi soldiers.[65] The next day, they found two more.[66] On 25 November, they discovered ten additional victims of execution.[67] By 30 November, 50 bodies had been found. Most were thought to be security personnel.[68] The very next day, U.S troops fought a gun battle with insurgents in Mosul.[69] By 3 December, the body count of assassinated security personnel had climbed to 66,[70] and insurgents were still manning checkpoints and engaging in running street battles.[71] When U.S. forces dropped a 500-pound bomb inside the city on 11 December,[72] a repeat of the Fallujah catastrophe seemed certain. Just before Christmas, a suicide bomber infiltrated a nearby U.S. base and blew himself up in the mess tent.[73] Three days after the holiday, militants attacked another Mosul police station.[74]

Meanwhile, there had been action elsewhere. By 20 November,

guerrillas were stilling attacking the police stations in Baqubah and Beiji.[75] In Baqubah a week later, a police official was assassinated, and a group of National Guardsmen car-bombed while trying to disarm an improvised explosive device (IED).[76] On 5 January 2005, the Baqubah police chief was killed, and a car bomber blew himself up at a police checkpoint.[77]

Outside the U.S. poster city of Samarra, a convoy had been attacked on 23 November 2004.[78] Six days later, insurgents stormed a police station just west of town.[79] On 1 December, there were clashes between U.S. troops and insurgents in Samarra.[80] A week later, militants raided a police station, stole its weapons, and blew up the building.[81] That was the same day a car bomb detonated at the Samarra city center.[82] On 2 January 2005, four policemen were killed on patrol inside the city.[83]

Ramadi also stayed volatile throughout this period. As late as Christmas 2004, only one fourth of its 2,000 policemen had returned to duty. On 28 December, a deputy province governor was assassinated there.[84]

Three days after Christmas, Muslim insurgents cut the throats of 12 Tikrit policemen. They then blew the police station.[85]

The insurgents had also added other Sunni-Triangle towns to their counterattack. On 27 November, they overran city hall and two police stations in Khalis, 40 miles north of Baghdad.[86] All the while, Iskandariyah—at the edge of the Sunni Triangle some 30 miles south of Baghdad—remained a rebel stronghold.[87]

Also Under Attack Was a U.S. War Machine Prerequisite

As of 21 November 2004, there had been no fewer than six attacks in ten days against the northern portion of Iraq's petroleum infrastructure.[88] In early December, insurgents blew up an oil pipeline at Beiji.[89] But they were not just after income-producing oil; they were after their occupier's biggest and most vulnerable requirement.

> The Department of Defense now has about 27,000 vehicles in Iraq—and every one of them gets lousy gas mileage. To power that fleet, the Defense Logistics Agency must move [in] huge quantities of fuel . . . in truck convoys. . . . Every day some 2,000 [U.S.] trucks leave Kuwait alone. . . .

... The U.S. military now uses about 1.7 million gallons of fuel a day in Iraq. . . .

[O]ver the past several decades the Pentagon has bought billions of dollars worth of tanks, trucks, and other vehicles with little or no consideration to their fuel efficiency. In decades past, U.S. Army logisticians assumed that 50 percent of the tonnage moved onto a battlefield was ammunition, 30 percent was fuel, and the rest was food, water, and supplies. Today the fuel component may be as high as 70 percent.[90]

— *Atlantic Monthly,* May 2005

[T]he Defense Logistics Agency and the Iraqi interim government must move vast quantities of fuel into the country. . . . Not enough is getting through. . . .

. . . In Iraq, the average G.I. uses about 22 times more fuel than a comparable American soldier did during World War II. . . .

Osama bin Laden sees America's energy vulnerability more clearly than the Joint Chiefs of Staff. Last Thursday (16 December 2004), he delivered another message to his followers about the evils of the oil industry, telling them to try their best "to stop the biggest theft in history." On Sunday, bin Laden's al Qaeda allies inside Saudi Arabia posted their own message, calling on "all mujahideen" in the Arabian peninsula to attack "the oil resources that do not serve the nation of Islam."

The insurgents [of all religious preferences] in Iraq appear to be listening. On Saturday, [rebel] bombers hit three different pipelines: one that carries refined products near Beiji, a line that supplies oil to the Daura refinery in Baghdad (which had been shut down for 17 days from a previous sabotage), and a crude oil pipeline 53 miles west of Kirkuk. The attacks halted Iraqi oil exports through the pipeline that terminates in Ceyhan, Turkey. The Kirkuk to Ceyhan pipeline has been bombed dozens of times since June of 2003 and the Northern Iraq Oil Company has only been able to sell oil from the port at Ceyhan on a sporadic basis.

On December 18, bombers struck again, hitting pipelines near Kirkuk and Samarra. After one of the bombings, a statement circulated in Beiji said that al-Qaeda leader

Abu Musab al-Zarqawi had blown up one of the pipelines, following orders from "supreme commander Osama bin Laden." . . .

[The] U.S. and its allies in Iraq, and elsewhere in the Persian Gulf, have to defend every pipeline, every truck convoy, and every fuel depot–a task that is ultimately unsustainable. Iraq has 4,400 miles of pipelines.[91]

— Initial draft of *Atlantic Monthly* article

Figure 1.1: Little Chance to Fix the Infrastructure

(Source: Courtesy of Sorman Info. & Media, illustration by Wolfgang Bartsch, from *SoldF: Soldaten i fält*, © 2001 Forsvarsmakten, Stockholm, p. 253)

Fallujah Was Occupied But Not Fully Pacified

The only official acknowledgment of an ongoing battle for Fallujah was the steadily rising casualty count of those who invaded. As of 5 December 2004, that count had risen from 46 to 71.[92] A day later, the Red Crescent Society pulled out saying the city was not secure enough for relief work.[93]

The rubbling of an urban area makes it easier to defend in many ways. It blocks traffic and permits more areas to be covered by long-range fire. A jump in Anbar Province Marine casualties in mid-December inferred more guerrilla activity in Fallujah. On the 14th of that month, there were reports of small guerrilla bands still roaming the city. Among other things, they were "emerging out of tunnels and crossing between rooftops on ladders."[94] Further U.S. airstrikes the city were also reported. The guerrillas had attacked the forces sent to clear the rubble from the November offensive.[95] Apparently, three complete sweeps of the city had enjoyed about as much success as the hundreds of sweeps across every inch of Vietnam.[96]

As late as 23 December, three more Marines had been killed in Fallujah, and U.S warplanes and tanks were still bombarding guerrilla positions.[97] It would be a long time before the city would be re-inhabitable. (See Figure 1.1.)

The Glaring Absence of Shiite Offensive

Before the U.S. assault on Fallujah, al-Sadr and al-Zarqawi took turns attacking Coalition forces. After that assault, the radical Shiites appeared to lose interest in open warfare. Of all the cities under attack, only Baqubah, Tal Afar, Samarra and Baghdad matched those of the Sadr rebellions.[98] If the Mahdi Army was creating diversions, it wasn't taking credit for them. However, on 8 November 2004, 12 National Guardsmen were abducted and executed near Najaf.[99] The ensuing trouble in Tal Afar and Qaim may also have been *Hezbollah* inspired. Both are on the Syrian border. Rutba—the site of the kidnapping of 31 policemen—is right next to Jordan.[100] On 22 November, one of the southern oil pipelines was destroyed.[101]

Finally starting to "get it" as things happened elsewhere, Iraqi police arrested 160 al-Sadr loyalists in Najaf on 19 November.[102] Then a reason for the apparent lack of Shiite activity began to materialize. A game of chess was being played, and it was almost time for checkmate from an unsuspected source.

> Shiites generally have refrained from joining the Sunni-led insurgency, believing they will gain power in Iraq anyway through the elections because of their force of numbers. Shiite clerics for the most part avoided public criticism of the Fallujah offensive.[103]
> — Associated Press, 28 November 2004

Other *Hezbollah*-Like Intrigue

With the assassination of two members of the influential Sunni Association of Muslim Scholars in Sunni towns (Muqdadiyah and Mosul) on 23 November 2004,[104] one suspects Shiite involvement. Such assassinations would further alienate the Sunni community, thus making it more likely to boycott the election. The Sunnis would not assassinate their own leaders, and the Coalition has not yet resorted to such tactics. That leaves the Shiite militants as probable culprits.

When al-Zarqawi accused the Sunni clerics of being too docile on 25 November,[105] the red flag of suspicion was definitely raised. That is not what a Sunni militant would do, unless his *al-Qaeda* affiliation or very existence was in doubt. When al-Zarqawi took credit for the Mosul counteroffensive four days later,[106] the insurgency's goals became more apparent. Implicit in al-Zarqawi's admission was his new headquarters' location. This would further indict the Sunnis, evoke a heavy-handed U.S. response, and thus remove Sunni representation from the election process.

Fallujah Had Been Turned into a Sunni "Alamo"

By acknowledging Lebanese *Hezbollah* and Iranian *Sepah* involvement in the Iraqi insurgency, one sees why Fallujah was billed as an al-Zarqawi stronghold. The Muslim militant method is more psychological and political than it is martial. It depends on the

Western occupier using so strong a hand as to alienate the local population. As such, it encourages that occupier's overreaction to ongoing events. When the *London Times* published a press release from "insurgent commanders . . . inside Fallujah" on 8 November 2004, it unwittingly furthered the opposition's agenda. That release casually mentioned that the insurgents had "118 car bombs . . . and 300 volunteer foreign suicide bombers lined up to take on the advancing American units."[107] Then—during the initial stages of the assault—when Marines reported "entire buildings that were boobytrapped" at the city's outskirts, the rumor quickly spread that many structures throughout the city had been rigged for demolition.[108] Such reports and rumors might have prompted casualty-conscious American commanders to destroy any vehicle, person, or building suspected of harboring high explosives.

While most of the U.S. troops probably showed great courage and restraint during the assault, there was still evidence of a firepower-heavy format. As they moved through the city, they shot at many of the vehicles, people, and dogs they saw up side streets. "Expecting and finding countless explosive devices and boobytraps, American units took few chances as they moved methodically through the city. Every vehicle is treated as a potential car bomb; every person a possible enemy."[109] While probably not universally true, some units were "shooting anything that moves."[110] It was obvious from the televised coverage of the battle, that many buildings came under heavy bombardment from bomb-dropping fixed-wing aircraft, "Hellfire"-missile-firing helicopters, tanks, and anti-tank weapons.

Khomeini's Successors Were Far Too Contented

With all the firepower, the U.S. was playing right into Iran's hands. In separate statements before the U.S. election, Iran's clerics and security council supported the incumbent American president for another term.[111] When Osama bin Laden then said in a videotape that he hated that incumbent, he may have been using reverse psychology. At least, that's what the former U.S. antiterrorism czar volunteered.[112] On 29 November 2004, *al-Qaeda's* real leader—al-Zawahiri—said that his organization opposed U.S. foreign policy but didn't care who got elected.[113] The enemy's political banter resembled an old criminal investigative technique—the "salt-and-pepper" approach to obtaining a confession.

Despite the Sunni-Triangle security lapses after the Fallujah assault, the Supreme Council for the Islamic Republic in Iraq (SCIRI) affirmed support for the 30 January 2005 Iraqi election.[114] That would have been good news if SCIRI didn't have close ties with *Sepah*. SCIRI had been spawned by the Iraqi *al-Da'wa* party but was first based in Tehran.

> Iran's official media has confirmed the close links between SAIRI [SCIRI] and the Guard. In the last days of the Iran-Iraq war, the Guard publicly called for a mobilization of SAIRI volunteers (Iraqis who had defected to Iran) to the warfront with Iraq ("IRGC Announces SAIRI . . . ," Tehran Domestic Service, 14 July 1988).[115]

SCIRI maintained a paramilitary wing (the Badr Brigade) of about 10,000 trained men. After the fall of the Baath regime in Iraq, its members began infiltrating back into the country.[116] As of 6 April 2004, SCIRI was one of Iraq's two biggest Shiite political parties and had a seat on the governing council.[117] During the subsequent "Sadr Rebellions," it encouraged U.S. forces to "negotiate with al-Sadr, rather than press the confrontation."[118]

The Political Cost of Too Much Firepower

While the retaking of Fallujah was legitimate, its particulars alienated the Sunni residents of other towns. Allawi was Shiite.[119] That might have been why he did not object to piecemeal destruction of the city.

> On Tuesday [9 November], a group of Sunni clerics announced that they will boycott the upcoming election. The Iraqi Islamic Party, the dominant Sunni group supporting the interim government, now says it is withdrawing its backing due to assault of Fallujah.[120]
> — *Christian Science Monitor,* 10 November 2004

As humanitarian organizations were forced out of Iraq, the U.S.

military had less reason to use minimal force. It had not fully considered the political cost of precision airstrikes within highly populated areas.

A team of international researchers, led by Les Roberts of Maryland's John Hopkins University, estimates that 100,000 Iraqi civilians have died due to violence since the 2003 invasion. The findings are much higher than previous estimates, and don't even include the recent siege of Fallujah.[121]

— *Christian Science Monitor,* 23 November 2004

Baghdad Drew Much of the Post-Fallujah Heat

On 3 December 2004, militants stormed two police stations in Baghdad.[122] A month later, they killed the governor of Baghdad Province and the police chief of Sadr City.[123] It stands to reason that the violence would shift to Baghdad, but the Sadr City incident deserves a second look. Who would stand the most to gain from the killing a Shiite neighborhood police chief? In Sadr City, the Mahdi Army provides most of the security.

The Green Zone Was the Guerrillas' Favorite Target

On 14 October 2004, a suicide bomber and his apparent handler penetrated the electronic surveillance, razor wire, and U.S. sentry posts that protect Baghdad's four-mile-square, super-secure "Green Zone." They subsequently detonated their explosives at a market and cafe. How they got in, or if the handler escaped, is unknown. The Zone is crisscrossed by sewers, and Saddam did have a penchant for secret tunnels. The bombers may have just passed themselves off as two of the Green Zone's several thousand Iraqi residents. A waiter at the restaurant said that the men carried back packs and spoke with a Jordanian accent.[124] Another explosive device was later found inside the Green Zone.[125] As of 25 November, that Zone was being routinely mortared and rocketed,[126] in much the same way Kabul had been during the Soviet-Afghan War.

On 4 December, car bombs were detonated simultaneously at a police station across the street from the main entrance to the Green

Zone.[127] Ten days later, another car bomb was set off near that front entrance with no apparent target.[128] Its only purpose was to discourage entry. Throughout December 2004 and early January 2005, car bombs continued to go off at the edge of the protected enclave.

A Hidden Entity Tries to Capture the Election

In a 4th-generation war, one expects the combining of martial and political initiatives. On 8 December 2004, the Sunni President of Iraq and the King of Jordan both warned of Iran trying to influence the upcoming Iraqi elections.[129] With the right Shiites in power, Iraq's "Party of God" would eventually emerge. Then, Iraq would become a Shiite state and go the way of Iran or Lebanon. There, *Sepah* and *Hezbollah* hold the real power. They don't work for the prime minister; they work for the supreme ayatollah.

> The leaders of Iraq and Jordan warned yesterday that Iran is trying to influence the Iraqi elections scheduled for Jan. 30 to create an Islamic government that would dramatically shift the geopolitical balance between Shiite and Sunni Muslims in the Middle East.
> Iraqi President Ghazi Yawar charged that Iran is coaching candidates and political parties sympathetic to Tehran and pouring "huge amounts of money" into the campaign to produce a Shiite-dominated government similar to Iran's.
> Jordanian King Abdullah said that more than 1 million Iranians have crossed the 910-mile border into Iraq, many to vote in the election—with the encouragement of the Iranian government. "I'm sure there's a lot of people, a lot of Iranians in there that will be used as part of the polls to influence the outcome," he said in an interview.
> The king also charged that Iranians are paying salaries and providing welfare to unemployed Iraqis to build pro-Iranian public sentiment. Some Iranians, he added, have been trained by Iran's Revolutionary Guards and are members of militias that could fuel trouble in Iraq after the election. . . .
> If pro-Iran parties or politicians dominate the new Iraqi government, he said, a new "crescent" of dominant Shiite

movements or governments stretching from Iran into Iraq, Syria and Lebanon could emerge, alter the traditional balance of power between the two main Islamic sects and pose new challenges to U.S. interests and allies. . . .
. . . Syria is ruled by the minority Allawites, an offshoot of Shiism. Shiites are the largest of 17 recognized sects in Lebanon, and Hezbollah is a major Shiite political party, with the only active militia.[130]
— *The Washington Post,* 8 December 2004

Despite Sunni and Kurdish threats to boycott the January 2005 election, the U.S. administration went through with it. To squash what it believed to be a Sunni revolt, Washington was willing to chance a Shiite state. In what was possibly the same divide-and-conquer strategy that had served the British so poorly in India, U.S. foreign policy had risked everything. One could only hope that Iraq was not headed down the same road that Lebanon had taken. Then, only in appearance would it be a republic. Below the surface, it would be an Iranian satellite controlled by a single *mullah* and his armed militia.

A cleric with links to Iran [possibly al-Sistani's pick] leads the candidate list of a powerful coalition of Iraq's mainstream Shi'ite Muslim groups for next month's election, an aide said yesterday. The list includes former Pentagon favorite Ahmad Chalabi [who took refuge in Iran while under investigation] and some followers of radical cleric Muqtada al-Sadr [with ties to Lebanese *Hezbollah*].[131]
— *The Washington Times,* 11 December 2004

Many Americans were now closely monitoring the Iraqi political front. Who would compete against Allawi in the January election? Would there be any surprises from the pro-Iranian Shiite camp?

Heading the al-Sistani-backed United Iraqi Alliance [UIA] list is Abdel-Aziz al-Hakim, leader of the pro-Iranian Supreme Council for the Islamic Revolution (SCIRI) and chief of its armed wing, the Iran-based Badr Brigade, during Saddam's rule.[132]
— Associated Press, 16 December 2004

When Iraqi Defense Minister Hazem Shaalan warned that Iran was heavily involved in the war and now trying to create an Islamic dictatorship,[133] Coalition officials ignored it.

> The interim government's defense minister, Hazem Shaalan, upped the ante yesterday by telling a news conference in Baghdad that the main Shiite slate was an "Iranian list."
> The Iranians "are fighting us because we want to build freedom and democracy and they want to build an Islamic dictatorship and have turbaned clerics to rule in Iraq," Mr. Shaalan said.
> Shaalan was referring to the United Iraqi Alliance [UIA], a list of mainly Shiite candidates that was put together at the behest of Grand Ayatollah Ali al-Sistani, Iraq's preeminent religious figure. The Shiite list—which most Iraqis refer to simply as "Sistani's list"—is widely believed to be the front-runner in the elections so far, so it will be significant competition for Allawi.[134]
> — *Christian Science Monitor,* 16 December 2004

A week before the election, the principal UIA candidate divulged his party's post-election agenda.

> The Shi'ite Muslim cleric tipped to become prime minister after next Sunday's election in Iraq has said it will be the duty of the new government to demand the withdrawal of American forces "as soon as possible." [135]
> — *London Sunday Times,* 23 January 2004

Right after the election, the same person said he should be prime minister whether or not the UIA won a clear majority of votes.[136]

The Militants' Pre-Election Offensive

With the Green-Zone-entrance car bomb of 14 December 2005, the insurgents' pre-election strategy began to emerge.[137] It would be decidedly 4GW in nature—a diabolical combination of intimidation and disinformation. With acts of terror against low-level officials, they would manipulate the occupier, government, and voting population. With disinformation about who perpetrated those acts, they would disenfranchize the Sunnis. To get what they wanted, they were perfectly willing to inflict collateral damage on their own people. Had not their previous focus been on killing security personnel and collaborators? Three days earlier, the Beiji police chief, three Baghdad police commanders, and two Shiite clerics had been killed.[138] Perhaps, the clerics had also cooperated with authorities.

Iraq's security and police forces were nowhere to be seen on 19 December, when armed gunmen started setting up checkpoints on Haifa Street—Baghdad's main thoroughfare. Only after those gunmen had executed three election workers did a U.S. helicopter finally make a cursory appearance.[139] On 2 January 2005 in Balad, a suicide-bomber detonated his explosive-laden car next to a bus carrying Iraqi National Guardsmen.[140] Three days later, a car bomb exploded next to a police academy in Hillah (60 miles south of Baghdad) killing 20 people.[141] Then the media remembered that some 1,300 Iraqi policemen had been killed during the last four months of 2004.[142] On 10 January, Baghdad's deputy police chief was gunned down. Baghdad's governor and police officials from Jebala, Samarra, and Baqubah, had just met the same fate.[143] Particularly at risk during this period were the National Guardsmen. Unlike the police, they were not allowed to take home their weapons at night.[144]

Right before the election, a fully loaded Marine CH-53 went down in what was described as "bad weather" in Western Iraq.[145] Two days later, a British C-130 crashed on take off just north of Baghdad. The British admitted to a shoot-down only after militants released a videotape of missiles being fired and the crash site.[146] Sometime during the night before the election, the U.S. embassy in the heavily protected Green Zone was hit by a single rocket "from nine miles away."[147] As a lucky hit from that range is highly unlikely, one suspects advanced technology or an infiltrator.

Trying to Attribute Shiite Holy-City Bombings to the Sunnis

On 19 December 2004, car bombs were exploded at a Najaf funeral procession and Karbala bus station. The first was detonated near where Najaf's governor and police chief were standing.[148] The second involved strategically important transportation. While both were conveniently blamed on the Sunnis, they may have had other perpetrators. There had been an ongoing Shiite power struggle, and its victors were supported by *Sepah*. They seldom admitted to any wrongdoing. A spokesman for confirmed liar al-Sadr went so far as to suggest that al-Zarqawi had done it.[149] Al-Zarqawi's alleged perpetration of every crime in northern Iraq had, after all, given the Mahdi Army a well-deserved rest in September. Here's what the Najaf police chief had to say after the attack.

> Najaf police chief Ghalib al-Jazaari said 50 people had been arrested in conjunction with the bombings. Some of them confessed to having links with intelligence services of neighboring Syria and Iran, he claimed.[150]
> — Associated Press, 21 December 2004

Right after the Najaf attack, Allawi dismissed the allegations of his defense minister. Hazem Shaalan had long accused both Iran and Syria of supporting terrorism in Iraq.[151] Then SCIRI head Abdel Aziz al-Hakim offered to protect the polls with a Badr Brigade that had grown tenfold over the last two years to around 100,000 men.[152] On 24 January 2005, someone claiming to be al-Zarqawi tried projection and exaggeration to quell the rumors. He accused "the Americans of engineering the election to install Shiites and claimed that four million Shiite Muslims had been brought from Iran to skew the vote."[153] Only an expert in Eastern deception would use blatant exaggeration to obscure an imbedded truth. Might the murderous phantom have a well-educated puppeteer?

Al-Zarqawi's Not-Too-Convincing Anti-Shiite Rhetoric

Al-Zarqawi's berating of Iraqi Shiites on 20 January 2005 could be viewed as evidence that he hates all Shiites and supports only *al-Qaeda*.[154] But radical fundamentalists often consider their more conservative brethren as traitors. Many of the indigenous soldiers who participated in the assault on Fallujah were Shiite. "Commando 36 . . . was the first Iraqi . . . unit into Fallujah. . . . Shia militia veterans and Kurdish *peshmerga* guerrillas dominate the unit."[155]

By 7 May 2005, U.S. authorities claimed to have gotten 20 of al-

Zarqawi's top lieutenants and to have narrowly missed him (in February).[156] Still, one suspects a loose alliance of Sunni groups with little or no organizational structure. The so-called "lieutenants" might be heads of barely affiliated insurgent groups.

Deja Vu on Inconsistencies

The attempted car-bombing of SCIRI chieftain Abdul Aziz al-Hakim on 27 December 2004 was widely interpreted as a Baathist act of reprisal or *al-Qaeda* attempt at civil war.[157] Unfortunately, it looked much more like the successful truck-bombing of his predecessor Mohammed Baqir al-Hakim in August 2003. The previous al-Hakim had threatened to cut ties with Iran after junior cleric Muqtada al-Sadr had been feted during his visit to that country in June 2003.[158] That's the way fundamentalist Shiites ensure the loyalty of other Shiites. Al-Sadr, after all, was already suspected of killing the moderate Shiite leader Abdel-Majid al-Khoei in April 2003.[159] On 13 January 2005, terrorists assassinated two of Ayatollah al-Sistani's top aides. His office was careful not to assign the blame.[160] If the heavily watched al-Sistani were not his own man, uncooperative aides might have to be disciplined. Five days later, a suicide bomber detonated his vehicle in front of the headquarters of what was formerly the largest Shiite political party in Iraq (SCIRI).[161] Could that blast have been a feint? Its perpetrator was never determined. In Southwest Asia, one must look beyond what is too obvious.

Polling Station Violence

The 30 January 2005 Iraqi elections were not as heavily contested as one might expect in a Sunni insurgency. Militants struck at only about 100 of the 5,200 polling stations across Iraq.[162] Overall, there were 260 incidents.[163] Roughly 35 voters were killed, and nine suicide bombers were involved.[164] There was a short pause in the fighting after the election, but there were political and economic developments to worry about from the standpoint of 4GW.

The UIA Just Misses a Clear Majority of the Votes

Luckily, the UIA only took 48% of the vote in the 30 January 2005 election. A clear majority would have given it *carte blanche* with Iraq's new constitution and top-job roster.

UIA was a coalition of Shiite parties and individuals put together by Ayatollah al-Sistani. About half of the candidates came from Shiite parties with close ties to Iran: SCIRI and the *Dawa*. Their respective leaders were al-Hakim and Ibrahim al-Jaafari. Ten percent of the remainder were affiliated with militant cleric al-Sadr. Also on the list was Ahmed Chalabi—the architect of the U.S. invasion who, while under investigation for leaking secrets to Iran, took refuge in Iran.[165]

What Happened after the Election

The instigator of the insurgency did not take long to establish a post-election strategy. There were ominous signs of it soon after the voting. Hundreds of Iraqi police uniforms were discovered missing, and four police cars.[166] On 2 February, a minibus full of recruits was stopped (presumably at a checkpoint) and 12 executed.[167] The next day, there were three attacks on police or National Guardsmen in Baghdad, one in Ramadi, and another in southern Iraq at Samawah.[168]

On 7 February, a car bomb blew up outside a Baqubah police station killing 15 prospective recruits. On the same date in Mosul, insurgents mortared another police station, and a suicide vest bomber killed 12 security personnel.[169] The very next day in the same city, a suicide bomber blew himself up in a crowd of Army recruits, killing 21 of them.[170]

On 10 February, just south of Baghdad, gunmen ambushed a large group of policemen who were searching houses for weapons. Before the two-hour gun battle was over, 14 police lay dead, and 65 wounded. That was the same day that police and National Guardsmen were attacked in Baquba and Ramadi.[171]

On 28 February, 115 people were killed by suicide car bomb in Hillah (60 miles south of Baghdad) while queuing up for government jobs outside a health center.[172] Hillah is just outside the Sunni Triangle.

A Signal to the New Legislature

On 16 March 2005 inside the Green Zone, the newly elected legislators were sworn in after enduring several mortar barrages.[173] Four days later, gunmen killed a regional police commissioner on his way to work in Baghdad.[174] Then in Mosul, a suicide-car bomber assassinated Walid Kashmoula, the head of the Iraqi police anticorruption unit.[175]

Was someone trying to send the Iraqi legislature a message? Was it to stop collaborating with the occupier, or start supporting the Iranian agenda? There were definite similarities to Mafia jury tampering.

A Suspicious Rash of Not-Too-Ruinous Anti-Shiite Activity

Eastern armies use proxies. This is one of their "36 Stratagems." When one pursues the hypothesis that Iran is ultimately behind the Iraqi insurgency, one finds evidence of a fairly elaborate disinformation plan. Near the end of the 40 days of mourning for legendary Imam Hussein (just before the religious festival on 31 March 2005), there were six attacks against Shiites in Iraq. In the first, two soldiers and three civilians were killed outside a shrine by a suicide car bomber. In the second, gunmen ambushed a truck carrying pilgrims but killed only one. In the third, another pilgrim was killed. In the fourth and fifth, two police officers and two pilgrims were killed. In the sixth, a roadside bomb injured six policemen on patrol near Basra.[176] If Sunni insurgents were intent on killing Shiites, they could do a lot better than that at a festival attended by hundreds of thousands. One of four things happened: (1) Sunni bungling, (2) a string of inconsequential coincidences, (3) the Iranian assassination of a few policemen and spies, or (4) an Iranian disinformation campaign. Such a campaign would so discredit the Sunnis as to ensure their election day defeat.

Al-Sadr Reappears in a New Role

On 9 April 2005, Muqtada al-Sadr organized a peaceful demonstration at central Baghdad's Firdos Square at which tens of thousands of people demanded that U.S. forces go home. He went so far as to ask for Iraqi police and National Guard protection. When Mahdi Army personnel set up dual checkpoints, no one objected.[177] That a sister rally was held in Sunni Ramadi suggests much more than just coincidence.[178] Might there be a Shiite presence or Mahdi Army proxy in Ramadi? If so, how many of the anti-Coalition attacks are its doing?

Similar demonstrations had just forced the Syrians out of Lebanon. Jaafari had stated in January that his first mission as prime minister would be the removal of U.S. forces.[179]

True to new form, al-Sadr launched more anti-American rallies in Sadr City, Najaf, Kufa, and Nasiriyah on 20 May. Again, their participants were demanding that U.S. forces go home.[180]

Spring and Summer Activity outside the Sunni Triangle

From April to August 2005, most insurgent attacks occurred inside, or at the edge of, the Sunni Triangle. Only a few happened in predominantly Shiite areas. Either Sunni insurgents couldn't enter Shiite zones and had to subsequently harm their own civilians, or Shiite insurgents could enter Sunni zones and thus spared their own civilians. The Iraqi police in Basra, Al'Amarah, or Hillah got most of the attention. But, the Japanese and British occupiers were also reminded of their fading welcome.

On 6 April 2005, the headless bodies of seven Iraqi soldiers and three policemen were found in Hillah (60 miles south of the capital). Then a provincial council member was gunned down in Babil, and a policeman in Basra.[181] Four days later, 15 Iraqi soldiers were found shot to death in a truck over 30 miles south of the capital.[182] On 29 April, a roadside bomb targeted Iraqi soldiers in Basra.[183] After a few days, another roadside bomb killed a British soldier in Al'Amarah.[184] On 12 May, a bomb exploded at Iraq's largest fertilizer plant in Basra, and several others in Samawah where the Japanese forces are based.[185] On 10 June, the dean of the police academy in Basra was killed.[186] At the beginning of July, a suicide bomber detonated his belt of explosives at a police checkpoint at the center of Hillah. Within 10 minutes, another suicide vest bomber entered the crowd of police and civilians who had come to help. This evoked memories of the second deadliest attack since the fall of Saddam Hussein. At the same town in February, a suicide car bomber had attacked a large group of police and army recruits.[187]

Shortly after those claiming to have committed the London transit bombings demanded the withdrawal of all British forces from Iraq, there were some telling incidents in the southern part of the country. On 16 July, three British soldiers were killed by an IED in Al'Amarah.[188] Six days later, it was announced that the British were planning to cut their 8,500-man contingent to 3,000.[189] On 30 July, a British-consulate convoy was attacked by IED in Basra. Thirty-eight days later, an American diplomatic convoy met the same fate in Basra.[190] Someone in Southern Iraq was trying to send the Coalition governments a message. There were clues to that message in what had transpired politically since April.

The Possibility of High-Level Intrigue

First, a car bomb had exploded outside the Iraqi Interior Ministry in Central Baghdad on 14 April 2005.[191] Twelve days later, a member of the new parliament was assassinated in her home.[192] Then on 28 April, the parliament approved Jaafari's list of cabinet ministers by a vote of 180 out of 185 possible, with one third of the 275-member parliament absent. After the largely ceremonial post of defense minister went unfilled, the key post of interior minister went to Bayan Baqir Jaber—an "Islamist" and top SCIRI leader.[193] Chalabi became one of the four deputy prime ministers and acting oil minister.[194] Jaafari temporarily doubled as defense minister.[195] On 8 May, the unfilled cabinet posts were confirmed by those legislators still willing to come to work. Saadoun al-Duleimi, a Sunni defector from Saddam's army, would become defense minister. Abed Mutlak al-Jiburi, a former Baathist general and Sunni, would be deputy prime minister. Osama al-Nujaifi, also a Sunni, would take the position of industry minister. Ibrahim Bahr al-Uloum, a Shiite member of the former governing council, would continue on in the oil ministry post. Mihsub Shlash, another Shiite, would assume the role of electricity minister. Al-Inizi would be minister of national security.[196] Of 37 cabinet seats, seven would be Sunni. One of the four deputy prime ministers would also be Sunni.[197]

Political Subtleties

About mid-May 2005, it became obvious that the predominantly

31

Shiite assembly was squelching Sunni representation. Its initial 55-member "constitution" committee contained only two Sunnis.[198] Its chairman would be a SCIRI deputy by the name of Sheikh Homam Baqr Hamoudi.[199]

Then, to no one's surprise, the Iranian foreign minister—Kamal Kharrazi—visited the new government during the week of 20 May. He conferred with al-Sistani and then Jaafari. Out of one side of his mouth came a denial of Iran's involvement with the insurgency. Out of the other came a veiled threat. Within a well-seasoned reporter's analysis lies the blueprint for Iran's hidden intentions.

> Analysts say that in the aftermath of the 2003 U.S. invasion, Iran believed that it might be the U.S.'s next target, and so set up networks that could apply pressure in Iraq, if a decision was made to do so. . . .
>
> Iran analysts described Tehran's aim as "managed chaos," a tricky balancing act that would keep U.S. forces and officials tied down in Iraq, but not spark the kind of breakdown that would threaten Iran. . . .
>
> "Had the Islamic Republic of Iran exploited the situation in Iraq to interfere in Iraq's affairs and allow terrorists to enter Iraq from Iran," Kharrazi added, "the situation in Iraq would have been much worse." . . .
>
> "I'm not sure how much of the [Iran-Iraq *detente*] is love and real friendliness," says Ali Ansar, an Iran expert at St. Andrews University in Scotland. "The Iranians are making the most of it, reminding the Americans and Europeans that if things get hot on the nuclear issue, that Iran has a big influence in Iraq." . . .
>
> Iraqi Prime Minister Ibrahim al-Jaafari for years led an anti-Saddam group in Iran. . . .
>
> On the Kurdish side, Iran has had the closest ties with the Patriotic Union of Kurdistan lead *[sic]* by Jalal Talebani, Iraq's new president.[200]
> —*Christian Science Monitor,* 20 May 2005

Brief Interruptions to the Flow of Enemy Reinforcements

As U.S. forces achieved one so-called "tactical victory" after another on sweeps to the south and west of Baghdad during the summer of 2005, the capital's troubles continued. Apparently, the opposition now had enough instructor cadre, Iraqi volunteers, and cached supplies to absorb temporary setbacks along its western manpower conduit. As most U.S. units lacked trackers, they seldom located the strategically important underground way stations. Within hours of their departure, the enemy conduit would be up and running. On a sweep of Tal Afar—the principal point of entry near the Syrian border—on 10 September, several hundred insurgents put up a spirited fight in the city's ancient Sarai district and then mysteriously disappeared.[201] There is only one place they could have gone— into the city's subterranean ruins. A day later, the deputy chief of staff for Coalition forces in Iraq admitted to a network of "escape tunnels" beneath Sarai.[202] He didn't realize that the insurgents were probably still below his soldiers' feet—just waiting for them to depart.

It was only through an informant's tip that U.S. forces found one of these underground facilities on 4 June. In Karmah (50 miles west of Baghdad), Marines uncovered a huge bunker hewn out of a rock quarry. It had living spaces, kitchen, showers, air conditioning, and a fully stocked armory. The black uniforms, ski masks, compasses, and night vision devices would indicate an operations center that doubled as a way station.[203]

Iraq's Elite Security Unit Likened to Defacto Shiite Militia

Since the autumn of 2004, many city police departments and Iraqi National Guard units have had to be disbanded throughout Anbar Province because of low morale, absenteeism, and enemy infiltration. To provide security for Fallujah, the Iraqi Interior Ministry sent in its "Public Order Brigade." That brigade is comprised almost entirely of Shiites from Baghdad and Basra. In August 2005, Fallujah "residents accuse[d] the battalion of being a defacto Shiite militia."[204] After reports in July that the Mahdi Army had all but taken over control of Basra's police department,[205] the Fallujans' accusation was more troubling.

America's new adversary was showing a remarkable degree of resilience and ingenuity in the nonmartial arenas of 4GW. His battlefield tactics were also improving.

The Iraqi Insurgents' Tactical Methods

- Are the militants depleting U.S. strategic assets?
- Which of their tactics have been the most successful?

THE REBELS MAKE THE COMMUNITY THEIR BASE

(Source: *DA PAM 550-31* (May, 1988), p. 67)

Muslim Tactics Do Not Obey Western Conventions

One must assess the Iraqi insurgent's martial ability within the context of his principal 4GW fronts—politics, religion, and economy. He will sometimes fall back in combat so as to advance on another front. His initial objective is to expel the Western occupier from Muslim territory. To do so, he depends on that occupier's over-reaction to limited combat.

For many years, the U.S. military has preferred firepower to maneuver. By encouraging this preference, the Muslim insurgent gains much of his popular support. In two separate incidents on the same day in February 2005, the U.S. military did what was expected. First to extract a patrol, one unit resorted to airstrikes in a heavily populated area. Then, another unit killed the driver of a pickup truck that got too close to its convoy.[1] Such errors were to be often repeated in the months to come.

How Fallujah Was Defended in October 2004

Fallujah's mosques played an important role in its defensive scheme. Many were found to contain munitions and fighters,[2] and many were connected by tunnels.[3] Their minarets would have provided an excellent view for observers, and their prayer chants an obscure way to sound the alarm. In addition, Coalition forces found weapon caches at five-block intervals on the south side of town.[4] In the yard of every other house was an apparent spider hole.[5] As houses are often the targets of aerial bombardment, those spider holes would have been the "bombproof shelters" so crucial to the Eastern style of defense. Strongly indicated is a series of strongpoint islands throughout the city—each with a mosque at its center and outposts along its periphery. As the outposts collapsed, the fighters moved into their religion-protected mosque and then, if need be, below ground to another zone of action. There were no reports of alternate streets being subsequently defended as was the case in Hue City.

More Evidence of a Tunnel War

A large, well-maintained tunnel network was found in Fallujah during the assault on that city.[6] The tunnels were steel reinforced, some big enough for bunk beds and trucks.[7] Others connected the mosques.[8] U.S. troops also found tunnels between houses and evidence of sewer movement.[9]

On 14 December 2004, *Hezbollah*-affiliated *Hamas* videotaped its third successful tunnel attack in six months on an Israeli outpost. When this videotape was widely aired, it reminded Iraqi insurgents of the next, evolutionary step in tactics against a technologically superior foe. The Israelis had spent millions on tunnel detection devices to no avail.[10] While the *Hamas* tunnel extended

900 yards and contained more than 2,000 pounds of explosives,[11] the tunnel on 26 June 2004 extended 1,000 yards and contained 3,300 pounds of explosives.[12] It was just a matter of time, before the Iraq insurgents would attempt something similar. The North Koreans had, after all, been helping the Iranians to build tunnels around their nuclear reactor.[13] On 26 March 2005, a 600-foot tunnel was discovered at Iraq's biggest prison—Camp Bucca. The prisoners had poured the tailings of their excavation down the toilets.[14]

The Urban Equivalent of a *"Haichi Shiki"*

The "inverted closing-U" ambush, known throughout America's 20th-Century wars as the *haichi shiki,*[15] may have been employed in Fallujah. A Marine armored unit was lured into a trap by six incoming RPG rounds. Once inside, the Marines noticed earthen berms to their front and one side. While they later described the ambush site as "L"-shaped, they may have failed to notice Muslim snipers along the non-fortified third side.[16] When the *haichi shiki* is sprung, fire teams assault from one side of the "U" to segment the column. Then the "closing circle of annihilation" begins on each segment. As that circle tightens, some of its members climb trees to get a better shot. Near the town of Hit, a Marine unit was taken under fire by people atop palm trees.[17]

Signs and Signals

A safehouse in Fallujah looked like every other house except for "two new bricks hanging from a cord on the outer wall."[18] A single brick hanging from a string meant "weapons cache."[19] Much of the signaling to enemy maneuver elements in Iraq has been done by cell phone or flag. In the Soviet-Afghan War, the removal of one's headdress also constituted a signal.

Additional Detail on the Enemy's Urban Tactics

During the assault on Samarra in early October 2004, U.S. troops encountered some fairly sophisticated guerrilla tactics. One U.S. company was delayed for hours by three snipers and then "ambushed" from the rear. That alone would not be noteworthy. What was noteworthy was that the ambusher had gotten between his quarry and another company on the other side of the river. Thus, he triggered a friendly fire fight.[20]

After two Chechen snipers killed 15 Marines during a single day in Fallujah,[21] U.S. officers said that "the remaining rebels are smart, and adapting to changing battle conditions."[22] Then, those rebels started firing from behind curtains to mask their muzzle flashes.[23] They also put machineguns in living rooms to cover the front gate of patios.[24] In addition to spider holes away from the buildings, there were hidden walls within buildings.[25] All of this led to a much tougher fight than had been expected.

Inside the Hue City Citadel, the North Vietnamese had used recessed positions and narrow sectors of fire to keep the Marines from returning accurate fire as they crossed streets. Something similar—but not nearly as lethal—was found in the older sections of Fallujah. After moving quickly through the ragtag militia at the city's outskirts, the Marines encountered a whole different class of defender. He was smart, well trained, and determined. Worst of all, he appeared to have past experience at urban combat. By not challenging the armor and blending into the background, he denied the Marines any specific target. With weapons and ammunition staged in every house, he easily gave way to the Western juggernaut. As the Marines were drawn more deeply into the inner city, they found a complex scheme of boobytrapped doors, car bombs, trip wires, rooftop spider holes, ceiling-dropped grenades, preregistered machineguns, RPG volleys, roof- and minaret-top snipers, mortar barrages, and land mines. While the Hue City defender had concentrated on street crossings, this new foe paid more attention to what went on inside buildings. He was totally familiar with the structure in which he hid. He fought from places that gave him the best angle to fire on the Marines without being seen.[26]

While the Marines searching the buildings well, a few enemy cells still escaped their attention. As the bypassed cells reemerged, they changed location every day or so. One moved to a house directly across the street from a Marine unit and started a firefight. When the Marines reoccupied the house, they found a corpse that had been boobytrapped with a grenade.[27]

In Fallujah, the enemy tactically withdrew in the face of armor as the Chechens had in Grozny in 1999. They employed boobytraps and an idea so innovative as to rarely appear in the annals of urban combat—dropping grenades on one's foe through a hole in the roof.[28] Despite each house being recleared by follow-on forces, lead units found militants popping up behind them. As the Germans had done in the Warsaw ghetto, those lead units then started to bulldoze pockets of resistance.[29] So doing may have suppressed the immediate opposition, but it also jeopardized the war's outcome. American service personnel were no longer perceived as the "liberators" of civilians who had been told to stay in their houses. As with the preparatory bombing, this was not lost on the rest of Iraq's Sunni population.

While martyrs fought to the death in some buildings, guerrillas fought for a while in others and then withdrew perpendicular to the Marines limit of advance. Upon entering the structures, Marines were shot through mouse holes in the walls and grenaded from apertures in the ceilings. Many of the fortified positions were on the second floor. Within the rooms facing hallways were often machineguns.[30] In effect, the insurgents had adapted their tactics to the terrain.

> The streets are narrow and are generally lined by walls. The walls canalize the squad and do not allow for standard immediate action drills when contact is made. . . .
> The houses are densely packed in blocks. The houses touch or almost touch the adjacent houses to the sides and rear. This enables the insurgents to escape the view of Marine overwatch positions. The houses also are all made of brick with a thick covering of mortar overtop. . . .
> Almost all houses have an enclosed courtyard. Upon entry into the courtyard, there is usually an outhouse large enough for one man. The rooftops as well as a large first story window overlook the courtyard. Generally, all the windows in the house are barred and covered with blinds or cardboard, restricting visibility into the house.
> The exterior doors of the houses are both metal and wood. The wood doors usually have a metal gate over top on the outside of the house, forming two barriers to breach. The doors have two to three locking points. Some doors are

even barricaded from the inside to prevent entry. There are generally two to three entrances to the house. The entrances are the front, the kitchen, and the side or rear.

. . . Interior doors only have one locking point and most of them can be kicked in. All doors inside and outside of the house are usually locked and must be breached.

The layout of all the houses is generally the same. Initial entry in the front door leads to a small room with two interior doors. The two doors are the entrance to two adjacent open-seating rooms. The size of the rooms varies according to the size of the house. At the end of the sitting rooms are interior doors that open up into a central hallway.

The central hallway is where all the first floor rooms lead and it contains the ladderwell to the second deck. The second deck will contain more rooms and an exit to the middle roof top. The middle roof top will have an exterior ladderwell leading up to the highest rooftop.[31]

— 3d Battalion, 5th Marines "Lessons Learned"

When Fallujah was finally "secured," the trouble did not end. Rebel bands reappeared in the rubble on 14 December 2004. They could be seen coming up out of tunnels and crossing between rooftops on ladders.[32]

Ominous Developments in Enemy Technique

In theory, urban terrain can be so laced with explosives as to be virtually unsurvivable. On 28 November 2004, U.S. Marines found an elevated outpost (overlooking the main highway through Fallujah) that could observe and then explode IEDs at eight different locations.[33] On 29 December, insurgents lured Iraqi police into a building with an anonymous tip that it was an insurgent hideout. Then they command detonated the entire building. Seven police died in the blast.[34]

On Operation Matador in May 2005, a Marine was killed through a building's floor grate by someone in the basement.[35] While such an event may seem commonplace, it isn't. Not since Stalingrad's darkest days have urban-assault troops been regularly ambushed through the floor boards of a first-story room.

Bad News for Mechanized Infantry

Though seldom realized by the Pentagon, mechanized infantry is routinely at more risk than straight-leg infantry. For a foot soldier, the only thing worse than riding inside an armored troop carrier is riding inside one with the hatch closed. Predictably, on 5 January 2005, the buried-bomb tank-killing method that had worked so well against Israeli Merkava tanks was applied to a heavily armored U.S. Bradley. The Bradley's seven passengers were killed instantly. On 8 January, it was confirmed that the insurgents had simply buried a bigger charge than usual.[36] Such an explosion does not penetrate the vehicle's skin, it simply creates enough concussion to set off its ammunition and fuel. An M-1 Abrams tank or another Bradley was blown up five days later.[37] On 3 August, 14 Marines were killed by a huge explosion beneath their armored amphibian near Haditha. To leave no evidence of a buried bomb, the enemy had tunneled beneath the road. This is a Lebanese *Hezbollah* trick. Might that movement be operating the infiltration route along the Euphrates River? The enemy now also uses upward-facing shaped charges and antitank mines in stacks. Some have a steel plate at their base to direct the charge upward. Others fire a solid steel projectile that can pierce a Bradley's skin.[38]

U.S. armor is not just vulnerable from below. Since 1992, Muslim rebels have known how to penetrate side-mounted reactive armor.

The rebels in Tadjikistan in 1992 applied this same technique when attacking T-72 tanks equipped with reactive armor. Since they lacked the anti-reactive armor PG-7VR tandem warhead, the first gunner would hit the tank to blow a hole in the reactive armor and the second and third gunner would fire the kill shots at the exposed area. This "double-teaming" also usually took out the tank's vision blocks, so if the tank survived, it was blind allowing the RPG gunners time to reposition, reload and reengage. Another "trick of the trade" was to throw a fragmentation grenade on the T-72's front deck to take out the driver's vision block before the massed RPGs opened up on the tank. The optimum shot for the Tadjik rebels was against the rear section of the T-72 turret.[39]

The U.S. Army's 1st Cavalry Division suffered the loss of 28 main battle tanks during its single year in Iraq. Most were destroyed in Sadr City.[40] While that number may seem a little high, it simply reproves the old axiom that tanks can't properly maneuver or return fire in urban terrain. There, the imaginative foot soldier reigns supreme.

Convoy Attacks

Most effective of the convoy attacks is ramming. (See Map 2.1.) On 30 October 2004, eight Marines were killed outside Fallujah when a white suicide sports utility vehicle (SUV) rammed their convoy.[41] On 6 November, 16 U.S. soldiers were wounded when a suicide police car rammed their convoy in Ramadi.[42] On 17 November, a suicide car bomber rammed a convoy during the fighting in Beiji.[43]

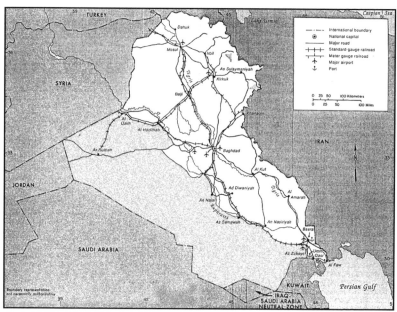

Map 2.1: Iraqi Transportation Network
(Source: *DA PAM 550-31* (May, 1988), fig. 10, pp. 164, 165)

Two weeks later, a suicide car bomb rammed a U.S. convoy on the Baghdad airport road. The very next day, the aspiring martyrs added a trick—drive slow and let the convoy pass.[44] Some 200 convoys were moving daily in Iraq as of 15 February 2005, and of that number 20% were being somehow attacked.[45]

The Emergence of the VBIED

On 1 April 2005, the vehicle-borne improved explosive device (VBIED) became the third greatest casualty producer. In first place was still small-arms fire, and in second IEDs. A VBIED is nothing more than a parked car that can be command detonated.[46]

VBIEDs would limit the restoration of basic services. When roads are blocked or too risky to travel, commerce suffers. When commerce suffers, people don't get what they need to live.

Then There Were the Vehicle-Borne Assaults

The Iraqi insurgency may be the first in which maneuver elements use civilian transportation. There have been rolling ambushes in which Coalition vehicles are surrounded by other cars. There have been drive-by shootings. There have been attacks on government compounds in which the assault element approaches the main gate by vehicle.[47]

With Enough Insider Help, One Doesn't Need Tactics

When a military organization becomes infested with turncoats and spies, it becomes much more susceptible to attack. On 29 October 2004, an "inside job" was suspected when an unobservable Iraqi National Guard formation was hit by mortar rounds.[48]

The Muslim militants used a fake checkpoint to gun down 50 National Guardsmen on 24 October.[49]

Closing In on Stormtrooper Technique

On 2 December 2004, militants stormed an Iraqi police station on the road to the Baghdad airport. This was nothing out of the ordinary. That the militants did so before dawn from behind a mortar barrage was.[50] A nighttime assault that follows a mortar barrage and then mimics its sound is state of the art. One wonders if the attackers withheld their small-arms fire and used only grenades. One also wonders if any of those grenades were of the concussion variety. During Operation Plymouth Rock south of Baghdad later that month, the 24th Marine Expeditionary Brigade captured some enemy "flash-bang grenades."[51]

Whereas German stormtroopers regularly used bangalore torpedoes to breach Doughboy barbed wire, militants sometimes use car bombs to penetrate an outer wall. So far, such cars have been reserved for front entrances and have not done enough damage to permit entry.

Commando Operations

During *Hezbollah's* Jerusalem Day parade in Beirut in November 2003, a "special battle force" practiced crossing a bridge between rooftops, rappelling down buildings, and assaulting an outpost. The bridge was made out of two taught wires, one above the other. The first of the wires must have been positioned by crossbow and grappling hook. All the while, marchers carried posters of Ayatollahs Khomeini and Khamenei and chanted "al Quds"—the name for Iranian Revolutionary Guard Special Forces.[52]

The Jeddah Consulate Attack

At the heavily fortified U.S. Consulate in Saudi Arabia, Muslim militants easily entered its outer perimeter on 6 December 2004.

The men avoided the heavily guarded main entrance on Palestine Street, choosing to use a secondary entrance on the east side of the compound. Reserved for diplomatic vehicles, this entrance was less well guarded.[53]

They approached by car as the compound's gate was remotely opened for a returning embassy vehicle, darted on foot through the automatically closing gate, shot briefly at the car, and then silenced the sentries with grenades.[54] It is not known whether any of those grenades were of the concussion variety, but some were incendiary or smoke.[55] They may have been intended for screening, mortar round simulation, or just media show. Then to advance, the attackers used human shields.[56] According to CNN, they had studied how cars entered the compound.[57] When the attack was first reported, there was also mention of insurgent activity along the compound's back wall.[58] While those reports may have been erroneous, a thought-provoking comment appeared in the prestigious *Christian Science Monitor* on 7 December. "The assault, which started around 11 A.M., involved a team of militants with rifles and bombs that scaled a wall and fought their way into the U.S. compound."[59]

The Abu Ghraib Prison Attack

At dusk on 2 April 2005, 40-50 insurgents attacked the Abu Ghraib prison, presumably to free its inmates. There were initial reports of car bombs on opposite sides of the camp. At least one had been followed by mortars and RPGs.[60] Later coverage indicated that the attack had begun with a mortar barrage.[61] Either way, a 40-minute firefight ensued in which over 40 Americans were wounded.

In an attempt to gain access to the prison, terrorists launched a simultaneous attack in multiple locations using indirect fire, rocket-propelled grenade fire, small-arms fire and a vehicle-borne improvised explosive device [VBIED]. Just as the sun was setting, indirect fire from 81mm and 120mm mortars began impacting the operating base. This was followed by multiple RPG attacks and a large volume of small-arms fire focused on two guard towers, one on the northwestern and the other on the southeastern corner on the operating base. Using the cover of the mortar fire and the intense fire on the guard towers, the terrorists launched a VBIED to penetrate the perimeter wall near the southeastern guard tower. Marines defending the base returned fire and the VBIED exploded before it reached the perimeter. Marines in the tower were forced to evacuate but were quickly reinforced by a quick reaction force.

The terrorists, using residential areas for cover and con-
cealment, then conducted a ground assault towards the
southeastern tower. With reinforcements from the quick
reaction force, Marines and Soldiers halted the advance of
the terrorists.[62]
— Official CENTCOM News Release, April 2005

"Al-Qaeda in Iraq" took credit for the attack, claiming that 20 of
its people had scaled the prison walls and one reached the top of a
prison tower. Having reconnoitered their objective from the inside
and out, they admitted to losing ten killed, including seven suicide
bombers.[63] Another American military spokesman said, "the insurgents staged simultaneous assaults on multiple locations, focusing
on two guard towers, and then using a car bomb to try to penetrate
a gate." After attack helicopters and artillery pushed back the assault, Abu Ghraib defenders failed to retrieve any injured insurgents.[64]

While not of stormtrooper quality, this attack did have a certain degree of sophistication. It was launched at a time when night
vision devices are useless and guards just returning from chow. It
attempted to seize the tower tops. Had those tower tops been occupied, the attackers would have gained an advantage in observation.
That's why tall structures have so much strategic significance in
urban combat.

A Conventional Ground-Attack Trend Emerges

The Muslim attackers have been trying to keep U.S. defenders'
heads down to give their suicide vehicles a better chance of breach-
ing U.S. obstacles. At Abu Ghraib, they started out with mortars
and RPGs and then took two observation towers under small-arms
fire. In an April 2005 attack on an American outpost near Husaybah
on the Syrian border, they remembered the mortars but forgot tower
suppression with small arms. Manning the guard tower that day
were Marine L.Cpl. Joshua Butler and PFC Charles Young, both of
Altoona, Pennsylvania. With fire through the windshield, L.Cpl.
Butler was able to detonate the first truck bomb. Then a fire engine approached from a different direction (along a road from town).
Amid the chaos of the first blast and supported by 30 dismounted
gunmen, the fire engine was almost to the compound. Luckily, PFC

Young slowed it with a grenade launcher round just long enough for Butler to recover. Despite Kelvar body armor and bullet proof glass, its driver and passenger were no match for the Marine L.Cpl. His fire prematurely detonated their bomb. A third vehicular bomb of unknown description then also detonated before it could do any damage. During the ensuing firefight, Cpl. Anthony Fink of Columbus, Ohio, killed 11 of the gunmen with his grenade launcher.[65] This is a perfect example of what small, loosely controlled U.S. contingents can do when initiative is encouraged.

On the evening of 20 April, a similar event took place at a U.S. outpost in Ramadi. This time PFC Bryan J. Nagel was manning the tower. Shortly after receiving small-arms fire, he watched a mid-sized passenger car explode at, and breach, the outpost's main entrance. Then, as a yellow sewage tanker truck came charging out of the smoke, Nagel directed a long burst from his squad automatic weapon (SAW) at its driver. The tanker instantly swerved and detonated harmlessly. The Beirut tragedy was not to be repeated this day.[66] Low-ranking Marines once again had the authority and confidence to do their jobs.

The enemy technique—in its simplest form—is to let a suicide car precede others filled with assault troops.

Evidence of Short-Range Infiltration

When the suicide bomber blew himself upside the Mosul mess tent right before Christmas 2004, an unsettling video was released by the perpetrators. It showed the plan and its execution. It claimed that a weak spot in the base wire had been penetrated during a shift change.[67] It was generally accepted that the bomber had then donned the disguise of an Iraqi soldier.

More than one Marine commander has found evidence of tampering with protective barbed wire. Hopefully, whoever is trying to get in will not look to the North Koreans for instruction.

Ramadi Provides a Rare Glimpse into Foe's Urban Tricks

Early in May 2005, U.S. Marines saw in Ramadi how enemy tactics were evolving. First, there were events of an intelligence gathering nature: "[1] people standing where they shouldn't, cars

47

suddenly U-turning, [2] people jumping out of vehicles with binoculars, [3] mosques cranking [up] the volume of their PA [public address] systems in unison, and [4] people just not showing up for work."[68] Then, after a few days, similar events turned deadly. First, there was a man on top of a distant building with a black flag. Then, a bus with approximately 50 middle-aged males drove past the government center. After going two more blocks, it suddenly stopped and dropped them off. In less than 30 minutes, snipers, automatic riflemen, RPG gunners, and a mortar crew had taken the facility under fire. Also reported from Ramadi was the exploitation of children. They were used to position a wheel-barrow-mounted rocket launcher.[69]

On the way to the "Assassin's Gate" into Baghdad's Green Zone, a U.S. soldier plainly saw rooftop sentries using their cell-phones to alert or reposition an ambush element. In South Lebanon in late 1998, a lone *Hezbollah* stalker doomed Israeli commandos and ended an occupation. He used his cell phone to tell a roving claymore ambush which path they had taken.[70]

Preparing to Limit Coalition Reinforcement

During the first al-Sadr Rebellion of April 2004, insurgents tried to sever the main roads into Baghdad: (1) the one to the west at Fallujah, (2) the one to the south at Muqdadiyah, and (3) the one to the north at Baqubah. The other southern arteries cross the Tigris at Al Kut and the Euphrates at Nasiriyah. Ominously, Fallujah marks the spot where the western road crosses the Euphrates.

As of 2 December, the ground-supply routes were being cut so frequently that some supplies had to be delivered by C-130 airlift.[71] This is all too reminiscent of what happened to the Soviets in Afghanistan. Saddam Hussein had, after all, promised to attack U.S. supply lines.

Turning the National Guard against the Coalition

A whole battalion of the new U.S.-trained Iraqi security forces refused to fight at Fallujah.[72] During renewed fighting in Al'Amarah in August, hundreds of Iraqi National Guardsmen promised to join al-Sadr until U.S. forces left Najaf.[73]

An Eastern guerrilla will intentionally create distrust between an occupier and his local defense force. Thus, the Muslim militant will discredit the National Guard in the Coalition's eyes, and the other way around. Early in the war, it was al-Sistani who blamed the Coalition for a lack of security after every atrocity. On 27 October 2004, interim prime minister Allawi allowed himself to fall into the same trap.

When 50 National Guardsmen were executed while heading home from training, Allawi accused "some Coalition forces" of not better securing their departure information. While Defense Minister Hazem Shaalan subsequently blamed the Guardsmen for leaving early along an unauthorized route, the damage had already been done. Someone should have stopped the Guardsmen from traveling unarmed along the Iranian border.[74]

Intimidating the Police

During the first al-Sadr Rebellion of April 2004, many Iraqi policemen opted to change sides.[75] At Mosul in November, the entire police department—some 5000 souls—deserted.[76]

As it became clear that the foe's primary target was the Iraqi police establishment, that establishment began to fall apart. Of its 80,000 members, only 20,000 showed up for work on 3 December.[77] The intimidation had started with the storming of police stations and ended with group beheadings.

The Attack on Infrastructure

To cripple Iraq's infrastructure, the enemy has only to attack its oil pipelines. They produce the income needed for reconstruction. In the last week of February 2005 alone, four separate pipelines were blown in the northern section of the country.[78] (See Map 2.2.)

Without enough infrastructure, a nation can't provide basic services to its people. That's when they look elsewhere for security, sustenance, and jobs. In many neighborhoods, al-Sadr's Mahdi Army (and SCIRI's Badr Brigade) are ready and able to provide all three

For almost a week, nearly half of Baghdad has been with-

out water, thanks to what the government says is an insurgent attack on one of its water mains.[79]
— *London Financial Times,* 22 January 2005

Boycotting the Coalition

By systematically assassinating Coalition workers, the militants have effectively boycotted the governing establishment. On 6 December 2004, gunmen ambushed a bus carrying 30 workers for a Coalition weapons dump in Tikrit.[80]

Since the January 2005 elections, there have been fewer attacks on governmental workers. Either the security is better, or the militants are happy with the new government.

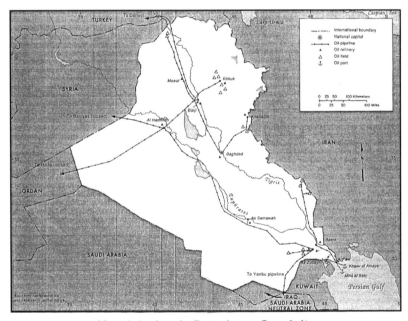

Map 2.2: Iraq's Petroleum Conduits
(Source: *DA PAM 550-31* (May, 1988), fig. 8, pp. 138, 139)

Hostage Taking

As of 15 September 2004, 100 foreigners had been seized in high-profile cases, with two dozen being killed. It was obvious that freelance kidnappers had swelled the total by selling captives to extremist groups.[81] While al-Zarqawi's *Tawhid and Jihad* took much of the credit, the identity of both the perpetrator and the "fence" are far from certain. Hostage taking is a Lebanese *Hezbollah* tactic. Falsely crediting another group would be a good way to divert attention. It was only a matter of time before the price for releasing kidnapped loved ones would be suicide bombing. That which is morally reprehensible is easily combined.

Intimidating the Entire Population

On 24 April 2005, a suicide car bomber drove into a crowd and blew up outside a Baghdad ice cream shop. Minutes later, as police and bystanders rushed to help the victims, a second bomber struck.[82]

Key facilities or people have been targeted before by static, command detonated car bombs in sequence. Bases have been hit by tandem suicide car bombers. But, this may be the first time that the tactic's only apparent goal was to terrorize civilians.

The 4GW Factor

In 4th-generation warfare (4GW), one can use battlefield maneuver to further his political agenda. From August 2004 to January 2005, there was more trouble in the Sunni north than in the Shiite south. While this statistic is often given as proof that the trouble makers are Sunni, it may mean something else. If the enemy's strategy were winning a clear majority of the vote to control the legislature, would he try to discourage the voting in opposition areas? Thus, one wonders to what extent insurgents who favored the United Iraqi Alliance (UIA) may have instigated trouble in the predominantly Sunni areas. If all the opposition party headquarters were bombed, could not a bomb outside UIA headquarters be only for show?

The Sunni Triangle Shiite force . . . was secretly trained and prepared over the past year by thousands of Iranian Republican [Revolutionary] Guards infiltrators. . . . This force numbers an estimated 5,000 combatants.[83]
— Israeli intelligence bulletin, 7 April 2004

In Asia Minor, not much is what it too obviously appears to be. Clearly, there have been three principal insurgent movements in Iraq—the Baathists, al-Zarqawi's "Al-Qaeda in Iraq," and al-Sadr's Mahdi Army. Only the last has tried to create alternative infrastructure. Baathists have been recruiting soldiers, al-Zarqawi's people have been executing "criminals," but only al-Sadr and his *Hezbollah / Sepah* mentors have been providing public services— police, courts, jails, clinics, food/clothing distribution points, financial-aid institutions, etc.[84] From the outset, Muqtada al-Sadr declared his own government and fully intended to use it.[85] That he represents Iranian interests is no longer speculation; it is a matter of public record.

In March 2003, days after the American invasion of Iraq, Tehran sent al-Sadr into the country, well-padded with Iranian weapons, intelligence, combatants, and cash, which are still on tap.[86]
— Israeli intelligence bulletin, 5 April 2004

U.S. officials have long suggested that al-Sadr receives direct support from Iran's Revolutionary Guard and Lebanon's Hezbollah. One London-based Al-Sharq Al-Awsat newspaper quoted what it called a Revolutionary Guard source who described three military camps on the Iran-Iraq border for up to 1,200 Mahdi army recruits.[87]
— *Christian Science Monitor,* 19 April 2004

During the long hot summer of 2004, al-Sadr's Mahdi Army was obviously under the tutelage of Iranian forces. They even participated in the fighting. On 15 July 2004, the *Christian Science Monitor* reported al-Sadr's forces were regrouping and rearming in Najaf with the help of 80 Iranian agents.[88]

Al-Zurufi, the Najaf governor, . . . said 80 of the fighters at

the cemetery were Iranian. "There is Iranian support to al-Sadr's group and this is no secret," he said.[89]
— Associated Press, 7 August 2004

Down to the last detail, al-Sadr's method matches that of the Iranian Revolutionary Guards and Lebanese *Hezbollah*. As of 4 August 2004, he had a gunman on every street corner in the holy cities and East Baghdad.[90] The Iranian Revolutionary Guard and Lebanese *Hezbollah* deploy sentries the same way.[91] To what extent does one's local city councilman take part in the democratic process?

Bankrupting the Occupier

By some estimates, the Iraqi war has been costing U.S. taxpayers $5 billion a month.[92] In the economic arena of a 4th-generation warfare, that is a significant amount. Even the world's richest nation can't afford to keep that up for long.

Could many of the insurgents' tactics have been intended only to cost the occupier money? From the beginning, they have focused on the U.S. resupply effort. Realizing that armor was doing U.S. forces little good, they still burned one whole truckload of assault personnel carriers (APC's).

A Terrible Mutation of Methods

Many of the Islamic militant's tactics make little sense to any world citizen who rejects martyrdom as a tool of war. The world was shocked when someone started taking Iraqi hostages and then forcing them—through threats to their families—to become suicide bombers.

On 11 June 2005, a fully accredited member of the Iraqi Wolf Brigade walked into his unit's highly secure compound after being absent without leave (AWOL) for weeks. While it has been speculated that the man was after his leader (Maj.Gen. Mohammed Qureishi), that leader was nowhere around when the man blew himself up at morning roll call.[93] While *"Al-Qaeda in Iraq"* claimed responsibility, their involvement is doubtful. The suicide vest is an

Iranian invention that has—more than once—been used against fellow Shiites. Of the 176 Iraqi police officers found to have terrorist connections, some had left their fingerprints on bomb debris.[94]

On 21 June, someone dressed like an Irbil policeman detonated his vehicle during morning roll call. To get that close, he had to be a member of the unit.[95] Just five days earlier, a suicide vest bomber had gotten into an Iraqi mess tent in Khalis.[96] Perhaps, he too belonged there. If so, these three events could mark a strategically significant change to the hostage bomber method. When the members of a military (or paramilitary) unit no longer trust each other, they lose "cohesion." Without it, they fight less hard and have more trouble winning.

On 14 July, Coalition forces were able to prevent a terrible mutation of technique outside the Green Zone. Two suicide vest bombers were planning to approach the crowd that gathered around a suicide car bombing.[97]

On 16 July, the enemy introduced another monstrosity of method in Musayyib, a religiously mixed town 40 miles south of Baghdad. A suicide bomber attacked a petroleum tanker as it made a gas station delivery near Shiite mosque. This prompted a call by Shiite legislators to empower their popular militias.[98]

What All of This Means to Iraq's Future

The Muslim militant's infantry tactics are not particularly sophisticated, but they have improved since the fall of 2004. That, in itself, worries those who realize how little leeway the average U.S. squad leader has in adapting his tactics to a changing situation. Iraq's urban guerrillas haven't won any major battles, but they haven't been seriously cornered either. For all practical purposes, they still control the vast majority of strategically important neighborhoods.

While none of this makes much difference to an American "big-picture" policy maker, it should. All the Iraqi insurgent has to do is drag the war out long enough for the Iraqi army and police forces to become sufficiently infiltrated. Then, whenever the U.S. Congress finally tires of funding the occupation, Iraq will inexorably metastasize into a fundamentalist Islamic Republic. To alter what is about to happen, one must go to its source.

The Iraqi Militants' Point of Origin

- *Where are all the suicide bombers coming from?*
- *Which movements recruit expendable foot soldiers?*

A PLACE FOR DEBARKATION AND TRAINING

(Source: *DA PAM 550-24* (December, 1987), cover)

How Much of the Insurgency Is Home Grown?

In March 2003 (right before the U.S. invasion), *jihadists* from all over the Muslim world received visas at the Iraqi embassy in Beirut to go to Iraq as martyrs.[1] That may have been what Iranian envoys discussed with Saddam Hussein at the last moment. For two years, he had been talking to Syria about how to conduct guerrilla warfare.[2] Since his ill-fated invasion of Kuwait, he had been designing a viable defense for his own country.

Izzat Ibrahim al-Duri had been Saddam Hussein's crony and Revolutionary Command Council vice chairman for years. He was

55

also a religious mystic. In January 1993, he hosted a convention at which the representatives from 51 countries were urged "to conduct holy *jihad* against the U.S. and its allies."[3] Six months before, Saddam had told his top leaders that Iraq could not defeat a U.S. invasion militarily but could prevail with "resistance tactics." One of the key players in this resistance would be al-Duri. Another was Saddam's intelligence chief, Gen. Taher Jalil Habush al-Tikriti. As of February 2005, neither had been captured. Also on the loose were Abd al-Baqi Abd and Rashid Tann Kazim—former Baathists who have been recruiting and funding resistance fighters.[4] At least one Marine battalion has witnessed Baathist recruiting inside Iraq.[5] After the Al-Sadr Rebellions died down, it seemed as if disgruntled Sunnis were the only problem.

Major General Muhammed Abdalluh al-Shahwani, director of the Iraqi National Intelligence Service, has estimated the number of gunmen who are carrying out the attacks and bombings in all parts of Iraq . . . at between 20,000 and 30,000 [no Shiites included]. He said they have the sympathy of around 200,000 persons. . . .

. . . He said former Iraqi Vice President Izzat al-Duri, former Regional Command member Muhammad Yunis [al-Ahmad], and Saddam's half brother Sab'awi Ibrahim al-Hasan are supervising the [Baathist portion of the insurgency]. . . . He pointed out that these leaders "are in Syria and move easily the to Iraqi territories." He also reported that the Ba'th Party has split into three wings and that Na'im Haddad and Tayih Abd-al-Karim are now operating inside the Iraqi territories. . . .

"They [the gunmen] are the Ba'thist remnants, hardline extremists, and others." . . .

"These [the Baathists] do not need any financial backing. As it is known, the Ba'th Party is the richest in the world." . . .

"[The defenders of Fallujah came from] the Ba'th Party and the extremist fundamentalist organizations, which are the "Ansar al-Sunnah", "Monotheism and Jihad", "Ansar al-Islam", "the 1920 Revolution", and other appellations. They total around 12 groups." . . .

. . . "[T]he support [from Iran and Syria] is continuing so as to achieve their interests." . . .

"They wrongly called it the Sunni triangle even though there are very hot areas like Diyali where the Shiites constitute almost half the population."[6]
   —Al-Sharq al-Awsat (London), 5 January 2005

In March 2005, Iraqi intelligence claimed that a Syrian security agency was arming, training, and moving Saddam's *Fedayeen.* Once in Iraq, those *Fedayeen* were targeting the police in Mosul and Ramadi.[7] Yet, even with massive Syrian assistance, Saddam's henchmen could not have generated what was to come. That would take the combined effort of many local militias and *jihadist* groups, each with its own support establishment. Soon, there would be people from all over South Asia, the Middle East and North Africa contesting the occupation. As hostage taking and suicide bombing became their weapons of choice, one would expect sponsors with a similar history.

Might Some of the Sunni Rebels Be Iranian Proxies?

As later chapters will show, Islamic states use local proxies to influence occupied neighbors. Iran is no exception in Iraq.

[I]ran is encouraging its proxies to stage attacks against the U.S.-led Coalition. Military intelligence officers describe their Iranian Revolutionary Guard Corps counterparts' strategy as one of using "nonattributable attacks" by proxy forces to maximize deniability.[8]
   — *Time Magazine,* 22 August 2005

Just as Sunni *Hamas* and *Palestinian Islamic Jihad (PIJ)* are proxies of Shiite Lebanese *Hezbollah,* so too might some of the Sunni factions in Iraq be proxies of the Iranian Revolutionary Guard *(Sepah).* There is ample evidence of *Hezbollah / Sepah's* collaboration with al-*Qaeda* since 1993. Bin Laden has met with Mughniyeh, and al-*Qaeda* operatives have been trained in the Bekaa Valley more than once.[9]

If Iran has its own Sunni proxies in Iraq, the most probable are *Ansar al-Islam* and *Tawhid and Jihad.* That would explain why the former spawned *"Ansar al-Sunna"* in May 2004 and the latter became *"Al-Qaeda in Iraq"* one month later. The new names would reinforce the belief that America was only fighting disenfranchised Sunnis and *al-Qaeda*. By November 2004, *Ansar al-Islam* had *Sepah* support, 650 fighters and 2,000 members. Its leader Mullah Krekar spent many years in Iran and sent his wounded there. Iran also provided *Ansar al-Islam* with logistical support, safe haven, and official processing of foreign fighters (mostly Syrians, Saudis, and Yemenis). *Iraqi News* found proof that *Ansar al-Islam* has *Hezbollah* advisers. *Ansar al-Sunna's* videos show *Hamas*-style suicide pacts and *Hezbollah*-style vehicle bombings.[10] By late 2004, *al-Qaeda in Iraq* had only a few hundred members (all dispersed in underground cells), and *Hezbollah* had been reportedly "supporting" al-Zarqawi.[11]

As of the previous April, there were Shiite forces in the Sunni Triangle that had been trained by Iranian Revolutionary Guard infiltrators. Imad Mughniyeh coordinated that effort, so some of those infiltrators probably now advise Sunni-militias. Mughniyeh was, for a while, Lebanese *Hezbollah's* director of operations. He now serves as *Sepah's* liaison officer with *al-Qaeda*.[12]

Where Are All the Foreign Fighters Coming From?

The instigators of the trouble in Iraq have intentionally concealed the specifics of their manpower pipeline. They did so to maintain deniability. To discover those specifics, one must establish a working hypothesis. The most promising is as follows: (1) *al-Qaeda* and *Sepah* are working together, (2) the Muslim Brotherhood recruits fighters from all over North Africa and sends them to Sudan, (3) *Sepah* trains them in Sudan and flies them in tiny increments to Beirut Airport (a *Hezbollah* stronghold), (4) *Hezbollah* sends the most dedicated to advanced or suicide training in the Bekaa Valley and the rest to Iraq through Syria. Continually added to the mix—with falsified papers—are well-seasoned Iranians, Lebanese, Palestinians, and North Africans. That is not to say that other Iranians, Afghans, Chechens, and Pakistanis do not cross the Iranian border, or that Wahhabi recruits do not transit the Saudi border. *Al-Qaeda* may even have its own small conduit through *Ansar al-Islam* in northeastern Iraq. But the majority of foreign fighters are coming in through Syria.

In late January 2005, Gen. George Casey admitted to only 1,000 foreign fighters, or 10% of the total number of estimated insurgents. At the same time, Iraq's Interim Interior Minister—Falah al-Naqib—

said the largest contingent was from Sudan.[13] Wherever they come from, they fit into four categories: (1) tactical advisers, (2) small-unit leaders, (3) common foot soldiers, and (4) suicide bombers. Some of the tactical advisers may come from *al-Qaeda*, but most are probably from *Hezbollah* or *Sepah*. To become a small-unit leader, one has only to be Moslem and have military experience. The common foot soldiers are those with average skill and dedication but no experience. Most of the rest—with a core cadre of Palestinians—become voluntary suicide bombers. That way, the formation of an international *Baseej* cannot be traced back to Iran.

As of 20 May 2005, 53% of the foreign "martyrs" were from Saudi Arabia. They were young, inexperienced, and without military training—i.e., foot soldiers or unsuspecting ordnance-delivery systems. They and their more experienced cell commanders (from Egypt, Sudan, Algeria, etc.) were entering Iraq through Syria. So too were Palestinians being delivered to al-Zarqawi.[14] So much for the naive belief that radical Shiites and Sunnis can't cooperate. *Hezbollah* depends almost entirely on its Sunni proxies in Occupied Palestine.

That more armed fighters are not crossing the Iranian border does not mean that Iran is not providing them. With false papers and a plane ticket to Damascus, who could tell? In early June 2004 (right before the second al-Sadr Rebellion), 10,000 Tehran residents signed up for suicide attacks against Israel and U.S.-led forces in Iraq. They were recruited by an organization calling itself the "Commemoration of Martyrs of the Global Islamic Campaign."[15] On 12 November, the "Headquarters for Commemorating Martyrs of the Global Islamic Movement" signed up 4,000 more Tehran residents for the same mission. While in theory, a semiofficial agency that helps the families of *Baseej* members (civilian militiamen) killed in the Iran-Iraq War, this organization appears to be more interested in future martyrs. One volunteer was asked to follow in his *Baseej* father's footsteps by participating in a new war.[16] As of 30 November, this "Martyrs' Movement" had already recruited 30,000 volunteers and chosen 20,000 of them for training. It is not hard to explain why the Tehran regime could profess neutrality but still tolerate such a movement. Recruiting and training ordinary citizens was the principal role of *Sepah* during the Iran-Iraq War. It would be only natural for it to assist with the regional progress of Khomeini's "Islamic Revolution." *Sepah* is an autonomous part of the Iranian government. It has close ties to Lebanese *Hezbollah* and its respective proxies. This is not conjecture. The Martyrs'

Movement meeting in June 2004 was attended by former *Sepah* member and now hard-line lawmaker Mahdi Kouchakzadeh and present *Sepah* member (and possible chief) Gen. Hossein Salami.[17]

Very possibly, the Tehran volunteers were motivated by more than just religious zeal. The world has long known that *Hezbollah* and *Hamas* lure destitute Palestinians with large recruiting bonuses. Insurgents in Iraq are paid as much as $3,000 for a successful attack on U.S. troops.[18] Thus, the families of the Iranian "suicide" volunteers would be well taken care of.

Iran is an Islamic state. That means its real power lies with "supreme leader" Grand Ayatollah Khamenei, his Guardian Council, and his semi-autonomous *Sepah*. To keep up appearances with the West, Iran still goes through the motions of electing a president. One candidate for the May 2005 election wanted to increase the size of the *Baseej (Sepah*-run people's militia) to 20 million to accomplish internal security and "military" missions.[19] There was a telling event during a December wargame inside Iran. The participants recruited suicide attackers to defend Muslim soil.

> Simultaneously, some 25,000 volunteers have so far signed up at newly established draft centers for "suicide attacks" against any potential intruders in what is commonly termed "asymmetrical warfare." [20]
> — *Asia Times,* 16 December 2004

Still, according to most media studies, the majority of Iraq's car bombers are from Saudi Arabia or Yemen. Many may be unaware of their missions and then detonated by remote control. The wearers of a suicide vest are different. To properly deploy their weapon, they must be willing. Thus, they are carefully selected. The suicide vest was, after all, first used in quantity by Lebanese *Hezbollah*. *Al-Qaeda* may have now adopted *Hezbollah*'s car-bombing tactic, but it has yet to fully master its psychological preparation for voluntary suicides. Sadly, two of its Pakistani religious-group affiliates are trying. One has hundreds of bombers in training for Iraq.

The Source of Willing Suicides

Lebanon allows a fully armed militia with Iranian roots *(Hezbollah)* to guard its southern border. Until just recently, it was also occupied by Syrian troops. On 2 September 2004, the United Nations Security Council narrowly adopted a resolution calling for the withdrawal of all foreign forces and the disbanding of all militias.[21] By amending its constitution to allow President Lahoud a second term, the Lebanese parliament effectively ignored that resolution. That Lebanese *Hezbollah* has been recruiting for the Iraqi war is no surprise. On 21 May 2004, thousands of Shiites marched in Beirut after *Hezbollah* leader Sheik Hassan Nasrallah accused the U.S. of desecrating holy shrines in Iraq. The marchers were wearing white shrouds to symbolize their willingness to die in defense of the holy cities of Najaf and Karbala. On the same day, a similar demonstration took place outside the British embassy in Tehran. To anyone wishing martyrdom against the Israelis, *Hezbollah* was willing to pay $100,000.[22] Lebanese *Hezbollah* has no shortage of funds. Its raises a good portion of those funds in the same way the Afghan Taliban does.

In the mid-1980's, the *Hezbollah's* use of the illicit drug trade as a funding source and a weapon against the West was sanctioned by an official *fatwa* (religious edict) issued by *Hezbollah:* We are making these drugs for Satan America and the Jews. If we cannot kill them with guns, so we will kill them with drugs.[23]

Hezbollah has been doing more recruiting and training in Lebanon than it requires for its current level of activity against Israel. In October 2003, a Popular Front for the Liberation of Palestine General Command (PFLP-GC) leader admitted that his group, *PIJ, Hamas,* and *Hezbollah* all trained at the same camp(s) in Lebanon and Syria.[24]

A source very close to the Revolutionary Guards said that the leader of the Islamic Jihad [PIJ] movement, Ramadhan Shalah, had visited Iran last week heading a large delegation that included the Islamic Jihad [PIJ] leadership, Hamas representatives, and Ahmad Jibril, leader of the PFLP - General Command, to participate in a symposium held in Tehran in support of the Intifada. . . .
[Shalah] met twice with [Iranian] Supreme Leader 'Ali

Khamenei who promised him that his movement's budget would be . . . expanded by 70% to cover the expense of recruiting young Palestinians for suicide operations. . . .

According to a Revolutionary Guards source, the Al-Quds Forces will continue training Islamic Jihad [PIJ] fighters inside Iran.[25]

— Middle East Media Research Institute, June 2002

Obviously, Shiite *Hezbollah* has no problem with the fact that most Palestinians are Sunni. Nor would it have a problem with preparing for suicide the most promising of the North African Muslim Brotherhood recruits. All the while, the Lebanese government claims to be against *al-Qaeda*. On 22 September 2004, it went so far as to arrest its "top *al-Qaeda* operative."[26]

By 21 December, all but a few of the Iraqi border posts along the Syrian border had been "routinely attacked." Many had been abandoned and burned down.[27] The reasons were obvious. The Iraqi insurgency depended—for its resupply of personnel—on a porous Syrian border.

The Outside Source of Involuntary-Suicide Bombers

In December 2004, National Broadcasting Company (NBC) News did a study on the background of 31 suicide bombers in Iraq. Half had come from Saudi Arabia; the others, from seven other countries (mostly North African).[28]

While doing a story near the Syrian border in 27 December, American Broadcasting Company (ABC) News reported that the majority of suicide bombers were from other countries. The story implied that many were destitute Palestinians recruited by *Hezbollah*.[29] They would be the willing suicide-vest bombers. Car bombers need only be idealistic.

Al-Qaeda had no history of suicide bombing in the Soviet-Afghan or the first Chechen Wars. It has only just recently copied the *Hezbollah* tactic. It can most easily acquire *jihadists* from Wahhabi Saudi Arabia. There is evidence that many of the Saudi *jihadists* are unaware of any suicide requirement. On Christmas morning of 2004, a Saudi volunteer was ordered to park his tanker truck full of explosives next to the Jordanian embassy in Baghdad. He didn't know of the other terrorists traveling at a safe distance behind him with a remote control trigger. Against all odds, the tanker truck driver survived to tell the story.[30]

For the *jihadists* who are somewhat willing to be martyred, there is another method. On 20 June 2005, a U.S. Army general provided the details. Three cars approach the target in column. In the first is the navigator. In the second is the bomber. In the third is the detonator. The bomber is closely escorted and never knows the exact second of detonation. Thus, he has much less opportunity to lose his nerve. There is no inconsistency here. The majority of suicide attacks are by car bomb (479 from January to February 2005), and most of the drivers are from non-Shiite countries. That's how the architects of the strategy maintain their deniability.[31]

A New Internal Source of Involuntary-Suicide Bombers

Kidnapping is one of *Hezbollah's* favorite tactics. On 2 May 2005, the inevitable came to light. The driver of an un-exploded suicide car in Iraq told authorities that "he had been forced to carry out the attack to protect kidnapped family members."[32]

An opportunistic foe might be expected to combine successful strategies. But, only one who was deranged would recruit suicide bombers through threats to his family. Unfortunately, the radical Muslim militant can in this way acquire an unlimited number of precision-munition-delivery "systems."

There May Be Whole Units Entering through Syria

On 17 April 2004, just over a hundred Muslim fighters attacked a Marine battalion at Qusaybah (Huseiba) on the Syrian border, fought for 24 hours, and inflicted a score of casualties.[33] Their degree of audacity and deception suggests an organized unit. First, a roadside bomb was detonated at Baath Party headquarters as a decoy. Then, the responding unit was met with machinegun and RPG fire. Finally, U.S. reinforcements were mortared and taken under small-arms and RPG fire from both sides of the road. When several Marines went to clear a house, they were ambushed in its courtyard. Their killers were wearing black uniforms and laughing.[34] As Lebanese *Hezbollah* members routinely parade in black, they have to be prime suspects. Marine intelligence speculated on Ramadi or Fallujah rebels but not their organization or reason for being at the Syrian border.

About the same time nearby, two distinct lines of insurgents were encountered on roughly parallel routes. One was on the main road from Syria, and the other was on an adjacent city street. When those on the city street were engaged, they broke contact and headed through a heavily populated area toward their comrades. Along the main road from Syria, those comrades were now firing machineguns at other Marines from between the buildings.[35] This sounds a lot like a contact made by 1st Battalion, 4th Marines just south of the Vietnamese Demilitarized Zone (DMZ) in the fall of 1966. There too, the enemy was fighting along a linear front. In fact, Asians are well known for hastily defending themselves from parallel lines instead of a perimeter. It was later discovered that this contact took place where an important "interior" leg of the Ho Chi Minh trail exited the DMZ.[36] The Marine battalion had encountered an NVA battalion in transit.

Enemy Foot Soldiers Hail from Many Lands

Clearly, the enemy is also recruiting foot soldiers internationally. Some 2,500 Saudis have already gone to Iraq.[37] Many others are coming from North Africa. People are signing up to fight the Americans out of more than just religious duty.

Contract killers are being offered as little as $US50 ($67) to hunt down Coalition troops . . . on the streets of Iraq. The mercenaries are being lured to Baghdad from poor neighboring countries in the Middle East with the promise of cash payments for every Western soldier they kill.[38]
— *Sydney Sunday Telegraph,* 12 December 2004

Some of the Specialists Come through Iran

During the Shiite holy weeks, tens of thousands of pilgrims cross the Iranian border with little, if any, identity check. (See Map 3.1.) It is no secret that *al-Qaeda* personnel have been allowed to freely

Figure 3.1: Grand Ayatollah Ruhollah Khomeini
(Source: *Corel Gallery*, Historical Portraits, #01C071)

transit Iran. Thus, bomb-making specialists and Chechen advisers may be coming over from Afghanistan. Still, the biggest concern is with how many advisers Iran itself provides.

Iran Has Been Buying Some Interesting Equipment

On 5 December 2004, two Iranians were arrested in Austria for attempting to purchase 3,000 sets of sophisticated, helmet-mounted night vision devices. Iran has already bought night vision equipment, global positioning systems (for land navigation), and body armor from Britain and France. It has also purchased thousands of high-powered armor-piercing sniper rifles in Austria.[39] Sadly, .50 caliber sniper rifles (that can shoot over a mile) are also easily obtainable through mail order from the U.S. market.

With substantial deposits of oil, Iran is not a poor country. Its Lebanese proxy has independent sources of income: (1) growing opium and hashish in the Bekaa valley,[40] (2) mining diamonds in Africa, and (3) enforced tithing all over the world.

Syria's Role in the Festivities

An article appeared in the *Christian Science Monitor* on 23 December 2004 claiming that the finding of Syrian photographs in Fallujah might mean that Iraqi Baathists were running the insur-

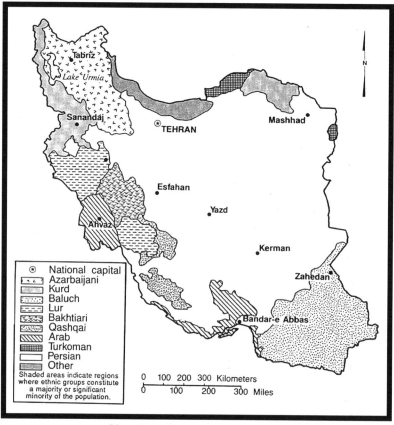

Map 3.1: Iran's Ethnic Areas

(Source: *DA PAM 550-68* (September, 1987). fig. 5, p. 86)

gency from Damascus. [41] This would have reinforced the official view that Sunnis were the problem, if Syria's Baathist leaders were not Allawite (an offshoot of Shiism). The Iraqi and Syrian Baath Parties have seldom gotten along. [42]

Striking Similarities between Sistani and Khomeini

Al-Sistani carries an Iranian passport. One of only a handful of grand ayatollahs, he is also the spiritual leader of much of the Iranian and Iraqi population. As Shiites pledge a fifth of their disposable income to their personal *marja,* al-Sistani has considerable financial clout. So far he has insisted that Iraq's new constitution be in line with Islamic principles and recognize Islam as the nation's religion. On the January 2005 recruiting posters, he looked just like Khomeini. (Refer back to Figure 3.1.) The extent to which he shares Khomeini's vision of a government regulated by fundamentalist Islamic thought is yet to be determined.

Rudhollah Khomeini . . . lived in exile in Najaf before leading Iran's Islamic revolution and called for a *wilayat al-faqth,* or the guardianship of the jurisprudent. But Sistani has also written about the need for clerical influence in political life.

"Sistani in his *fatwas* does talk about . . . the guardianship of the jurisprudent in social issues," says Mr. Cole, the history professor (at the University of Michigan). Sistani's preference is "that clerics mostly leave running the state to lay persons. But the implication is that Shiite lay persons will be influenced by Sistani's *fatwas* on legislative issues."

Analysts note that one of the main differences between Shiite and Sunni Islam is the hierarchical nature of Shiism. Almost all Shiites adopt an "object of emulation," or *marja al-taqlid,* a senior cleric whose rulings on what is permitted under Islam they closely follow. Sistani is the most widely followed *marja* in Iraq. [43]
— *Christian Science Monitor,* 20 January 2005

According to *Newsweek,* "Sistani has pledged not to interfere in politics, but [for the 30 January election] he made it a religious obligation to vote for his list. [44]

67

Evidence That Iran Is Helping the Sunni Insurgents

On 24 December 2004, a captured commander of the Baathist Sunni organization Mohammed's Army—Muayad Yassin Aziz al-Nasiri—was videotaped saying that both Iran and Syria were providing funds and equipment. On 7 January, the Iraqi Defense Minister—Hazim Shaalan—played the tape during a news conference in Baghdad. He had been saying for several months that both countries (Iran and Syria) were aiding the insurgency movement in Iraq—including Saddam Hussein loyalists—with cash, operatives, and equipment. U.S. officials and commanders have already confirmed many of al-Nasiri's assertions.[45]

So much for the theory that Iran only supports Shiite separatists. Iran will help any group that defies a Western occupier. Once that occupier is gone, Iran easily asserts its dominance. That's how Eastern powers fight 4th-generation wars—by publicly professing to abstain from what they are really doing. The *Tehran Times* runs an occasional article about how much it dislikes *al-Qaeda* (memo for record).[46] Yet, after the U.S. invasion of Afghanistan, many of *al-Qaeda's* top leaders found political asylum in Iran.[47]

> According to European, Saudi, and U.S. government sources, several high-level members of al-Qaeda are either in Iran or moving freely across the Afghan-Iran[ian] border. Those include Osama bin Laden's No. 2, Zayman al-Zawahiri; Mr. bin Laden's son, Saad bin Laden; the No. 3 in charge of military operations, Said al-Adel; and Abu Gheith, al-Qaeda's spokesman. Up to a dozen "serious al-Qaeda members" are there, and a total of some 50 foot soldiers, as well as family members, swelling the total figure to about 300.[48]
> — *Christian Science Monitor,* 24 October 2003

In December 2004, a London-based CNN contributor claimed to have evidence that Osama bin Laden was in Iran instead of northwest Pakistan.[49] This is certainly possible, as he would want to be with his family.[50] In February of that year, a high level *Sepah* defector by the name of Zakiri confirmed that Imad Mughniyeh had helped several *al-Qaeda* personnel to enter Iran, including bin Laden's wife. He speculated that bin Laden may have been assisted as well.[51]

Once the director of operations for Lebanese *Hezbollah,*

Mughniyeh is now the leading *Hezbullah* operative in Iran with connections to *al-Qaeda.* Zakiri (the *Sepah* defector) also claimed that Mughniyeh delivered a letter from al-Zawahiri to the leaders of Iran right before 9/11 asking for help in attacking the "Great Satan." He went on to say that the request had been denied.[52] Mughniyeh has since been busy in both Palestine and Iraq. His coordination has not been strictly between Shiite elements.

Zakiri further asserted that the *Ansar al-Islam* organization in Iraqi Kurdistan had won the support and protection of *Sepah* intelligence.[53] That would explain why it (or al-Zarqawi's group) purportedly attacked every time al-Sadr's forces needed a rest.

Indeed it [al-Sadr's rebellion] was prepared well in advance at the behest of Tehran—with the collaboration of Damascus and the Hezbollah—by the Shiite master terrorist Imad Mughniyeh. Its purpose: to trigger Iran's Spring Offensive against the Americans in Iraq.

Sunday night [4 April 2004], the young radical cleric al-Sadr told cheering followers in Kufa: "From now on we are the beating arm of the Hezbollah and Hamas in Iraq." The crowds, raising clenched fists, declared: "The occupation is over! Sadr is our ruler!"[54]

— Israeli intelligence bulletin, 5 April 2004

Iran's Degree of Complicity

The extent of Iran's meddling into the affairs of its western neighbor would impress the most discerning of East-Asian "36 Stratagems" experts. Iran has created a politically viable "big picture" while unobstrusively altering tens of thousands of "little pictures." It has convinced U.S. authorities that they face a Sunni-inspired insurrection.

On April 6, the London Arabic daily *Al-Hayat* discussed recent Iranian activity in Iraq: "In the last 2 [two] days, there has been repeated talk in the Governing Council of Iraq about the major Iranian role in the events. . . . "The direct Iranian presence in . . . political, security, and economic affairs can not be ignored anymore. This presence is accompanied by a vigorous Iranian effort to create bridges with different forces in Iraq; first, *by material and logistic aid to parties other than the Shi'a* [italics added], and secondly through the traditional Iranian influence in the religious seminaries *[hawza]* and in the *Marja'iya* [religious Shiite authorities] institutions. "A member of the Governing Council told *Al-Hayat* that the Iranians have recently managed to activate a known *Marja'*, Kazem al-Ha'iri, who lives in the city of Qum in Iran, and is known to be close to al-Sadr's movement. . . . [S]ources [recalled] . . . Al-Sadr's statements that his movement is an extension of the Lebanese *Hezbollah* and of *Hamas.* . . . [They] said that the visit of an assistant of Muqtada Al-Sadr to Fallujah before the last uprising and al-Sadr's statement that his movement is an extension of *Hamas* were both messages to his *new allies among the Iraqi Sunnis* [italics added]. . . .

The London Arabic-Language Daily *Al-Sharq Al-Awsat* quoted extensively the former Iranian intelligence official in charge of activities in Iraq, identified as Haj Sa'idi, who recently defected from Iran: "Haj Sa'idi told *Al-Sharq Al-Awsat* that the Iranian presence in Iraq is not limited to the Shi'ite cities. Rather, it is spread throughout Iraq, from Zakho in the north to Umm Al-Qasr in the south, and the infiltration of Iranian Revolutionary Guards and the Al-Quds [special-forces-led] Army into Iraq began long before the war [U.S. invasion]. . . . "After the war, the Iranian intelligence sent its agents through the uncontrolled Iraq-Iran border; some of them as students and clerics, and others as belonging to the Shi'ite militias. "Haj Sa'idi said that the assassination last summer of Ayatollah Muhammad Baqir al-Hakim, who headed the Supreme Council of the Islamic Revolution in Iraq (SCIRI), was a successful operation carried out by the intelligence unit of the Iranian Al-Quds Army. He also revealed that there was a failed attempt on the life of the highest Shi'ite *Marja*, Ayatollah Ali al-Sistani, at the Eid Al-Adha holiday last year, and that there was another plan to assassinate Ayatollah Ishaq al-Fayad. "Haj Sa'idi claimed that some of the Iranian intelligence officers in Iraq are known to everybody, for example in Al-Suleimaniya and Derebendikhan in the north." However, he said, the real threat comes not from the officers that are known, but from those that are unknown. Amongst them are 18 Shi'ite charities in Kazimiya, in Al-Sadr city in Baghdad, in Karbala, Najaf, Kufa, Nasiriyah, Basra, and other cities with a large Shi'ite majority. In those offices, new agents are recruited every day, under the guise of financial aid, medicine, food, and clothing for the poor. "Haj Sa'idi said that the Iranian plan to turn Iraq into another Iran is a wide-ranging plan, and it involves the recruitment of thousands of young Shi'ites for the next stage, which will take place with the [first] parliamentary elections in Iraq." Those recruited now are supposed to enlist their relatives to vote for candidates that will be endorsed by the Iranian intelligence apparatuses. "Haj Sa'idi also mentioned that more than 300 reporters and technicians who are working now in Iraq for television and radio networks, newspapers, and other media agencies are in fact members of the Al-Quds Army and the Revolutionary Guards intelligence units." "He also mentioned that the Iranian money allocations for activities in Iraq, both covert and overt, reached $70 million per month. . . ." "Haj Sa'idi added that the attempt by the Kurdish authorities in northern Iraq to act against the Iranian activities there prompted a reaction by the Iranian Revolutionary Guards to incite the Turkmeni Shi'ites in the region against the Kurds. He claimed that many Turkmen Shi'ite commanders traveled to Iran and got huge financial support, as well as guarantees that Iran will stand by them in case of clashes between them and the Kurds."

A source in the Quds Army of the Iranian Revolutionary Guard revealed to *Al-Sharq Al-Awsat* information relating to the construction of three camps and training centers on the Iranian-Iraqi borders to train elements of the "Mahdi Army" founded by Muqtada al-Sadr. The source estimated that about 800-1200 young supporters of al-Sadr have received military training including guerilla [sic] warfare, the production of bombs and explosives, the use of small arms, reconnoitering and espionage. The three camps were located in Qasr Shireen, 'Ilam, and Hamid, bordering southern Iraq which is inhabited largely by Shi'a Muslims.

During his recent visit to Iran, al-Sadr met with Hashemi Rafsanjani, head of the Expediency Council, as well as the head of the revolutionary guard intelligence, Murtadha Radha'i, and the commander of the Al-Quds Army responsible for Iraqi affairs, Brig. General Qassim Suleimani and other government and religious leaders. . . . The source indicated that elements of the Al-Quds Army and the Revolutionary Guard Intelligence lead many of the operations directed against the coalition forces.[55]

— Excerpts from London-based Arabic newspapers,
Al-Hayat and *Al-Sharq Al-Awsat,* April 2004

After the January 2005 elections, the extent of al-Sistani's support (whether willing or otherwise) for an Islamic state became painfully clear.

Iraq's Shiite leader Grand Ayatollah Ali al-Sistani and another top cleric staked out a radical demand that Islam be the sole source of legislation in the country's new constitution. . . .

Sistani leads the five most important clerics, known as marja al-taqlid, or objects of emulation, who had portrayed a more moderate stance going into the election.

The surprise statement was released by Sheikh Ibrahim Ibrahimi, a representative of Grand Ayatollah Mohammad Ishaq al-Fayad, another of the marja. . . . A source close to Sistani announced soon after the release of the statement that the spiritual leader backed the demand.

Sistani and the other top clerics mainly live in the central holy city of Najaf. On top of [in addition to] Sistani and Fayad, there are the ayatollahs Bashir al-Najafi and Mohammad Said Hakim. A fifth, Ayatollah Kazem al-Ha'iri, lives in Iran.[56]

— Agence France-Presse, 6 February 2005

While no one appeared to notice or care, al-Sistani's election poster visage was almost identical to that of Khomeini. Their black turbans and white beards were identical. All that varied was facial detail. After the election, there were four United Iraqi Alliance (UIA) front runners for the post of prime minister: (1) Ibrahim Jaafari (*Dawa* Party chieftain), (2) Adel Abdul Mehdi (SCIRI choice), (3) Ahmed Chalabi (pro-Iranian U.S. confidant), and (4) Hussein al-Shahrastani (al-Sistani's choice).[57] On 14 February, Mehdi posed for a "victory photo" next to the apparent image of Iran's Ayatollah Khamenei.[58] On 16 February, it was reported that Mehdi had dropped out of the race and the "moderate" Jaafari was in the lead. While Jaafari was vowing moderation and U.S. support, the platform on his party's website "explicitly urges for the 'Islamization' of the Iraqi society and the state, including the implementation of Sharia, or Islamic law." [59] Then Chalabi was in the lead. On 17 February, he promised to drop all charges against Muqtada al-Sadr.[60] Two days later, he said, "[H]e would seek to establish an agreement to govern [limit] the presence of U.S. troops, and open the heavily fortified Green Zone . . . to the Iraqi people." [61] The Shiites were working well together. With a mutual parent, people are less prone to power struggles.

The True Identity of the UIA

In the post-election bargaining for key posts in the new government, it appeared as if the Kurds would permit a pro-Iranian *Dawa* Party prime minister in return for Jalal Talebani as president. SCIRI's Mehdi also looked like a good bet for minister of interior— the person who controls every aspect of domestic security and intelligence. His Badr Brigade could greatly augment the security apparatus.[62]

SCIRI has enjoyed good relations with both main Iraqi Kurdish factions—the [Patriotic Union of Kurdistan] PUK and the Kurdish Democratic Party (KDP), especially the former, as PUK leader Jalal Talebani has been a key ally of the Islamic Republic [Iran] for more than 2 [two] decades.[63]

Finally, in late February 2005, al-Sistani threw his support behind Jaafari and the debate was over.[64] This sparked renewed interest in the *Dawa* Party's background. That SCIRI has its own conventionally armed militia—the Badr Brigade—is common knowledge. That the *Dawa* Party had a very proficient unconventional warfare wing is not. It was a secretive, cell-based network of bombers and assassins that earned a reputation as Saddam Hussein's most fearsome enemy.[65]

According to *Newsweek,* the *Dawa* Party was traditionally fundamentalist.[66] It also had close ties to Iran and Lebanese *Hezbollah.* In fact, it was a direct descendent of the "Party of Islamic Call" *(Hizb ad-Da'wa al-Islamiya)* that spawned Ayatollah Khomeini and

Hezbollah's clerics. The Shiite activist revival did not originate in Iran in 1979; it originated in Najaf, Iraq in the 1960's. Its leader was Muhammed Baqir al-Sadr (Muqtada's grandfather). From then on, the Party of Islamic Call "propagated . . . a revolutionary transformation of society among Shi'i communities in Iraq, Iran, the Persian Gulf, and Lebanon."[67]

> Militant Lebanese clerics [are] affiliated with the Lebanese branch of Al-Da'wa, a radical Iraqi Shi'ite fundamentalist group. . . . Most of the radical clerics who formed the nucleus of Hezbollah's leadership [in 1982] had been educated in the Shi'ite seminaries of southern Iraq, particularly Najaf, where Iranian Supreme Leader Ayatollah Khomeini . . . spent many years in exile.[68]
> — *Middle East Intelligence Bulletin,* February 2003

On 11 March 2005, the Kurds agreed to Jaafari for prime minister, as long as they got Talebani for president, control over oil-rich Kirkuk, a share of the region's oil revenues, the right to maintain the *peshmerga* militia, and a bigger share of the national budget.[69] More about the UIA surfaced on 15 March during the first meeting of the newly elected assembly. There, Abd Aziz al-Hakim, brother and replacement of murdered SCIRI leader Mohammed Baqir al-Hakim, was the keynote speaker.[70] He was now the head of UIA.[71]

On 6 April, Iraq's new leaders were finally chosen by its parliament. Talebani would be president, Ghazi al-Yawer (a Sunni) one vice president, Adel Abdul Mehdi (a Shiite) the other vice president, and Jaafari prime minister. Thus, Iraq now had the head of the *Dawa* Party for prime minister and a SCIRI chieftain for a vice president.[72] Only left to be determined was the interior minister. Ominously, the Kurds were allowing the UIA to control the ministries of interior, finance, electricity, transportation, communications, oil, and health.[73] These just happen to be the same parts of infrastructure that Muslim militants erode.

Iran's Backing of Muqtada al-Sadr

On 1 March 2005, the U.S. administration finally acknowledged that al-Sadr was working for the Iranians. Still, he remained at large.

[Defense Intelligence Agency] DIA Director Vice Adm. Lowell Jacoby told the Senate Select Intelligence Committee that the Iraq insurgency has grown "in size and complexity over the past year." . . . [T]he agency said the Iranian-backed Mahdi Army, headed by Shi'ite cleric Muqtada Sadr, was preparing to expand its role. "We judge Sadr's forces are re-arming, re-organizing and training," Jacoby said. "Sadr is keeping his options open to either participate in the political process or employ his forces." [74]

Iran's Manipulation of al-Sistani

Al-Sistani will continue to lead the Shiite world as long as that leadership is deemed useful by the Iranian Revolutionary Guard. Many of the houses in al-Sistani's neighborhood have recently been purchased by Iranians.[75]

Most of Iran's charities double as food/clothing distribution centers and recruiting stations. One, however, has a different role. Ahl ul Bail World Assembly opened an office in Najaf to promote the doctrine of clerical rule. It intends to incorporate the *Sharia* into Iraq's new constitution.[76]

The Possibility of Political Hardball

On 17 April 2005, kidnappers purportedly took 100 Shiites hostage at Madaen on the southern edge of the Sunni Triangle. Their demand was that all Shiites leave the town.[77] When Iraqi and U.S. troops surrounded and searched Madaen, they found no evidence of foul play. More than one source reported the hostage taking a hoax.[78] Even Iraqi's acting Interior Minister, Falah Naqib, confirmed that no hostages had been found.[79] Two days later, some 55 bodies of indeterminate origin came floating down the Tigris River.[80] While newly elected president Talebani felt obligated to infer that they were the missing hostages, others pointed to inconsistencies in his theory. There was no conclusive evidence that the bodies had all been retrieved at once, had come from the Salman Pak area, or had even been Shiite.[81] Domestic kidnapping (for any number of reasons) is commonplace throughout the upstream area, and bodies routinely float to the surface in the spring.

According to local police, as well as reports from Iraqi journalists who reached Madaen, most of the corpses were uni-
dentified young men who had been killed elsewhere and
dumped in the river. Iraqi police said the victims who could
be identified came from cities and villages up and down the
Tigris valley, particularly from towns astride the highways
that connect Baghdad to the south.[82]

— *Newsweek,* 2 May 2005

Then the plot thickened. A young Shiite by the name of Hussein
Hashimi came up with a computer disk (CD) full of photographs of
the missing men and a list of their Sunni abductors.[83] In a com-
puter-oriented society, such a discovery would be perfectly natural.
In Iraq, it's not. Next, the personal effects and ID card of Margaret
Hassan—the murdered CARE envoy—were found during a raid on
Madaen.[84] All the while, the UIA's choice—Jaafari—was working
under a 7 May deadline to form a cabinet or abdicate as prime minister.[85]

The kidnapping victims and waterlogged bodies had either been
one and the same, or someone had gone to a lot of trouble to allege
that they were. Either way, the casual American reader became
more convinced than ever that the only insurgents in Iraq were
Sunni, and that the rightful rulers of Iraq were Shiite.

Hours after an Allawi-affiliated legislator was gunned down in
her own home, Jaafari got his cabinet list approved (with some temporary fillers) on 27 April. Thus ended a three-month-long stale-
mate.[86] Then came nine straight days of concerted attacks against
Iraqi security forces that killed over 300 people.[87] Most were by car
bomb and in Baghdad, but a few were elsewhere and by suicide
explosive. On 29 April alone, 10 went off in Baghdad's Sunni neighborhoods and two in Madaen,[88] the site of the alleged massacre of
Shiites. On 2 May, a car bomb killed 25 at a rite for a Kurdish
official in northern Iraq. Two days later, a suicide bomber killed 50
police recruits in Kurd-controlled Irbil.[89]

So one has to wonder—were all of these bombings coincidental
or somehow connected to the political process? Were the Sunnis
mad because only four of their seven ministries (out of 37) and deputy
premiership had been initially filled?[90] Or was there a more sinister plot afoot—like getting the legislature to fill out the cabinet before Jaafari's deadline? That legislature rejected ten Sunni nomi-
nees for defense minister before finally agreeing on one. On 8 May,

the nominations for the last six cabinet posts were confirmed by the legislature with the Sunni human-rights minister declining his appointment.[91] The country did not experience another major bombing until 11 May. It happened in Tikrit—Saddam's home town. The very next day, Kurdish Kirkuk endured several.[92] There was still the little matter of a trilateral constitution to be worked out by 15 August.[93] After two of the 14 Sunni members of the 71-member constitution committee were assassinated during the week of 18-22 July, the other twelve returned to the negotiating table.[94] During the one-week extension to the 15 August deadline, the Sunnis again boycotted the discussions. Then three members of their political party were executed while working on voter registration.[95] In the realm of 4GW, that which is tactical can be combined with that which is media related or political. Mughniyeh is world renown for erasing evidence trails. In which would he be more interested—obscuring the identity of a town's bully or of a theocracy's architect?

The Real Power in an Islamic Revolutionary Theocracy

In Iran, the supreme leader—Ayatollah Khamenei—wields most of the actual power. The Iranian Revolutionary Guards work for him alone. Thus, President Khatami's hands have been largely tied in the running of Iran.[96]

In the presidential elections of 17 June 2005, Mohamad Baqer Qalibaf was supposedly Khamenei's choice, but there were other less-obvious *Sepah* candidates in the race. Amid allegations that *Sepah's Baseej* (morality police) had rigged the voting, Mahmoud Ahmadinejad earned and then won a run-off against the favored Rafsanjani (president from 1989 to 1997). (See Figure 3.2.) After organizing the assault on the U.S. embassy in 1979, hard-liner Ahmadinejad became a *Sepah* commander and Tehran mayor. That *Sepah* could now win elections did not bode well for the future. While Ayatollah Khamenei has the last say on all important decisions, the Iranian president still sets the tone and agenda. In March 2005, Rafsanjani made several "vitriolic public harangues" against U.S. troops in the region. In one speech, he accused the U.S. of waging war against all of Islam and called on all Muslim nations to confront the U.S.[97] Ayattolah Khamenei doesn't want a softer tone, he wants total loyalty. Rafsanjani tried occasionally to reason with the supreme leader.

Figure 3.2: Ali Akbar Hashemi Rafsanjani
(Source: *Corel Gallery*, Political Portraits, #01F170)

The Hidden Instigator Consolidates

While Coalition forces worked hard to contain *al-Qaeda*, Baathist, and *Ansar al-Islam* terrorist cells in the north, the real enemy consolidated the south. Something similar had happened in southern Lebanon.

In Basra these days, it's not uncommon to see armed men from Shiite religious groups standing at the gates of Basra University, scrutinizing female students to make sure their dresses are the right length and their make-up properly modest.

"No alcohol, no music CDs, woman forced to wear [head covering] *hijab,* people murdered in the streets—this is not the city I remember," says Samir, an editor of one of Basra's largest newspapers. (His name, and others, have been changed for security reasons.) "In the past, Basra revolted against attempts to make it too Islamic." . . .

With the fall of Saddam Hussein in April 2003, Shiite organizations, many with close associations with Iran, seized political control of the south. The Jan. 30 elections solidified their power, especially in Basra, where 35 out of the 41 members of the province's Governing Council (GC) belong to such groups as *Dawa Islamiyya* or the Supreme Council for Islamic Revolution in Iraq (SCIRI). . . .

Others contend that devotion to extreme Islam does not itself solve Basra's problems. "These people held power for two years, and what did they accomplish?" says Samir. "Basra is in shambles, we are without electricity, fresh water, and security. They didn't even give us hope."

Others criticize GC members. . . . (A Ministry of Defense official in Basra claims that "50 percent" of the GC have ties to the Islamic Republic [Iran]). . . .

As for the bans on alcohol, music CDs, or general mingling of the sexes, "This is Iranian, too," says Mr. Wendy. "In the past, Basra had bars, casinos, nightclubs—it had life. Basra has really become an Iranian city. I no longer recognize it." . . .

Another major source of extremist mores is firebrand cleric Muqtada al-Sadr. Last March, Mr. Sadr's followers disrupted a picnic held by Basra University students. . . . The militias have also harassed Basra's media. . . .

According to Iraqi officials, nearly 1,000 people—most of them Sunni Muslims—have been killed in the city over the past three months, with 100 murdered in one week in May alone. . . .

While no one is certain about the killers' identities, Basrans have their suspicions. Echoing sentiments one hears throughout the city, "I believe intelligence agents from Iran identify the victims and then hire gunmen affiliated with the religious parties," says a Sunni sheikh in Zubair, a city southwest of Basra.[98]
— *Christian Science Monitor,* 13 July 2005

Jaafari's same-day news conference may have been a coincidence, but it still evoked images of enemy strategy.

[H]e [Jaafari] said security in many of Iraq's 18 provinces—notably in the Shiite south and the Kurdish-controlled north—has improved so that Iraqi forces could assume the burden of maintaining order in cities there.

"We can begin with the process of withdrawing multinational forces from these cities to outside as a first step that encourages setting a timetable for the withdrawal process," al-Jaafari said at a news conference with U.S. Deputy Secretary Robert Zoellick.[99]

— Associated Press, 13 July 2005

On 3 August, a free-lance investigative journalist was yanked from the streets of Basra by the occupants of a police car and subsequently shot.[100] (See Figure 3.3.) Steven Vincent had just written

Figure 3.3: Basra's Already Compromised Police Force

(Source: Courtesy of *The New York Times* and the artist, from "Switched Off in Basra," by Steven Vincent, 1 July 2005, illustration by M.K. Perker, ©2005 M.K. Perker)

an article for the *New York Times.* Parts of that article are reprinted below. Mr. Vincent is also the author of the 13 July *Christian Science Monitor* piece with which this paragraph began. It will be a terrible shame if the momentous discoveries of this brave American go unheeded by his own countrymen.

> As has been widely reported of late, Basran politics (and everyday life) is increasingly coming under the control of Shiite religious groups, from the . . . Supreme Council for the Islamic Revolution in Iraq [a UIA component] to the bellicose followers of the rebel cleric Muqtada al-Sadr. . . .
>
> In May, the city's police chief told a British newspaper that half of his 7,000-man force was affiliated with religious parties. This may have been an optimistic estimate: one young Iraqi officer told me that "75 percent of the policemen I know are with Muqtada al-Sadr—he is a great man." And unfortunately, the British seem unable or unwilling to do anything about it. . . .
>
> An Iraqi police lieutenant . . . confirmed to me the widespread rumors that a few police officers are perpetrating many of the hundreds of assassinations . . . that take place in Basra every month. He told me that there is even a sort of "death car": a white Toyota Mark II that glides through the city streets, carrying off-duty police officers in the pay of extremist religious groups to their next assignment. . . .
>
> In other words, real security reform requires psychological as well as physical training. Unless the British include in their security sector reform some basic lessons in democratic principles, Basra risks falling further under the sway of Islamic extremists and their Western trained police enforcers.[101]
>
> — *New York Times,* 31 July 2005

What the U.S. government had tried so hard to prevent was occurring right under its nose. Its exit strategy of returning security to the locals had backfired. Yet, no one in Washington seemed overly concerned with the problem. On 22 July, it was announced that the U.S. hoped to hand over to Iraqi forces the security of 14 out of 18 provinces by early 2006, thereby cutting its troop levels from 176,000 (at their highest level) to 66,000.[102]

What was happening could not have been more obvious. In early August 2005, Baghdad's major Alaa al-Tamimi was run out of office by Shiite militiamen (presumably from Sadr City). Then, a month later, there were reports of Karbala being infiltrated at every level of power by Iran's Ministry of Intelligence and Security. When an independent Iraqi daily claimed that "thousands of intelligence agents from the Iranian regime have been given Iraqi citizenship," [103] American policy makers should have noticed the Basra and Karbala parallels. What chance will Iraq's overt democratic process have with a covert Islamic revolution in progress?

The "Working Relationship" between Shiite and Kurd

After missing three deadlines, the Iraqi parliament produced a draft constitution on 28 August 2005. Favoring a federation of Shiite and Kurdish states, it was instantly rejected by the Sunni members. This set up a crucial showdown at the national referendum on 15 October. If two-thirds of the voters in three of the four Sunni provinces reject the charter, it will be defeated, prompting the reelection of parliament by 15 December.[104]

All of this was interesting, but nearly as interesting as what went on concurrently. As with the parliamentary leadership deliberations, corpses started to appear. On 26 August, 36 men with baggy Kurdish trousers had been found executed near the Iranian border. The same day, 15 of Kurdish President Talebani's bodyguards were gunned down in an assassination attempt.[105] The Kurds were not the only ones being nudged. There had just been several clashes between the Shiite Mahdi Army and Shiite Badr Brigade over the issue of federalism.[106] While al-Sadr's Mahdi militia represented *Sepah/Hezbollah*, SCIRI's Badr militia was aligned with Iraq's pro-Iranian ruling party—the UIA. The former wanted nothing short of a Shiite Republic, but the latter had just settled for a federation of semiautonomous Shiite and Kurdish states. That's all it took to light the spark. It was not the Sunnis or al-Qaeda doing the killing. It was the hidden mentor encouraging its entourage to stick to the original plan.

This type of thing is neither new to the region nor attributable to a disenfranchised part of the population. It is the way a radical-Islamic lead faction consolidates its power. It does not do so by political agreement, diplomatic compromise, or financial compensation; it does so by threats, intimidation, and murder. It can treat a tentative member of its own religious sect worse than an infidel. Shiite infighting occurred in Lebanon in the 1980's. As Sepah-launched *Hezbollah* consolidated, it engaged in active combat with Syrian-backed *Amal*.[107] The differences in their viewpoints were subtle. While *Amal* sought security for southern Lebanon, *Hezbollah* wished to extend the fight into Israel.[108] *Amal* desired no armed Palestinian presence in Lebanon and a greater role for Shiites in a secular government. *Hezbollah* wanted help from armed Palestinians in expelling the Israelis from an Islamic Republic.[109] In other words, only *Amal* would have settled for a federation. As the two vied for power,[110] *Hezbollah* had the decided edge. From the Islamic Revolution in Iran, its founders had experience in dislodging other guerrilla factions, suppressing ethnic uprisings, providing internal security, and prosecuting open warfare.[111]

Sepah, Hezbollah, and their various Sunni proxies cannot be appeased. They will keep expanding their territory. As Israel completed its pullout of the Gaza Strip on 27 August, thousands of *Hamas'* fighters celebrated victory. Then, their leader, Jebaliya Deif, vowed that his people would continue their attacks against Israel.[112] Thus, America's Iraqi focus must shift back to counterinsurgency. A Muslim revolution depends for its life's blood on the indoctrination and training of small units. While the U.S. military should be aware of the foe's political maneuvering, it must concentrate on his combat training facilities.

A Synopsis of Iraqi Insurgent Training Sites

As of February 2005, Muslims of every sect and nationality were contesting the U.S. occupation of Iraq. Some of the Sunnis may have come from *al-Qaeda* affiliated camps in Pakistan, Kashmir, or Georgia's Pankisi Gorge (see Chapter 6). Others were trained in Iraq, Iran, Lebanon, Syria, and Sudan. One cannot assume that their instructors were Sunni. There is considerable evidence to the contrary.[113] There are three Sunni factions that are closely linked to, and heavily supported by, Iranian and Lebanese *Shiites*. They are *Hamas*,[114] the *PIJ,* and the PFLP-GC.[115] All share training facilities with Shiite *Hezbollah*.

According to the U.S. 9/11 Commission, *al-Qaeda* personnel were attending *Hezbollah's* Bekaa Valley camps as early as 1993.[116]

Inside Iraq

Along the Iran-Iraq border, al-Sadr's "Mahdi Army" is known to have trained at three camps: Qasr Shireen, 'Ilam, and Hamid. Those camps can handle up to 1,200 recruits at a time.[117]

After being retrained and re-outfitted in Syria, Saddam Hussein's elite *Fedayeen* are being "organized" in Al Qaim.[118] On Operation Matador (7-15 March 2005), U.S. forces swept the area. As soon as they departed Al Qaim, heavily armed insurgents returned to its streets. Near there, "cave complexes" were found just north of the Euphrates River.[119] The *Fedayeen* and other insurgents in transit may have escaped detection just as the Viet Cong did 40 years ago—by using an "underground hide facility."[120] Unless its main or rear entrances are found, such a facility remains inviolate. To find those entrances, the U.S. military would need trackers.

On 21 March, Iraqi commandos discovered an insurgent training camp at Samarra. It contained boobytrapped cars, suicide vests, and the papers of trainees from several Arab countries. Among those trainees were Saudis and Syrians.[121]

On June 18, U.S. Marines found another training facility near Al Qaim at Karabilah. Then, they raided a third on the marshy shores of Lake Tharthar, north of Baghdad.[122]

Of course, a few camps also exist along Iraq's northern border with Iran. While they technically belong to *Ansar al-Islam,* many have an *al-Qaeda* presence. After *Ansar al-Islam's* base at Khurmal was attacked, its offshoot's headquarters appeared in Mosul.[123]

Ansar al-Islam's primary bases are located in the mountains along the Iran-Iraq border. Assessments by the PUK [Patriotic Union of Kurdistan] indicated that in 2002, a second group *[Ansar al-Sunna]* affiliated with Ansar al-Islam was formed in Baghdad and controlled from the city of Mosul (Taylor, "Taliban-Style Group . . . ," *Christian Science Monitor,* 15 Mar. 2002). The city of Halabja was a base for many of the group's al-Qaeda-affiliated members (Goldberg, "The Great Terror," *The New Yorker,* 25 Mar. 2002). Ansar also maintained strongholds in the villages of Kharbani, Zardahal, and Bayyarah. Following significant defeats in battle with the PUK, Ansar subsequently retreated from these areas, eventually settling in the Darka Shikhan area, a remote village on the border between Iraq and Iran ("Ansar al-Islam Confirms . . . ," BBC, 7 Jan. 2003). Ansar's shura council most recently operated from the village of Beyara (Chivers, "Threats and Responses . . . ," *New York Times,* 13 Jan. 2003).

. . . It is believed that many of Ansar's most militant members are Afghan Arabs who [have] crossed into the Northern border through Iran ("Iraqi Kurdish PUK Official Cited . . . ," BBC, 23 Aug. 2002).

The group maintains training camps which instruct participants on tactics, suicide bombings, infantry weapons, and assassinations [as of November 2004].[124]

— Internat. Policy Instit. for Counter-Terrorism

Iran

Iran has made little attempt to limit the number of foreign *jihadist* training camps on Iranian soil. The main facility for SCIRI's Badr Brigade was just west of the Vahdati air force base in Dezful.[125] Leader/adviser courses were at "Imam Ali" camp in northern Tehran. Courses for urban combat were at Isfahan. Near the town of Khoum, "Imam Rada" camp trainees underwent courses on sabotage and demolition. Various specialist courses were held at Mashad.[126]

Most international guerrilla training is conducted by the Iranian Revolutionary Guard. In the 1980's, *Sepah* ran camps patterned after the *Hashishins'* Alamut in north Tehran's Manzariyeh Garden and just north of Qom.[127] Now, it is their special forces or (al-Quds) branch that trains the foreign fighters.

The Quds force seems to control many of Iran's training camps for unconventional warfare, extremists, and terrorists. . . . It has at least four major training facilities in Iran. The Quds force has a main training center at Imam Ali University that is based in the Sa'dabad Palace in Northern Tehran. Troops are trained to carry out military and terrorist operations, and are indoctrinated in ideology. There are other training camps in the Qom, Tabriz, and Mashhad governates, and in Lebanon and the Sudan. These include the Al Nasr camp for training Iraqi Shi'ites and Iraqi and

Turkish Kurds in northwest Iran, and a camp near Mashhad for training Afghan and Tajik revolutionaries. The Quds seems to help operate the Manzariyah training center near Qom, which recruits from foreign students in the religious seminary and which seems to have trained some Bahraini extremists. Some foreigners are reported to have received training in demolition and sabotage at an IRGC facility near Isfahan, in airport infiltration at a facility near Mashad and Shiraz, and in underwater warfare at an IRGC facility at Bandar Abbas (Venter, "Iran Still Exporting Terrorism," *Jane's Intell. Review*, Nov. 1997, 511-516).[128]

— Center for Strat.Internat.Studies, December 2004

Lebanon

Captive (non-Lebanese) insurgents report visits to the Bekaa Valley.[129] They were either in transit or trained at Iranian or *Hezbollah* camps. While the most famous is "Sheikh Abdallah" near Baalbek, there have been five others since 1984.[130] *Hezbollah* welcomes non-Shiites to its camps. According to the Iranian News Agency (IRNA), "the Palestinian Islamic Jihad [PIJ] is one of the many fruits on our leader Khomeini's tree."[131] *Hamas* and *PIJ* both follow Sunni ideologies.[132] Or the captives were trained at PFLP-GC camps. That organization also has extensive facilities in the Bekaa Valley.[133] On 20 May 2000, the Israelis bombed the PFLP-GC base at Dir al-Raza.[134]

After Iranian intelligence *(Sepah)* took steps to consolidate all Palestinian terrorist organizations in the spring of 2000, *al-Qaeda* terrorists were sent to Lebanon for intensive training by *Hezbollah*. They did not set a precedent. *Al-Qaeda* operatives had gone—for training—to the Bekaa before. In 1993, several were instructed on the finer points of tall-building demolition.[135]

In late July [2000], Iran arranged a meeting in Afghanistan between Osama bin Laden's new Lebanon team and a Palestinian delegation. As a result, *al-Qaeda* terrorists were sent to Lebanon for intensive training by *Hezbollah* in the laying of ambushes, bomb construction and diffusing techniques, local booby-trapping techniques, and clandestine communications, as well as in the forging of documents. At the same time, with *Hezbollah's* help, *al-Qaeda* operatives were smuggled into the PA [Palestinian Authority]-controlled territories to help train members of *Hamas,* the *[Palestinian] Islamic Jihad,* the PFLP-CG, Arafat's al Aqsa Martyrs' Brigade, and other Palestinian terror organizations.[136]

Since the summer of 2000, two hundred *al-Qaeda* operatives and several senior commanders have been allowed to take up refuge in the Palestinian refuge camps around Sidon, Lebanon.[137] They could easily function as recruiters for the Iraqi conflict. Most would be in *Asbat al-Ansar* (Band of Partisans) led by Abd al-Karim al-Sa'di (a.k.a. Abu Mohjen). Its base camp used to be at Ayn al-Hilweh.[138]

Syria

There have been reports of Sunnis being recruited and trained in Syria by Iraqi Baathists,[139] but no one knows for sure who is responsible. The training probably happens at the PFLP-GC camps south of Damascus. One is about 25 miles outside the city.[140] The two main PFLP-GC camps are in the Yarmouk Refugee Camp near Damascus.[141] In these camps, Iranian-funded instructors teach Sunnis.[142]

PFLP-GC and *PIJ* share a base at Ein Sahib. Though the Israelis bombed it on 5 October 2003, it is probably now back in operation. *PIJ* follows the Iranian model of Islamic Revolution and is sponsored by Iran.[143] Lebanese *Hezbollah* also runs several training centers for terrorists inside Syria. The most famous is Ayn Tzahab.[144] It is 12 miles north of Damascus and possibly on the main road to Baalbek.[145]

In Syria, as in Lebanon, it is extremely difficult to differentiate one camp from another, because PFLP-GC, *PIJ, Hamas,* and *Hezbollah* often train together. Syrian military intelligence reportedly provides support to Palestinian and Lebanese extremist groups alike.[146]

Sudan

Prior to 1991, the Iranian Revolutionary Guard instructed both the Sudanese Army and "Islamic fundamentalist militants from [other countries]" at camps in Sudan.[147] In 1993, thousands of Muslims from all over the world were being trained at other camps built by Osama bin Laden.[148] "By early 1995, Iranian funding enabled the National Islamic Front [NIF] and al-Qaeda to establish twenty-three training camps throughout Sudan." At some of these *al-Qaeda* camps were *Hezbollah* and *Sepah* trainers.[149] The following stayed open after Osama's departure in 1996: "two camps for Arabs at Merkhiyat; one camp for Eritrean, Ethiopian, Ugandan, Somali, and occasionally Palestinian Islamists at Al-Qutanynah; one camp for training Palestinian, Libyan, Iranian, Iraqi, Yemeni, Chinese, and Fillipino Islamists in Jabel al-Awliya; one for training Egyptians, Algerians, and Tunisians in Shendi, near Port Sudan; one for treating casualties in Soba; [and] . . . one in Sejara near Omdurman [that] controlled training throughout Sudan."[150] *Al-Qaeda* had also used a protected quay at Port Sudan's mechanized infantry barracks and a base at the remote island of Ras Komboni.[151] The facilities inherited by the Sudanese government may have been shut down after Turabi's arrest in 2001,[152] but those belonging to *Sepah / Hezbollah* were probably not. That would make the sovereign nation of Sudan the main portal into the Iraqi insurgents' manpower pipeline.

Pakistan
  Lashkar e-Toiba (LET), the military wing of the Pakistani *Jamaat ul-Dawa* has volunteers in Iraq. It also has up to 2,000 militants in training for suicide operations there.[153] (See Chapter 6 for its training sites.)

Are There *Madrasas* Involved?

Large numbers of fundamentalist *madrasas* still operate in Yemen and Pakistan.[154] With a state religion of Wahhabism, Saudi Arabia may have many as well.

If the Soviet experience in Afghanistan is any indicator, the fundamentalist rhetoric and militaristic training at these *madrasas* must be contained. *Jihad* is a concept. Like any concept, it is subject to governmental interpretation.

Some Enemy Trainers Get Schooled in North Korea

That North Korea has been providing military technology to Iran is common knowledge. That North Korea may have also been sharing its light-infantry expertise with Iran isn't. In February 2003, *Sepah* defector Zakiri, talked of attending training camps in North Korea. Among his high level associates was one of the *jihadist*-training-camp commanders from Sudan.

> Zakiri told of bin Laden's stay in the Sudan, during the period when the Iranian Revolutionary Guards maintained an extensive presence there. According to him, Hezbollah and the Palestinian Islamic Jihad . . . had a massive presence in the special training camps supervised by Guards officers such as Dhu-Al-Qadr. . . .
> Zakiri: "I went to North Korea twice, as our relations with it are special. Over the years, we sent a number of groups of Revolutionary Guards personnel and security [forces personnel] to North Korea. Among those who received combat training were Revolutionary Guards Commander Rahim Safavi and his deputy Dhu-Al-Qadr." . . .
> The first time I went for 40 days and participated in special courses on psychological warfare and counter-espionage, and the second time, I stayed in North Korea again for 40 days and participated in a special course for protecting nuclear and other secret installations." [155]
> — Middle East Media Research Inst., February 2003

If Iran is interested enough in its western neighbor to train infiltrators in North Korea, one has to wonder how interested it is in its eastern neighbor.

Developments in Afghanistan

- *How is the new Afghan rebellion different from the last?*
- *What role will drugs play in its outcome?*

LITTLE TO SHOW FOR SWEEPS AND CORDONS

The New Regime's Make-Up

After the Iranian backed Northern Alliance captured Kabul in late 2001,[1] its leader—Mohammad Fahim (Massoud's replacement)—was installed as Afghanistan's new defense minister.[2] About that time, President Karzai (a Pashtun Tajik) slightly restructured the traditional *Loya Jirga* to function as an interim parliament. Some very interesting veterans of the Soviet-Afghan War headed up five of its ten committees working on the constitution.[3] First, there was Burhanuddin Rabbani, founder of the Afghan chapter of the Pakistani fundamentalist *Jamiat-Islami (JI)* party and leader

91

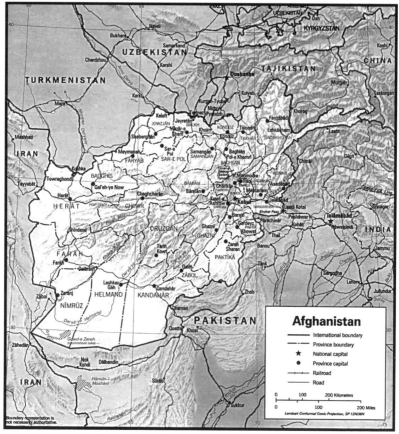

Map 4.1: Afghanistan's Provinces
(Source: Courtesy of General Libraries, University of Texas at Austin, from their website for map designator "afghanistan.jpg")

(with close ties to Iran) of one the seven original Pakistani-supported *mujahideen* factions.[4] Next, there was Abdul Rasul Sayyaf, fundamentalist leader of another of the seven Pakistani-supported factions.[5] Then came Ahmad Nabi Mohammadi, leader of an independent faction that operated along the Iranian border, accepted Iranian arms, and took refuge in Iran.[6] In addition, there was Ustad

Farid, one of pro-Iranian Hekmatyar's former commanders.[7] Rounding out the list was Mohammed Asef Muhsini, founder (in Iran) of a Shiite *mujahideen* faction that operated around Kandahar.[8] That's a lot of Iranian influence. Now that Iran is suspected of fanning the Iraqi insurgency and Hekmatyar is known to be fighting Coalition forces in Afghanistan,[9] pro-Iranian revolutionaries should not be making too many high-level decisions. After all, infiltrating the government is one of the *jihadist's* principal strategies. The democratic process will solve this problem, but only if it gets enough time. Much would depend on the outcome of the September 2005 elections.

On 9 October 2004, the Afghan presidential election succeeded despite Taliban threats to disrupt it. (See Map 4.1.) Estimating guerrilla strength at 2,000, the U.S. expected more trouble than it got. First, three U.S. soldiers were killed, then a suicide car bomb mangled three American contractors hired to train Afghan police, and finally vehicle-borne attackers killed nine policemen on two checkpoints.[10] But the polling stations remained relatively secure for the election. Then the guerrilla activity gradually started to increase. It started with a suicide bombing by a man with grenades strapped to his chest in Kabul.[11] In the next few weeks, there were more bombings (this time by remote control) and kidnappings.[12] Then, winter set in.

All eyes were on the guerrilla tactics of the 2005 summer. If they remained the same as those of the Soviet-Afghan War, the Taliban (and its Pakistani mentor) would be the only instigator. If they started to mirror those being used in Iraq, it would mean one of two things: (1) more Iranian involvement, or (2) *al-Qaeda* copying *Hezbollah* tactics.

Hostage Taking

On 28 October 2004, three U.N. aid workers were abducted from their vehicle in Kabul.[13] A group calling itself *Jaish-e-Muslamin* (Army of Islam) took the credit. Formed in December 2001 by Syed Akbar Agha, this Taliban offshoot is undoubtedly affiliated with the now outlawed Pakistani *Jaish-e-Mohammed (JEM).*[14]

During the Soviet-Afghan War, there was no hostage taking.[15] This is a tactic that has apparently been copied from Lebanese *Hezbollah.*

Foreign-Aid Workers Targeted

On 28 November 2004, 30 Taliban insurgents drove up in six vehicles and stormed the offices of the Voluntary Association for the Rehabilitation of Afghanistan in Delkaram, a town in southeastern Nimroz province.[16]

As the foreign-aid workers retreated, the reconstruction effort slowed. Without it, Afghanistan would remain a collage of independent fiefdoms, each with its own agenda, and each with its own hidden arms cache.

Vendettas Get in the Way

Through bad intelligence, U.S. forces bombed a wedding party in July 2002. U.S. officials admit that they can often not tell the difference between a genuine lead and a vendetta fabrication.

In a region so famous for its tribal feuds,[17] one automatically alienates the population by depending too heavily on aerial and artillery bombardment.

Cultural Reasons for the Unrest

For the residents of an Afghan village not to resist the repeated entry by U.S. forces may also breach the Pashtun code of ethics— *Pashtunwali.* It would be more culturally correct to surround the village and send some one in to ask about its militant activity.[18]

The Expanding Poppy Business

On 2 March 2005, the International Narcotics Control Board warned that drug production in Afghanistan was so widespread that it "has become a severe threat to this new democracy, as well as the stability and economic recovery of the country as a whole." Its president, Hamid Ghodse, also told reporters, "Once it becomes a narcotic state, the rule of the law, the democracy, everything, will go out of the window." [19]

By late 2003, poppy growing accounted for more than half of

Afghanistan's gross domestic product and yielded 75 percent of the world's heroin. Even then, U.N. experts warned that Afghanistan was in danger of becoming a "narco-state" like Colombia.[20]

Antonio Maria Costa, head of the U.N. Office on Drugs and Crime, has seen Iranian intelligence photos of a 60-vehicle drug convoy with armed escorts crossing from Afghanistan into Iran. Unfortunately, Iran appears to be using its purported "war on drugs" as an excuse to obtain high-tech surveillance equipment from the West.[21] It has also just built a new road to Herat. One wonders about the timing. The poppies are grown in Western Afghanistan. Perhaps Iran needs a new source of income for its expansionist activities.

As of 16 May 2005, the Afghan government's eradication efforts had succeeded in Nangrahar province but been delayed by heavy snows or met with armed resistance elsewhere.[22]

More Trouble in the Offing

As of 21 February 2005, U.S. forces had doubled to about 600 the number of troops embedded within the Afghan armed Forces. While those troops were predominantly National Guardsmen, they had been specially trained to call in airstrikes for the Afghans. Meanwhile, a senior leader of the ousted (Taliban) regime vowed that the violence would pick up after one of the harshest winters in years.[23]

When the U.S. Secretary of State visited in March 2005, a car bomb blew up in Kandahar.[24] As a declared Islamic State,[25] Afghanistan still lies nestled between other Islamic states.

Only the Afghan presidential election was completed in October 2004. Due primarily to security concerns in outlying regions, the parliamentary elections had to be postponed until May 2005 and then again to September 2005.[26]

The Air War Heats Up

On 6 April 2005, a U.S. helicopter crashed southwest of Kabul killing 16 Americans. According to initial reports, a sandstorm was to blame.[27] Later, eyewitnesses reported cloudy skies, high wind, and a damaged rotor blade.[28]

That would be the end of the story if not for a few haunting coincidences. Another helicopter had crashed in Western Afghanistan a month earlier, and there had been others before that. (See Figure 4.1.) In late January, a sandstorm had been blamed for the loss of a fully loaded U.S. helicopter in Iraq .[29] Another sandstorm was also initially linked to the collision of two F-18's over Iraq in early May.[30]

Figure 4.1: How U.S. Units Routinely Announce Their Presence
(Source: Courtesy of Sorman Info. & Media, illustration by Wolfgang Bartsch, from SoldF: Soldaten i fält, © 2001 Forsvarsmakten, Stockholm, pp. 22, 23)

The Easterner will hide effective military technique to keep his foe from defending against it. To do this for anti-air technique, he would normally need incomplete reporting or disinformation. But, because the U.S. military's aversion to failure, the Easterner often requires nothing at all.

The Dry-Season Offensive Begins

On 21 April 2005, rebels rocketed a U.S. ground base in the volatile southeastern portion of Afghanistan. This came four days after U.S. and Afghan security forces had exchanged fire with suspected Taliban rebels in Zabul province, and a week after Afghan forces had been ambushed on a mountain pass near Khost.[31] In early April, U.S. gunships had also fired upon and killed 12 insurgents in Paktia province.[32]

On 24 April, U.S. and Afghan soldiers fought again with the insurgents near the border with Pakistan. It was reported that such confrontations had all but curtailed reconstruction throughout the southern and eastern part of the country.[33]

On 3 May, six U.S. soldiers were wounded in a firefight in the Dehchopan district of Zabul province.[34] The U.S. military said the fighting started when gunmen attacked American soldiers and Afghan police investigating the reported beating of an Afghan man.[35] Afghan officials claimed it began when Taliban fighters attacked a checkpoint manned by Afghan police.[36] Either way, it was probably a carefully laid trap.

On 8 May 2005, two U.S. Marines were killed while tracking terrorists near Jalalabad in eastern Afghanistan.[37] They may have been looking for the exact trace of a major infiltration route. During the Soviet-Afghan War, the most sophisticated of these routes originated in Parachinar and then traversed Pakistan's "Parrot's Beak" (just to the south of Jalalabad).[38]

Morale-Boosting News from Pakistan

On 3 May 2005, al-Qaeda's director of operations—Abu Faraj al-Libbi—was captured at Mardan in Pakistan.[39] As al-Qaeda has little structure, his loss will not be felt. In fact, he is the fourth purported No. 3 leader of al-Qaeda killed or captured since 9/11.[40]

Al-Libbi made the mistake of talking over his cell phone. He was then captured by Pakistani agents, some of whom had dressed in "burqas" as women. Under interrogation, al-Libbi initially hinted that bin Laden was hundred of miles from where he was previously thought to have been (Baluchistan or Iran perhaps).[41] This man is not the same as Ibn al-Shaykh al-Libi captured in 2001.

Noms de guerre are common to the region, but this book makes no attempt to identify their owners. High-level leadership is less important to a bottom-up organization.

Portent of Things to Come

Throughout the spring of 2005, events in Iraq grabbed most of the U.S. headlines. Yet, American service personnel returning from Afghanistan still spoke of considerable danger in that theater. Besides the Taliban, they were now facing the militia of legendary Hekmatyar.

As a proportion of their total numbers, U.S. troops in Afghanistan recently have been dying at a slightly higher rate than in Iraq. . . . [B.Gen. Greg] Champion said the militants are comprised of more than just the Taliban. They also include smaller elements like the Hezb i-Islami Gulbuddin, or HIG, an extremist group founded by Gulbuddin Hekmatyar, an Afghan who ran training camps in the 1990's.[42]

— Associated Press, 22 May 2005

On 21 May, Taliban-led rebels attacked a Coalition patrol in Paktika province. They crossed the Pakistani border to do so.[43] Two days later, rebels in the Uruzgan province of central Afghanistan fired on Coalition forces as they left their helicopter. Others fled into a nearby cave to escape the aerial bombing that predictably followed.[44] At the end of May, a clerical opponent of the Taliban was killed in southern Afghanistan.[45]

As the summer of 2005 began, the firefights intensified. About 1 June, a suicide bomber struck in Kandahar. Six days later, a Pakistani fuel tanker was attacked as it delivered fuel to a U.S. base in the southern Afghan district of Pin Boldak.[46] On 8 June—in the third incident along the border in a week—militants ambushed a joint American/Afghan patrol in Paktika province.[47] That's the same day a U.S. base was rocketed near the Pakistani border.[48] On 13 June, a suicide car bomber blew himself up next to a U.S. military vehicle on a road just west of Kandahar. Several roadside bombs had just been discovered inside Kandahar.[49]

On 15 June, there were three incidents: (1) the workers in a free clinic were massacred in Khost province near the Pakistani border, (2) a tribal elder who supported Karzai was assassinated south of Kandahar, and (3) a joint patrol was attacked near the border of Kandahar and Uruzgan provinces.[50]

At the end of May, there had been a precedent—the attack of a police station in Zabul province.[51] The tactic was not new to Afghanistan, but it was new to the current insurrection. It was also common to a rebellion raging 1,000 miles to the west. On 18 June, Taliban rebels copied another tactic from Iraq—ambushing a police convoy and taking 10 officers and a District police chief hostage.[52]

Four days later, there was one of the biggest battles since the ouster of the Taliban. It occurred on the border between Kandahar and Zabul provinces when Afghan policemen and soldiers found an enemy camp. Some 50 *jihadists* were killed by supporting arms before they could reach their caves.[53]

On 25 July, rebels attacked a patrol in southern Uruzgan province. The day before, there had been a firefight in neighboring Helmand province and an IED attack on a U.S. convoy in eastern Kunar province.[54]

Everyone's Worst Nightmare

With the exception of Northern Alliance leader Massoud's assassination in 2001, there has been only one suicide-vest-type attack in Afghanistan. It occurred on 27 January 2004 when a man with artillery and mortar rounds strapped to his chest blew up next to a North Atlantic Treaty Organization (NATO) convoy. According to Associated Press, this was "a tactic previously unknown to Afghanistan."[55]

Unfortunately, there was another suicide-vest bombing in Afghanistan on 1 June 2005. The bomber walked into a Kandahar mosque and killed 20 people including Kabul's police chief.[56] Either the police chief was the target, or the religious and psychological complexities of 4th-generation warfare had come to Afghanistan.

Pre-Election Violence

Afghanistan's parliamentary elections were scheduled for September 2005. Throughout that dusty summer, the insurgents attacked but not in such a way as would seriously hinder the voting. All the while, the deployed GIs wondered if a nation that had never been successfully occupied could be still be pacified. They did not know of the extent to which Iran influenced its new government. They heard mostly about the Taliban. Now "village type" attacks were being attributed to Taliban revenge.

On 26 July, the enemy orchestrated again what had worked so well at Jalalabad—a popular demonstration. Staged right outside Bagram Air Base where it would get plenty of media attention, the riot included "Death to America" chants, stone-throwing at a convoy, and attempts to break down the gate.[57] As in Iraq, the foe was turning to the nonmartial aspects of 4th-generation warfare.

Post-Election Warning

Afghanistan's parliamentary elections went off without a "hitch" (or much media analysis) on 18 September 2005. Americans hoped that the democratic process had finally defused its 26-year-old Islamic revolution. A week later, those hopes were dashed. Another U.S. helicopter was down,[58] and the Taliban claimed responsibility. Concurrent disclosures made that claim hard to ignore. First, a commander from *Jaish-e-Muslimin* (a Taliban affiliate) admitted that his people and *HIG* had recently uncovered a large cache of American "Stingers" inside Afghanistan. He further advised that the whole insurgency was now well funded. Those assertions correlated well with known facts. Over 2000 Stingers had been sent to Afghanistan in the late 1980's, and a U.S. unit had found a 30-missile cache in 2002. With the recent infusion of drug money, the insurgency would be well funded. In fact, Afghan authorities had recently noted other improvements in enemy technology. Along the roads were now shape charges and remote-detonation devices similar to those being supplied to the Iraqi rebels by Iran.[60] Afghan roadside bombings had increased 40 percent over the last year.[61]

With advanced threats to ground and air travel, occupation forces would be much less likely to stray from their bases. Whether U.S. or NATO, those forces were being slowly isolated.

The Afghan Guerrillas' Tactical Trends

- Will the Afghan insurgents stay in the mountains?
- Have they started to copy any of the Iraqi rebels' tactics?

TIME IS ON THE SIDE OF THE OPPOSITION

(Source: *DA PAM 550-65* (January, 1986), p. 139)

The Afghan Resistance Adopts Maneuvers from Iraq

There were car and truck bombs during the Soviet-Afghan War, but none were set off by their drivers. The *mujahideen* also frowned on kidnapping. Of late, Afghanistan has experienced both suicide bombing and hostage taking. The government continues to provide a token presence in the outlying areas. Most at risk from direct attack are its police and army outposts. They would not be hard to isolate. The way to disrupt their resupply/reinforcement has already been perfected. When the Iraqi fever wanes, thousands of *jihadists* will re-infiltrate Afghanistan.

Just as the war in Iraq, the Afghan insurgency has acquired more and more of a 4GW dimension. While not too heavily waged in the arenas of politics/media or religion/psychology, it has taken its toll on economics/infrastructure. From the standpoint of politics, local warlords still control most of the countryside. In the realm of religion, U.S. troops are still viewed as attacking Islam. As for infrastructure, Afghanistan still has very little. Might the enemy's strategy have changed since the war with the Russians? What nonmartial strategy would be powerful enough to destabilize Afghanistan and unassuming enough to be befuddle a Western capitalist?

The Proven Way to Oust an Occupier

All it took to evict the Soviets from Afghanistan was money and what it could buy. Three factors led to the their demise: precipitous terrain, adept guerrillas, and sophisticated weaponry. The first is inescapable. The other two can be bought. *Al-Qaeda* and its subsidiaries can recruit any number of new fighters (whether suicide or otherwise) by simply paying larger enlistment and martyrdom stipends. It can hire the world's best trainers of light infantrymen. It can buy hand-held anti-air and thermobaric weapons on the open market. With an adequate source of revenue, it could take back Afghanistan.

While in power, the Taliban may have had a fundamentalist outlook, but they did permit drug growing and smuggling.[1] On 26 April 2005, an Afghan drug kingpin by the name of Noorzai was caught smuggling half a ton of heroin into the United States. According to U.S. Attorney David Kelley, Noorzai had been protected by the Taliban for years. From 1990-2004, he "provided demolitions, weapons, and manpower to the Taliban." "In exchange, the Taliban allowed Noorzai's business to flourish," he said. While his drug factories and smuggling routes were being guarded, Noorzai also shared his proceeds with the Taliban.[2] With that big a source of income, the Taliban could become a much greater threat to the region. Also disturbing is the inference that the Taliban may be undermining America at home.

With the opium growing and heroin production now gaining momentum in Afghanistan, the Taliban (and *al-Qaeda*) could afford the world's best military advisers and equipment. When combined with the diversionary chaos of a narco-state, tactically adept guerrilla bands with advanced hand-held weaponry could prove quite a challenge for U.S. forces. If the Taliban had any money left over from its drug trade, it could even fund diversionary uprisings in other countries.

Other 4GW Initiatives

While the war against the Soviets had some political, religious, and economic overtones, it was primarily martial. With *al-Qaeda* learning more about 4th-generation warfare from Lebanese *Hezbollah* and the Iranians, this new *jihad* is bound to be different. The first signs of a change occurred on 11 May 2005. It took the form of public unrest—much like that which had engulfed Fallujah right after the U.S. invasion of Iraq. Acting on rumors that the Koran had been desecrated at Guantanamo, 1,000 demonstrators took to the streets of Jalalabad. Shouting "Death to America," they threw stones at a U.S. convoy, attacked government offices, and forced the evacuation of two U.N. foreign-aid agency buildings.[3]

Those who see no harm in such an event might find India's Sepoy Rebellion interesting. In 1857, Muslim segments of the Indian Army slaughtered their British officers and many British civilians after hearing a rumor that their cartridges had been encased in pig fat.[4] In this part of the word, rumors of desecration are dangerous.

The Metastasis of Traditional Methods

The Muslim militant tries to subvert and undermine his government. In the past in Afghanistan, he did so through bribes and threats. As the drug lords gain more influence, government workers will be easier to subvert.

As early as the late spring of 2005, a world-renown U.S. biweekly was reporting that America's greatest fear was at hand—Afghanistan had already become a "narco-state." It inferred that more cabinet ministers, regional governors, and local police chiefs were involved than not.[5]

Afghanistan now produces 90 percent of the world's opium—most of it ends up . . . as heroin. European officials warn

this fledgling democracy is being undermined as Afghan officials make decisions based on what is good for the drug trade, rather than the electorate.[6]
— *Christian Science Monitor,* 13 May 2005

With the Taliban insurgents now able to buy sophisticated weaponry and government protection, how long can the occupier expect to hold out? Government corruption was the excuse used for America's failure in Vietnam.

Additional Evidence of the Foe's Primary Strategy

On 18 May 2005, "suspected Taliban militants killed five Afghans working on a U.S. funded project to help end opium farming."[7] This is not what an angry farmer would do. One can therefore conclude that *al-Qaeda,* the Taliban, and their Pakistani supporters were using the drug trade to destabilize the country. If the Afghan government lost popular support, the occupier would have little choice but to depart. In 4GW, martial and infrastructure initiatives can be combined.

Just a day later, Taliban insurgents killed six more Afghans working on the same antidrug project. According to the U.S. State Department, the company managing the endeavor subsequently withdrew all personnel from southern Afghanistan.[8] To make matters worse, one of the demands for the return of the kidnapped CARE coordinator was "more aid to opium farmers."[9]

After the Taliban captured Kandahar in the early 1990's, it immediately went after Helmand province. It is in these two regions, that 60% of Afghanistan opium is grown.[10]

Within the Training Lies the Essence of Infantry Tactics

Two of the same factions that were active in Afghanistan for years—the Taliban and Hekmatyar's militia—are now contesting the U.S. occupation. Their fighters are being prepared by the same Pakistani *madrasas* and camps that supplied the *mujahideen.* Thus, one can reasonably conclude that their tactical skills will be about the same.

At *al-Qaeda's* training camps, recruits were daily required to crawl 25 meters in 21 seconds.[11] Their other subjects included map reading, celestial navigation, remaining motionless while lying in wait, and maintaining their alignment while being closely supported by flank machinegun fire.[12] Because *al-Qaeda* had little, if any, organizational structure, each camp determined its own training syllabus. Unimpeded by standardization, its students acquired the initiative and tactical-decision-making ability that is so important in short-range combat. Their training consisted of "battledrills" that were run against simulated casualty assessment and subsequently modified.[13]

The above skills are associated with advanced close combat. Because of *al-Qaeda's* short-range focus and experimental process, it's just a matter of time before it discovers the state of the art in infantry technique. On offense, that amounts to "stormtrooper-squad-assault" and "short-range-infiltration." On defense, it is the "below-ground-strongpoint matrix."[14]

The Return of the Helicopter Ambush

For months, there had been warnings that the Afghan insurgency was about to assert itself. No one was really sure whether it would try the same tactics as before. The answer came on 28 June 2005. It was on that date that a U.S. Chinook helicopter was hit by RPG near the Eastern Afghan town of Asadabad in the Shagal district of eastern Kunar province. It flew on a mile, made a hard landing, and then slid into a ravine. All 16 of its Army and Navy passengers were killed. They had volunteered to assist in the extraction of a four-man reconnaissance patrol. The four were later found—one alive and three dead. Though the Taliban claimed to have a videotape of the shoot-down, it was never aired (possibly due to execution footage). An actual *al-Qaeda* contact would be more consistent with this location.[15]

With a single round and a camera, the enemy had scored three victories: (1) grabbing the headlines, (2) killing/discrediting America's finest, and (3) destroying a high-dollar item. The helicopter ambush was back. It does not require a reverse-engineered "Stinger." Its principal goal is to discourage government or occupier presence in outlying areas. As the outposting and patrolling of those areas decreases, the guerrilla incrementally takes over the country. The U.S. special-operations patrol had made the mistake of getting spotted or followed. Guerrillas have been following U.S. patrols since WWI. Most of the line infantry units in Vietnam were never reminded of this fact.[16] Either way, the RPG's effect on the low-flying chopper was catastrophic.

On 15 August, 17 Spanish peacekeepers were killed when their chopper crashed near Herat. As the Spanish Defense Minister did not rule out hostile fire, that's probably what happened.[17] NATO is scheduled to take over all Afghan security by the end of 2006.[18] This may be the way members are discouraged from participating. It worked in 1987 and 1988.

The Afghan Guerrillas' Most Versatile Weapon

For helicopter danger in Afghanistan, Americans generally think of "Stingers." "During 1987 . . . 900 U.S. Stinger anti-aircraft systems, and probably three times that number of missiles, reached Pakistan for distribution to the Mujahideen for use in Afghanistan. Only a portion of them reached their destination."[19] Khalis let four launchers and 16 missiles fall into the hands of the Iranians that same year.[20] The Soviets later claimed the *mujahideen* had "sold 33 U.S. Stingers to Iran, and 10 to drug traffickers."[21] Then, London's *Sunday Times* cleared up the confusion. Khalis had sold 32 Stinger systems to Iran, some of which had ended up on Iranian naval vessels.[22] If the Pakistan Munition and Ordnance Depot explosion near Islamabad in April 1988 included any intrigue,[23] the number of mislaid Stingers may be considerably higher. In any case, Iran and North Korea have been trying for some time to reverse engineer the missile. Unfortunately, light-infantry-inspired guerrillas do not need the latest gadgetry. They prefer to combine a "low-tech" weapon with tactical deception. Their favorite is the RPG-7.

Where combatants are 10-30 meters apart in constricted terrain—mountains, forest, or city—supporting arms are of little use to an occupier. It is here that Muslim militants turn RPG-7's into tank killers, helicopter destroyers, and antipersonnel mortars. With RPG-7 volleys, they can deliver indirect, preparatory fire in support of an infantry assault. When hunting a tank or helicopter, they can preclude accurate return fire by simply shooting from every direction and level at once.[24]

When fighting the Soviets, the *mujahideen* formed armored-vehicle hunter/killer teams. These teams could have as many as 15 RPG gunners and up to 15 riflemen, snipers, and machinegunners. The role of the latter was to suppress accompanying infantry. Normally, five or six hunter/killer teams would simultaneously attack a single armored vehicle. If it had reactive armor, members of the same team would put two or three RPG rounds into the same spot. That way the first round would make way for the others. When not firing from a prepared position, the RPG gunners would change location after every shot. When dug-in, they would often soak the area behind themselves with water to decrease their backblast signature.[25]

While attacking dug-in firing positions, the *mujahideen* would fire just above those positions. The resulting ricochet of shrapnel and rock was often enough to kill their occupants.[26]

To ambush helicopters, the *mujahideen* staked out likely landing zones with RPG men and machinegunners. Whenever a helicopter landed, it was instantly fired upon. On 23 May 2005, Afghan insurgents fired on U.S. and Afghan forces as they boarded a Chinook helicopter in Uruzgan province. The attackers then took refuge (from the predictable airstrike) in a nearby cave.[27]

Of course, one can also use larger, ground-mounted rockets to damage helicopters. In a way often observed in Vietnam,[28] insurgents went after a U.S. helicopter on the ground on 8 June 2005. Four rockets of indeterminate size landed nearby, as U.S. troops were unloading that helicopter at their base camp in Eastern Afghanistan.[29]

Shoulder-fired missiles are also occasionally fired at U.S. aircraft. Such an incident occurred during the first few days of June.[30]

There Are Other Ways to Destroy Planes on the Ground

During the Soviet-Afghan War, the *mujahideen* also went after opposition planes at their airfields. They did so by long-range rocket or sabotage (two means often combined in the East—the former to divert attention from the latter). In June 1984, *HIK* said it destroyed 25 aircraft by rocket at Bagram Air Base. A year later, someone left the gate open at Shindand Air Base, resulting in the loss of 20 aircraft and execution of several Afghan air force personnel.[31]

One might expect something similar during the next phase of

the current insurgency. There is only one way to stop it—aggressive patrolling by combat support personnel who have been trained in certain light-infantry skills—like tracking and chance contact techniques.

Subversion Remains the Enemy's Principal Tactic

With an accomplice inside every governmental facility, the Afghan insurgent would not need state-of-the-art penetration tactics. Thus, he will continue to infiltrate Afghanistan's already pro-Iranian regime at every echelon. Once in, he will do whatever it takes to limit cooperation with the occupier. On 10 September 2005, there was startling evidence of subversion. That is when Afghanistan's soldiers tried to assassinate Rahim Wardak, its Defense Minister.[32]

"Ward chairmen" can also have considerable, collective influence over elections. While contesting the Soviet occupation, the *mujahideen* used the traditional Afghan system of *Shahmans* (night letters) to secretly convey instructions and threats to homes.[33]

Another Taliban Tactic from the Past

On 10 July 2005, Taliban fighters in four, four-wheel-drive pickup trucks attacked a 25-member government patrol in opium-rich Helmand province. While the severing of 10 soldiers' heads may have set a precedent,[34] the use of 4x4 pickup trucks did not.

In August 1995, Taliban troops retreating in the face of an offensive by government troops suddenly counterattacked, ambushing the government's spearhead forces while mobile units mounted in 4x4 pickup trucks outflanked the government army and cut the roads connecting it with its rear-area supply depots. Retreating government units tried and failed to establish a defensive line as Taliban units in pickup trucks—many armed with antiaircraft cannon and rocket launchers—repeatedly outflanked the new positions and attacked from the rear, leaving the paved roads at will and driving their vehicles across open ground and rugged, hilly terrain. The pickup trucks, whose delivery was facilitated

by Pakistan, introduced a kind of mobile warfare that had not been seen in the fighting before (A. Davis, "How the Taliban . . . ," in *Fundamentalism Reborn,* ed. Maley, n.d.).[35]
— *Human Rights Watch* Report, July 2001

Tricks from Lebanon and Iraq

What has worked so well for the Iraqi insurgent is just now starting to appear in Afghanistan. The same armor-killing charges that drove the Israelis out of Southern Lebanon are unfortunately included. Initially reported as roadside IEDs, they are more probably remotely detonated shape charges or stacks of antitank mines under the road. Such things are almost impossible to detect when inserted by tunnel. On 4 August 2005, one device was exploded on a U.S. military vehicle of unknown configuration in eastern Afghanistan.[36] Two weeks later, another killed two Americans in an armored vehicle north of Kandahar.[37] Shortly thereafter, someone detonated a bomb under a Zabul province bridge just as an American convoy was passing over it.[38] Unfortunately, Afghanistan has it s fair share of culverts. During the last week in August, there was another explosion beneath an armored HMMV.[39] The enemy had established a pattern. In this new Afghan War, he would use more below-ground IEDs than roadside ambushes to isolate his opponent. With a large enough charge, he could kill a main battle tank.

On 28 September, a uniformed man detonated his motor bike outside an Afghan army training center where soldiers were waiting to take buses home.[40] While nothing out of the ordinary for Palestine and Iraq, this type of suicide bombing set a precedent in Afghanistan. It may herald a new and terrible "urban" phase to the enemy's offensive.

The Afghan Rebels' Base of Support

- *Where did al-Qaeda go?*
- *To what extent is Pakistan involved in the insurgency?*

THE HINDU KUSH ALLOWS ONLY SUMMER ACCESS

(Source: *DA PAM 550-35* (September, 1991), cover)

A Two-Pronged Attack on the Coalition

There are two militias now contesting the U.S. occupation of Afghanistan—Mullah Mohammed Omar's Taliban and Gulbuddin Hekmatyar's *Hezb i-Islami Gulbuddin (HIG)*. They have previously fought each other, and the latter has ties to Iran. Thus, their current liaison seems illogical. A brief review of contemporary Afghan history may help to explain it.

In one sense, Pakistan and Iran have traditionally vied for Afghanistan. In another, they have cooperated. The two compete for the Islamic orientation of the Afghan government (whether it will

111

be Sunni or Shiite). They conspire to remove its non-Islamic influences. While occasionally backing opposing militias, they both seek a fundamentalist regime. While occasionally shifting allegiance, these militias share the same goal—the establishment of an Islamic state. Once their support establishments are exposed, the details of their cooperation will emerge.

In the mid-1970's, Afghanistan's traditionalist government was opposed by the "Afghan Muslim Brethren." It contained Hekmatyar, Massoud, Rabbani, and Khalis. All shared the same fundamentalist dream—to turn Afghanistan into an Islamic state like that of Iran.[1] They would form the *Hezb i-Islami (HI)*, a Pakistan-based militant organization with Hekmatyar at its head. In Afghanistan, *HI* was also called the "Muslim Brotherhood."[2] Massoud conducted most of its raids into Afghanistan's Panjshir Valley.[3] At about the same time, Rabbani formed what was for all practical purposes the Afghan chapter of *Jamaat i-Islami (JI)*, a Pakistani religious party that supported Hekmatyar.[4] *JI* had ties to the Muslim Brotherhood of Egypt.[5]

During the Soviet occupation, Pakistan formed a "Seven-Party Alliance" of eastern *mujahideen* factions. Those led by Hekmatyar, Khalis, Rabbani, and Sayyaf were fundamentalist; those led by Nabi, Gailani and Mujaddadi were moderate.[6] Each fundamentalist militia had its own acronym(s): (1) Hekmatyar had *HIH (HI Hekmatyar)*, (2) Khalis had *HIK (HI Khalis)*, (3) Rabbani had *JIA (Jamiat i-Islami Afghanistan)* or IA (Islamic Association); and (4) Sayyaf had *IIS (Itehar i-Islami Sayyaf)* or IULA (Islamic Unity for Liberation of Afghanistan).[7] Osama bin Laden had conferred with Rabbani and Sayyaf in 1979.[8] Khalis and Rabbani enjoyed the closest ties with Iran.[9] Pakistan wanted Hekmatyar's forces to eventually take over Afghanistan. When the Soviets left that country in 1988, their puppet regime (though controlling only 20% of the country) hung on for four more years. Due to political rangling between the pro-Iranian Shia and pro-Pakistani Sunni factions, the former *mujahideen* were not able to establish a coalition government.[10] While Hekmatyar tried to control the Pashtun groups, Massoud combined most of the non-Pashtun groups into the United Front. (The United Front is now known as the Northern Alliance.[11]) During this period, *al-Qaeda* moved to Sudan.

Pakistan sought to avoid building up the strength of Pashtun nationalist groups that might subsequently want to carve an independent Pashtun state from Pakistani and Afghan territory (interview with senior Pakistani military officer, Lahore, 1999). . . . Thus, Pakistan came to throw its support behind the *Hezb i-Islami [HI]* of Gulbuddin Hekmatyar, a Pashtun-dominated group that espoused an Islamist rather than nationalist agenda. . . . Hekmatyar's failure to defeat the Afghan government forces under Defense Minister Massoud and take Kabul, left Pakistani policy temporarily at a loss in 1993-94 and searching for a new partner. . . .

Iran has represented the principal source of military assistance to the United Front [Northern Alliance], providing significant levels of weapons and training. . . .

Iran's involvement in the conflict in Afghanistan dates back to the Soviet occupation of 1979-1988, when some two million Afghans fled to Iran and founded at least nine resistance groups in exile. The Iranian government was instrumental in creating and supporting several pro-Iranian Shi'a resistance groups within Afghanistan, including *Hezb i-Wahdat* [a Shiite coalition], *Nasr [Sazeman-e-Nasr],* and *Sepah* [Iranian Revolutionary Guards]. . . .

. . . [I]n late 1991, Iran signed a trilateral treaty on cultural cooperation with the government of Tajikistan, *Hezb i-Wahdat,* and . . . Rabbani's *Jamiat-i Islami [JIA],* aimed at spreading Iranian influence in Afghanistan. . . . Also at this time, Iran established contact with Isma'ili Shi'a and Uzbek groups in Afghanistan—contacts that catalyzed the formation of the United Front [Northern Alliance] coalition. In 1992, these forces—under the command of Tajik commander Massoud, Uzbek Gen. Abdul Rashid Dostum, Isma'ili Shi'a leader Jaffar Naderi, and the Hazara leader of *Hezb i-Wahdat,* Abdul Ali Mazari—seized Kabul.[12]
    —*Human Rights Watch* Report, July 2001

On 26 April 1992, two *mujahideen* armies were poised to take Kabul: (1) Hekmatyar's from the south, and (2) Rabbani/Massoud's from the north. Technically part of the Northern Alliance,[13] Khan's Iran-supported *Hezb i-Wahdat* controlled Herat and the central Hazara region stretching almost to Kabul.[14] Rabbani/Massoud's forces entered the city first. Three days later an interim government (formed without Hekmatyar's consent) arrived from

113

Peshawar.[15] Hekmatyar's army, previously supported by ISI,[16] would continue to attack the capital (and Rabbani/Massoud's forces) for several more years.[17] During this period, he was offered the post of prime minister but refused it.[18] Frustrated by Hekmatyar's failure to conquer Afghanistan, Pakistan sent in the Taliban in 1994.[19] Invading from Quetta, Taliban units were initially contested by Hekmatyar's soldiers. In 1995, Hekmatyar did finally become Rabbani's prime minister for a brief period.[20] The Taliban defeated Kabul's defenders (the combined forces of Rabbani and Hekmatyar) in September 1996.[21] While Massoud kept on fighting the Taliban with his Northern Alliance, Hekmatyar changed the name and location of his militia. Now calling itself *Hezbul Mujahideen" (Hezb)*, that militia was about to become quite active in Kashmir. (At a *JI* conference, *HIH* had been merged with *Tehrik ul-Mujahideen* to form the *Hezb.[22])* About this time, *al-Qaeda* returned from Sudan and took up residence with the Taliban.

With Pakistani support in 1997, Taliban forces seized Herat from Khan's Shiite army but were stymied at Mazar-e-Sharif by the rest of the Northern Alliance.[23] The two sides would trade blows for four more years. All the while, the Taliban received operational advice and logistical assistance from Pakistan,[24] and the Northern Alliance from Iran.[25]

Pakistan also provided some direct military support to the Taliban. In late 2000, Pakistani aircraft ferried Taliban troops and Pakistani artillery may have helped to capture Taloqan.[26] This was not the first time that the Taliban's effectiveness had abruptly improved on the eve of a pivotal battle. Its use of Pakistani 4x4 pickup trucks at Herat in 1995 has already been documented. A senior Pakistani military officer claimed in 1999 that up to 30 percent of the Taliban's fighting strength was made up of Pakistanis serving in units organized by Pakistani political parties.[27] The principal contributors were *Harakat ul-Ansar (HUA)* and *Lashkar e-Toiba (LET)*, the military wings of *Jamiat Ulema-i-Islam Fazlur Rehman (JUI/F)* and *Markaz-ud-Dawa-wal-Irshad (MDI)*, respectively.[28] (See Figure 6.1.) These religious-party recruits boarded trucks in Peshawar or Quetta and were required to show no documentation at the border. They later served in fighting units of 20 to 30 men. These units were led by people claiming to be former Pakistani military personnel.[29]

Iran's support of the Northern Alliance (United Front) was remarkably similar. It had fewer overland supply routes after the fall of Taloqan. "To channel aid to the *Hezb i-Wahdat,* Iran built a big airstrip at Yakaloang." [30] During the fight for Mazar-i Sharif in 1997 and 1998, it used scores of C-130 flights to resupply the Northern Alliance with ammunition. [31] Later, it was forced to send heavy weaponry and ammunition by train through the former Soviet Union. In October 1998, such a train was intercepted in Kyrgyzstan. [32] The Iranians also provided instructors and advisers to the Northern Alliance.

> The Iranian government has also been involved in training anti-Taliban forces in northern Afghanistan (interviews of Iranian expatriates). When Human Rights Watch visited United Front [Northern Alliance]-controlled areas in June 1999, military training was being provided by small teams of approximately five to eight military instructors who arrived from Iran periodically to lead courses at a training center near the village of Farkhar in Takhar province (Shah, "Russia . . . , Iran Giving Military Advice," AP, 24 Feb. 2001). [33]
> — *Human Rights Watch* Report, July 2001

Then came the U.S. invasion. On 7 November 2001, General Dostum led a body of North Alliance militias against Mazar-e-Sharif and evicted the Taliban. On 18 November, Herat was retaken by a Northern Alliance pincer movement led by Ismail Khan. [34] Meanwhile Dostum was moving on Kabul. On 19 November, the Taliban abandoned it and withdrew to Kandahar, where they prepared for guerrilla war. [35] Initially, Rabbani was reinstalled as president. [36] Then Karzai, a Pashtun, took his place.

From Which Location Does the Taliban Now Operate?

The Taliban was founded by Mullah Mohammed Omar (from the central Afghan province of Urguzgan) and Mullah Akhtar Mohammed Usmani. Many of its members wear black turbans. [37] As late as June 2005, one Western tourist was followed by black turbans in Islamabad. [38] According to National Public Radio (NPR), "most of the Taliban's leaders and camps are in Pakistan." [39] (See Map 6.1.)

Pakistan has four provinces, each with its own cities: (1) Punjab with Rawalpindi and Lahore, (2) Sindh with Karachi, (3) the North-

115

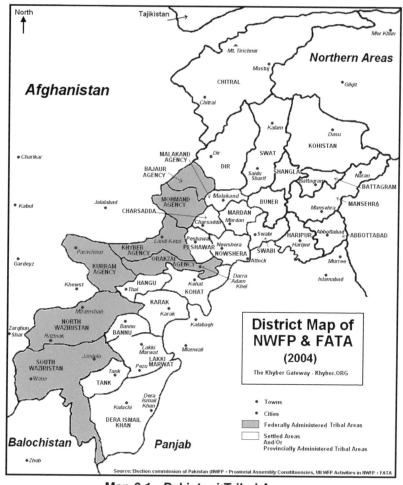

Map 6.1: Pakistani Tribal Areas

(Source: Courtesy of www.khyber.org from map designator "nwfpmap01.gif," copyright © Khyber Gateway)

west Frontier Province (NWFP) with Peshawar, and (4) Baluchistan with Quetta. The Federally Administered Tribal Areas (FATA) lie between the NWFP and the Afghan border. Certain areas within NWFP are also designated as tribal areas and not subject to normal government jurisdiction.[40] The same holds true of certain areas within Baluchistan.

Pakistan is somewhat of a political enigma. It is a military dictatorship with a democratically elected national assembly. It exerts limited control over its four provinces. They too have democratically elected provincial assemblies.[41] Though President General Musharraf came to power by coup, he is considered by most U.S. leaders to be Pakistan's best hedge against Islamic fundamentalism. That fundamentalism has—in varying degrees—permeated Pakistan's military and intelligence communities since President Zia-ul-Haq required it from 1977 to 1988.[42] Having depended on fundamentalist-party militias throughout the Soviet-Afghan, Taliban, and Kashmiri experience,[43] the nearly autonomous Inter-Service Intelligence (ISI) could have trouble divesting itself of that *modus operandi*. Thus, President Musharraf may have little more control over the ISI than Iranian President Khatami had over *Sepah*. Both presidents have been using the same rhetoric—wanting to "reconcile" with the West.[44] To succeed, Musharraf must not only rein in his agency, but also control huge geographical areas that are virtually autonomous. Still, he has made some headway. He has expanded freedom of the press and the emancipation of women. He promises a presidential election in 2007.[45] At the two-day Organization of Islamic (Countries) Conference (OIC) in Rawalpindi on 30 May 2005, he advised against "confrontation in dealing with the Western world." [46]

While Pakistani troops keep close watch on Wana in the federally administered tribal area of South Waziristan, "many senior Taliban are believed to live in . . . Quetta [Baluchistan] and the tribal regions around it."[47] As most trouble now occurs in Afghanistan's southeastern provinces, one suspects Mullah Omar (whose headquarters was in Kandahar). His principal safe area would be near the *JUI/F madrasas* that provided his personnel. That would put it just across the Pakistani border, near Quetta, Baluchistan. In a world of satellite-generated intelligence, the Taliban's expeditionary forces would not have the same safe haven as the defenders of *al-Qaeda* headquarters.

Where Is *al-Qaeda's* New Safe Area?

Al-Qaeda recruits, trains, and advises *jihadists*. It does not have its own army. After the bombing of its Afghan camps, it may have moved in with its Pakistani support establishment. In the

117

1990's, *al-Qaeda* enjoyed a close working relationship with *Harakat ul-Mujahideen (HUM), Jaish e-Mohammed (JEM), Hezb,* and *LET.*[48] Its lone assault unit—Brigade 055—was largely comprised of people from these and other religious-party factions. Fully integrated into Mullah Omar's Taliban Army, Brigade 055 was based at Rishikor and operated just north of Kabul.[49] To support Brigade 055, *al-Qaeda* would need a headquarters complex straddling the border.

Osama bin Laden was thought to be spending much of his time in Afghanistan's inaccessible Kunar province northeast of Jalalabad. He had established an autonomous area there during the war with the Soviets.[50] More likely, he is in Iran with the rest of his family, while his second-in-command runs the war from the upper reaches of the Kunar Valley. Al-Zawahiri would no longer be in the Waziristans, but just across the Pakistani border from Kunar—in the Bajaur portion of FATA or Chitral district of NWFP.[51] (See Map 6.2.) The Chitral Valley and its Kunar River span the frontier, making it a historic invasion route. The valley provides all sorts of sustenance in summer and is landlocked in winter. Large areas of Afghanistan's Kunar province are crisscrossed by supply trails.[52]

Where Is Hekmatyar's Current Base of Operations?

Before creating the Taliban, Pakistani ISI supported Afghanistan's Pashtun (Sunni) factions. Its favorite then—legendary Gulbuddin Hekmatyar—is now back in the fight. In November 2001, he was thought to be joining Taliban forces in Kunar province after a self-imposed exile in Iran.[53] Perhaps, he was just coordinating with a Taliban-protected al-Zawahiri in Kunar before moving on to his own theater of operations. While he may cooperate with Mullah Omar, he would prefer his own command. The ISI did, after all, shift their allegiance to the Taliban in 1994. With hidden sponsor *JI,*[54] Hekmatyar's contingent would now make a powerful ally. From different directions, the two could take turns contesting the occupation. One could attack from just inside Pakistan south of the "Parrot's Beak." The other could attack from the Khakrez mountains just north of Kandahar. That would leave *al-Qaeda's* Kunar refuge relatively free of combat. Either contingent could operate from Afghanistan's interior, but is more likely to be Omar. In late June 2005, radio conversations between Taliban commanders Dadullah and Brader were intercepted at the boundary between of

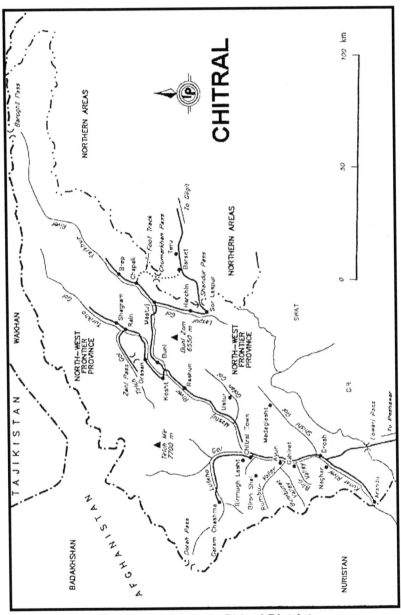

Map 6.2: Pakistan's Chitral District

(Source: Courtesy of Pakistan & Karakoram Highway and Loney Planet from Khyber Gateway map designator "chitraldistrict.gif," © 2005 by Lonely Planet Publications)

Afghanistan's Zabul and Kandahar provinces. Hekmatyar had used the border town of Spin Buldak (on the road to Kandahar) and an old ammunition dump at Spina Shaga (in Paktia province) as bases during the Soviet-Afghan War.[55] (They may be one and the same.) In 1995, *Hekmatyar* had a stronghold in the town of Chaikar.

Hekmatyar's most likely base of operations is in North Waziristan. That's where the *JI* flags were flying all along the border during the Pakistani sweeps into South Waziristan.[56] Pashtuns here have always freely flowed across this border. Of course, South Waziristan and Kurram are also possible. For sensitive equipment or personnel, Hekmatyar could use the tunnels into Afghanistan's "Zawwhar Kili" cave complex. This old *HIK* base (30 kilometers southwest of Khost) has subterranean passages leading to Pakistan. With scores of cave openings, it covers a full three-square-miles. That's too large an area to adequately search or monitor.[57]

Hekmatyar's Mixed Allegiance

Should the time come for a joint venture, Hekmatyar would feel just as comfortable in the Khakrez mountains. It was from there that the *Harakat i-Islami-yi Afghanistan (HIA)* operated during the Soviet-Afghan War and cooperated well with Hekmatyar's faction. Mostly Shiite and founded in Iran by Ayatollah Asef Muhsini, it had several bases in the region. One was near the *HIK* base of "Islam Dara" behind Shawadan mountain. There was also "Char Dewal" in the Malajat suburbs of Khandahar and "Char Bagh" in the Arghandab River Valley northwest of Kandahar.[58] *Harakat i-Islami* allied with Rabbani's *JIA* in 1993-1995.[59] Hekmatyar's founding of a faction with a similar acronym may be coincidental, but his years in Iran are more troubling.[60]

In May 1996, Hekmatyar did ally himself with the pro-Iranian leader of the Northern Alliance—Massoud. In 2002, he was accepting *Sepah's* support through Ismail Khan.[61] In this part of the world, former adversaries form new alliances. Just as they will attack from more than one direction, they will also resort to more than one offensive method. What sometimes results is parental representation on opposite sides of a dispute. On the surface, Pakistan and Iran are at odds. Beneath the surface, their intelligence agencies have been cooperating on many things. To confuse the opposition, they may be playing name games. It may be no coincidence that some of the *"H's"* are *"Harakat"* and others *"Hezb,"* or that some of the *"J's"* are *"Jamaat"* and others *"Jamiat."* That way, the West might naively assume that all were outlawed. *"Hezb"* means party, while *"harakat"* means movement. Similarly, *"jamaat"* means party, while *"jamiat"* means society or organization.

The Opposition's Recruiting Pipeline

If the Taliban is still working for ISI, it gets its reinforcements from *LET*,[62] the military wing of Pakistan's *MDI* group.[63] *MDI* is now called *Jamaat-ul-Dawa,* whereas *LET* is referred to as *Khairun Naas.*[64] *MDI* and *LET* have Wahhabi roots.[65] Most of their training bases were in Kashmir.[66]

The five components of Brigade 313 that helped the Taliban contest the U.S. invasion of Afghanistan were *JEM, Harakat ul-Jehad i-Islami (HUJI), LET, Lashkar-e-Jhangvi (LJ),* and *Harakat ul Mujahideen al-Alami (HMA).*[67] Thus, any one (under an assumed name) may still be involved in the resistance. Despite a terrorist designation by the U.S. State Department, *LET* and its parent *Jamaat-ul-Dawa* were not rebanned by Pakistan in November 2003. They were moved instead to the watch list of Pakistan's Interior Ministry.[68] It was the Interior Ministry that launched the Taliban.[69]

Hekmatyar would get his reinforcements from *JI's Hezb* establishment. While told to "turn in its weapons" at two camps in Kashmir, it may still produce *jihadists.*[70] Pakistan has a long history of furthering its military agenda through religious-party proxies.

Pakistan's Role in the Soviet-Afghan War

The Soviets were not kicked out of Afghanistan by *al-Qaeda,* they were kicked out by a coalition of *mujahideen* factions. Providing strategic guidance and material support to that coalition was the Pakistani government.

The Soviet defeat was orchestrated by Pakistan's ISI.[71] Its director until 1987—Gen. Akhtar Abdul Rehman—coordinated the *mujahideen* effort by distributing arms according to each party's strategic contribution. "In practice some 70 percent of [the] logistic support was given to the fundamentalist parties," according to his

121

Afghan Service Bureau chief.[72] The militias of Hekmatyar, Khalis, Rabbani, and Sayyaf all qualified, but that of Hekmatyar *(HIH)* got most of the money.[73]

The ISI's Involvement with the Taliban

The ISI's Afghan Service Bureau had been providing the *mujahideen* with training contact teams and tactical advisers as late as 1987.[74] To replace Hekmatyar with the Taliban, the Pakistani Dept. of Interior needed ISI support. "At the request of Pakistan's Interior Minister, Maj.Gen. Naseerullah Babar, the ISI got the military wing of the Taliban off the ground in August 1994, providing them with munitions, supplies and advisers."[75] Some Pakistanis call Hamid Gul (ISI director from 1987 to 1989) "the godfather of the Taliban."[76] Before the Taliban occupied Kabul in September 1996, Gul went to a Sudanese conference at which bin-Laden was present.[77] Probably the al-Turabi-sponsored Islamic People's Conference of 1995, it was attended by *al-Qaeda, Hezbullah, Hamas, Palestine Islamic Jihad,* and terrorist contingents from Algeria, Egypt, Tunisia, and Pakistan.[78] Since the Taliban's 1994 invasion of Afghanistan, strange things had been happening to its leadership.

> The Taliban [at first] were good, honest people," [President Hamed] Karzai told me. . . . "They were connected to the *madrasas* . . . in Quetta and Peshawar and were my friends from the jihad . . . against the Soviets. They came to me in May 1994. . . . I had no reservations about helping them. . . . It was only in September of 1994 that others began to appear at the meetings—silent ones I did not recognize, people who took over the Taliban movement. That was the hidden hand of Pakistani intelligence."
> I heard versions of this story from several former commanders of the jihad, who told me how they had supported the Taliban only to be deceived by the Pakistani intelligence agents who were behind the movement.[79]
> — Robert. D. Kaplan, *Soldiers of God*

If the ISI took over the Taliban's political arm, it may have also directed its military operations. Ahmed Shah Massoud—the North Alliance's legendary leader—claimed that Taliban forces had Pakistani advisers as late as mid-1999.[80]

But for the past seven years [since October 1994] Pakistan has been the main provider of military supplies, fuel and food to the Taliban army, and Pakistani officers have advised the Taliban on their military campaigns. Over the same period, up to 60,000 Pakistani Islamic students, three-quarters of whom were educated in Pakistani madrasas, or religious schools, have fought in Afghanistan for the Taliban. One year ago, when the Taliban captured Taloqan in northeastern Afghanistan, then headquarters of the anti-Taliban United Front [Northern Alliance], more than sixty Pakistani military officers and a small unit of the Special Services Group—Pakistani commandos—were supporting and advising the Taliban force of 12,000 troops, which included some 4,000 non-Afghan militants.[81]

As soon as the Taliban took Kabul, the ISI turned its attention to Kashmir. To maintain deniability, it needed proxies there as well.

Successive Pakistani governments used the *jihadi* training and operational infrastructure on the Pakistan-Afghanistan border to arm, train, and finance up to two dozen Kashmiri groups. Although there is no evidence that the Pakistani intelligence establishment directly supported *al-Qaeda,* they did help its associate Pakistani and Kashmiri groups for the specific purpose of using them as proxy military forces to undermine Indian control of Kashmir.[82]

An Indication of Things to Come

The March-April 1995 Sudanese conference had been preceded by two others—one in December 1993 and another in April 1991. In attendance at the 1991 conference were Gulbuddin Hekmatyar (the ISI's fair-haired boy), Ibrahim Ghawah (spokesman for *Hamas),* Yasser Arafat, and Osama bin Laden.[83]

Hekmatyar's joining of the anti-U.S. resistance in May 2004

123

may have signaled more ISI involvement in ousting the Americans.[84] Hekmatyar had received the "lion's share" of the aid during the Soviet-Afghan War. His was the most fundamentalist of the seven *mujahideen* factions.[85]

To this day, Taliban members operate out of Pakistan's rugged border region.[86] (See Map 6.3.) That they share ethnicity with its Pashtun tribesmen would not totally protect them. They must also enjoy some sort of political immunity. That border is long and precipitous. The Taliban could easily enter Afghanistan through its old network of infiltration routes and way stations.

The Pakistani Groups Most Closely Linked with the Taliban

After the Soviet forces were driven from Afghanistan in 1989, many Pakistani *jihadist* groups began to shift their attention to Kashmir.[87] It was only then that people began to speculate on which others may have joined the Taliban. Their identities would be of interest to any future occupier.

Late in 1994, Afghanistan witnessed the rise of an improbable militia that would go on to unite 90 percent of the country and declare the Islamic Republic of Afghanistan. After almost eighteen years of Soviet occupation followed by civil war, a seemingly endless cycle of carnage and chaos was abruptly reversed by the astonishing success of a new Islamic movement.

Late in 1994, as if out of nowhere, the predominantly Pashtun Taliban, a band of madrasa students who had been living as refugees in Pakistan suddenly appear. . . . Within two years they swept across the country, overwhelming the Northern Alliance of non-Pashtun minorities. . . .

. . . [B]y 1998 they had subdued 90 percent of the country. . . .

. . . [The Taliban's] political expression and ideology were transformed with Pakistan's Jamiat- i-Ulema-i-Islam [JUI], a religious party with a rigid, militant, anti-American, and anti-non-Muslim culture. Many of the Taliban were trained in hundreds of JUI madrasas. Often run by semi-literate mullahs, these schools were first set up for Afghan refugees in the Pashtun-dominated areas of Pakistan, along the border with Afghanistan. Many were supported by Saudi funding that brought with it the influence of an ultraconservative Wahhabi Islam. Students received free education, religious, ideological, and military training. . . .

When they came to power, the Taliban turned over many of their training camps to JUI factions, who in turn trained thousands of Pakistani and Arab militants as well as fighters from South and Central Asia . . . in their radical jihad ideology and tactics. Assisted by military support from Pakistan and financial support from the Wahhabi in Saudi Arabia, with JUI mentoring and influenced by Osama bin

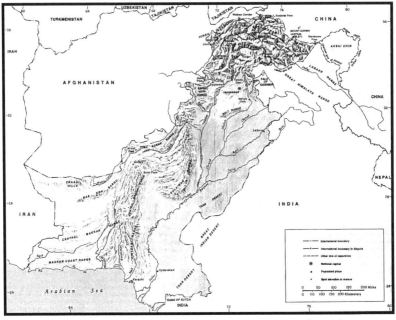

Map 6.3: Difficult Terrain along Pakistan's Frontier
(Source: *DA PAM 550-48* (April, 1994), pp. 84, 85)

Laden's evolving radical jihadist political vision, the Taliban promoted their own brand of revolutionary Islam.[88]
— U.S. Marine Corps Combat Develop. Cmd., 1995

One *JUI* faction *(JUI/F)* has a military affiliate that has previously operated mostly in Kashmir. "Closely linked with Osama bin Laden's al-Qaeda group . . . the Harakat ul-Mujahidin *[HUM]* operates terrorist training camps in Afghanistan in conjunction with al-Qaeda."[89]

> The HUM is an Islamic militant group based in Pakistan that . . . is politically aligned with the radical political party, Jamiat-i-Ulema-i-Islam['s] Fazlur Rehman faction [JUI/F].
> [It is] based in Muzaffarabad, Rawalpindi, and several other towns in Pakistan, but members conduct insurgent and terrorist activities primarily in Kashmir. The HUM trained its militants in Afghanistan and Pakistan.[90]
> — U.S. State Dept., *Patterns for Global Terrorism*

There may be as many as 50 militant factions in Pakistan.[91] Some are allied with lawful political parties. Among the most interesting of the 27 Pakistani parties in the *CIA Fact Book* of October 2004 is *JUI/F* with its current leader Fazlur Rehman Jalili.[92] It spawned *HUM*. After the terrorist attack on Indian Parliament on 13 December 2001, India demanded that Pakistan crack down on *HUM, JEM,* and *LET.*[93] *JEM* is an offshoot of *HUM*. *LET* has its roots in a fundamentalist Wahhabi sect of Saudi Arabia.[94] *LET* also has links to *LJ.*[95]

The Students

The word *taliban* translates as "students" or "seekers." Which students joined *mujahideen* leader Mullah Mohammed Omar in 1989 to take over Afghanistan? It is known that they were predominantly Pashtun and from border (often refugee camp) *madrasas*. But one wonders how many were native Pakistanis. *JI* was the pioneer religious party and leading Islamist movement.[96] It had an active student organization:

In 1947 Maududi [the 1941 founder] redefined the JI's purpose as the establishment of an Islamic state in Pakistan. . . .

. . . Under party chief Mian Tufail Muhammad, the JI supported the Zia regime's Islamization program, but it clashed with him over the 1984 decision to ban student unions because this ban affected the party's student wing, the Jamiat-i-Tulaba-i-Islam. . . . The Jamiat-i-Tulaba-i-Islam had become increasingly militant. . . . Aspiring student activists, supportive of religious issues, have flocked to the Jamiat-i-Tulaba as a means of having an impact on national politics. . . . The JI envisions a state governed by Islamic law and opposes Westernization. . . .

. . . The JI and its [original] political umbrella group, the Pakistan Islamic Front, captured only three seats in the National Assembly.[97]

JI had operated a branch office in Afghanistan since 1974. When the Soviets invaded in 1979, it easily got involved. Before Abdallah Azzam founded the *Makhtab al-Khidmat* (Services Office) to receive foreign *jihadists, JIA* (in conjunction with the Pakistani ISI) was setting up reception committees to greet them.[98] Near the end of the war, it supported the birth of *al-Qaeda.*[99] With ISI advisers, Mullah Omar and these students might have become a fairly efficient fighting force. ISI chief—Gen. Akhtar Abdul Rehman—had, after all, long favored the creation of an Islamic state in Afghanistan.[100]

In 1996, the Taliban got some help. According to a July 2002 report by the South Asian Analysis Group, "cadres of the Sipah-e-Sahaba [SSP], Lashkar-e-Jhangvi *[LJ]*, Lashkar-e-Toiba *[LET]*, and Harakat ul-Mujahideen *[HUM]* encouraged by the Inter-Services Intelligence [ISI] entered Afghanistan in numbers of thousands to help the Taliban in its successful assault on Jalalabad and Kabul." After the capture of Kabul, they stayed on to fight the Northern Alliance. Their infrastructure may have become that of Osama bin Laden. When the Taliban got evicted from Afghanistan in 2001, that infrastructure moved back into Pakistan.[101] *HUM* is associated with *JUI/F, LET* with *MDI*, and *LJ* with *SSP*. It is unlikely, therefore, that *JI* provided the first batch of "students." Both *JI* and *JUI/F* had extensive *madrasa* networks.[102] Instead of a student organization, *JUI/F* had sent *madrasa* graduates. Of note, *JI* and *JUI/F* were now in "not-so-friendly" political competition with each another. (See Figure 6.1.)

The Difference between *JI* and *JUI*

These Pakistani religious parties have similar goals but different roots. Both existed at Pakistan's birth in 1947. While *JI* wanted an "Islamic state," *JUI* wanted to let the *ulama* (community of learned men) "expand traditional Islamic education, reform the teaching of Islamic law, and promote that law's application in contemporary Muslim society." [103] *(Ulama* means "body of senior Muslim religious clerics.")* As *JI* also wanted to represent the *ulama,* the difference may have been in the *ulama's* power or method.

Prominent in political life since independence, the JI was the dominant voice for the interests of the *ulama* in the debates leading to the adoption of Pakistan's first constitution.[104]

— *Pakistan,* Library of Congress Country Study

The subtle differences in perspective between *JI* and *JUI* are well beyond the purview of this book. It is known that *JI* followed the Egyptian Muslim Brotherhood model, whereas *JUI/F* became interested in the Saudi Wahhabi model.[105] *JI* was Pakistan's traditional equivalent to the Egyptian Muslim Brotherhood.

During the Soviet-Afghan War, *JI* supported Hekmatyar's militia.[106] Its interest in Afghanistan may not have ended with the Soviet defeat. In May 2004, "Hekmatyar joined the remnants of the Taliban and promised to drive out the foreign troops." [107] Just two months earlier, *JI* had again gotten involved during the Pakistani Army raid into South Waziristan.

An hour's drive from where Pakistani troops are waging their biggest assault ever against al-Qaeda, men of fighting age stream back and forth across the border unhindered by lounging Pakistani guards. . . .

Flags of Pakistan's ultraconservative Jamaat-i-Islami [JI] religious party hung among the buildings on the Pakistan side of the border. . . .

Parent Political Party/Group	Name Identify Progression	Probable Leader(s)	Date Banned	Afghan Cause/Comment	Fought with Taliban
Supported the Taliban in 1994					
JUP@ of MMA	HUM became HUA* which in turn became JUA*	Fazlur Rahman Khalil+ / Maulana Farooq Kashmiri+	Nov. 2008** =	yes* **/in Afghanistan May 2004&;	yes* ** < ‡
JUF** of MMA	HUJI is HUA offshoot* that contributed to JUA* and JEM**	Qari Saifullah Akhtar***! / Amin Rabbani*** / Maulana Ahmed Utaer*	banned, no date Œ	yes** >	yes‡
JUF** # of MMA	JEM (aka Mohammed's Army##) is HUM offshoot# that split into two sects:	(once Maulana Masood Azhar*#)	prob. Nov. 2008** =	yes#, Taliban ties *, al-Qaeda funds*	yes*‡
	KUI**	Maulana Abdullah Shah Mazhar+ / Maulana Abdul Rauf+	Nov. 2008** =	unknown	yes*
	JUF**	Maulana Abdullah Shah Mazhar% / Abdul Jabbar%	Nov 2008** =	unknown	yes**
probably JUUF of MMA	HMA is offshoot of JUA* and linked to LJ*		banned, no date Œ	unknown	yes‡
probably JUUF of MMA	TKI contributed to JUF%	Maulana Masood Azhar%	prob. Nov. 2008 ◊	Azhar says Taliban will rise again/%	unknown
Moved Most Operations from Kashmir to Afghanistan in 2002					
Sipah-i-Sahaba Pakistan (SSP)**	LJ has ties with HMA* and LET,# anti-Shiite, suicide oriented	unknown	Jan. 2002‡	yes-/sought refuge with Taliban**	yes‡
Markaz-ud-Dawa-wal-Irshad (MDI)** LET (aka Army of the Poor and Righteous##) has links to LJ# / not a political party, roots are Saudi Wahhabi /now "Jamaat-ul-Dawa"/I	LET now called Khairun Naas0	unknown	not rebanned Ø	yes**	yes‡
May Be Now Be Shifting Its Focus from Kashmir to Afghanistan					
Jamaat-i-Islami (JI) of MMA	Heab is merger of Hekmatyar's Heab-e-Islami and Tehrik ul-Mujahideen=	Syed Salahuddin =	told to stop=	unknown	unknown
unknown	Hizb-ul Tahrir	unknown	Nov. 2008=	unknown/wants US out of Iraq$	unknown
(possibly *Tehrik-e-Islami* of MMA)	Islami Tehrik Pakistan (may be Shiite "Tehrike-Millat-e-Islami Pakistan")	unknown	Nov. 2008=	unknown	unknown
(possibly *Tehrik-e-Islami* of MMA)	Millat-i Islamia (may be Shiite "Tehrike-Millat-e-Islami Pakistan")	unknown	Nov. 2008=	unknown	unknown

Abbreviations:

Heab — Heab-ul Mujahideen
HMA — Harakat-ul Mujahideen Al Alami
HUA — Harakat ul-Ansar
HUJI — Harakat ul-Jihad-i-Islami
HUM — Harakat-ul Mujahidin
JEM — Jaish-e-Mohammed
JI — Jamaat-i-Islami

JUA — Jamiat ul-Ansar
JUP — Jamiat ul-Furqan
JUUF — Jamiat Ulema-i-Islam Fazlur Rehman Jalili faction
KUI — Khuddam ul-Islam
LET — Lashkar-e-Toiba (or Tayyiba)
LJ — Lashkar-e-Jhangvi
TKI — Tehrik Khuddam-ul Islam

MMA — Mutahida Majlis Amal
TKI — Tehrik Khuddam-ul Isla

Source Code:
* — pakistan-facts.com
** — Patterns of Global Terrorism
# — Pearl, *A Mighty Heart* (72-74)
$ — uk.news.yahoo.com
+ — rediff.com
± — Mir (128, 130)
Œ — tkb.org

— State Dept. Public Notice 4561
@ — military.com reference page
% — dailytimes.com.pk
& — worldthreats.com
= — globalsecurity.org
‡ — Gunaratna (217)
◊ — hellodiplomatic.com

! — fas.org
> — Pearl (168,232,233)
< — Pearl (173,176)
√ — Pearl (173,176)
‡ — Mir (95, 96)
‡ — Mir (81)
Ø — Mir (103,104)

Figure 6.1: Pakistani Party Schematic

Afghan officials in Paktika province, across the border from South Waziristan, also voiced skepticism about the raid. They said it was a show put on by Pakistan for the Americans—repeating the common charge by many Afghanis that Pakistan, a one-time patron of the Taliban, continues to support the hard-line militia privately while publicly aiding the United States.[108]
— Associated Press, 21 March 2004

Then, instead of launching more raids against Islamic militants in South Waziristan, the Pakistani military made peace with them. On 24 April 2004, the Peshawar Corps Commander went so far as to decorate former Taliban Commander, Nek Mohammad. Under pressure from Washington, President Musharraf rescinded the amnesty and ordered new raids against the Taliban sanctuary. In June 2004, Nek Mohammad made the mistake of doing a news interview and was targeted with a precision-guided missile. With no new government raids into the region since then, Pakistanis worry about a widening insurgency.[109]

It was *JUI's madrasas* that spawned the Taliban,[110] but there is no evidence of an Afghan chapter. Thus, *JUI* may have preferred to limit its involvement to recruiting and education. It does, however, have some heavily defended camps near Karachi.

A Closer Look at *JUI*

JUI is almost as old as *JI*. Originally part of the Deoband Movement, *JUI's* focus has always been the application of Islamic law through education by the *ulama*. While most Deobandis wanted a united India, a group that favored the creation of another nation called Pakistan later emerged as the core of the Jamiat-ul-Ulama-i-Islam party in 1947.

Since 1947 the JUI has undergone a number of organizational and program changes. It developed strong support in the North-West Frontier Province and Baluchistan. In 1972 it joined the NAP [National Awami Party] to form governments in those two provinces. In 1977 the JUI contested the National Assembly election as a component of the Paki-

stan National Alliance. The JUI did not sympathize with General Zia's Islamization program, and in 1981 the JUI joined the MRD to pressure Zia to hold free elections. The JUI won six seats in the National Assembly in the 1990 elections. In the 1993 national elections, the JUI was the main component of the Islami Jamhoori Mahaz, which won four seats in the National Assembly.[111]
— *Pakistan,* Library of Congress Country Study

On 23 February 1998, Osama bin Laden issued a *fatwa* announcing the formation of the World Islamic Front for the Jihad (Struggle) against Jews and Crusaders (WIFJ). Sheikh Mir Hamzah, Secretary of *JUI* was a co-signer of that document.[112]

More about *HUM*

HUM is *JUI/F's* military wing. Once quite active in Kashmir, it may now have diverted most of its attention to Afghanistan. In 1998, its leader (Fazlur Rehman) was also a co-signer of Osama bin Laden's *fatwa* against the West.[113] Under an alias, *HUM* probably still trains fighters for the Taliban.

HUM is an Islamic militant group based in Pakistan that operates primarily in Kashmir. It is politically aligned with the radical political party, Jamiat Ulema-i-Islam Fazlur Rehman faction (JUI/F). . . . HUM operated terrorist training camps in eastern Afghanistan until Coalition airstrikes destroyed them during fall 2001. In 2003, HUM began using the name Jamiat ul-Ansar [JUA], and Pakistan banned the successor JUA in November 2003. . . .
. . . HUM lost a significant share of its membership in defections to the Jaish-e-Mohammed . . . *[JEM]* in 2000.[114]
— *Patterns of Global Terrorism,* U.S. Dept. of State

Al-Qaeda . . . serves as [an] . . . umbrella organization for a worldwide network that includes many Sunni Islamic extremist groups, . . . and the Harakat ul-Mujahideen *[HUM].*[115]
— U.S. Dept. of State

Jamiat ul-Ansar (JUA)

To divert unwanted attention, *HUM* used the name *HUA* for a while. Then *HUA* became *JUA*. In 2003, Pakistan banned *JUA*.[116] Its members may have since adopted a new name.

In May 2004, Muhammad Sohail (age 17) was captured fighting with the Taliban in Afghanistan. He claimed to have been recruited and trained for eight months by *JUA*. He also claimed to have had his military training in a camp near Islamabad and then to have been sent with several other Pakistanis to Afghanistan.

> Intelligence officials said they found on him a Jamiat-ul-Ansar *[JUA]* membership card and a list of phone numbers of high-level party officials.[117]
> — *New York Times*, 4 August 2004

Jaish-e-Mohammed (JEM) (Army of Mohammed)

JEM is a Pakistani extremist group formed by Masood Azhar upon his release from prison in India in early 2000. When *HUM* started getting too much attention, Pakistani ISI shifted its support to one of *HUM's* offshoots—namely, *JEM*.[118] Like *HUM, JEM* is aligned with *JUI/F*.[119] As of 12 March 2003, *JEM* had renamed itself *Khuddam ul-Islam (KUI)*.[120]

> By 2003, JEM had splintered into Khuddam ul-Islam (KUI) and Jamaat ul-Furqan (JUF). Pakistan banned KUA [an alias of KUI] and JUF in November 2003. . . .
> . . . Most of the JEM's cadre and material resources have been drawn from the militant groups Harakat ul-Jihad-i-Islami (HUJI) and the Harakat ul-Mujahidin (HUM). The JEM had close ties to Afghan Arabs and the Taliban. Osama bin Laden is suspected of giving funding to the JEM.[121]
> — *Patterns of Global Terrorism*, U.S. Dept. of State

"[T]he group *[JEM]* claims to have sent thousands of fighters into Kashmir and says its bi-weekly magazine has a circulation of 50,000 in Pakistan and abroad." Until the fall of 2001, it had training camps in Afghanistan. It has its headquarters in Bahawalpul, a city in Pakistan's northern Punjab province.[122] Something calling itself *"Jaish Mohammed"* issued its first statement in Iraq about 5 December 2004.[123] It is unknown whether the two organizations are related. *JEM* is often called the Pakistani representative in *al-Qaeda's* worldwide network.[124]

Jamaat ul-Furqan (JUF)

JUF is an offshoot of the banned *JEM*. It is led by Abdul Jabbar, who was released from Pakistani custody in August 2004.[125]

This group is not the same as the America-oriented *Jamaat ul-Fuqra* that has training facilities in Abbotabad, Pakistan.[126]

Harakat ul-Jihad-i-Islami (HUJI)

HUJI is a Sunni extremist group that follows the Deobandi tradition of Islam. It was founded in 1980 in Afghanistan to fight in the *jihad* against the Soviets. It also is affiliated with the *JUI/F*. *HUJI*, led by Qari Saifullah Akhtar and chief commander Amin Rabbani, is comprised mostly of Pakistanis and foreign Islamists who are fighting for the liberation of Jammu and Kashmir and its accession to Pakistan.[127] *HUJI* provides headquarters cadre and material resources to the *JEM.*[128]

According to the U.S. Dept. of Homeland Security, Pakistan has banned *HUJI*. Along with former members of *LJ* and *HMA,* some of *HUJI's* members may still operate as "313."[129]

Harakat ul-Mujahideen Al Alami (HMA)

HMA was formed as an offshoot of *JUA* in 2003. Along with *JEM, HUJI, LET,* and *LJ,* it contributed fighters to the Brigade 313 that helped the Taliban to contest the U.S. invasion of Afghanistan.[130] The U.S. Dept. of Homeland Security says that Pakistan has banned *HMA*. Some of *HMA's* members are in "313."[131]

Lashkar-e-Toiba (LET) (Army of the Righteous)

When *HUM* and its offshoots became too well known in Kashmir, the Pakistani ISI shifted its support to *LET*. *LET's* parent organization is Wahhabi.[132] Like *JUI/F, SSP* and *MDI* would support the Taliban or *al-Qaeda*. (See Figure 6.1.) Now, many of *LET's* suicide bombers are headed for Iraq.[133]

> The LT [LET] is the armed wing of the Pakistan-based religious organization, Markaz-ud-Dawa-wal-Irshad (MDI)—a Sunni anti-U.S. missionary organization formed in 1989. The LT is . . . one of the three largest and best-trained groups fighting in Kashmir against India; it is not connected to a political party. . . . The group was banned, and the Pakistani Government froze its assets in January 2002. . . .
> . . . The LT is also suspected of involvement in the 14 May 2002 attack on an Indian Army base in Kaluchak that left 36 dead. Senior al-Qaeda lieutenant Abu Zubaydah was captured at an LT safehouse in Faisalabad in March 2002, suggesting some members are facilitating the movement of al-Qaeda members in Pakistan. . . .
> . . . Almost all LT cadres are foreigners—mostly Pakistanis from madrasas across the country and Afghan veterans of the Afghan wars. . . .
> . . . The LT trains its militants in mobile training camps across Pakistan-administered Kashmir and had trained in Afghanistan until fall of 2001.[134]
> — *Patterns of Global Terrorism*, U.S. Dept. of State

LET deserves further scrutiny. It and its parent were moved to a Pakistani "watch list" in 2003 (instead of being rebanned).[135]

While re-banning the various jihadi organizations associated with al-Qaeda in 2003 under their new names, [President] General Pervez Musharraf refrained from re-banning the *Jamaat [Jamaat ul-Dawa or MDI]* and the *Lashkar [LET or Khairun Naas]*. Instead he put them on the so-called watch list.[136]

Lashkar-i-Jhangvi (LJ)

LJ runs a sizable terrorist network in Karachi. Like *JUI/F*,

MDI, and *SSP, LJ* would support the Taliban or *al-Qaeda.* (See Figure 6.1.) *LJ* is believed to be *al-Qaeda's* "delta force." It is suicide oriented and has female bombers.[137] Because of its distinctly anti-Shia orientation, *LJ* would be less likely to be currently involved in Iraq.

> Lashkar-i-Jhangvi (LJ) is the militant offshoot of the Sunni sectarian group Sipah-i-Sahaba Pakistan (SSP). The group focuses primarily on anti-Shia attacks and was banned by Pakistani President Musharraf in August 2001 as part of an effort to rein in sectarian violence. Many of its members then sought refuge with the Taliban in Afghanistan, with whom they had existing ties. . . .
> . . . [P]ress reports have linked LJ to attacks on Christian targets in Pakistan, including a grenade assault on the Protestant International Church in Islamabad in March 2002 that killed two US citizens.[138]
> — *Patterns of Global Terrorism,* U.S. Dept. of State

Hezbul Mujahideen (Hezb)

Hezb used to be the most powerful Pakistani militant group fighting in Jammu and Kashmir. With many of its leaders killed by the Indian Army, it may be looking for a new place to fight for its founder.

Originally created by *JI, Hezb* now denies the tie. It's commander, Syed Salahuddin, controls a 20,000-man-strong *jihadi* cadre based at Muzaffarabad in Azad Kashmir. The Pakistani government has done little more than ask its Tabela and Haripur camp occupants to turn in their weapons. Though seldom mentioned in the context of Afghanistan, *Hezb* may now be a player there. It is, after all, the merger in 1989 of Hekmatyar's *HIH* and *Tehrik-ul Mujahideen.* Thus, Gulbuddin Hekmatyar—America's new adversary in Afghanistan—is generally considered to be the founder of *Hezb.*[139] Thus, while *JUI/F, MDI,* and *SSP* support the Taliban, *Hezb* supports Hekmatyar. (See Figure 6.1.)

With Pakistan's history of military backups, one would expect secondary support for Hekmatyar. Its source is not yet clear. That religious or political faction would have no affiliation with *JUI/F.*

Khuddam ul-Islam (KUI), Hizb-ul Tehrir, and Other Groups

Few details have been published about *KUI*. Like *JUF*, it was an offshoot of *JEM*. *JUA, JUF,* and *KUI* were all banned in November 2003. *Millat-i Islamia, Islami Tehrik Pakistan*, and *Hizb-ul Tehrir* were also banned at that time. The first two may be affiliated with the Tehrik-e-Islami religious party. On 29 October 2004, *Hizb-ul Tehrir* conducted demonstrations in Peshawar against U.S. forces in Iraq.[140]

Where the Enemy Went after the U.S. Invasion

By the end of Operation Anaconda, an estimated 400 hard-core *al-Qaeda* personnel had escaped to Pakistan. Of these, 75 are believed to be in Yemen or Saudi Arabia, 30 in Iran, 225 scattered throughout Pakistan's four provinces, and 75 in Karachi. After resisting the U.S. invasion, 10,000 Taliban are reported to have returned to their respective villages in Afghanistan and Pakistan. Some 5,000 others, including Mullah Mohammad Omar, stayed together and moved to safe havens in NWFP and Baluchistan. Some may now have returned to the Khakrez mountains north of Kandahar. Before October 2001, the International Islamic Front (IIF) had five components: *LET, JEM, HUM, HUJI,* and *LJ.* Its combined strength was 35,000. Some 30,000 managed to survive U.S. airstrikes and move back to Karachi, Lahore, Faisalabad, Rawalpindi, and Azad Kashmir.[141] (This IIF may have been bin Laden's local coalition, whereas the IIFJ was his world alliance.)

Bin Laden's Whereabouts

As of 28 February 2005, bin Laden was probably no longer in Pakistan. Before then he was thought to be in the Bush Mountains of Shawal, North Waziristan.[142] He may now be in Iran.

Pakistani Political Parties

Among the 27 parties listed in the U.S. Central Intelligence Agency (CIA) Fact Book of 19 October 2004 are the following: (1)

Awami National Party (ANP) with leader Wali Khan; (2) *JUI/F* with leader Fazlur Rehman Jalili; (3) two other *JUI* factions; and (4) *JI* with leader Qazi Hussain Ahmed.[143]

The *JUI/F* leader above is not the same as Fazlur Rehman Khalil—the bin Laden associate who signed the *fatwa* in February 1998 calling for attacks on U.S. and other Western interests.[144]

Awami National Party (ANP)

While the ANP is known as one of the three moderate political parties in Pakistan, it has ties to the radical left. In the past, it cooperated with *JUI*.

> The Awami National Party *(awami* means "people's") . . . depends on Pashtuns of the North-West Frontier Province and northern Baluchistan as its political base. . . . In 1956 Wali Khan joined the National Awami Party (NAP), led by a charismatic Bengali socialist, Maulana Bhashani. In 1965 the NAP split into two factions, with Wali Khan becoming president of the pro-Moscow faction. In 1972 the party was strong enough to form coalition provincial governments, with its partner the Jamiat-ul- Ulama-i-Islam (JUI) in the North-West Frontier Province and Baluchistan. These govern-ments were short-lived. . . . Wali Khan was . . . jailed, . . . released, . . . and ultimately formed the Awami National Party.[145]
> — *Patterns of Global Terrorism,* U.S. Dept. of State

According to the *Christian Science Monitor,* the most recent con-figuration of ANP was formed in 1986 by the "merger of several left-leaning parties." When ANP seized the *Mutahidda Majlis-e-Amal (MMA)* coalition's majority in the NWFP elections of August 2005, something very interesting happened. *MMA* member *JI* "chose to join hands with ANP" despite their ideological differences.[146] Thus, ANP should no longer be considered as moderate.

NWFP's Government Has Always Leaned toward the Left

For a while in 1972, *JUI* and *NAP (ANP* forerunner) controlled the governments of NWFP and Baluchistan. The former province is still under considerable influence by *JUI / F.* As such, it has mixed emotions about the Taliban.

> Mualana Fazil ur Rehman Khalil . . . seems to have got *[sic]* a new lease on life following electoral gains by the x *[MMA]* in the 2002 elections. Sources say he is being protected by some MMA ministers. The NWFP government has also freed over 100 arrested activists of Khalil's group.[147]

This is the same Fazlur Rehman Khalil who with Osama bin Laden signed a *fatwa* in February 1998 calling for attacks on U.S. and Western interests.[148]

Baluchistan Is Also a Safe Haven for the Taliban

In January 2005, militants blew up Baluchistan's only natural gas plant at Sui.[149] Perhaps bin Laden's December 2004 call to attack oil facilities worldwide was being pursued inside Pakistan. Local autonomy arrangements have kept the peace in Baluchistan since the 1970's. A rollback by Pashtun and Baluch tribesmen could limit Islamabad's ability to rid the region of *al-Qaeda.*[150]

More about the *MMA* Religious-Party Coalition

In the spring of 2005, an alliance of religious extremist parties—the *MMA*—again took center stage in Pakistani politics. Since 2002, it had held 45 of the 272 national-assembly seats, ruled the NWFP, and emerged as a major coalition in Baluchistan. Those are the provinces that border Afghanistan.

In mid-May, *MMA* was reported to be gaining strength for the July election. Its president—Qazi Hussain Ahmed—announced plans for a global demonstration on 27 May, in which *Hamas, Hezbollah,* and the Egyptian Muslim Brotherhood would participate. They would protest the initially alleged, and then later retracted, desecration of the Koran at Guantanamo.[151] Such a plan suggested considerable cooperation and collusion between some of the world's most dangerous militant sects.

As of 1 June, the *MMA* consisted of six sub-parties: (1) *JI*, (2) *JUI/F*, (3) *Jamiat Ulema-e-Pakistan* of the late Shah Ahmed Noorani, (4) *Jamiat Ulema-e-Islam* of Maulana Sami ul Haq, (5) *Jamaat Ahle Hadith* of Senator Professor Sajid Mir, and (6) *Tehrik-e-Islami* of Allama Ajid Naqvi. *(Ahle Hadith means Wahhabi).*[152] Of note is the working relationship between *JI* and *JUI/F.*

Iran's Continuing Involvement

Iran's ties to the Northern Alliance of non-Pashtun minorities are well documented. The Northern Alliance was largely Shiite. It had Iranian arms, and its important prisoners were sent to Tehran for questioning.[153] By backing the Northern Alliance, the U.S. may have unwittingly helped Iran to pursue its revolutionary goals.

The *[Sepah]* Quds force seems to control many of Iran's training camps for unconventional warfare, extremists, and terrorists. . . . These include . . . a camp near Mashhad for training Afghan and Tajik revolutionaries.[154]
— Center for Strat.Internat.Studies, December 2004

Past *Sepah* leader and presidential candidate, Mohsen Rezaie, claims that *Sepah* members fought alongside and advised the same Northern Alliance troops who helped the U.S. to overthrow the Taliban.

Former CIA Afghan team leader Gary Schroen says there were two Iranian Guard colonels attached to a Northern Alliance commander, Bismullah Khan. . . .
"We knew they were on the ground," says John McLaughlin, former deputy director of the CIA.
Two officers who served with Task Force Dagger . . . say they knew Iranian agents or troops were present.
. . . An Army Special Forces commander says he encountered an Iranian intelligence agent in Kunduz, scene of one of the war's biggest battles. A third Army officer says U.S. forces reported the presence of Iranians in the city of Herat with alliance leader and warlord Ismail Khan. . . .
. . . Defense Secretary Donald Rumsfeld told [Columbia Broadcasting System] CBS' *Face the Nation* on Nov. 11, 2001,

two days before the fall of Kabul, that there were places in Afghanistan "where there are some Iranian liaison people, as well as some American liaison people," working with the same Afghan forces.

James Dobbins, a former [U.S.] State Department official . . . , says the Iranians "were equipping and paying the Northern Alliance." . . .

. . . Rezaie says "some" guard commanders were there [at the fall of Kabul]. "They were special forces for urban warfare (with) experience . . . during the Iran-Iraq War (1980-1988). They were very effective and very active." [155]
— *USA Today,* 10 June 2005

A Radio Free Europe story confirms the claim. Iran has adequately demonstrated its designs on Afghanistan. Unfortunately, American officials appear unwilling or unable to counter this dual threat.

Mohammad Yusef Pashtun, an aide to Kandahar Province Governor Gul Agha Shirazi, claimed that senior Iranian military officers have been operating in Farah, Nimruz, and Helmand provinces. He said that Iranian generals using the names "Baqbani" and "Dehqan" were offering cash and other incentives in an effort to lure local warlords from their commitments to the administration in Kabul, according to reports in the 24 January issues of "The New York Times" and "The Los Angeles Times."

Iran has sent about 20 trucks filled with money for Ismail Khan [Herat warlord] to pay his troops, "The Guardian" reported from Herat on 24 January. Some of Ismail Khan's commanders say that the approximately 12 trucks a day that come from Iran carry weapons, uniforms, and other war materiel. Indeed, the troops in Herat are better outfitted than those in Kabul. And on 21 January, Kandahar intelligence chief Haji Gulali said that Ismail Khan was working with the Islamic Revolution Guards Corps (IRGC) and allies of Gulbuddin Hekmatyar, the mujahideen commander who has been based in Iran for the last few years, to arm and fund opponents of the interim administration.

Meanwhile, there is increasing concern about possible Iranian involvement with the creation of a national Afghan army. Defense Minister Mohammad Fahim was in Tehran in mid-January, at which time he met with the heads of the IRGC and the Ministry of Defense and Armed Forces Logistics.[156]

— *Radio Free Europe,* January 2002

As of 28 January 2005, there was a new road between the Dogharoun region of northeastern Iran and Herat, Afghanistan.[157] Also in the works was a natural-gas pipeline that would connect Iran with the Pakistani ports. The U.S. oil company, UNOCAL, has wanted to run a pipeline across Afghanistan from Central Asia to those ports for years.[158] This is the same oil company that the Communist Chinese attempted to purchase in early July 2005.[159]

Lebanese *Hezbollah's* Link inside Pakistan

Lebanese *Hezbollah* has provided assistance to *Sipah-e-Mohammed,* a militant Shiite organization that defends Shiites against militant Sunnis.[160]

Where Are the Enemy Training Camps Now?

Before the U.S. invasion of Afghanistan, there were Taliban training camps at Kandahar and Jalalabad. It is there that it processed Pakistani refugee camp recruits. In the early 1990's, those camps contained 3.5 million people.[161] That is fertile recruiting ground for *JUI/F.*

During the Soviet-Afghan War, Pakistani religious parties had a number of training camps along the Pakistan-Afghanistan border.[162] (See Map 6.4.) Thousands of the graduates of *Hezb, LET, JEM, and HUM* camps went on to wage war against Indian occupation forces in Jammu and Kashmir. As each faction had its own camps at the Afghan border,[163] one would expect a few in Kashmir as well. As recently as 2004, *Hezb* ran the Tarbela and Haripur camps at Muzaffarabad in Azad Kashmir.[164] Despite an official ban on three of the four factions listed, the leaders of all four continue to enjoy freedom of movement and speech in Pakistan.[165] Thus, one or more may currently be providing manpower to the insurgency in Afghanistan.

141

While there may be many factions running such camps, only HUM has been officially reported.[166]

During the Soviet-Afghan War, many of the *HUM* camps were in Afghan territory—in the Paktia province and just across from

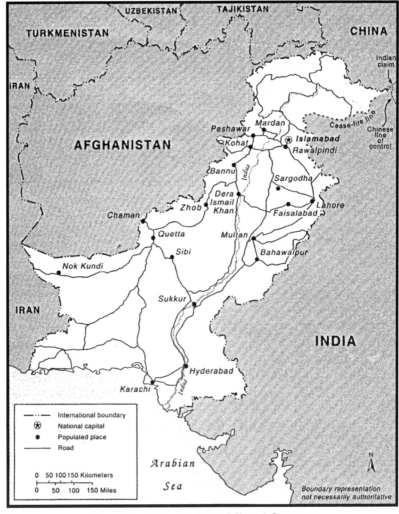

Map 6.4: The Pakistani Road System

(Source: *DA PAM 550-48* (April, 1994), p. 190)

Miram Shah in NWFP.[167] Later, they were probably moved back across the border. Atta-ur Rehman, a militant cell leader from Pakistan, claims he sent his men to training camps in Pakistan's remote tribal areas.[168] In late 2001, there was also a *JEM* camp called (or at) "Balakot." [169]

Initially, *al-Qaeda* had training camps in the Peshawar suburb of Hayatabad. Its first training site inside Afghanistan was called al-Ansar. It was located near the Afghan village of Janji (or Jaji or Jiji) in Paktia province.[170] In 1987, a well-supported Soviet/Afghan relief force could not break an insurgent siege of its border garrison.[171] Among *al-Qaeda's* other Afghan camps were Sidda,[172] Darunta, Jihad Wal, Khaldan, Sadeek, Khalid ibn Walid, al-Farouq (probably the same as Farook in Khost),[173] Zhawar and al-Badr in Khost,[174] Durante,[175] and al-Masada at the Afghan-Pakistan border.[176] *Al-Qaeda* also shared a Kunar camp with *LET.*[177] While bin Laden wanted a headquarters at al-Masada, he settled for one in Khost (Farook was where recruits got ideologically indoctrinated; Zhawar and al-Badr were part of the Zawwhar Kili al-Badr complex near the Pakistani border).[178]

This Zawwhar Kili complex is located 30 kilometers southwest of Khost astride the Pakistan border. Formerly run by *HIK,* it sits just inside Afghanistan on a hillside atop a series of caves. When the Soviets tried to attack it in 1986, its defenders escaped at the end of a three-week battle through subterranean passages to Pakistan.[179] The complex is huge, covering a full three-mile-square area with at least 50 caves. While U.S. forces have repeatedly searched the area and sealed most of the visible caves, they cannot be sure they've gotten them all.[180] In the Zazi mountains of Paktia, bin Laden blasted enough roads, tunnels, and caves to accommodate field hospitals, arms depots, and a training facility for hundreds of fighters. That complex stretched over several kilometers as well.[181] There were other *al-Qaeda* complexes in Kabul, Khost, Mahavia, Jalalabad, Kunar, Kandahar, and (presumably supply) depots at Tora Bora and Liza.[182] After the U.S. invasion, *al-Qaeda* tried to regroup near Gardez.[183]

No one knows how many *al-Qaeda*-affiliated training camps are still left in Afghanistan. If any, they are probably in the Kunar region. During the latter stages of the Soviet-Afghan War, there were pro-Wahhabi *LET* training camps in the eastern Afghan provinces of Kantar and Paktia. At the end of the war (after gaining favor with the ISI), *LET* moved its operation to Kashmir.[184] In turn,

143

al-Qaeda shared instructors with a *HUJI* camp. Soon, most of the training camps for the Afghan *mujahideen* in Pakistan, Azad Kashmir, and Afghanistan were turned over to the Kashmiri resistance (fundamentalist) groups, and other camps established in Kashmir. Another *HUJI* camp sprang up at Kapran, Anantnag in 1993.[185]

Of course, the Taliban still needed recruits for this fight with the Northern Alliance. In Afghanistan, there was a *LET* camp at Khost and various *HUM* training facilities (one at Rishikor garrison southwest of Kabul). According to *Human Rights Watch,* Rishikor was the main training center for Pakistani volunteers, processing over 1,000 every 40 days.[186]

There was a "Yawar" camp run by the Khalis faction of *HI.*[187] Its former graduates would have fought for the Northern Alliance, but its present graduates may fight for another *HI* leader— Hekmatyar. On the other hand, "Yawar" could be just another facility in the Zawwahr Kili complex taken over by *al-Qaeda* and the Taliban.

The U.S. State Department has indicated that the Azad Kashmir camps were still operational as of June 2004. The largest was in the Jungle-Mangal area. According to the Indian Home Ministry, it trained mostly "foreign mercenaries" (Pakistanis). As *LET* is the only *jihadist* group still operating from Azad Kashmir, it has probably inherited most of these camps (including "Muaskar Abu Bashir").[188] It had some of its own.

> *[LET]* keeps a comparatively larger group of activists at its *Muaskar-e-Toiba* and *Muaskar-e-Aqsa* camps in Muzaffarabad from where young jidahis are reportedly launched after being trained at the *Jamaat ul-Dawa's* Muridke headquarters. . . .
> . . . The Muridke camp is the first step for recruits who are vetted for their suitability for jihad before . . . (getting) a 21-day basic course . . . and a three-month advanced course . . . geared toward guerrilla warfare.[189]

Thus, nowhere is President Musharraf's unfinished business more visible than at Muridke, 45 kilometers from Lahore. There exists a sprawling 200-acre, barbed-wire-enclosed compound of *Jamaat ul-Dawa* and *LET,* complete with AK-47-toting guards. The vast area between Lahore and Gujranwala has already been transformed into an Islamic state that prohibits music, television, and smoking. There, like *Hezbollah* in southern Lebanon, this *Jamaat ul-Dawa* headquarters (called *Markaz Dava Wal Irshad*) runs a huge network of social services: 16 Islamic institutions, 135 secondary schools, five *madrasas,* and a multi-faceted medical mission. Its initial funding came from the Palestinian who helped to found *Hamas* and later did found *al-Qaeda*—none other than Abdullah Azzam.[190] Now, some money comes from sympathetic Saudis. *Markaz Dawa Wal Irshad* covers north and central Punjab. In southern Punjab, there is now a *Markaz Yarmuk* in Pattoki.[191] The growth is disturbing.

As of late 2004, there were six Taliban training camps in Baluchistan.[192] They are probably part of the *JUI/F* network.

Madrasas That Man the Taliban and Hekmatyar Militias

As of 2004, there were 1,000,000 Pakistani youths studying in 20,000 to 50,000 local *madrasas.* Most have never heard of Musharraf's promised reforms.[193] Since 1994, most of the Taliban's replacements have come from *madrasas* along the Baluchistan-Afghan border.[194] They were religious-party-recruited Afghan refugees. The majority came from two schools: (1) "Dar-ul Uloom," established by Maulana Abdul Haq at Akora Khattak, and (2) the "Binori Chain" of *madrasas,* with their center at Binori Town in Karachi.[195] As of 27 July 2005, Haq was still running the Dar-ul Uloom *madrasa* in the same "refugee-camp-turned-town" location.[196]

During the Soviet-Afghan War, *madrasa* graduates were most prominent in the *mujahideen* factions with Iranian ties: Mawlawi Muhammed Nabi Mohammadi's *Harakat-i Inqilab-i Islami* (Islamic Revolutionary Movement or IRMA) and Mawlawi Yuni Khalis' *HIK.*[197] Of course, the Pashtun factions were supported by *madrasas,* too. Mullah Omar had been deputy commander of IRMA.[198] He is now most often associated with *"JUI*-Taliban stronghold" at Karachi's Binori Mosque.[199] (There may be another at Karachi's Bionsi town mosque.[200]) *JUI* does, after all, share Iran's dream of a clergy-dominated government.[201]

JUI is the faction most closely linked with the training of the Taliban.[202] Its *madrasas* are located at several locations throughout Pakistan. In the 1980's, they were within the Frontier and Baluchistan provinces.[203]

145

During the Soviet-Afghan War, Hekmatyar, Khalis, Rabbani, and Mohammadi got their replacements from *"JI"* *madrasas* near the Pakistani refugee camps.[204] They may still exist. There is now another *madrasa* player. Initially put on the Pakistani watch list and then later banned, *SSP* for a time had the fastest growing chain of *madrasas.*

A secret survey . . . by the government of Punjab in 1997 showed the growth of only one sectarian organization . . . *Sipah-e-Sahaba Pakistan,* based in Muridke (Sheikhupura district). This organization runs 28 centers in Punjab, 2 center in Baluchistan, 3 in interior Sind[h], and 43 in Karachi [as of 2002]. This study also showed that "there were 2,512 functioning deeni [traditional] madrasas. . . in Punjab.[205]

An Afghan Army liaison officer with the U.S. 82nd Airborne Division at the Pakistan border claims that Pakistani *madrasas* are now producing fighters of the U.S. occupation.

Captain Islamuddin is more blunt. "Pakistan is interfering in Afghanistan. They are sending the bad guys here. They say they are cooperating, but they are not." . . . "There are some stupid Afghans among them," he says. "But most of them are Waziris [from Pakistan's Waziristan tribal agency], Chechens, and Arabs. They are all coming from the madrasas [religious schools] in Pakistan.[206]
  — BBC News, July 2005

As of 5 December 2003, President General Musharraf was still defending all *madrasas.*[207] After the British transportation system attack in July 2005, Pakistani authorities "rounded up 300 religious extremists" at *madrasas* affiliated with the banned *JEM* and unbanned *LET.*[208]

Recruitment Incentives

Pakistani recruits for the ongoing conflict in Afghanistan are being well paid for their trouble. "For the *jihadis,* the work can be lucrative—they are paid $170 to $340 a month."[209] While not much of a wage by U.S. standards, this is a significant sum for South Asia.

Foreign *jihadis* get more. While there are no current statistics available, one can easily imagine what heroin proceeds might afford. During the Soviet-Afghan War, 1,000 Algerian recruits received $1500 a month.[210]

In Asia Minor, One Needs All the Dots to See a True Picture

This and the third chapter have categorized the ways in which Muslim *jihadists* discourage the U.S. occupation of Iraq and Afghanistan. In both places, the *jihadists'* strategy is "death by 1,000 cuts." Individually, many of those "ways" are only mildly deceptive. When combined however, they have so fooled the West as to be yet undefeated. At every echelon within the U.S. military, the pattern of this combination must be fully understood. It will only perplex those who have made no effort to think like an Asian.

Muslim militants operate at a scale that most Western strategists deem insignificant. To study their ruses, one needs an accepted standard of combat deception. Throughout Asia, that standard is the ancient *36 Stratagems*. To each of six situational categories, it assigns six ruses. Each category will have its own chapter, and each ruse its own section. As the war in Iraq has been the hotest of late, it will get the majority of attention.

Part Two

Insurgent Tricks of the Militant Muslim

"The overall military strategy . . . to drive the Soviets out
[of Afghanistan] was . . . death by a thousand cuts."
— Gen. Abdul Akhtar Rehman
Pakistani Inter-Services Intelligence Head

7 ___ Stratagems When in a Superior Position

- How does the Islamic militant cross an open area?
- What have U.S. forces left unguarded?

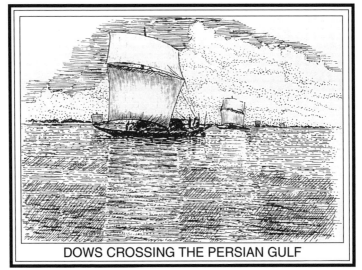

DOWS CROSSING THE PERSIAN GULF

(Source: *DA PAM 550-175* (September, 1988), cover)

The Ancient Blueprint for Deception

Throughout history, Eastern combatants—to include those from Mongol-controlled Asia Minor—have depended much more upon battlefield ruses than their Western counterparts. To fully appreciate this obscure part of their heritage, one must examine a compilation of combat tricks dating back to 200 B.C.—*The 36 Stratagems.* All modern versions descend from a single tattered copy that was found in mainland China in 1941. Its fascinating contents did not become available to the general public until 1979 in Beijing.[1]

151

These 36 categories of deception are further separated into six sets of circumstances: (1) when in a superior position, (2) for confrontation, (3) for attack, (4) for confused cases, (5) for gaining ground, and (6) for desperate times. As the fifth set of circumstances is also a Maoist-guerrilla-warfare stage, they all may prove useful in understanding the latest installment of Eastern intrigue.

In both Iraq and Afghanistan, the U.S. military has easily occupied ground and killed enemy. Yet, Iraq is still convulsed with insurgency, and Afghanistan is close to becoming a narco-state. While painful to admit, America has been badly fooled again. Its strategic planners must now learn how Easterners win while appearing to lose. If they can't or won't, they face a century-long war with radical Islamic factions. This chapter will be dedicated to the ruses of a well-positioned foe.

When One Has the Upper Hand in War

After getting the better of Westernized, "high-tech" armies in South Lebanon and Chechnya, the Muslim militants have become overconfident. Thus, they are tempted to do the following in Iraq or Afghanistan: (1) openly cross an open area, (2) seize something of value that their adversary has left unguarded, (3) use the enemy against himself, (4) make the foe come to them, (5) capitalize on a natural disaster, or (6) pretend to attack from one side while actually attacking from another. If U.S. forces had to leave Vietnam, they might be tricked again.

Openly Cross an Open Area

To consistently win in war, one must continually achieve surprise. A wary foe won't fall for the usual ruses. By demonstrating in a nonthreatening way, one can cause him to relax his vigilance. When he no longer takes notice of frequently repeated actions, a follow-through can work. Originally, this axiom took two forms: (1) "Cross the sea without heaven's knowledge," or (2) "Fool the emperor to cross the sea."

To cross an open area in Iraq, the insurgent has only to ditch his weapon and don civilian clothes. For this reason, it has been almost impossible to stem the flow of jihadists into the country. Those coming from Iran claim to be Shiite pilgrims on a short visit to nearby holy sites. Those coming from Syria pretend to be part of the normal smuggler traffic.

[T]o cross the sea without heaven's knowledge, one had to move openly over the sea but act as if one did not intend to cross it.[2]

Another literal application of this axiom helps the urban guerrilla to approach his target.

By prestaging weapons and individually moving along streets and alleys, any number of Muslim assault force members can secretly approach their objective.

People who take ample precautions are liable to be off guard. Familiar sights do not rouse suspicion. *Yin* is the inner instead of the opposite aspect of *yang* [the subtle is embedded in the obvious].[3]

Within this axiom also lies the intentional manipulation of an opponent's psyche. His psyche becomes the sea. Then one exploits a perfectly normal aspect of his character, like pride.

The U.S. military has always claimed to be the world's best at everything. Trying to limit its casualties through advanced technology and centralized control, it is really only the world's best at standoff range. By ordinarily fighting at short range, Iraqi and Afghan insurgents built their own confidence while eroding the confidence of American troops. As enemy body counts are often inflated, U.S. commanders never suspect either problem.

One who thinks that his safeguards are well conceived is apt to relax his vigilance. Everyday occurrences will not arouse his suspicion. Thus secret plans against him can take place in the midst of common everyday occurrences.[4]

This parable can also refer to the passing along of one's own relaxed mood to the enemy. With less vigilance, he becomes easier to deceive. Then, one's security elements can pose as farmers, supply columns as refugees, and infiltrators as normal foot traffic into a city. To avoid alienating the populace, an occupier will seldom treat everyone like an enemy sympathizer.

Firepower-oriented defenders work hardest to protect their installations from forced entry. They seldom perceive passive infiltration as a legitimate threat. They do not look for people in disguise at their public entrances. Disguised as Iraqi officials, suicide bombers have so far penetrated the Green Zone and a U.S. base. It is only a matter of time before someone tries to impersonate a U.S. soldier. That's how the Persian Hashishins used to operate.

Each military maneuver has two aspects: the superficial move and the underlying purpose. By concealing both, one can take the enemy completely by surprise. . . . [I]f it is highly unlikely that the enemy can be kept ignorant of one's actions, one can sometimes play tricks right under its nose.[5]

Moving about in the darkness and shadows, occupying isolated places, or hiding behind screens will only attract suspicious attention. To lower the enemy's guard, you must act in the open, hiding your true intentions under the guise of common every day activities.[6]

Take Something of Value the Foe Has Left Unguarded

One must approach a more powerful opponent carefully. While preoccupied with his next objective, he may leave behind and inadequately secure a strategic asset. It can then be successfully attacked. When his forces quit their offensive to rescue what has been lost, they will become disheartened and easy to trap. Literally, this precept translates, "Besiege Wei to rescue Zhao."

By repeatedly breaking contact during the U.S. invasion, Iraqi defenders diverted unwanted attention from their ammunition dumps. By so doing, they may have accomplished two things: (1) preserving the ammunition for their insurgency, and (2) encouraging U.S. forces to underdefend their logistics. Since that time, those Iraqi defenders have focused more on the Coalition's resupply convoys and storage facilities than on its maneuver elements.

When the enemy is too strong to attack directly, then attack something he holds dear. Know that in all things he cannot be superior. Somewhere there is a gap in the armor, a weakness that can be attacked instead. If the enemy is on campaign, his home defense will be weak, if his army is fast, his baggage trains will be slow, if the army is well equipped, the treasury will be at a loss.[7]

This stratagem's application can be either physical or psychological. Its objective may be nothing more than to manipulate an opponent's perception. Among its central themes is the countering of enemy mass. If the opposing force is too large, it is made to disperse so that its separate elements can be beaten one at a time. It is by stringing small victories together that the Asian establishes momentum. If any element is too strong, he waits for it to make a mistake.

Through IEDs and sniping, Muslim militants encourage a Westernized occupier to patrol by vehicle. Now instead of an irresistible force, their hidden cells have only to deal with two poorly protected HMMVs on a lonely road. In effect, the occupier has put expensive equipment, priceless occupants, and overall mission at risk. Those occupants no longer enjoy the survivability of a foot patrol, nor do they get as many tips on enemy activity. They have become effectively isolated from the indigenous population—one of the Islamic militant's primary objectives.

Instead of attacking headlong a powerful, concentrated enemy, break it up into smaller, vulnerable groups. Instead of striking first, bide your time and strike only after the enemy has struck.[8]

This axiom says to "relieve the besieged by besieging the base

155

of the besiegers." [9] If skirmishes are generated in greater numbers than enemy supporting arms can handle, then the subsequent thrust will be uncontested by supporting arms. In this way, a besieged and understrength unit can still make a strategic contribution.

By precipitating many incidents per day, the Muslim militant ensures that no single incident can be fully handled. This gives the few with strategic significance more chance of succeeding. If one is an attack, it frequently involves quarry encirclement. With trouble on every side, that quarry has less opportunity to thwart a random thrust.

Attack where he is unprepared, appear where unexpected. [10]
— Sun Zi (Tzu)

Use the Enemy against Himself

In a military endeavor of indefinite duration, one must frugally expend resources. Instead of endangering personnel, he uses trickery and deception to deplete the opponent's strength. One way is helping that opponent to hurt himself. Originally, the principle said, "Kill with a borrowed knife or sword."

The Muslim militants have done to America in Iraq what they did to Russia in Afghanistan and Israel in Lebanon. They have capitalized on their adversary's political aversion to casualties. By "preceding every soldier with a bullet" and "answering every sniper round with a tank shell," America has badly exposed itself to public criticism. Every time the insurgents evoke a heavy-handed response, they gain more popular support.

"Borrow" can mean making use of the enemy to cause its self-destruction. Use ruses to sow discord among the enemy and make them kill one another; this is making use of the enemy's own knife. To get hold of the enemy and use them is borrowing the enemy's resources. To sow discord among the enemy's generals, making them fight among themselves, is to borrow the enemy's generals. To find out the enemy's strategy and turn it to one's advantage is to borrow the enemy's strategy.[11]

While stalling for time, the Asian stays close enough to his foe to ascertain intentions and capitalize on opportunity. In past wars, this "close embrace" has caused many a U.S. unit to shell or bomb itself.

While few friendly fire accidents have been reported from Iraq, the U.S. has hurt itself in another way. It has littered the Iraqi countryside with enough aerial and artillery duds to keep the IED factories supplied for years. The Muslim insurgent has only to capitalize on his opponent's style of war.

We need not act by our own [inertia] but just sit and wait for things to happen. When something is found to be difficult to do, we simply get someone else to do it.[12]
— Bing Fa Bai Yan, *A Hundred War Maxims*

U.S. infantrymen carry much more than the "one-third their body weight" recommended by S.L.A. Marshall.[13] In a desert climate, the enemy has only to wait until mid-afternoon to confront them. By then, the GIs have been sufficiently weakened by operational tempo, high heat, and heavy load.

To destroy a U.S. unit's momentum in Iraq, all the Muslim militant has to do is to create a single casualty that must be medically evacuated. To facilitate casualty removal in Fallujah, many U.S. units defied tactical protocol by frontally assaulting, and then clearing from the bottom up, contested buildings.[14]

When you do not have the means to attack your enemy directly, then attack using the strength of another. Trick an ally into attacking him, bribe an official to turn traitor, or use the enemy's strength against him.[15]

An insurgent faces two enemies—the foreign occupier and his own government. He does whatever he can to divide them.

By subverting and demoralizing Iraqi security elements, the insurgents have caused U.S. forces to distrust those elements. Every time a U.S. trainer yells at an Iraqi National Guard recruit, that recruit "loses face." [16] *In the Middle East, losing face can lead to resentment, a poor self image, or worse. To capitalize on any lapses in patriotism, the rebels have a few of their own people in each session.*

In dialectic terms, another man's loss is your gain.[17]

Make the Enemy Come to You

While it is sometimes advantageous to hurry onto a battlefield to take advantage of terrain, weather, or some other circumstance, it is generally not a good idea. If one's opponent already occupies that space, he better understands the situational nuances. The idea here is to allow the enemy to experience the loss of energy and certainty that is associated with entering an unfamiliar area. Word for word, this axiom suggests, "Wait Leisurely for an Exhausted Enemy."

In Iraq, the Muslim militant lacks supporting arms and precision munitions but still manages to destroy point targets. He brings those targets to him—most notably, the Coalition vehicles to his IEDs.

To weaken the enemy, it is not necessary to attack him directly. Tire him by carrying out an active defense, and in doing so, his strength will be reduced, and your side will gain the upper hand.[18]

By fighting in unfamiliar areas, U.S. forces lose their firepower advantage. With enough time and initiative, a skilled defender can turn all but the most unobstructed terrain into a death trap.

In Iraq, U.S. forces do most of the moving into unfamiliar territory (on raids and such). Because of the enemy's highly sophisticated community watch apparatus, those forces seldom surprise anyone. Continual failure can be disheartening.

Most importantly, build up one's forces before deploying them. Use small to counter big, the unchanging to deal with the changing, the stationary to deal with the mobile.[19]

While waiting for an opening, one can still explore—through ruses and demonstrations—the enemy's intentions and weaknesses. This will further tire and confuse him. There is no way for a public demonstration to backfire if its participants flee at the first sign of government crackdown. A small force can wear out a big force by continually harassing it—alternately fighting and falling back.

U.S. forces have been susceptible to manipulation in the past. In Vietnam, those wanting to use one route were lured by enemy activity onto another; those nearing enemy base camps were dissuaded by boobytrap mazes from entering; and those inadvertently camping over a strategic burrow were encouraged by inactivity to leave. When used in combination, such distractions can cause a foe to feel almost powerless. The Iraqi insurgent has tried—through his own portfolio of tricks—to control U.S. movements.

It is possible to lead the enemy into an impasse without fighting. The active is weakened to strengthen the passive.[20]

Of course, a less literal translation of this parable is also possible. The idea here is to passively manipulate one's foe. It will keep him tired and off balance.

U.S. personnel expend huge amounts of energy in planning and executing each raid. Just by creating dummy targets and cursorily defending them, Iraqi and Afghan insurgents severely tire U.S. forces.

Tempt the enemy with profit to make it come forward; forestall it with danger to keep it from coming. In this way, we can exhaust the enemy when it is reposed, starve the enemy when it is well fed, and provoke the enemy when it is calm.[21]

— Sun Tzu, *Art of War*

Capitalize on a Natural Disaster

The world's civilizations suffer from starvation, disease, and war. The disruption of the first two can be significantly exploited during the third. The ancient stratagem renders, "Loot a burning house."

In many parts of Iraq, the security forces are nonexistent and the infrastructure in shambles. Unable to acquire basic services from the duly elected government, the people turn to the insurgents for help. Weakened by their living conditions, they become more susceptible to rabble rousing and subliminal intimidation.

An enemy's troubles can come from two sources. . . . External threat [is one]. The enemy is invading our country! Internal difficulties [are the other]. Natural disasters [happen]. Corrupt and dissolute officials [exist]. Internal strife [occurs].[22]

Natural disasters come in many shapes. Widespread civil disorder would definitely qualify.

By intimidating and corrupting security officials, the Islamic insurgents gain access to more than just sensitive information. They also gain access to attack objectives. When a gate is left open, one needs much less tactical expertise to penetrate a Coalition compound.

When the enemy falls into a severe crisis, exploit his adversity and attack by direct confrontation.[23]

Poverty can sometimes become so prevalent as to permeate an entire segment of society. Only the most unscrupulous of combatants would take advantage of the destitute.

The most dangerous of Iraq's insurgents keep whole segments of the own populations destitute while pretending to help them. In the Shiite neighborhoods for example, they field an alternative governing apparatus, complete with many of the basic services that people need. That way the charities can double as recruiting centers for prospective martyrs.

When a country is beset by internal conflicts, when disease and famine ravage the population, when corruption and crime are rampant, then it will be unable to deal with an outside threat. This is the time to attack.[24]

There is a psychological equivalent to this stratagem that is highly obscure. It takes its inspiration from an Asian tradition—only fighting the battles for which victory is virtually assured. The opportunity lies in the opponent's predictable failure.

By seeking engagement before victory, the Western commander overemphasizes body count and de-emphasizes strategy. His Eastern counterpart takes advantage of this tradition's effect on unit morale and war outcome. The Muslim creates so many engagements that the U.S. commander can do little more than react.

In ancient times, one who was good at warcraft attained victories that were easily attainable. Therefore, the victory brought him neither fame for wisdom nor merit for courage. Each victory was certain, for it was gained by defeating an enemy that had already lost. Thus a victorious army gains victory before seeking engagement whereas a doomed army seeks victory during the engagement.[25]
— Sun Tzu, *Art of War*

Pretend to Attack from One Side and Attack from Another

An adversary will reinforce whichever side is threatened. To do so, he must reduce his vigilance in other sectors. This makes him easier to attack. Verbatim, the axiom advises, "Make a clamor or feint to the East while attacking to the West." It can be applied at either a tactical or socio-political level.

The Iraqi opposition has managed to paint a politically correct "big picture"—that the insurgency is al-Qaeda and

Baathist inspired. All the while, Iran-sponsored terrorists continue to inflict cuts so small as to seem unimportant to U.S. leaders.

When the enemy command is in confusion, it will be unprepared for any contingencies. . . . When the enemy loses internal control, take the chance and destroy him.[26]

The Asian uses ordinary forces to capture his foe's attention, and extraordinary forces to beat him. What's visible of his initial formation is a feint. If the extraordinary forces wish to escape after penetrating their objective, they create a commotion in one sector and leave through another.

Many portions of Iraq have been beset by widespread violence. Yet, the strategic damage to security forces and infrastructure has been accomplished by tiny assault squads and lone suicide bombers.

To use military strategies skillfully, move east then west, advance then retreat. Never let others know when you'll strike. When others expect you to act, don't act. When others don't expect you to act, take action. If the enemy is taken in by the stratagem and becomes confused, strike decisively to grab victory.[27]

Stratagems for Confrontation

- *Which sinister intentions are being masked with smiles?*
- *How is the enemy increasing his odds?*

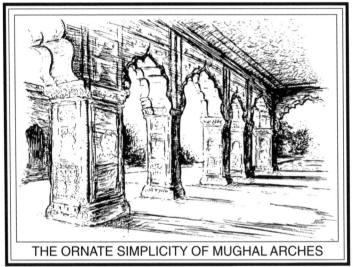

THE ORNATE SIMPLICITY OF MUGHAL ARCHES

(Source: *DA PAM 550-21* (January, 1985), p. 459)

When One Is Confronted in War

After being directly challenged by a more powerful foe, one might do the following: (1) make something out of nothing, (2) give Murphy's Law time to work on the enemy, (3) mask sinister intentions with a good impression, (4) sacrifice minor concerns for the sake of the overall mission, or (5) seize the chance to increase the odds.

The Iraqi insurgents have held their own despite being challenged by the most technologically advanced army on earth. One wonders which of the ancient stratagems they may have preferred.

Make Something out of Nothing

"Sun Zi (Tzu) wrote that the direct attack and the indirect attack are interchangeable depending on the enemy's expectation."[1] Thus, any diversion—no matter how subtle—can be turned into an attack. Precisely, the axiom translates, "Create something from nothing."

Thanks largely to the insurgent assault on infrastructure, Iraq has no shortage of uncollected trash or rickety vehicles. That every pile of roadside refuse or component of traffic flow can suddenly turn lethal exemplifies this axiom.

Design a counterfeit front to put the enemy off-guard. When the trick works, the front is changed into something real so that the enemy will be thrown into a state of double confusion.[2]

Western armies can have great trouble solving a problem that "nothing" created. Theirs is a top-down culture, in which only big things matter.

Due to the threat of IED or car bomb, U.S. vehicular patrols normally usurp the right of way and move quickly. They honk and sometimes push other vehicles aside. Having no sirens, they occasionally surprise a civilian driver. He or she does not always get out of the way in time.[3] If their gunners become too used to these types of occurrences, they become susceptible to suicide car bomb. If they overreact, they kill noncombatants. Either way, the population is alienated. Here, the Muslim militant acquires tremendous strategic gain out of nothing.

Make a false move, not to pass it for a genuine one but to transform it into a genuine one after the enemy has been convinced of its falsity.[4]

To use this precept, one must pay close attention to his opponent's disposition. He who has recently occupied a defensive position will often be "trigger happy." It would be unwise to attack him the first night. Here, timing is everything.

More than one car bombing in Iraq has been preceded by a decoy car. In the 13 November 2003 bombing of the Italian barracks in Nasiriyah, the offending truck was preceded by a decoy car going the other direction.[5] When Red Cross headquarters and three police stations were car-bombed on 27 October 2003, two of the bombers used disguises. The Red Cross bomber drove an ambulance. One police station bomber was dressed as a policeman and drove a police car.[6] In three of those attacks, another vehicle first distracted the perimeter guards.[7]

False and then real is the most effective. In using this stratagem, bear in mind two factors. Firstly, the character of the enemy (leader). . . . Secondly, the timing. When the enemy is blind to your intention, change from false to real and mount a surprise attack.[8]

This particular ploy can be strengthened by employing two, identical diversionary actions in succession. The third time the opponent sees the action, he will assume it a diversion and not react to it.

The Eastern infiltrator likes to generate a series of false alarms at his intended point of entry. As soon as the security force gets tired of responding, he makes his move. While this ruse has yet to be reported from Iraq, infiltrators have been active.[9]

Use the same feint twice. Having reacted to the first and often the second feint as well, the enemy will be hesitant to react to a third feint. Therefore, the third feint is the actual attack catching your enemy with his guard down.[10]

Finally, the axiom advises being able to employ either extraordinary or ordinary forces on any occasion, so as to befuddle the enemy.

A couple of infiltrators can often do what a powerful force cannot. Before attacking a position en masse, an Eastern unit often uses one or two sappers to investigate its internal layout and a stormtrooper squad to breach its outer defenses.

If this lone sapper or vanguard squad can destroy the position's strategic contents, there is no longer any need for a follow-up attack. While the Iraqi insurgents have not yet acquired enough skill to do such things, they soon may. After the April 2005 attack on Al Ghraib prison, "al-Qaeda in Iraq" claimed to have fully reconnoitered their objective from inside and out.[11]

One who is good at the art of war can employ either extraordinary or normal forces on every occasion, so that the enemy is deprived of judgment. Therefore he can achieve victory by either using normal or extraordinary forces.[12]
— *Li Jing's Reply to Emperor Taizong of Tang*

Attack from One Side and Switch to Another

The well-seasoned adversary may not fall for a feint. One must sometimes assault him from one side and then switch to another, or at least approach him from one side and then attack on another. In Chinese, the precept says, "Advance to Chencang by a hidden path."

In both Iraq and Afghanistan, the enemy often fires simultaneously on every outpost in a given locale. By so doing, he not only draws attention from his intended objective, but also keeps it from being reinforced.

Make a false move to tie up the main force of the enemy.[13]

To pin down the enemy, expose part of your action deliberately, so that you can make a surprise attack somewhere else.[14]

This axiom advises blatant attack to conceal covert maneuver. In the Orient, that which is visible is routinely intended to deceive. For example, by avoiding contact, an Eastern vanguard might lead its pursuers into a trap. What differentiates this stratagem from "Make a clamor in the East and attack in the West" is the idea of a converging assault.

Inherent to the Eastern style of defense is continual with-drawal. In Fallujah, frontline Marines warned that they were being pulled into a trap.

Attack the enemy with two convergent forces. The first is the direct attack, one that is obvious and for which the enemy prepares his defense. The second is the indirect attack, the attack sinister, that the enemy does not expect and which causes him to divide his forces at the last minute, leading to confusion and disaster.[15]

Give "Murphy's Law" Time to Work on the Enemy

According to colloquial "Murphy's Law," what can go wrong in combat generally will. It applies to all participants. He who hesitates can often discover a weakness that his foe did not initially possess. If his first chance slips away, he will get another. Frequently the prize will be revealed as not worth fighting for, or obtainable later with less effort. Literally, the stratagem recommends, "Watch a fire from across the river."

Patience is just as much a part of the Iraqi culture as it is of the East Asian. In both places, time is viewed as a continuum, and difficult projects are expected to take a while. That the Iraqi insurgent may be working on a 10-year plan to remove the occupier is difficult for a poll-driven society to comprehend. His initial steps may make little sense. Only when they converge may their true power be felt.

To remain disciplined and calm while waiting for disorder to appear amongst the enemy is the art of self-possession.[16]
— Sun Tzu

Though much has been said about swiftness in battle, the Easterner masters the art of delay. Before engaging a powerful foe, he discovers an opportunity. Such is the basis of all delay-oriented strategies.[17] Every time a Western unit returns fire, it must work harder to maintain its alignment and thus impedes its forward progress. The resulting loss of momentum is something on which all Easterners count. Whenever a Western headquarters issues an order that defies common sense at the squad level, it creates communication gaps and halfhearted execution. These are problems that can also be exploited.

Since the Sadr Rebellions, Iraq's Shiite militant factions have rested their combatants, enlarged their militias, expanded their alternative infrastructures, and participated in official elections. At the same time, the Coalition has permitted—as prime minister—the leader of the region's original activist Shiite movement and all but precluded Sunni political opposition.

When the enemy finds itself in a predicament and wants to engage us in a decisive battle, wait; when it is advantageous for the enemy but not for us to fight, wait; when it is expedient to remain still and whoever moves first will fall into danger, wait; when two enemies are in a fight that will result in defeat or injury, wait; when the enemy forces, although numerous, suffer from mistrust and tend to plot against one another, wait; when the enemy commander, though wise, is handicapped by some of his cohorts, wait.[18]
— Bing Fa Bai Yan, *A Hundred War Maxims*

This stratagem does not imply that one should sit idly by while the war goes on around him. When the time is ripe, one should strike to destroy the enemy.[19]

Whoever controls the largest militia in Iraq will become its unofficial ruler. That's what happened in Lebanon. According to all official accounts, only the occupiers and Sunnis have been fighting since the fall of 2004. As of 1 January 2005, the Badr Brigade had grown tenfold in two years to around 100,000 men.[20] No one is quite sure just how big the Mahdi Army has become. Its three training bases along the Iran-Iraq border can handle up to 1,200 recruits at a time.[21] During the Najaf standoff along, the Mahdi Army recruited 3,000 suicide bombers.[22]

Delay entering the field of battle until all the other players have become exhausted fighting amongst themselves. Then go in full strength and pick up the pieces.[23]

Mask Sinister Intentions with a Good Impression

In war, the enemy can be lulled into a false sense of security by causing him to believe that he is in no danger. Originally, the precept advised, "Hide your dagger behind a smile."

To establish rapport with the U.S. government, some of the most dangerous militants in Iraq have only had to join the political process. Al-Sadr was never pursued.

One way or another, make the enemy trust you and thereby slacken his vigilance. Meanwhile, plot secretly, making preparations for your future action to ensure its success.[24]

The stroke, when it comes, must be smooth and unobtrusive. It should be the product of considerable planning (reconnaissance and rehearsal).

Muslim militants sometimes take years planning a ground assault. Often they have rehearsed in a life-size mock-up of their objective.

Reassure the enemy to make it slack, work in secret to subdue it; prepare fully before taking action to prevent the enemy from changing its mind.[25]

Forty years ago, the enemy made the nationalization of another war so expensive that Congress could no longer afford it. One truly adept at this axiom might lead a losing foe to believe that he was winning.

By all accounts, U.S. forces believe that they, and their indigenous allies, are winning the war in Iraq. To claim overall victory, one's proxies must still be in control years later.

Speak deferentially, listen respectfully, follow his commands, and accord with him in everything. He will never imagine you might be in conflict with him. Our treacherous measures will then be settled.[26]
— *The Six Secret Teachings of Tai Gong*

169

The so-called "good impression" can be nothing more than an adversary failing to realize the consequences of damage.

While U.S. forces have lost a lot of equipment in Iraq, they see little, if any, significance in that fact. To eventually win, the militants have only to keep running away every time they destroy an expensive vehicle.

When the enemy is strong and cannot be easily overcome, we should puff it up with humble words and ample gifts and wait until it reveals its weak point to subdue it once and for all. The principle goes, "When the enemy is humble, make it proud." [27]
— *A Hundred Marvelous Battle Plans*

Sacrifice Minor Concerns for the Sake of Overall Mission

To gain a thing, one must sometimes lose another. Trying to hold on to everything can, in the end, cause the loss of everything. To accomplish a major goal, it is wise to sacrifice minor concerns. Verbatim, the saying renders, "Sacrifice the plum tree to save the peach."

The best example in Iraq was when the Mahdi Army agreed to stop fighting in the early fall of 2004. It may have lost a little face, but the much-needed respite gave it time to re-outfit and re-train.

There are circumstances in which you must sacrifice short term objectives in order to gain the long term goal. This is the scapegoat strategy whereby someone else suffers the consequences so that the rest do not. [28]

On more than one occasion in history, weak elements have so tied up their opposition that one such element was able to take down a target of strategic significance. The idea is to risk small units to keep the bulk of an opposing force occupied, while gathering up other units to wipe out a part of that force. As long as withdrawing from a battle does not risk that battle's strategic goal, so doing can conserve limited resources. When properly covered (by terrain and fire) and prerehearsed, tactical withdrawal can be relatively safe.

Tiny contingents that were willing to alternately fight and pull back could keep American combat formations indefinitely at bay in Iraq.

Pit your least strong horse against his strongest. Your strongest against his less strong. And your less strong against his least strong. Although I lost one race, I won two.[29]

The Asian sees no shame in strategic retreat or tactical withdrawal. He knows that both are necessary to achieve final victory against a formidable opponent. He sees dishonor in refusing to withdraw when strategically useful.

The Iraqi insurgent has sacrificed much to achieve his long-term goal. He neither revels in small victories, nor agonizes over small defeats.

Know contentment, and you will suffer no disgrace. Know when to stop, and you will meet with no danger. You can then endure.[30]
— Lao Zi

One who looks into the distance overlooks what is nearby; one who considers great things neglects the details. If we feel proud of a small victory and regret over a small defeat, we will encumber ourselves and lose the opportunity to achieve merits.[31]
— Li Su, a Tang Dynasty general

Seize the Chance to Increase the Odds

Victory is not totally assured to the most diligent of military planners. Chance always enters into the equation, so windows of opportunity must be sought out and quickly exploited. The "word-for-word" translation suggests, "Seize the opportunity in passing to lead away the sheep."

The U.S. government wants its forces out of Iraq as soon as possible. It has conveniently forgotten that it initially supported Saddam Hussein to blunt Iranian expansionism. A 4th-generation war can be lost politically. That the pro-Iranian Dawa Party and SCIRI won the election is problematic, to say the least.

Exploit any minor lapses on the enemy side, and seize every advantage to your side. Any negligence of the enemy must be turned into a benefit for you.[32]

Again inferred by this axiom is the need for timely action. This strategy requires one to be totally responsive to changing circumstances.[33]

Most ground attacks require some degree of surprise. Asian maneuver elements routinely abort any attack for which the planned degree has been too badly eroded. This is more a sign of common sense, than of weakness. It increases the odds of eventual success.

In both Iraq and Afghanistan, the Islamic guerrilla has mounted few attacks in which he kept coming after his initial surprise had been compromised. While pulling back upon being discovered may seem logical and commonplace, it is not part of the U.S. military tradition.

To seize opportunity, nothing is more significant than the element of surprise. Therefore, when losing its natural defenses, a fierce beast may be driven away by a child with a spear. . . . This is because the danger emerges too suddenly for one to retain one's presence of mind.[34]
— Jiang Yan, *The Art of Generalship*

Oriental armies have learned to exploit the slow and methodical way in which U.S. forces attack without much reconnaissance or rehearsal.

The Iraqi insurgents have little trouble telling when there are Americans nearby. If there are Americans nearby, they hear the sound of internal combustion engines.

Just before a large army enters battle, its shortcomings will be exposed. Exploiting them will lead to victory.[35]

Taking a goat in passing without being noticed is tantamount to striking a blow in passing without being felt. If this were possible, the same subtle raid could be used on the same objective over and over. U.S. headquarters in Vietnam never realized that its bases were being repeatedly penetrated by tiny units. Because those penetrations produced few casualties, they were assumed to have been unsuccessful. Actually, the enemy assault squads were more interested in destroying targets of strategic significance. They would "secretly penetrate by force" one side of a perimeter using an indirect-fire deception. Then, they would blow up a command bunker or artillery piece, throw down an 82mm mortar fin, and sneak out the other side. When U.S. defenders only found the fin and a couple of bodies in the morning, they assumed that they had successfully defended their base.

The Islamic insurgent has no rules and regulations to squash his initiative. He is more able to react to unforeseen events than Western foot soldiers.

While following the rules of strategy and tactics, be prepared to take advantage of circumstances not covered by conventional thinking. If opportunities present themselves, then the leader should be flexible in his plans and adapt to the new circumstances.[36]
— Sun Tzu

173

Stratagems
for Attack

- *Which tactical feints do the insurgents use?*
- *Is the U.S. being given room to end its occupation?*

THE PLOWER APPROACHES AN OUTPOST

(Source: *DA PAM 550-21* (January, 1985), p. 337)

When One Wants to Attack in War

If interested in taking the fight to the enemy, one might do the following: (1) make a feint to discover the foe's intentions, (2) steal the enemy's source of strength, (3) draw the enemy away from his refuge, (4) give a retreating adversary room, (5) discover a foe's intentions by offering him something of value, or (6) damage the enemy's method of control.

All of these ploys will weaken him—either physically or psychologically. All will lessen his chances of successfully defending himself.

Make a Feint to Discover the Foe's Intentions

An inexperienced or nervous opponent will overreact to a feint and thus reveal his overall plan. In war, thwarting an enemy's strategic intentions can be as helpful as accomplishing one's own. In Chinese, the axiom reads, "Beat the grass to startle the snake."

The Iraqi insurgent has attacked U.S. forces to keep them occupied and sample their reaction to his version of asymmetric warfare. He knows that he has only to beat the Iraqi security forces to win the war.

When you cannot detect the opponent's plans, launch a direct, but brief, attack and observe your opponent's reactions. His behavior will reveal his strategy.[1]

The Asian routinely uses a "sucker" formation to discover Western intentions. He prefers to make the first follow-through, not the first move. To do so, he must know what his opponent has in mind.

The Iraqi insurgent has learned (as did the Afghan mujahid) that a "high-tech," Westernized opponent will respond to almost every incident with armored vehicles or attack helicopters. Thus, he has little to fear from a light-infantry ground assault.

Any suspicion about the enemy's circumstances must be investigated. Before any military action, be sure to ascertain the enemy's situation; repeated reconnaissance is an effective way to discover the hidden enemy.[2]

There are any number of ways to apply this axiom in war. One of the more common is deploying a large force to attract the foe's attention and a small force to secretly reconnoiter or do damage. Sometimes the enemy never realizes that the small force even exists.

By creating a riot near a police station, the Iraqi insurgent can determine the Coalition's predisposition toward reinforcing that station. While a riot was raging at the front entrance of a security facility its occupants might not notice a suicide car bomber approaching their back gate. As many Iraqi police stations have been overrun, diversions of this type have almost certainly occurred.

Whether in Iraq or Afghanistan, the Muslim insurgent attacks every outpost in a particular area at the same time. By so doing, he draws attention away from that which is his ground assault objective. On 5 August 2005, the current Iraqi variant of the traditional maneuver became clear. Four collocated outposts were initially attacked—two by small arms or RPG, and two by suicide car bomb. Only the latter were subjected to a later ground assault.[3]

In warfare, employ both large and small forces to observe the enemy's reaction, push forward and pull back to observe the enemy's steadiness, make threats to observe the enemy's fear, stay immobile to observe the enemy's laxity, take a move to observe the enemy's doubt, [and] launch an attack to observe the enemy's solidity. Strike the enemy when it hesitates, attack the enemy when it is unprepared, subdue the enemy when it exposes its weakness, and rout the enemy when it reconnoiters. Take advantage of the enemy's rashness, forestall its intention, confound its battle plan, and make use of its fear.[4]
 — Sima Fa, *Law of Master Sima*

Sometimes, the Asian will wage a battle just to study his opponent. Only when a battlefield has strategic value, can the side that controls it claim to be the winner.

At first, the overseers of Iraq's insurgency used any way they could to accomplish their overall objective—utter chaos. They now favor three procedures: (1) driving foreign countries out of the Coalition, (2) blowing up revenue-producing oil and Coalition fuel, and (3) undermining Iraqi security forces (most notably the police). By watching their occupier, they learned that economic, political, and media initiatives are more effective than pronounced combat. By periodically attacking him, they can still divert his attention from the nonmartial aspects of 4GW.

177

If we and the enemy have not engaged yet and are therefore unacquainted with each other, we can sometimes dispatch a band of troops to test the enemy's strength and weakness; this is called a tasting battle. For the tasting battle, we should allow it to be neither grave nor long and should withdraw the troops after a brief engagement. Coordinating forces should be sent to cope with emergencies and prevent the loss of the tasting army, which may bring about the defeat of our main force.[5]
— Wu Bei Ji Yao, *An Abstract of Military Works*

Steal the Enemy's Source of Strength

Philosophies, institutions, traditions, and procedures all have varying degrees of moral and emotional power. Those of the enemy can be appropriated. For example, Mao Tse-tung—an avowed atheist—treated prisoners well in his war with Chiang Kai-shek to stimulate recruitment and dispel rumors of barbarism.[6] There are two ways in which this principle can be interpreted: (1) "Find reincarnation in another's corpse," or (2) "Raise a corpse from the dead."

America has always prided itself on being able to deliver supplies and reinforcement throughout a war zone. With IEDs, the Iraqi insurgents have interrupted that process and often literally steal the source of U.S. strength—its wherewithal. They have so effectively inderdicted the roads that the 3d Infantry Division had to shift to helicopter transport on its second deployment.[7] While in the past America depended on aerial bombardment to interdict roads, the Muslim insurgent depends on buried bombs.

Take an institution, a technology, or a method that has been forgotten or discarded and appropriate it for your own purpose. Revive something from the past by giving it a new purpose or to reinterpret and bring to life old ideas, customs, and traditions.[8]

Embedded in this axiom is the idea of looking for little ways to manipulate one's opponent and thereby keep him off balance.

With less concern for the final casualty count, the Muslim militant can deploy thousands of tiny maneuver elements. In that way, he controls the tempo of the fight.

Instead of being controlled by others, be in control. . . . In military strategy, it means using all available means to boost one's standing.[9]

To successfully apply this parable, one must be able to differentiate actual events from propaganda. Because the Eastern leader more readily acknowledges defeat, he does more to correct deficiencies.

The Muslim militant has been exposed to a training method that is experimental in nature and thus superior to what a Western soldier experiences. Namely, jihadis practice tactical techniques in life-size mock-ups against simulated-casualty assessment. If too many mock kills are recorded, local instructors have the authority to change what they teach. What the instructors learn this way gets shared. As other instructors attempt to improve on it, everyone becomes more proficient at close combat. Nothing demoralizes a powerful opponent more than getting embarrassed at short range.

In warfare there are no ever-victorious generals but there are many who taste defeat.[10]

By facing tanks and aircraft with tiny, irregular infantry detachments, the Asian creates the impression of a righteous cause. As the long-suffering underdog, he more easily wins the hearts and minds of the people.

The Islamic militant draws attention to every battlefield mistake and cultural excess of his Western adversary. By so doing, he creates the mistaken impression that America has been attempting to destroy the Muslim way of life.

The pivot of war is nothing but name and righteousness. Secure a good name for yourself and give the enemy a bad name; proclaim your righteousness and reveal the

unrighteousness of the enemy. Then your army can set forth in a great momentum.[11]
— *A Scholar's Dilettante Remarks on War*

Draw the Enemy Away from His Refuge

As a rule, one doesn't attack a foe who has the edge in terrain, defensive works, or home ground. Through trickery and deception, that foe must be lured away from his comfortable sanctuary. Exactly, this stratagem renders, "Lure the tiger off the mountain."

While there are few hilltops in central Iraq, there are plenty of heavily fortified U.S. bases at the outskirts of its cities. To draw the occupants of those bases out where they can be more easily attacked, the Iraqi insurgent has many ploys. One of his favorites is to set off a car bomb at a government facility near the city's center. The reaction force is automatically canalized into what often turns out to be a carefully prepared kill zone.

With regard to heights, if you occupy them before the enemy, you can wait for the enemy to climb up. But if he has occupied them before you, do not follow but retreat and try to entice him out.[12]
— Sun Tzu

Never directly attack a well-entrenched opponent. Instead lure him away from his stronghold and separate him from his source of strength.[13]

Implicit in this stratagem is the kind of ground suitable for a trap. Asian ambushes often start out as sniping incidents to get American forces to fully deploy across relatively open ground. At that point, the U.S. forces become vulnerable to grazing machinegun fire from the flanks.

Multistory buildings and narrow streets pose a great risk to armored vehicles. By continually drawing vehicle-borne U.S. troops into the center of town, the Muslim militant puts them at a severe disadvantage.

Use unfavorable natural conditions to trap the enemy in a difficult position. Use deception to lure him out. In an offensive that involves great risk lure the enemy to come out against you.[14]

Also implicit in this axiom is the advantage gained from making an opponent move onto unfamiliar ground. Because U.S. forces seldom establish a base at the center of town, they never become well enough acquainted with its streets to sufficiently adapt their tactics.

Every time a few Muslim jihadists die disabling one U.S. "Stryker" vehicle, their parent cell has won an engagement. Those jihadists are too easy to replace to have much strategic value. The Stryker vehicle cost hundreds of thousands of dollars. If enough are destroyed over a long enough period of time, Congress will stop funding the war.

If the enemy is led on to the battlefield, its position is weak. If we do not have to reach for the battlefield, our position is always strong. Use various methods to make the enemy come forward and lie in wait for it [him] at a convenient locality; we can thereby achieve certain victory.[15]
— *A Hundred Marvelous Battle Plans*

Give a Retreating Adversary Room

A desperate fugitive may turn to fight. By letting him go, one can reduce his eagerness for a last-ditch stand. Originally, this precept recommended, "To catch something, first let it go."

The instigators of the insurgency in Iraq have allowed America the same exit to which it resorted in Vietnam. They have helped to create a democracy with the explicit understanding that U.S. troops leave "as soon as possible." Before the election, this was publicly proclaimed by two UIA candidates: (1) a cleric (probably al-Sistani's choice of Hussein al-Shahrastani), and (2) Chalabi.[16] Since the election, al-Jaafari has repeatedly mentioned withdrawal while coyly avoiding its timetable.

Cornered prey will often mount a final desperate attack. To prevent this you let the enemy believe he still has a chance for freedom. His will to fight is thus dampened by his desire to escape. When in the end the freedom is proven a falsehood [unattainable,] the enemy's morale will be defeated and he will surrender without a fight.[17]

Inherent to this principle is patience. The enemy's will to fight is an important objective.

The Iraqi insurgent has not pressed his occupier as hard as he could have. Of late, he has directed most of his aggression toward indigenous security forces. He knows that as occupation forces make fewer contacts, some will go home. By increasing incident lethality, he indirectly keeps up the pressure.

Do not obstruct an army retreating homeward. If you besiege an army you must leave an outlet. Do not press an exhausted invader.[18]
— Sun Tzu

Press enemy forces too hard and they will strike back fiercely. Let them go and their morale will sink. Follow them closely, but do not push them too hard. . . . In short, careful delay in attack will help to bring destruction to the enemy.[19]

In warfare, if the enemy is outnumbered by our troops, it will be afraid of our strength and flee without fighting. We should not embark in hot pursuit, for anything forced to the extreme will develop into its opposite.[20]
— *A Hundred Marvelous Battle Plans*

This precept can be interpreted in many ways. By destroying targets of strategic significance without killing defenders, Asians lessen the resolve with which materiel-rich Westerners defend those targets.

The Iraqi insurgent has been targeting America's equipment, not its personnel. He has killed only enough Americans to evoke a heavy hand. With the war's cost soaring, he knows that the U.S. will be unable to stay long enough to prevent another theocracy.

By making the enemy feel lucky to get away, he'll lose the will to put up a good fight.[21]

Discover a Foe's Intentions by Offering Something of Value

He who knows where his foe plans to move has the edge. To find out, he offers an incentive to go there. Word for word, the strategy advises, "Cast a brick to attract a gem."

With rumors of terrorists at particular locations, the enemy may have fanned the five-month-long aerial bombing of Fallujah that caused many a pro-Coalition Iraqi to change sides. With the same bait, the insurgent has lured more than one security element into a trap.

One needs to bait the fish, so hook the enemy with the prospect of gain.[22]

Lure the enemy with counterfeits.[23]

Embedded within this principle is manipulating the whereabouts of one's opponent. Great advantage lies in choosing where a battle will be fought. For the Asian, detailed knowledge of the terrain can lead to every square inch of ground being covered by fire.

The Iraqi insurgent has fought most battles in his own backyard or a place unfamiliar to U.S. forces—e.g., Fallujah, Najaf, or Sadr City. There—by better knowing the terrain—he gave himself an edge. Seldom did he remove people from their natural environment to go after an American base.

[A]gainst the invasion of a hostile power, one should refrain from launching an attack into the enemy territory. Instead, it is best to allow the invading army to move in

183

and then defeat it on one's own ground. . . . First, the commander offers the enemy some bait, which can be a body of weak troops, [or] poorly guarded provision(s). . . . At the prospect of gain, the enemy will advance to swallow the bait. Thus the commander has gained the initiative by maneuvering the enemy at his will, and the battle has actually been half won before it is fought.[24]

Which incentive to offer depends on what the opponent deems important. The chance to corner a large number of enemy soldiers has more than once been enough to draw an American unit onto unfamiliar ground.

By encircling and assaulting Najaf and Fallujah, U.S. forces hoped to capture or kill large numbers of insurgents. In Najaf, most were spared by the cease-fire negotiation. In Fallujah, all but the suicide-prone rear party escaped the cordon.

Abandon goods to throw the enemy into disorder, abandon troops to entice it, and abandon fortresses and land to encourage its arrogance.[25]
— Bing Fa Bai Yan, *A Hundred War Maxims*

The Asian will sometimes bait his trap with the prospect of capturing two or three fleeing soldiers. Whether or not the Western unit pursues them, it will be mystified by their behavior.

Something similar occurred over and over in Fallujah. It is difficult to distinguish intentional bait from the practitioners of a retrograde defense. Still, many of the Marines felt as if they were being lured into a trap.

Prepare a trap, then lure your enemy into the trap by using bait. In war the bait is the illusion of an opportunity for gain.[26]

Bait them with the prospect of gain, bewilder and mystify them.[27]
— Sun Tzu

By ordinarily lying low and only temporarily defending non-strategic terrain, the Asian adds surprise to his strategic initiatives.

Whenever the Islamic insurgent shoots at a U.S. patrol, he evokes a predictable response. That response works for him in several ways: (1) it alienates the population, (2) damages the infrastructure, and (3) creates a diversion. Then, by leaving (offering the U.S. patrol a tactical victory), he can further assess its capacity for 4GW. It is only a worrisome foe if it continues on into the village or neighborhood to interact with the people.

One who is good at maneuvering the enemy makes a move so that the enemy must make a corresponding move, offers bait so that the enemy must swallow it, or lures the enemy with [the] prospect of gain and waits for it with one's main force.[28]

— Sun Tzu, *Art of War*

Damage the Enemy's Method of Control

Due to a stratified "top-down" structure, the Westernized unit's degree of effectiveness is largely dependent upon its command-and-control apparatus. By removing its leader, one can disrupt its whole mission. Verbatim, the principle says, "To catch rebels, first catch the ringleader."

The insurgent in Iraq has not attacked many U.S. leaders, but he has attacked hundreds of Iraqi leaders. By so doing, he has undermined the U.S./British bureaucratic model upon which most of Iraq's governmental agencies are now based. That makes them more susceptible to infiltration.

Destroy the enemy crack forces and capture their chief, and the enemy will collapse.[29]

This axiom is most often figuratively applied to the command echelon. Sometimes discrediting those in charge can be just as effective as removing them.

The Iraqi insurgency has worked hard to discredit the Coalition's ability to provide basic services. To emphasize the point, it routinely attacks the Green Zone—by car bomb on its edges and mortar at its center.

When our troops have penetrated deep into the enemy's territory and the enemy strengthens its defense works and refuses to engage in battle for the purpose of wearing us down, we may attack its sovereign, storm its headquarters, block its return route, and cut off its provisions. Thus it will be compelled to fight, and we can employ crack forces to defeat it.[30]
— *A Hundred Marvelous Battle Plans*

There are ten thousand artifices [tricks] of war, and one should not stick to any one of them. First seize the enemy's mainstay, and its strength will be weakened by half.[31]
— Hu Qian Jing, *Canon of the General*

Eastern insurgents want the occupation force gone. Killing its commanders might reinforce its commitment to stay.

There has been no high-level U.S. official killed in Iraq. With a few of the hundreds of U.S. "Stingers" that went to the mujahideen during the Soviet-Afghan war, the insurgents could have downed at least one. They must have seen more benefit in that official's peers pursuing disengagement.

If the enemy's army is strong but is allied to the commander only by money or threats, then take aim at the leader. If the commander falls, the rest of the army will disperse or come over to your side. If, however, they are allied to the leader through loyalty, then beware, the army can continue to fight on after his [the leader's] death out of vengeance.[32]

Thus, the Easterner tries harder to demoralize the Western occupiers' commanders than to kill them. Over the last half of the 20th Century, he learned how to undermine the pride of an attritionist adversary.

In Iraq, the insurgent commander does so by keeping the

stress level of his U.S. counterparts higher than his own. While they struggle to avoid daily casualties, he is relatively unconcerned with temporary setbacks and working on a long term plan. Now more than ever, the U.S. commanders have to worry about the 4GW consequences of their battlefield maneuvers.

When asked, "If the enemy troops are superior in number and about to advance in an orderly formation, how shall I cope with them?" I reply, "Seize something they treasure and they will become maneuverable." [33]
   — Sun Tzu, *Art of War*

10 Stratagems for Confused Cases

- *Which U.S. strength does the insurgency undermine?*
- *How does chaos help the enemy?*

THE NEIGHBORHOOD RABBLE ROUSER

(Source: *DA PAM 550-25* (December, 1988), chap. 4)

When Confused in War

After becoming disoriented in battle, one might do the following: (1) erode the enemy's source of strength, (2) create chaos to make an opponent easier to beat, (3) leave behind a small force to slow and deceive pursuers, (4) encircle the foe but let him think he has a way out, (5) concentrate on the nearest opposition, or (6) borrow from the enemy the instrument of his own destruction.

For America's adversaries in Iran and Afghanistan, electronic surveillance and standoff bombardment would generate considerable confusion.

Erode the Enemy's Source of Strength

In war, an opponent's strength usually comes from his wealth, material resources, or manpower. If wealth, cause him to incur expenses; if resources, disrupt the lines of distribution; if manpower, sow discord. Literally, the stratagem proposes, "Remove the firewood from under the cauldron."

As an affluent nation, America tries to provide its soldiers with the world's most technologically advanced equipment. By destroying that equipment one truckload at a time, the Iraqi insurgent has cost the American taxpayer many billions of dollars. He has so disrupted overland convoy routes that many U.S. units are routinely short key items.

Avoid a contest of strength with the enemy but seek to weaken his position.[1]

When confronted with a powerful enemy, do not fight them head-on but try to find their weakest spot to initiate the collapse.[2]

This axiom can also be applied psychologically. Asian defenders routinely hide below ground about to be captured. By so doing, they do more than escape capture. They sap a Western attacker's morale. With too few bodies to show for his effort, that attacker feels defeated. By fighting just long enough to inflict casualties, the Eastern defender also tempts the Western attacker to exaggerate the body count.

The Iraqi insurgent has found a different way to erode American morale. He capitalizes on the fact that U.S. infantrymen are now obligated to patrol by vehicle.[3] By covering the roads with IEDs, he creates in them a feeling of futility.

Don't fight a powerful enemy head-on, instead undermine its morale and deprive it of leadership. . . . Study the war situation carefully to find out the enemy's weak points and exploit them.[4]

When faced with an enemy too powerful to engage directly you must first weaken him by undermining his foundation and attacking his source of power.[5]

Then, there are the moral dilemmas with which the Asian distracts his opponent. He who doubts himself is less likely to win.

By sending suicide cars against convoys, the Iraqi insurgent creates a moral dilemma for the defender of every motorized contingent. Should he kill whoever gets too close? Every time he errs in judgment, he is emotionally scarred and / or accused of brutality.

In directing warfare and assessing the enemy, one should try to undermine the enemy's morale and destroy its discipline, so that it looks intact but loses its utility. This is the method to win by political strategy.[6]
— Wei Liao Zi, *Book of Master Wei Liao*

Create Chaos to Make an Opponent Easier to Beat

People will pay attention to anything out of the ordinary in their environment. Magicians, card sharks, pick pockets, and prize fighters all rely on this trait. That's how they redirect their quarry's attention while secretly achieving their goal. This axiom has two possible translations: (1) "Muddle the water to seize fish," and (2) "Fish in troubled waters."

In Iraq, the Muslim insurgent has done what Western strategists thought impossible. He has effectively harnessed what they have tried to minimize—the uncertainty of war. He has turned chaos—war's principal ingredient—into a tactic. By rousing rabble, fanning disorder, and rewarding criminals, he has befuddled the U.S. occupier and discredited the interim government. By attempting to respond to every incident, that occupier spread himself too thin. Unable to provide neighborhood security, the interim government lost credibility and popular support.

Before engaging your enemy's forces, create confusion to

weaken his perception and judgment. Do something unusual, strange, and unexpected as this will arouse the
enemy's suspicion and disrupt his thinking. A distracted
enemy is thus more vulnerable.[7]

When the enemy falls into internal chaos, exploit his weakened position and lack of direction and win him over to your
side.[8]

Whether on ambush, defense, or attack, Asians will often confuse their quarry by alternately firing from different locations. That
way the quarry has difficulty locating the source of the most dam-
aging fire. Another variation on this theme is to initially take one's
quarry under fire from every direction at once.

For the occupier of Iraq, a good example is the routine "hail"
of RPG rounds. With rounds coming from every direction,
it's hard to pinpoint their source. Not being able to accu-
rately shoot back can be highly demoralizing to a firepower-
dependent army.

Every day have the vanguard go forth and instigate skirmishes with them in order to psychologically wear them
out. Have our older and weaker soldiers drag brushwood
to stir up the dust, beat the drums and shout, and move
back and forth. . . . Their general will certainly become fa-
tigued, and their troops will become fearful. In this situation the enemy will not dare to come forward. Then when
we come forth with our three armies the enemy will certainly be defeated.[9]
— *The Six Secret Teachings of the Tai Gong*

There are any number of aspects to chaos. Each, in its own
way, weakens the enemy. Because a highly structured Western
army steers away from uncertainty, it only halfheartedly analyzes
those aspects.

In the name of security, U.S. units often fail to share crucial
pieces of information—something they or the enemy did that
works. Hezbollah and al-Qaeda don't have that problem.

They widely disseminate such information over their TV networks and websites. That leaves the normal media outlets free to accept disinformation. As in Vietnam, the U.S. intelligence apparatus still takes—at face value—most of what it sees or hears on the battlefield. It thus has trouble separating useful fact from enemy fabrication. To avoid embarrassment, it forwards vast reams of information to operating units to extrapolate. With neither the time nor the expertise to do so, those units are further confused.

One who is good at combatting the enemy, fools it with inscrutable moves, confuses it with false intelligence, makes it relax by concealing one's strength, causes it to hesitate by exposing one's weakness, deafens its ears by jumbling one's orders and signals, blinds its eyes by converting one's banners and insignias, eases off its vigilance by hiding what it fears, saps its will by offering what it likes, confounds its battle plan by providing distorted fact, and breaks its courage by showing off one's power.[10]
— *A Scholar's Dilettante Remarks on War*

Create chaos in the enemy camp and when it's weak and without direction, you can hold sway over them.[11]

Leave Behind a Small Force to Slow and Deceive Pursuers

Tactically withdrawing from an engagement takes discipline. It also takes a rear guard. The unit must create the illusion that no retreat is in progress. Word for word, the principle reads, "The cicada sheds its skin."

The volunteer martyr is the Muslim insurgent's rear guard, both literally and figuratively. He delays the attacker just long enough for the strategically important people and assets to be removed from the battlefield. He also occupies the opponent in the martial arena, just long enough for other 4GW arenas to be exploited.

When you are in danger of being defeated, and your only chance is to escape and regroup, then create an illusion.

193

While the enemy's attention is focused on this artifice, secretly remove your men leaving behind only the facade of your presence.[12]

It is important for the rear guard to closely mimic the front array of the departing unit. To do so, it may construct human dummies. Or it may have each of its people man more than one defensive position.

To more easily exit Fallujah, the enemy deployed a rear party of voluntary martyrs. While the East Asian equivalent would have saved themselves by hiding below ground or exfiltrating the encirclement, the Fallujah's martyrs fought to the death. As they were often barricaded with automatic weapons in upper-story rooms, they took their fair share of American lives.

Make your front array appear as if you are still holding your position so that the allied forces will not suspect your intention and the enemy troops will not dare to attack rashly. Then withdraw your main forces secretly.[13]

Inherent to this axiom is a prompt and obscure withdrawal. The false front will do little good if the enemy sees the rest of the unit falling back. One must pull away quickly while maintaining the appearance of inaction.[14]

In Fallujah, the enemy left behind martyrs so that U.S. forces could not tell when most defenders were falling back.

To "shed the skin" doesn't mean doing so out of panic, but keeping up appearances to preserve oneself while retreating, so that the enemy won't suspect anything amiss.[15]

The false front must simulate more than just the visible parts of the original formation; it must also imitate its ongoing activity. When encircled, an Asian force will often withdraw after directing machinegun fire at the opposing unit. It does so to keep its movements hidden from any supporting-arms observers.

When surrounded, an Afghan guerrilla unit has many ways

to escape. Normally, small contingents reconnoiter the opposition cordon and exfiltrate where possible. If what's left of the guerrilla unit is at all familiar with the Maoist method, it hides below ground while a few machinegunners create the illusion of a breakout. As the opposing unit's cordon tightens around the machinegunners, it passes over the top of the main party. Then the machinegunners hide or try to hold out until dark. If everyone wants to escape at once, they have only to use timed firecrackers as a breakout simulation.

Maintain the original shape and play out the original pose, so that . . . the enemy does not move.[16]

Encircle the Foe But Let Him Think He Has a Way Out

A cornered opponent is dangerous, but so too is one who gets loose. Leaving him a way out of his predicament and then removing that way will erode his will to fight. Verbatim, the precept says, "Bolt the door to catch the thief."

The closing-door, U-shaped ambush perfectly exemplifies this axiom. Before it is sprung, Coalition forces have a secure route of egress. After it is sprung, that route is blocked. Such ambushes have been occurring in both Iraq and Afghanistan.

When dealing with a small and weak enemy, surround and destroy him. If you let him retreat, you will be at a disadvantage pursuing him.[17]

This axiom can also be applied psychologically. One can lead a U.S. soldier to believe he'll be home for Christmas and then dash those hopes.

Some American units about to leave Iraq have experienced an increased level of violence. Their involuntary extension was hard on morale.

When one fights an opponent and it appears on the surface that he [the opponent] has been defeated, if his fighting spirit has not yet been eradicated in his heart of hearts, he will not acknowledge defeat. In that case, you must change your mental attitude and break the opponent's fighting spirit. You must make him acknowledge defeat from the bottom of his heart. It is essential to make sure of that.[18]
— Musashi Miyamoto, *Book of Five Rings*

Encirclement plays much more of a role in Eastern tactics than in Western. Sometimes the quarry is encouraged to move right over the top of a well-camouflaged emplacement. He can then be taken under fire from both front and back. The escape route does not have to be physically blocked. It can be also closed by indirect fire or delayed IED.

On more than one occasion, Coalition forces have been lured into a building just to have it destroyed around them.[19] Boobytrapped houses were discovered in Fallujah. The walls of a building form a type of encirclement.

The strategy points out that encirclement and annihilation is the best method to deal with [a raid]. . . . For instance, on learning of the enemy's plan for a night attack on your camp, you can pull away the troops and leave the camp empty. When the enemy enters the camp, you can lead the troops to close in from all sides and form a tight encirclement. Or you can use a bait army to lure the enemy into an ambush ring that allows no way of escape.[20]

Concentrate on the Nearest Opposition

The foe's chances largely depend on how quickly he can concentrate or disperse his forces. To beat him, one must score back-to-back victories. Taking a quick local victory, however small, can be the first step. With initial momentum, more difficult or distant targets become attainable. Here, final intentions are both facilitated and masked by exploiting a local opportunity. The Chinese translation recommends, "Befriend a distant state while attacking a nearby state."

*Hezbollah and al-Qaeda have focused more on their mu-
tual occupier than on any theological differences. Once the
occupier has left, they will vie for overall control with each
other.*

It is more advantageous to conquer the nearby enemies, because of geographical reasons, than those far away.[21]

The advantage lies in preempting the nearest foe's intentions.
A surprise attack from him could jeopardize one's overall plan.

*The Iraqi and Afghan insurgencies have directed most of
their combat power against indigenous security forces, not
the U.S. military. Those security forces are much easier to
beat. Once they have been sufficiently infiltrated, they will
be more docile. Ideally, they will be politically forced to
absorb intact guerrilla militias.*

When you are the strongest in one field, your greatest threat
is from the second strongest in your field, not the strongest
from another field.[22]

Stressed here is the need to beat a powerful foe piecemeal.
Avoided are battles that don't contribute to the overall war effort.

*Neither the Iraqi nor Afghan insurgent has yet tried to amass
enough people to try a major ground assault. For the time
being, he prefers to wear down his opponent with 1,000 tiny
cuts.*

[T]he strategy instructs the military leader to deal with
his enemies one by one. Also, one is cautioned against seeking superficial victories that do not bring about any concrete profit.[23]

Of course, this axiom can also be applied in a less literal context. He who cannot recognize nearby opportunities may lack the
flexibility to take minimal casualties in war.

*While the enemy in Iraq is incurring some casualties, he is
not incurring nearly as many as the North Vietnamese did*

40 years ago. That is probably because his cells are taking only what is locally available and not yet trying to form larger units or traverse the countryside.

When circumscribed [submersed] in situation and restricted in disposition [posture], seek profit from nearby and keep peril at a distance.[24]

Borrow from the Foe the Tool of His Own Destruction

There are two sources of opposition in war—the human adversary and unfavorable circumstance. Here one can reduce his own weakness by appropriating part of an enemy's strength and using it against him. In this way, he generates additional capabilities. One can take something from his adversary to reduce a shortage of materiel, for example, and then destroy him with that very same item. Precisely, the strategy advises, "Borrow a route to conquer Guo."

During America's massive bombing of Laos, a full third of all ordnance dropped turned out to be duds.[25] If one twentieth of the bombs and shells used on Iraq didn't detonate, the insurgents would have enough high explosive to keep up the current level of violence for a very long time.

Borrow the resources of an ally to attack a common enemy. Once the enemy is defeated, use those resources to turn on the ally that lent them in the first place.[26]

Literally the principle says to take from one's more wealthy opponent whatever is needed to win the war. With what can be stolen from convoys or police stations, the Iraqi insurgency could keep up the current level of violence for a very long time. Technology is America's strongest suit, but the Iraqi insurgent has access to similar items on the open market. It has exploited one aspect.

With increasingly sophisticated detonating devices, the Iraqi insurgents have suckered U.S. forces into their traditional solution to any problem. Instead of dismounting the vehicles, the U.S. has pursued electronic jamming and more armor. American units have killed or alienated many non-combatants while protecting their vehicles from suicide car bombs or IED. They could have more productively used foot patrols.

When a small state, located between two big states, is being threatened by the enemy state, you should immediately send troops to rescue it, thereby expanding your sphere of influence.[27]

Of course, the axiom can also be applied more subtly, like borrowing an opponent's appearance or intentions. Disguise is after all the trademark of the Iranian *Hashishin.*

In many parts of southern Iraq, al-Sadr has created a quasi-state—complete with alternative basic services. When not able to obtain those services from the local government, people turn to his organization for help. Through election-day irregularities, there are now other Islamist Shiites in the fledgling government. They will try to infiltrate the Interior Ministry, its subordinate security agencies, and all local police forces. Then, they will be able to use the "establishment" to promote their revolutionary agenda.

When somebody wants to use your territory to deal with an external threat, do not believe him so readily.[28]

11 ___ Stratagems for Gaining Ground

- *Which U.S. habits have Muslim insurgents encouraged?*
- *Were the Islamic rebels feigning lack of military skill?*

HEAVY INFANTRYMEN ENJOY LIMITED MOBILITY

(Source: Courtesy of Bates Creative Group, from *Marines Magazine*, January-March 2005, cover art by Seth Sirbaugh, © 2005 Bates Creative Group)

When One Wants More Territory in War

If the goal is a larger "friendly" area, one might do the following: (1) attack the enemy's habits to undermine his foundation, (2) make an example of someone to deter the enemy, (3) feign a lack of military ability, (4) lure the foe into poor terrain and cut off his escape route, (5) mislead the enemy with false information, or (6) secretly occupy an enemy-controlled area.

Gaining territory is a stage of Maoist guerrilla warfare. Insurgents do not gain territory by sweeping across and occupying all of it. They expand the number of hidden cells and friendly villages.

Attack the Foe's Habits to Undermine His Foundation

A large unit operates more out of habit, than logic. While invincible in one formation, it may be ineffective in another. By interfering with the rules and habits under which it fights, one can take away its physical and moral foundation. In Chinese, the principle advises, "Steal the beams and replace the pillars with rotten timber."

During the re-invasion of Chechnya in 1999, the Russians tried through blanket bombardment to keep any opposition at least 300 yards away from their lead elements. On the march up to Baghdad in 2003, U.S. forces did much the same thing. When the Iraqi Army did stand and fight, it "hugged" those forces to escape their supporting arms and take advantage of their close-combat inexperience.

On sweeps into the enemy's infiltration route west of Baghdad, American units have responded with overwhelming firepower to any sign of resistance. Along the Euphrates just south of where 21 Marines lost their lives in separate incidents in early August 2005, a Marine battalion swept into the town of Haqlaniyah. On the way in, one vehicle encountered a mine and another an IED. There was a smattering of mortar, RPG, and AK-47 fire. Then, the battalion opened up with its heavy weapons. By noon, F-18's had dropped two 500-pound bombs and done some strafing. After searching all day in the intense heat for an enemy base camp, the Marines were told by former Iraqi National Guardsman Munaf Khalaf that the insurgents had fled the town at their initial approach. Then, they found two buildings rigged for command demolition.[1] Might the guerrillas have used this axiom to create the illusion that the town was defended. What if two jihadists had occasionally fired their weapons while leaving the town. What if the IEDs had been remotely controlled and the mortars fired from outside of town? That would leave the Marines demoralized, residents alienated, and insurgents unchecked.

Disrupt the enemy's formations, interfere with their methods of operations, change the rules in which they are used to following, go contrary to their standard training. In this way you remove the supporting pillar, the common link which makes a group of men an effective fighting force.[2]

While this ploy could be applied to any of an opponent's rules or habits, it is aimed primarily at his formation. It can cause that formation to frequently change and subsequently fragment. One way is to separate the main body from its march (column) security elements.

Without enough advance and rearguard protection on a straight stretch of road, U.S. convoys can find themselves under a linear sheaf of long-range machinegun or mortar fire that precisely coincides with the road. To produce that sheaf, the Islamic guerrilla has only to position himself to the direct front or rear of the column, "direct-lay" his gun, and spin the elevation wheel between rounds.

Change the enemy's formation frequently, dislocate its main force and deal the blow when it tends toward defeat.[3]

Easterners will sometimes use a series of sudden maneuvers to thoroughly confuse a Westernized foe. On ambush, they may start with a feigned sniper attack from one side, and end up with a full fledged assault from another.

Iraqi insurgents have preceded their ground assaults against Coalition facilities with any number of diversions. The most effective of these diversions would tempt the facility commander to reinforce the wrong side of his defensive perimeter.

Make the allied forces change their battle formation frequently so that their main strength will be taken away.[4]

The axiom further advises the skilled warrior in an unfavorable position to proceed slowly.

A mechanized maneuver element makes quite a sight. Just

its tracked-vehicle noise and potential firepower alone seems to preclude opposition. Yet, by hiding in spider holes next to a road, Afghan mujahideen easily bypass security elements to get at tanks, refuelers, and command vehicles. One IED video from Iraq clearly shows two figures darting away from the explosion.

Similarly, a U.S. linear defense—with all of its advanced early warning devices, barbed wire, and machineguns—seems impregnable. Yet, to penetrate it, the Muslim insurgent has only to tunnel. At some point, he may learn (from his East Asian cousins) how—on the surface—to bypass early warning devices, crawl through barbed wire, and silence machineguns. Stopping an East Asian sapper with a Western-style perimeter has been likened to blocking water with a fish net. With an non-Western talent, that sapper has taken advantage of a Western habit. In Iraq, there has already been evidence of protective-wire tampering.

A typical battle formation has a central axle (heavenly beam) extending from the front to the rear and a horizontal axle (earthly pillar) connecting the right and left flanks. The two axles are made up of the best fighters.[5]

Any of an adversary's bad habits can be exploited. They are sometimes the product of competing priorities—like more truck traffic through a gate than would favor adequate inspection. Or those bad habits can be a product of a "top-down" organizational structure. As U.S. commanders more often hear what their immediate subordinates did well, they seldom learn of lower-echelon bad habits. For example, most company commanders have never been told that equitably distributing defenders across unevenly rippled ground will leave the door open to enemy short-range infiltration. They do not know that digging one's fighting hole just behind the military crest of a hill makes it approachable to within a few feet. They do not realize that, by checking the lines while upright, they are giving away the locations of their frontline positions.

Prior to the attack on the U.S. mess tent, there were trucks being cursorily waved into many bases.[6]
— DoD contractor in Iraq

When confronting a powerful enemy, adopt feints, sudden maneuvers, and split the enemy strength to weaken it.[7]

Make an Example of Someone to Deter the Enemy

A larger adversary will sometimes advance too cautiously after seeing the destruction of one of its subordinate elements. Originally, this axiom read, "Point at the mulberry tree and abuse the locust."

The Viet Cong ringed their base camp villages with boobytraps. Whenever a U.S. unit tripped one, it tended to skirt that village. There is evidence that the Muslim insurgents are also encircling their training facilities and ammunition stashes with IEDs. A string of command-detonated explosives was spotted on the main road into Fallujah.[8] Two IEDs were detonated near a U.S. raid site in late April 2005.[9]

To discipline, control, or warn others whose status or position excludes them from direct confrontation, use analogy and innuendo.[10]

Feigning an attack from the front will only momentarily distract the foe's attention away from his other sides. For this reason, the Asian will occasionally launch a frontal, human-wave assault. By so doing, he causes his future adversary to worry less about flanks and rear. In Iraq, the Islamic insurgent uses a different type of distraction—one that discourages the deployment of small teams.

While few U.S. soldiers have had their heads severed, al-Zarqawi's all-too-graphic execution of Iraqi security personnel has discouraged American commanders from adequately decentralizing control. Guerrilla wars are won by deploying thousands of tiny maneuver elements, each with the authority to track down a perpetrator. That's how the British defeated the Communist insurgency in Malaysia.

To dangle a carrot may not be enough to win someone over,

for he may be suspicious of your motives. But if you warn him subtly by using another as an example, he may take the hint.[11]

Feign Lack of Military Ability

Irrational behavior normally generates a sound or motion signature. But one can unobtrusively feign tactical ignorance. Literally this stratagem says, "Feign foolishness instead of madness."

Most U.S. and British troops have come to see all Muslim insurgents as tactically inept. They don't yet realize that their foe intentionally places poorly trained martyrdom volunteers in their path. With little strategic value, those volunteers are considered expendable. It is their handlers— the enemy recruiters/trainers/advisers—who must be stopped. Many are Iranian special operators and as tactically proficient as their U.S. counterparts. Their "throwaway" personnel have accomplished two things: (1) fooling the Coalition as to the real source and sophistication of the insurgency, (2) facilitating the handlers' escape.

At times, it is better to pretend to be foolish and do nothing than brag about yourself and act recklessly. Be composed and plot secretly, like thunder clouds hiding themselves during winter only to bolt out when the time is right.[12]

In Vietnam, the enemy threw satchel charges with no shrapnel into U.S. perimeters. At the time, Americans thought their foe to be stupid. As it turns out, the satchel charges were not intended to hurt anyone, only to keep their heads down during an assault. They were concussion grenades large enough to imitate impacting artillery shells. Enemy flash-bangs were found in Fallujah.

The foe in Iraq has not claimed tactical victory after every encounter. He cares more that the encounter happened. The event adds to the overall impression of chaos, thereby discrediting the Coalition's ability to establish order. Totally unconcerned with each event's success or failure, certain groups try to take credit for as many as they can. Mosul-based Ansar al-Sunna has claimed responsibility for incidents in almost every part of northern Iraq.

Secrecy begets success; openness begets failure. In military conflicts, it's better to conceal than to reveal moves, to play dumb than to act smart.[13]

In modern war, the side that first reveals its shape and intentions is often the one that loses. In every ostensible act, fake or otherwise, lies some clue to its underlying purpose in an overall plan. Total secrecy is frequently preferable to some type of deception. Of utmost importance to an Asian is remaining motionless upon the enemy's arrival.

A Muslim insurgency has no shape, because it has no organizational structure. It initially encourages every malcontent to add to the chaos, because it later intends to assume overall control. Among criminal elements and guerrilla groups alike, there is the unspoken understanding that the strongest will establish a ruling alliance. The best finisher in the region is the Iranian Revolutionary Guard and its Iraqi proxies.

Stay motionless and hide one's intention.[14]

To undertake military operations, the army must prefer stillness to movement. It reveals no shape when still but exposes its shape in movement. When the enemy exposes a vulnerable shape, seize the chance to subdue it.[15]
— Bing Lei, *Essentials of War*

In Iraq, enemy forces appear unwilling to maneuver against their U.S. counterparts. They prefer to let the U.S. forces come to them. Then, they watch for an opening.

The Asian equates Western pride with arrogance. He knows that the U.S. military claims to have won every battle since 1918 except for Bataan and Kasserine Pass. Under his more maneuver- (as opposed to firepower-) oriented definition of victory, such an accomplishment is statistically impossible. Thus, he considers the claim to be a fabrication and all U.S. commanders to be tyrannical automatons. He capitalizes on their blind acceptance of the U.S. interpretation of history. He does so by pretending to be less skilled at short-range encounters than he really is and to lose strategically important battles that he has really won. Most U.S. and British occupiers of Iraq will begrudgingly admit to their foe's courage but not to any tactical ability. Very possibly, the Israelis felt the same way about the Hezbollah-led Palestinians right before having to leave Southern Lebanon.

Hide behind the mask of a fool, a drunk, or a madman to create confusion about your intentions and motivations. Lure your opponent into underestimating your ability until, overconfident, he drops his guard. Then you may attack.[16]

Lure the Foe into Poor Terrain and Cut Off His Escape Route

Terrain can offer opposite advantages to different-sized forces. While narrow terrain will restrict a large force, it can protect a small force. The idea here is to lure the enemy into terrain that limits his activities while helping one's own. Word for word, the precept translates, "Climb onto the roof and remove the ladder."

The easiest terrain to defend is urban. The Iraqis waited for Baghdad to be fully occupied before seriously contesting it. They thereby forced their attacker to engage in widely dispersed, short-range combat (his shortest suit) in a place where electronic surveillance (his longest suit) made little difference.

With baits and deceptions, lure your enemy into treacherous terrain. Then cut off his lines of communication and avenue of escape. To save himself he must fight both your own forces and the elements of nature.[17]

One can employ any number of enticements. In Asia, the most common is the appearance of losing while flawlessly executing a retrograde defense. If the opponent tries to lengthen his string of easy "victories," he becomes overextended. It is then that his lifeline can be severed.

During the assault on Fallujah, enlisted Marines felt as if they were being drawn up certain streets into an ambush. Whenever they got ahead of their brethren on adjacent streets, their fear was often realized.

Provide the army with an apparent chance, entice it to advance, cut it off from coordination or reinforcement, and place it in an impasse.[18]

In one interpretation, the foe's retreat can be impeded by the terrain itself. Many kinds of terrain have this potential.

A built-up area consists of highly restrictive terrain. It is crisscrossed by high obstacles (the building fronts) and narrow passes (the streets and alleys). When a vehicular patrol is attacked from the side, it has a virtual cliff to its rear.

Avoid terrain that features cliffs and crags, narrow passes, tangled bush, and quagmires. While avoiding such places ourselves, try to lure the enemy into such areas so that when we attack the enemy will have this type of terrain at his back.[19]
— Sun Tzu

Normal terrain that has been covered by fire—a "firesack"—both impedes the enemy and blocks his escape. It may be what appears to be a gap in one's own lines. Then, any intruders are quickly decimated by grazing machinegun fire from both flanks. In the matrix of small forts that replaced defensive lines late in WWI, every opening between forts constituted a firesack. WWII Americans often successfully assaulted dummy lines only to find themselves caught in the crossfire between enemy squad- or platoon-sized strongpoints. Sometimes, they were allowed to advance past the first row of heavily camouflaged forts unchallenged. Then, when the enemy appeared at close range from all sides, the Americans were effectively cut off from reinforcement or resupply.

The occupants of Iraqi or Afghan farm compounds can cover each other by fire across intervening fields. A Coalition unit in their midst might encounter grazing machinegun fire from every direction. The walled compounds around al-Qaeda's supposed headquarters in northwest Pakistan actually comprised a strongpoint matrix. Each compound's entrance may have been covered by the fire of its rearward neighbors. That would explain why the Pakistani attackers were so badly mauled.[20] Concentric circles of walled compounds occur all across Southern Afghanistan. Their central building cluster may too have a long escape tunnel.

Expose your weak points deliberately to entice the enemy to penetrate into your line, then ensnare him in a death trap by cutting off his rear-guard support.[21]

Of course, this axiom need not be applied literally. There are any number of figurative applications.

It has been said that one fights hardest for his home turf. By fighting mostly in the cities against a firepower-dependent foe, the Iraqi insurgent has guaranteed himself an ample supply of willing reinforcements.

In battle, the "ladder" refers to deliberately exposing a weak spot to entice the enemy to advance towards you. Once he has entered your ambush ring, cut off his escape route. . . . The strategy can be used to entice and destroy the enemy, and to put one's own soldiers in a position with no way of retreat so that they'll fight with all their might.[22]

Like any other stratagem, this one can also be applied psychologically. To cause a superpower to go home, one must disprove enough predeployment claims to create a need for face saving. It is then that the axiom can be put into practice.

By creating chaos, the Iraqi insurgent has temporarily blocked his occupier's exit. That occupier cannot leave before restoring some semblance of order. By then, the replacement government will be sufficiently undermined.

Ladder refers to the means by which the enemy is lured into the ambush ring. It may be a gesture of weakness if the enemy commander is arrogant, an enticement of gain if the enemy commander is greedy, or repeated defeats if the enemy commander is hesitant.[23]

Mislead the Enemy with False Information

While important to determine an enemy's intentions, it is equally important to disguise one's own. Through the use of decoys, facades, and camouflage, one can conceal his own strengths and weaknesses. Verbatim, the axiom renders, "Tie silk blossoms to a dead tree."

There are any number of ways to disguise intentions. To hide a maneuver, one can operate behind some sort of screen. If the adversary has satellite-borne thermal imaging, he can move below ground or into a heavily populated area. However, the Asian will sometimes reveal part of his initial formation—that which a Westerner might construe as his own. When a Westerner attacks what he believes to be a defensive line, he may be actually entering an area swept by long-range fire.

The Iraqi insurgent, though not yet very tactically sophisticated, blends in well with an urban population. He can therefore mask many intentions with everyday activities. For example, his attack force members take turns crossing each street, thus attracting the least amount of attention. They also set up two-man security checkpoints around their intended target, thus secretly isolating it. With no reports of an approaching enemy unit, the quarry feels safe.

Use deceptive appearances to make your troop formation look much more powerful than it really is.[24]

Then, there are the noises that mask intentions. The most useful are extremely loud.

By firing at every combat outpost in an objective's vicinity, the Afghan rebel diverts unwanted attention from that ob-

211

jective and keeps it from being reinforced. He also covers the unmistakable sound of heavily armed men approaching on foot.

Deceptive appearances coupled with unusual noises can make up for the lack of military might to subdue the enemy.[25]

In addition, there are many ways to look stronger than one really is. This can draw unwanted attention from someone else.

Al-Zarqawi has been made to look much stronger than he really is. Since August 2004, he has taken credit for about half of all the incidents in northern Iraq. There is no way that he and his tiny "Al-Qaeda in Iraq" organization could have been responsible. Many think that he has closer ties to Lebanese Hezbollah.[26] On 20 February 2005, because of a lap-top computer containing "my pictures," al-Zarqawi was believed to have been almost captured.[27] How better to convince an electronics-oriented occupier that al-Zarqawi still exists or controls a network of operatives.

Tying silk blossoms on a dead tree gives the illusion that the tree is healthy. Through the use of artifice and disguise make something of no value appear valuable; of no threat appear dangerous; of no use, useful.[28]

By flaunting one's strength, one can seize the foe's attention and create a diversion for extraordinary forces (covert elements).

The Iraqi insurgent's strength is his IEDs. But Sepah and its Lebanese counterpart also have talented saboteurs. During Beirut's 2004 Jerusalem Day, black-clad Hezbollah personnel crossed wires between, and rappelled down, tall buildings. One can only guess at how many Ansar al-Islam and "Al-Qaeda in Iraq" incidents may have been their doing.

Displaying power to intimidate the enemy is a timeless strategy. . . . Feign advances that you have not secured, achievements that you have not made, strength that you

lack, and maneuvers to deceive the enemy. Flaunt your strength, subdue the spirit of the enemy, and use extraordinary plans to secure victory.[29]
— Bing Fa Bai Yan, *A Hundred War Maxims*

Appearing to be exceedingly strong can lower enemy morale. For example, infiltrators of a city's heavily guarded center might cause outskirts' defenders to lose confidence in their command. Or infiltrators of an installation's heavily guarded center might cause perimeter watch standers to worry about their rear.

So far, suicide bombers have succeeded at a restaurant inside the Green Zone and a mess tent inside a U.S. base. Both were put back into service, but not before the U.S. style of defense was impugned. As the insurgency drags on, radical fundamentalists will slowly infest all governmental agencies. At first (like the Iranian Hashishins), some may go to great lengths to obscure their backgrounds and beliefs.

[T]hings can be transformed and moved, and people can appear and vanish: We can therefore fool the enemy and deprive it of judgment.[30]
— *A Scholar's Dilettante Remarks on War*

There are many man-made devices with which to perplex an enemy—everything from prefabricated dummies to camouflaged suits. The Iraqi insurgent's favorite is the disguised vehicle.

So far, suicide bombers have approached Coalition targets in police cars, ambulances, and fire trucks. One hates to think of all the variants possible in normal urban activity.

Victory in war can be achieved by [one's] ingenuity. One who is conversant with a minor skill can launch great causes, and one who is versed in a minor art can attain great achievements. No skill is too lowly and no art too humble.[31]
— *A Scholar's Dilettante Remarks on War*

Then, there are the many types of disinformation. The most

effective are strikingly unique. Acting out—for everyone to see—a mistake that occurs rarely in one's own army could cause an opponent to underestimate his opponent's level of discipline.

The use of cognizant (Hezbollah) and unaware (al-Qaeda) suicide bombers might lead Western soldiers to believe that their enemy counterparts were drugged or insane. Leaving volunteer martyrs behind as a blocking force might cause U.S. soldiers to underestimate their foe's offensive capabilities.

People are accustomed to what they often see and are startled by what they rarely see.[32]
— Bing Lei, *Essentials of War*

Secretly Occupy an Enemy-Controlled Area

In battle, it's relatively easy to undermine and subvert a stronger adversary's power. The idea is to reverse the role of provider and recipient of an enemy-controlled variable. Originally, this principle recommended, "Reverse the positions of host and guest."

By repeatedly attacking the Green Zone, the enemy has undermined U.S. claims to winning the war. A short-lived American embassy attack diminished popular support for another war 40 years ago.

Before a battle, one can reverse the position of host and guest, and exploit a weak spot of the enemy to attack.[33]

One can sometimes reverse the role of occupant and occupier in an enemy-controlled area (e.g., to secretly take up residence in an enemy camp). In previous U.S. wars, enemy observers would hide within a defensive perimeter as it was built or sneak in afterwards.

To penetrate a Coalition facility in Iraq or Afghanistan, the Muslim militant has only to enlist as, or dress up like, a soldier or policeman. With subtle warnings and big money, he then can influence others.

Defeat the enemy from within by infiltrating the enemy's camp under the guise of cooperation. . . . In this way you can discover his weakness and then when the enemy's guard is relaxed, strike directly at the source of his strength.[34]

There are many ways that the host can usurp other aspects of the guest's environment and vice versa.

In Iraq, the insurgent can steal (or find lying about) much of what he needs to participate in a low intensity conflict. The United States, on the other hand, has had trouble winning the hearts and minds of the people with its "high-intensity" way of operating.

In Chinese military terminology, guest refers to the party that launches an attack into the territory of its enemy, and host is the party that takes up the defensive in his own territory. Though the guest holds the initiative of the attacker, he also has many problems. He has to transport provisions long distances, fight on unfamiliar ground, deal with a hostile populace, and lay siege to well-fortified cities. A skilled attacker can minimize these difficulties by raiding the enemy's base camp for supplies, befriending the local populace to recruit guides and agents, and feign weakness to lure the enemy out of his strongholds. In these ways, the guest can obtain the advantageous position of the host for himself.[35]

Then there is the psychological application of this principle— sneaking into an enemy's psyche to cause him to believe that some ideas are his own. To succeed, the mental intrusion must be progressive.

By doing so well in Iraq's election, the Shiite fundamentalists have legally entered into that country's decision-making process. They can now expect greater freedom to pursue their revolutionary vision.

Whenever there is a chance, enter into the decision-making body of your ally and extend your influence skillfully step by step.[36]

It is no accident that Asian small-unit tactical techniques initially mimic their opposite. Attack looks like defense and vice versa. By allowing an adversary to go first, the Asian gains the advantage.

Though having entered the new government, the Shiite fundamentalist does little to establish its credibility. By biding his time, he builds two things: (1) resentment against the occupier, and (2) popular support for himself.

The strategists have a saying: I dare not play the host, but play the guest; I dare not advance an inch, but retreat a foot instead. This is known as marching forward when there is no road, rolling up one's sleeve when there is no arm, dragging one's adversary by force when there is no adversary, and taking up arms when there are no arms.[37]
— Lao Zi

12 Stratagems for Desperate Times

- *How has the foe lulled U.S. forces into relative inactivity?*
- *How does refusing to fight help him to win?*

MUNDANE ACTIVITIES TO LULL THE OCCUPIER

(Source: *DA Pam 550-175* (September, 1988), p. 97)

When Desperate in War

When close to being beaten in combat, one might do one or more of the following: (1) lull the enemy to sleep with something beautiful, (2) reveal a personal weakness to cause the enemy to suspect a trap, (3) attack the enemy's cohesion from within, (4) feign injury to oneself, (5) combine stratagems, or (6) refuse altogether to fight.

When directly confronted by a full-fledged U.S. assault (one in which any hint of resistance gets heavily bombarded), one would almost certainly feel desperation.

Lull the Enemy to Sleep with Something Beautiful

A beautiful woman evokes feelings so powerful that all else is forgotten. Associated emotions—vanity, lust, jealousy, envy, and hatred—(from whatever source) can be equally disconcerting. Precisely, the axiom translates, "The beauty trap."

Most at risk from this ploy is the enemy commander. His emotions greatly influence his unit's chances.

U.S. military leaders have been traditionally expected to win every battle or engagement tactically. That this expectation is unrealistic makes them more susceptible to this ploy. Unless they experience an avowed foe's blatant aggression, they assume that he has lost his interest in fighting.

When faced with a formidable enemy [force], try to subdue their [its] leader. When dealing with an able and resourceful commander, exploit his indulgence of sensual pleasures in order to weaken his fighting spirit. When the commander becomes inept, his soldiers will be demoralized, and their combat power will be greatly reduced.[1]

The "beautiful woman" can be any pleasurable emotion. Leading an opposition commander to believe that he has won, when he really hasn't, might so greatly relieve him as to qualify. Easiest to sidetrack are those who have been led to believe that they must win every battle—an expectation so unrealistic as to encourage misrepresentations of the truth. By secretly withdrawing during the final stages of a defensive stand, the Easterner could tempt an attrition-oriented Western attacker to overestimate his kills. Any assault commander who so reacted would begin to lose touch with reality. Then, with winning assured, he might place less importance on the unique circumstances of the next engagement. As the door to fabrication got wider and wider, his tactical decisions would become increasingly less viable. Soon, he would have trouble distinguishing aspiration from truth.

High-level U.S. leaders seem greatly relieved that free elections have finally been held in Iraq. They apparently be-

lieve that democratic elections (however loosely monitored) will automatically defuse any insurgency. South Vietnam had free elections right before it fell.

When the general becomes inept and the soldiers listless, their fighting ability will decline.[2]

Of course, the enemy's rank and file can also be manipulated. Might artificially enhancing their pride give them less reason to improve? "As dripping water wears through rock, so the weak and yielding can subdue the firm and strong."[3] By waiting for the right time to fight, the Asian soldier unduly flatters his Western opponent.

Most U.S. fighters in Iraq have come to believe that killing more of the enemy (than he of them) is tantamount to winning tactically. That might be partially true if not for the following: (1) the differential in medical evacuation; (2) the supporting-arms hits are normally a guess; and (3) the small-arms hits are often the total of what each GI has seen (multiple countings). In WWII, Zhukov's East-Soviet riflemen often pretended to be shot while "firing and moving" so as not to be shot instantly when they popped back up. As American's in Iraq become more familiar with 4GW and Far-Eastern tactics, they more easily evaluate their degree of success. When an opponent abandons his rear party, they won't think him demoralized. That would only be a reasonable assumption if he did not have an unlimited supply of suicide volunteers and did not routinely practice retrograde defense. He has merely eroded their determination by appearing to give up.

Increase the enemy's excesses; seize what he loves. Then we, acting from without, can cause a response from within.[4]
— Si Ma Fa, *Seven Military Classics*

Reveal a Weakness to Cause the Enemy to Suspect a Trap

In times of crisis, unusual behavior evokes suspicion. Placing the slightest doubt in an enemy's mind creates opportunity. If the

219

gates to a lightly defended city (or position) were left open, a stronger opponent might hesitate to enter, fearing a trap. His hesitation could create just enough self-doubt to ensure his subsequent defeat. Here, one must have steady nerves to succeed. In Chinese, the stratagem reads, "The empty-city ploy."

Evidence of weakness did not fool U.S. forces on the way to Baghdad in April 2003. At its lightly defended gates, they feared no trap and plunged right in to its center. Only later at Fallujah, did the Iraqi insurgent successfully employ this axiom. When U.S. ground troops first entered Fallujah in April 2004, they encountered some resistance but not a sophisticated defense. Still, fearing too many casualties, their leaders opted to withdraw. This gave their people time to worry and the enemy time to fortify. While they would have suffered some casualties by staying, they might have ended up with an intact city and a less-polarized Sunni population.

When the enemy is superior in numbers and your situation is such that you expect to be overrun at any moment, then drop all pretense of military preparedness and act casually. Unless the enemy has an accurate description of your situation, this unusual behavior will arouse suspicions. With luck he will be dissuaded from attacking.[5]

This parable also tells the residents of an undefended city to keep quiet. Again suspecting an ambush, the attacker hesitates.

U.S. forces were initially dissuaded from overrunning Fallujah by former regime soldiers who promised to restore order. In effect, the Baathists kept quiet about al-Zarqawi's ability to control them. Despite the relative calm, the Coalition feared a blood bath and was willing to try anything.

When weak, appear strong; when strong, appear weak.[6]
— Sun Tzu

This axiom might also be applied to a standard operating procedure—e.g., by omitting a step to slow down the response of a suspicious foe.

*By initially abandoning Samarra, Muslim militants led
U.S. forces to believe that it had been pacified and set the
stage for a religious initiative. After touting Samarra as an
example of successful pacification, U.S. forces were somewhat embarrassed when it was re-attacked in November
2005. Samarra had once been the capital of the Muslim
Empire.*[7]

Bear a weak appearance when in a weak position to create
doubts in the already doubtful enemy.[8]

Attack the Enemy's Cohesion from Within

How well a unit functions in war has largely to do with how
well it understands its own capabilities. By sowing doubt, confusion, and discord within the enemy's ranks, one can undermine
their will to fight. Verbatim, the principle says, "Turn the enemy's
agents against him," or "Sow discord in the enemy's camp."

*By massacring the unarmed graduates of a National Guard
school near the Iranian border in October 2004, the enemy
sowed the seeds of distrust between Iraqi and U.S. forces.*[9]
*Throughout the Arab media, he created the impression that
the U.S. overseers of that school had somehow been remiss.
Even Allawi got dragged into the ploy. He was quoted (or
misquoted) as saying that the Americans had not properly
protected departure information.*[10]

Reduce the effectiveness of your enemy by inflicting discord among them.[11]
— Sun Tzu

Undermine your enemy's ability to fight by secretly causing discord between him and his friends, allies, advisers,
family, commanders, soldiers, and population. When he is
preoccupied settling internal disputes, his ability to attack
or defend is compromised.[12]

Here the value of sneaking into the enemy's camp is emphasized. When all of his strategic assets, machineguns, and obstacles have been premapped, the attacker has more of a tactical opportunity.

In December 2004, a suicide bomber got into the mess tent of a U.S. Army base in Iraq. He did so by dressing up as an Iraqi army officer.[13] If he could get in, so could the reconnaissance element for a ground assault. There is nothing quite as demoralizing at 3:00 A.M. than the shout of "enemy in the perimeter."

Spying is the best of all deceptive measures against the enemy. Use the enemy's spies to work for you and you will win without any loss.[14]

This axiom can also apply to starting rumors, planting false information through double agents, or allowing enemy agents to obtain false information and return to their own lines.

Was it not Chalabi who first talked the U.S. into invading Iraq? If he was such a close ally, why did he later take refuge in Iran?

In adopting this stratagem, one must first know the enemy's likely response to leaked information. Make him think it's to his advantage to follow a certain course of action and exploit his mistake.[15]

Politics and media go hand in hand. To cover every aspect of a fast-moving story, journalists have little choice but to use partially substantiated information from apparent eyewitnesses. Within such an environment, the highly deceptive insurgent has little trouble spreading disinformation.

There is no better way to attack an enemy's cohesion from within than to enter his election. With Zarqawi's affiliation very much in doubt, it is somewhat problematic to have Talebani (a longtime Shiite ally) and al-Jaafari (original activist Shiite party leader) as president and prime minister of Iraq.

Among the ways of deceiving the enemy is plunging him into a fog. Induce the enemy's spies to work for you. . . . Pretend to be unaware of the spies' activities and deliberately leak false information to them.[16]

Feign Injury to Yourself

One who pretends to be hurt is less of a threat to his enemy. When literally deciphered, this precept advises, "Inflict injury on oneself to win the enemy's trust."

At the start of the U.S. assault on Fallujah in November 2004, one group of insurgents waved a white flag as if to surrender. As soon as U.S. forces exposed themselves, they came under heavy, well-directed machinegun fire.[17] Near the end of the battle, another group did the same thing.[18] With such a blatant violation of the Geneva Conventions, the guerrillas' handlers may have had an ulterior motive. If U.S. troops had started to give no quarter, the number of civilian casualties would have skyrocketed. Whether intentional or not, peacekeepers who hurt those they are trying to help, suffer a moral setback.

People rarely inflict injuries on themselves, so when they get injured, it is usually genuine. Exploit this naivete.[19]

There are any number of ways to succeed after the enemy lets his guard down. They are only limited by one's degree of imagination.

At first, Iraqi insurgents approached their targets by ambulance. Then, they used ambulances as car bombs. Eventually, the Coalition got blamed every time an ambulance took too long getting to the hospital.

Espionage can be conducted when the enemy takes a false injury to be genuine.[20]

Nonphysical injuries can also be faked. A command-detonated

explosive might look to a TOW gunner like a secondary explosion and thus cause a pilot's wing man to drop his payload in the wrong location.

> *On 19 April 2005, this axiom was cleverly applied by a Shiite member of the newly elected Iraqi parliament. He tearfully claimed before the assemblage that he had been roughed up by U.S. soldiers at a checkpoint. He then tried to convince his fellow legislators that they too had been dishonored.[21] Had he not been linked to radical cleric al-Sadr, his antics might not have qualified as a trick. While "saving face" is every bit as important in Iraq as it is further east,[22] al-Sadr is well known for his anti-American sentiment and predisposition toward lying.*

The stratagem involves an element of self-sacrifice. The enemy is fooled into drawing a conclusion which is the opposite of the truth.[23]

Combine Stratagems

In war, victory belongs to the commander who can launch simultaneous attacks from left and right, outside and inside, above and below. That commander can choose which attack to follow through on, while his opponent may reinforce the wrong front. Here, the literal interpretation recommends, "Interlocking stratagems."

> *If the militant Muslim were fully adept at all of the "36 Stratagems," he could easily combine them. He has already displayed an amazing ability to combine techniques. For example, he now uses the suicide car in conjunction with ground assault and kidnapping in conjunction with suicide bomber recruiting.*

When the enemy possesses a superior force, do not attack recklessly. Instead, weaken him by devising plots to bring him into a difficult position of his own doing.[24]

Embedded in this stratagem is the idea of continually alternating supporting and main attacks, or intended feints and actual maneuvers. How easily victory is achieved will depend on how the defender reacts to the various initiatives.

By appearing tactically inept while embracing chaos, the Muslim militant melts into the background of malcontents. Now swimming freely in a school of looters, feuders, and vigilantes, he has less to fear from the shark. That shark— the occupier—will sometimes mistake bystander for combatant. If he does so often enough, sympathizers can so expand the militant's protective school as to make him virtually immune from attack.

Appearance and intention inevitably ensnare people when artfully used, even if people sense that there is an ulterior intention behind the overt appearance. When you set up ploys and opponents fall for them, then you win by letting them act on your ruse. As for those who do not fall for a ploy, when you see they won't fall for the open trap, you have another set. Then even if opponents haven't fallen for your original ploy, in effect they actually have.[25]

— Yagyu Munenori, *Family Book on the Art of War*

Do not repeat tactics which gained you victory in the past, but let your tactics be molded by the infinite variety of circumstances.[26]

— Sun Tzu

A more literal translation of this axiom is also possible. For example, switching one's focus of main effort might cause his opponent to shift his formation too often and thus tangle his forces.

The Muslim militant's tendency to attack a quarry from every side might cause that quarry's reaction forces to get tangled up with each other. If the type of attack further varied, that quarry might become very confused.

Do not engage an enemy that has many generals and numerous soldiers. Weaken its position by making its troops interlaced [entangled].[27]

225

An entanglement could occur in many ways. If two U.S. battalions were participating in a cordon operation and not completely sure of each other's location, they could be easily induced to shoot at one another. Firing at both, from defiladed ground in between, would almost certainly get the job done.

During the U.S. assault on Samarra in October 2004, a guerrilla force got between two U.S. companies before ambushing one from the rear. This effectively triggered a friendly firefight.[28] *Thus, the guerrillas had combined three stratagems: (1) secretly occupying an enemy-controlled area, (2) misleading the enemy with false information, and (3) using the enemy against himself. If the major "36 Stratagem" groupings were considered, he has combined what he would do if he wanted more territory and had the upper hand.*

If the enemy has superior strength, don't be foolhardy and engage them in battle. Instead, think of a way to entangle them for this will weaken them.[29]

Then more than one simultaneous deception might create additional confusion. Upon seeing through the first, the enemy would not suspect a second.

In the 13 November 2003 bombing of the Italian contingent barracks in Nasiriyah, the offending (explosive-laden) truck was accompanied by a "base-of-fire" vehicle and preceded by a decoy car that was going the opposite direction.[30] *That's a lot of deception all at once.*

A victory often results from a circumspect battle plan consisting of several interrelated ruses. . . . The first aim is to reduce the enemy's maneuverability, and the second to annihilate its effective strength. . . .
. . . Confronted with the enemy in the morning, one challenges it to battle and soon feigns defeat. After retreating for some distances, he stops and turns to challenge the enemy again, then feigns defeat and retreats. Eagerly seeking for a decision, the enemy follows in hot pursuit, with no time to take a rest. On the other hand, one has planned

the repeated retreats beforehand and is therefore able to use the intervals to rest and feed the troops. At nightfall, the enemy has become tired and hungry. Feigning defeat for the last time, one scatters cooked beans on the ground. When the enemy . . . arrives, [they] stop to feed. A great victory can be achieved if one fights back at this moment.[31]

Any ruse can be further exaggerated by combining it with tactics or obstacles. In the world of close combat, all are interchangeable.

In Iraq, decoy cars have almost certainly been combined with otherwise blocked roadways. In any way controlling the traffic would certainly magnify the decoy's effectiveness.

In important matters one should use several strategies applied simultaneously. Keep different plans operating in an overall scheme. In this manner, if any one strategy fails, you will still have several others to fall back on. Combining even weak strategies in unison has a greater effectiveness than applying them sequentially.[32]

Refuse to Fight

Only false pride could cause a commander to fight a battle with no strategic consequence. In the art of war, an often overlooked but highly useful talent is knowing when to run. Word for word, the axiom reads, "When retreat is the best option."

By finally refusing to fight for Najaf, al-Sadr gave his Mahdi Army new life. On 25 August 2004, Grand Ayatollah al-Sistani brokered a deal and brought in the pilgrims.[33] His "deal" had all the earmarks of a delaying and replacement operation. Now, that same Mahdi Army has all but taken over Basra.[34]

If it becomes obvious that your current course of action will lead to defeat, then retreat and regroup. When your side is losing, there are only three choices remaining: surrender, compromise, or escape. Surrender is complete defeat, compromise is half defeat, but escape is no defeat. As long as you are not defeated, you still have a chance.[35]

Under constant attack by Chiang Kai-shek's well-supplied army, Mao Tse-tung's forces retreated more than 6,000 miles across China from October 1934 to October 1935. In January 1949, they defeated the Chinese Nationalist army.[36] Refusing to fight and tactically withdrawing have been successfully employed against U.S. forces at Iwo Jima, the Chosin Reservoir, and throughout the Vietnam War. It is a tactic wholly consistent with maneuver warfare doctrine.

By curtailing all but the most obscure of Shiite insurgent activity, al-Sadr was able to reestablish the impression that the insurgency was strictly Sunni. This impression paid big dividends in the election.

If greatly outnumbered, then retreat. While it is possible for a small force to put up a great fight, in the end it will lose to superior numbers.[37]
— Sun Tzu

The Ultimate Deception

Just as the North Vietnamese Army (NVA) and Viet Cong did 30 years ago, the Iraqi insurgent has created the illusion that the U.S. is winning the war. He has lost more people, run from more firefights, and resorted to more dispersion. In fact, most of his tiny units now have no visible means of support, coordination, or control. The previously repressed majority has won the election. The number of well-dressed and well-equipped security forces is starting to grow. Yet, the country is in shambles. The restoration of basic services had to be put on hold. The unemployment rate is high. The new prime minister is pro-Iranian, and the new constitution will almost certainly obey fundamentalist Islamic law. The Shiite militias are the strongest in the country. In short, Iraq is well on the way to becoming another Lebanon—a nation that is only free in appearance.

Until U.S. military leaders admit to themselves that they have won only from the standpoint of outgunning their opposition, they will have little chance of creating a viable democracy. Like Vietnam, this is a war in which no amount of ordnance will make up for a deficit in tactical proficiency. Only highly skilled light infantrymen can project minimal force. The U.S. has had none since the days of Carlson's Raiders and Merrill's Marauders.

Part Three

Combating the Deception

"I will be damned if I will permit the . . . [U.S. military]—
its institutions, its doctrine, and its traditions—
to be destroyed just to win this lousy war."
— anonymous American general, 1970

(Source: *The Unchangeable War*, RM-6278-ARPA, by Brian M. Jenkins [Santa Monica, CA: RAND, 1970], p. 3)

Ways to Turn the Tide in Iraq

- *Who has been recruiting and training the foe's fighters?*
- *Which nation has helped both Sunni and Shiite to resist?*

IT'S ALL ABOUT THE NEIGHBORHOODS

(Source: Courtesy of Sorman Info. & Media, illustration by Wolfgang Bartsch, from *SoldF: Soldaten i fält,* © 2001 Forsvarsmakten, Stockholm, p. 287)

Unmasking the True Culprit in Iraq

To discover the true culprit in Iraq, one must look beyond the battlefield and into other 4GW arenas—particularly that of politics/media. In this part of the world, political process and open warfare are not opposites, but supplements. To find the hidden competitor for Iraq's future, one must look for the proven saboteur of a similar country's past. A close match is Lebanon. Over a third of its population is Shiite. From 1982 to 2000, it was occupied by a Westernized army. Since then, it has allowed a fundamentalist Shiite militia to control whole regions and amass political clout.

Iraqi Politics

Since the Second Sadr Rebellion of August 2004, U.S. officials have—for whatever reason—missed few opportunities to allege the strictly-Sunni nature of the insurgency in Iraq. While the fundamentalist Shiites may have temporarily stopped shooting, they appear to be still advancing on several of the other 4GW fronts. The most important of those fronts is political. They imported between one and four million Iranians to participate in the election.[1] Before the returns were even announced, UIA spokesmen were demanding their choice of prime ministers, an Islamic constitution, and the removal of U.S. troops.[2] Luckily, their party only won 48% of the popular vote, with the Kurds getting 26%, and Allawi's people 14%.[3] That was enough to acquire 140 out of the 275 parliament seats.[4] Still, to achieve their goals, the pro-Iranian UIA would have to cooperate with the Kurds. Once allied against Saddam Hussein, the Iranians and Kurds had since drifted apart. Yet, to acquire the post of president, the Kurds would agree to a UIA candidate for prime minister. At the top of the UIA list were Ibrahim Jaafari, Adel Abdel Medhi. Ahmed Chalabi, and Hussein al-Shahrastani.[5] With al-Sistani's blessing, Jaafari finally got the nod. Officially a physician, Jaafari was also a *mujtahid* or person who can make religious rulings. As late as October 2004, he had been in Iran conferring with its top clerics.[6]

Because most of the pre-election unrest occurred in Sunni areas, U.S. officials were quick to conclude that it was the work of Baathists or *al-Qaeda*. Because the Mongols controlled this region for over 200 years, its residents are predisposed toward battlefield deception. They are expert at doing what Western forces will not: (1) getting others to do their fighting, (2) playing a future adversary off against a current occupier, and (3) shifting the blame for indiscretions. Throughout Palestine and Iraq, most of the evidence trails lead eventually to Iran. Its ultimate intentions are not difficult to distinguish from its overall rhetoric. When confronted on the development of nuclear arms, Iran warned, "Any attempt to haul it before the Security Council for possible sanctions would lead to more instability in the Middle East."[7] Like China, Iran has a "revolutionary" government;[8] it views revolution as an integral part of the region's growth process. In Iraq and Palestine, Iran may draw little distinction between revolution and insurrection. Ayatollah Khomeini considered the *Pasdaran (Sepah)* to be "guardians of the Revolution." [9] Thus, the Iranian Revolutionary Guards may view Lebanese *Hezbollah* and al-Sadr's Mahdi Army as fellow guardians of a regional uprising. In Palestine, Shiite *Hezbollah* uses Sunni *Hamas* and Sunni *PIJ* as proxies to fight the Israelis. Why then in Iraq, could not Shiite *Sepah* use Sunni factions as proxies to fight the Americans?

Prophetic Events from Lebanon

On 14 February 2005, Lebanese President Lahoud's longtime rival—Rafik Hariri—was killed by a command-detonated bomb beneath a Beirut street. Because Hariri had been calling for the removal of occupation forces,[10] Syria became a prime suspect. But in the Middle East, one must look beyond what is too obvious. Hariri had also been opposing *Hezbollah* candidates, and Syria had been limiting *Hezbollah's* participation in the Lebanese parliament.[11] So one wonders, "Who stood the most to gain from harming both?" *Hezbollah* will remove a key official just as a reminder to the rest. While Lebanon's pro-Syrian prime minister Karami and his cabinet resigned, its president did not.[12] The assassination had forced an unscheduled reelection for the 128 parliament seats,[13] of which *Hezbollah* had previously held only 12.[14]

Soon, the plot thickened. On 7 March, 70,000 people filled Beirut's streets to demand a full Syrian withdrawal.[15] When the U.S. repeated the request, *Hezbollah* Chieftain Nasrallah organized a counterprotest to thank the Syrians for their presence.[16] Within the size and rhetoric of this counterprotest lay irrefutable evidence of Lebanon's true master. *Hezbollah* is its best-armed and best-organized faction.[17] Before the rally, Nasrallah defiantly told reporters that *Hezbollah's* fighters would never give up their arms.[18] According to a senior U.N. peacekeeper, nobody in the region had the strength to take them away.[19] Nasrallah's warning to America far exceeded that of a political adversary. What part of his ongoing military activity involves Americans?

Lebanon's state news agency estimated 1.5 million participants in Tuesday's [Nasrallah's] rally, but that seems high for a nation of 3.7 million. An Associated Press estimate put the crowd's size at 400,000 to 500,000. . . .

"Lebanon is not Ukraine," Nasrallah said [to the crowd], referring to the [that] country's "orange revolution" last year. If anyone thinks you can bring down a state with a few demonstrations, a few scarves, a few shouts, a few media, . . . he is wrong."
Nasrallah also warned Washington against any military action to achieve its goals.
"The fleets came in the past and were defeated. They will be defeated again," he said to supporters.[20]
— Associated Press, 9 March 2005

On 12 March 2005, there was another huge *Hezbollah* rally.[21] Two days later just as many anti-Syrian protesters showed up.[22] They accomplished little more than a cry for help. Present at all the demonstrations had been the Lebanese Army. Absent from all had been any objection to *Hezbollah*. A high-level Army officer explained that *Hezbollah* was the "resistance" to Israeli incursion and thus vital to Lebanon's security.[23] If Iran has a revolutionary government, it is only natural for its satellite state to require continual resistance.

With the Hariri bombing, *Hezbollah* may have been just trying to improve its political fortunes. When that bombing threatened to produce a full Syrian pullout, *Hezbollah* got worried. U.N. Resolution 1559 of September 2004 had called for the withdrawal of Syrian occupiers and the "disbanding and disarmament of all Lebanese and non-Lebanese militias." And Syrian military intelligence had been helping to run Lebanon's military, economy, and politics since 1991.[24] To pursue a covert war with Israel, *Hezbollah* depended on Damascus-sanctioned political cover.[25] It also depended on the Syrian "pipeline" of Iranian equipment and funding for its military units and social-service agencies.[26]

To no one's surprise, the ousted prime minister was reinstated on 10 March 2005. However, most of his cabinet ministers refused to return.[27] Thus, a parliamentary reelection was still needed in May.[28] Some saw the events as *Hezbollah's* way of rebutting both provisions to U.N. Resolution 1559.[29] Others saw them as *Hezbollah's* way of taking over the Lebanese political process. On 12 March, Associated Press said that "Hezbollah was planning to take a new role in Lebanese politics."[30] There is little doubt of *Hezbollah's* ultimate goal. In Lebanon, *Hezbollah* operates three hospitals, 17 medical clinics, and a commercial network that includes supermarkets, gas stations, department stores, and construction companies.[31] It also runs a huge social-welfare network that is largely funded by Iran.[32] In Iran, its parent—*Sepah*—has banks and amusement parks.[33]

On 3 April 2005, there was the fourth in a series of bombings of Marionite Christian areas.[34] They caused few casualties and were probably just intended to prevent any more protests.[35] Then, evidence surfaced that Hariri had been killed by a truck bomb. Right after the explosion, authorities buried what was left of a pickup truck in the crater.[36]

Then, Omar Karami again resigned as prime minister and pro-Syrian Najib Mikati tried to cobble together a cabinet. Finally, in mid-June, Lebanon held its parliamentary elections. While *Hezbollah* won a landslide victory in the south and gained seats in the central and eastern portions of the country, the anti-Syrian elements still managed a slim majority. Now, Saad Hariri (son of Rafik) is the most likely choice for prime minister. On 8 June, he wanted to bring Hezbollah into a ruling coalition.[37]

U.S. Urges *Hezbollah* to Join Lebanon's Political Mainstream

On 15 March 2005, the U.S. president "urged Hezbollah to disarm and to stay out of Israeli-Palestinian disputes, suggesting the militant group could . . . win U.S. backing for a role in Lebanon's political mainstream."[38] An identical offer was made to *Hezbollah's* representative in Iraq—Muqtada al-Sadr—in August 2004.[39]

While the policy appeared to support the democratic process, it also ignored 4GW theory. In a 4th-generation war, the foe can be beaten tactically and still win politically. Would al-Sadr be more dangerous as an insurgent or cabinet member? Until his Mahdi Army is disbanded, he should not be allowed any leadership role.

People worry that the U.S. may have made some sort of nonaggression pact with *Hezbollah* during the 1980's hostage negotiations. If so, it may still be clinging to that outdated accord. It may have promised not to attack *Hezbollah,* if *Hezbollah* does not attack Israel. Unfortunately, *Hezbollah* has been attacking Israel, just in obscure ways. Even the U.S. State Department admits that a major plank in *Hezbollah's* political platform is to fight all "western imperialism."[40]

237

Statistical Evidence of the Original Source of Iraqi Chaos

That much of the violence has occurred in the Sunni Triangle could mean that it is by Sunni design. Or it could mean, that its architect wanted its own streets safe and the Sunnis vanquished. From the Israel advocacy organization comes some very interesting lists. One shows all major suicide bombings between January 2000 and December 2004 worldwide, and the other just those in Iraq.[41]

While periodically used by almost every terrorist organization on earth, suicide bombing was first embraced as an instrument of war by the Iranian *Sepah* and Lebanese *Hezbollah*. Contrary to popular opinion, it was not used in Afghanistan until 9 September 2001—long after the end of the Soviet-Afghan War.[42] On that date (two days before 9/11), Northern Alliance leader Massoud was killed by suicide-vest bombers posing as journalists. Iran had long supported the Northern Alliance, but the legendary Massoud was nobody's "man." On 27 January 2004, a man with artillery and mortar rounds strapped to his chest blew himself up next to a NATO convoy in Kabul. According to Associated Press, this was "a tactic previously unknown to Afghanistan."[43]

Similarly, suicide bombing was not employed in Chechnya until 27 December 2002—long after the first and second Russian invasions of that country. That was when Riyad al-Salheyn Martyr's Brigade took the credit for a father and daughter ramming their bomb-laden truck into a government building.[44]

According to the Israeli list, there were 39 major suicide bombings in Iraq between 26 February 2003 and 21 December 2004. All but one occurred in a non-Shiite area or was claimed by al-Zarqawi, *Ansar al-Sunna,* or *al-Qaeda.* They occurred in Baghdad, Kirkuk, Fallujah, Ramadi, Beiji, Baqubah, Tikrit, Irbil, Iskandariyah, Zamaqi, Hillah, Khalis, Mosul, and just off the southern coast. Though Khalis and Baqubah have some Badr Corps present, neither is traditionally Shiite.[45] The only real exception involved police installations in Basra on 21 April 2004. However, according to another source, this attack did not involve suicide. In and around Basra on 21 April 2004, car bombs were simultaneously exploded outside three police stations and two police academies.[46]

The Israeli list, by its own admission, may be missing a few entries. For example, on 13 December 2003, a suicide car bomb (driven by a Palestinian from Lebanon) is known to have blown up at the Khaldiyeh police station killing 23 of its occupants.[47] Still, the study appears fairly reliable. During the first year of Iraqi occupation, another source says there were only 24 suicide bombings, of which six were by suicide vest.[48] There was also at least one additional suicide bombing in the Shiite south during this period. On 13 November 2003, a suicide truck-bomber attacked the Italian barracks in Nasiriyah killing 28 people.[49] Vehicle-mounted IEDs have been detonated in the Shiite holy cities as well. Still unclear is whose truck bomb killed SCIRI leader Mohammed Baqir al-Hakim. He had threatened to cut ties with Tehran after junior cleric Muqtada al-Sadr was feted during his visit to Iran in June 2003.[50] On 27 December 2003, the Karbala City Hall was car-bombed.[51] Al-Sadr is also suspected of killing the moderate Shiite leader Abdel Majid al-Khoei in April of 2003.[52]

Still, the implications are startling. For almost two years, there were no major suicide bombings against Iraqi targets in Shiite areas. That casts suspicion for the northern trouble onto the Shiites themselves—they who pioneered suicide bombing. Al-Sadr did, after all, threaten in 2004 to use suicide vest bombers.[53] And his Mahdi Army fighters did brag about recruiting 3,000 suicide bombers during the Najaf standoff.[54] During the invasion, American forces discovered hundreds of pre-assembled suicide-bomber vests and belts. Their interim location was linked to the M-14 Branch of the former Iraqi Intelligence Service,[55] but their points of manufacture and final delivery were never fully determined.

Only After the Election Was the Trend Momentarily Broken

It was a nonsuicide car bomb (intended for a dissident cleric) that killed so many people in Najaf in 2004. But, it was suicide cars that exploded during Shia's most holy "Ashoura" festival (commemorating the death of Imam Hussein) in 2005.[56] And it was a suicide car that killed 115 people in Hillah on 28 February 2005.[57] While the target was prospective security force recruits, the city was predominantly Shiite. A few days later al-Zarqawi took the credit, and Hillah demonstrators blamed the Baathists and Wahhabis.[58] That does not necessarily mean that the Sunnis did it, only that the previous trend had been momentarily broken.

On the same day of the 28 February blast, the *Philadelphia Inquirer* reported a possible explanation for the apparent shift in instigation. *Sepah* will only tolerate free-lance activity until it is time to consolidate.[59] The blast may have been directed at a breakaway faction or served as a warning to Shiite collaborators.

Since the Jan. 30 election, Shiite militants have begun a systematic program of assassination, targeting Saddam's former security and intelligence personnel. Shiite politicians are looking the other way, recognizing that while civil war is not in their interest, quietly eliminating their enemies is.[60]

— *St. Louis Post Dispatch,* 1 March 2005

On 10 March, what was thought to be another suicide bomb killed 47 people at a Shiite funeral in Mosul. It was directed at those working with U.S.-led forces.[61]

Iran's Longtime Effort to Unite the Muslim World

In the early 1990's, before the emergence of the Taliban in Afghanistan, there were some very interesting conferences going on in Sudan.

As of the summer of 1989, . . . the international network of the HizbAllah, under tight Iranian and Syrian control, actively prepared for an escalatory surge of operations against the West, and specifically against America and Americans. . . .

In early 1992, there was a major leap forward in the Islamics' preparations for a terrorist campaign. The Armed Islamic Movement, popularly known as "the International Legion of Islam," was consolidated from among the ranks of the Muslim Brotherhood worldwide with their world center in Khartoum, Sudan. The leading terrorists are known as 'Afghans,' having been trained with the mujahideen in Pakistan, and, for some, having also fought in Afghanistan.

A joint elite force of the Islamic internal terrorism was established by Iran last summer [presumably 1992] from among the very best terrorists and networks of both the HizbAllah and the Armed Islamic Movement [AIM] . . . .

... [T]he HizbAllah operational center in Lebanon, and the AIM operational centers in Sudan, Pakistan, and Afghanistan, are being reinforced by supplies and expert terrorists arriving from Iran, Syria and many other Islamic countries. An instrument of state policy, the HizbAllah-AIM terrorist system and its networks now await orders from Tehran. . . .

. . . The establishment of AIM [under Shaykh Hassan al-Turabi] essentially facilitated the institutionalization of the Sunni Islamic international terrorism and their complete integration into the Iran-dominated international terrorist system. These developments took place in the aftermath of the milestone visit by Hashemi-Rafsanjani and a large Iranian delegation to Khartoum in December 1991 and the comprehensive strategic agreements concluded between Iran and Sudan, agreements that in effect transformed Sudan into an Iranian fiefdom. . . .

. . . A major breakthrough took place in July 1992 when al-Zawahiri [the cofounder of *al-Qaeda*] arrived in Tehran after mediation by Turabi. Tehran agreed to assist with advanced training in Iran and Sudan, financing and providing weapons for the plans to escalate the Jihad against Cairo. The only condition Tehran put was for the Islamic Jihad [which later merged with *al-Qaeda*] to join the Arab Liberation Battalions of the IRGC Intelligence. In the late-summer, at Tehran's invitation, al-Istambuli [the brother of Sadat's assassin and an associate of al-Zawahiri] travelled to the Biqaa to inspect the HizbAllah facilities and discuss their assistance in training Egyptian 1 [One], already in Sudan. Thus, by the fall of 1992, the main Egyptian Islamic groups were being integrated into the Iranian-HizbAllah terrorist system. It is therefore not by accident that the Egyptian Islamic Jihad began issuing communiques from Tehran in December 1992.[62]
— Study based on Israeli research project

Al-Turabi, purported founder of AIM, was the leader of the Sudanese branch of the Muslim Brotherhood. He was also the spiritual director of the National Islamic Front (NIF) political party that took over Sudan in 1989 and then invited Osama bin Laden to live there. While himself Sunni, Turabi additionally allowed several thousand Shiite Iranian Revolutionary Guard and Lebanese *Hezbollah* personnel to run training camps in Sudan.[63] There is no further reference to AIM in the literature, but *al-Qaeda's* cofounder (al-Zawahiri) was from the Muslim Brotherhood,[64] and his movement did absorb several North African terror groups—most notably, Egypt's *Islamic Jihad* and *al-Gama'a al-Islamiyyama.*[65] That would make AIM a possible alias for the Islamic National Front (INF)—a coalition of militant sects that met in Sudan in the early 1990's. Thus, the core elements of *al-Qaeda* may have moved there to operate under Turabi's umbrella. That's what one author infers.[66]

From this and the previous book's research,[67] one can still conclude that Iran is behind most of the trouble in Iraq. Its designs on Iraq far exceed any that the Muslim Brotherhood might have. It is *Sepah* that provides the local population with alternative infrastructure. Thus, it is Iran that is best at 4GW. Iran's attempt to coordinate international terrorism has been well documented.

> Hizbullah, in conjunction with Iran, made great efforts to forge links with Sunni terrorist groups. Al-Qaeda and its affiliates made use of these opportunities and forged a strategic partnership. The relationship began [in the mid-1990's] in Sudan. . . . Al-Turabi facilitated meetings between Osama bin Laden, Iranian intelligence, and Hizbullah leaders. . . . Hizbullah training videos were used to train al-Qaeda operatives.[68]

Iran's Degree of Complicity in Iraq

Iran and its erstwhile Lebanese offspring—*Hezbollah*—were behind the two al-Sadr rebellions.[69] To give al-Sadr time to reorganize his militia, they shifted to the political arena in the fall of 2004. As in Palestine, they wanted to keep their opposition guessing.

> Matthew Levitt, of the Washington Institute for Near East Policy, says . . . "Hezbollah, Hamas, Islamic Jihad, al-Aksa Martyrs and others all at Iran's behest, are currently attempting to torpedo the nascent peace process."

Most notable, in Mr. Levitt's view, is Iran's support for

the radical terrorist group Hezbollah, and its targeting of Israel as well as Americans. He adds there is substantial evidence Iran is also behind terrorism in Iraq. "Iranian and Hezbollah elements are very active today in Iraq," he stated.[70]
— U.S. Congressional Testimony, February 2005

Like East Asian entities, Iran and *Hezbollah* are not the least bit hesitant to divert the blame for some covert attacks and use proxies for others. Since al-Sadr's ceasefire, their covert forces and Sunni proxies have been active. It is no secret that Iran has been behind much of the trouble in the Sunni Triangle.

The Sunni Triangle Shiite force . . . was secretly trained and prepared over the past year by thousands of Iranian Republican [Revolutionary] Guard infiltrators in conjunction with the Iranian protege, Lebanese Hezbollah terrormaster Imad Mughniyeh. This force numbers an estimated 5,000 combatants, who are better equipped, organized and trained than [al-Sadr's] Mahdi Army militiamen.[71]
— Israeli intelligence bulletin, 7 April 2004

As the number of IED attacks dramatically increased in the summer of 2005, it was disclosed where they were coming from.[72] Within a two-week period, shipments had been seized at both ends of the Iranian border. The southern seizure came near Maysan in the British sector.[73]

Many of the new, more sophisticated roadside bombs used to attack American and government forces have been designed in Iran and shipped in from there, United States military and intelligence officials said Friday. . . .
. . . [S]ome of these devices have been seized, including one large shipment . . . in northeast Iraq coming from Iran.[74]
— *New York Times,* 6 August 2005

With the IED link to Iran came another part of the puzzle. It seems that the same group killing U.S. armor has death squads (like the one that assassinated Steven Vincent in Basra). Still missing is the advisory and support network behind Iran's Sunni proxies.

243

The U.S. military's new nemesis in Iraq is named Abu Mustafa al-Sheibani, and he is not a Baathist or member of al-Qaeda. He is working for Iran. According to a U.S. military intelligence document obtained by TIME, al-Sheibani heads a network of insurgents created by the Iranian Revolutionary Guard Corps with the express purpose of committing violence against U.S. and coalition forces in Iraq. Over the past eight months, his group has introduced a new brand of roadside bomb more lethal than any . . . before; based on a design from the Iranian-backed Lebanese Hizballah. . . . According to the document, the U.S. believes al-Sheibani's team consists of 280 members, divided into 17 bomb-making teams and death squads. The U.S. believes they train in Lebanon, in Baghdad's . . . Sadr City district and "in another country" [Iran] and have detonated at least 37 bombs against U.S. forces this year in Baghdad alone. . . .

. . . [I]ranian funded militias helped organize a mob attack in . . . Majarr al-Kabir on June 24, 2003, that resulted in the execution of six British military-police officers. . . . [Implicated is] a cell of the Mujahedin for Islamic Revolution in Iraq (MIRI), a paramilitary outfit coordinated out of the Iranian Revolutionary Guard's base in Ahvaz, Iran. . . .

More sinister are signs of death squads charged with eliminating potential opponents and former Baathists. . . . In the southern cities [like Basra], Thar-Allah (Vengeance of God) is one of a number of militant groups suspect of assassinations. U.S. commanders in Baghdad and eastern provinces say similar cells operate in their sectors. The chief of the Iraqi National Intelligence, General Mohammed Abdullah al-Shahwani, has publicly accused Iranian-backed cells of hunting down and killing his officers.[75]

— *Time Magazine,* 22 August 2005

Iran's Non-Martial 4GW Strategies

The Iranians are masters at media manipulation and psychological warfare. Just as they publicly denounce *al-Qaeda* in their newspapers, so too do they deny any involvement in the Iraqi insurgency. Thus, one must expect their influence wherever they say it is absent. Their battlefield method is based on one ignored since

Korea by the West. To pursue it, their proxies need no heavy weaponry, technology, or organization. Whatever they require, they either find or steal. Unfortunately, the Iranian method is an obscene metastasis of its Maoist predecessor. While the latter harnesses chaos and subjugates the population, the Iranian version generates chaos and terrorizes the population.

While Western commanders try to manage chaos, Eastern commanders take advantage of it. They do so by decentralizing control over subordinates, thereby facilitating a quicker response to local disturbances. They also do so by exploiting popular opinion. At this, the Muslim militant is unusually adept. Resorting to psychological warfare, he plays upon the noncombatants' yearning for security. In their neighborhoods, they want some semblance of order. If they can't get it from the occupier, they look for it elsewhere. "Coalition commanders admit that, among the 125,000 policemen and soldiers trained so far [as of 2 February 2005], the rate of desertion is as high as 40 per cent." [76]

Iran knows that the U.S. Congress will only subsidize the Iraqi war for so long. American forces have been losing billions of dollars worth of equipment. The foe has repeated blown up Iraq's only money maker—its oil pipelines. Americans believe that the Cold War bankrupted Russia. Iranians believe that the Soviet-Afghan War got the job done. That's why they are going after high-dollar items—like vehicles and supplies. In a video aired by Arab TV on 29 October 2004, bin Laden boasted that al-Qaeda had spent $500,000 on 9/11, whereas the U.S. had forfeited $500 billion in its aftermath. All the while, more-than-adequate funding has been flowing easily to the Iraqi insurgency from "private" sources in Iran, Saudi Arabia, and Syria. [77]

The U.S. Must Gauge Its Response Carefully

Muslims don't take exception to Christians who like them or are neutral, only to those who invade, occupy, or otherwise oppress them. To keep from invoking the Muslims' *jihadist* duty, the U.S. must not look like the oppressor in Iraq. It may only be able to export those parts of democracy that follow a liberal interpretation of Islamic law.

The U.S. response must be transparent and virtually immune to criticism. Most active warfare must be done by Iraqi forces. To fully root out the insurgents, those forces must find and closely monitor Saddam's network of tunnels beneath the major cities. (See Figure 13.1.) Those forces must also establish a presence in each neighborhood. That would free up U.S. forces to work on the far more important infrastructure of the country. They must not only do good works, but also take credit for them in the media.

The Insurgents' Neighborhood Intimidation Plan

U.S. forces have occupied Iraq's main roads and streets, not its inner neighborhoods. It is in these neighborhoods that the 4GW battle has been fought and thus far lost. Below is a perfect example of the insurgent's method. In 2003, U.S. forces set up dozens of local councils to democratically govern Iraqi neighborhoods. Then, the councilmen began to die. In August 2004, four from Baghdad's

Figure 13.1: Attention to the Subterranean Threat

(Source: Courtesy of Sorman Info. & Media, illustration by Wolfgang Bartsch, from *SoldF: Soldaten i fält*, © 2001 Forsvarsmakten, Stockholm, p. 306)

Hay Somer neighborhood were killed. In decline ever since have been that neighborhood's basic services (like garbage collection) and its willingness to cooperate with the Coalition.[78]

> Though the murders were never fully investigated, Khalaf [a councilman's brother] and neighbors say . . . they were carried out by members of militant Shiite cleric Muqtada al-Sadr's Mahdi Army. . . . Khalaf says that in mid-September, four Mahdi gunmen were arrested as suspects in Rahim's [the councilman's] murder, but were released the next day after a pro-Sadr mob threatened to attack the local police station.[79]
>
> — *Christian Science Monitor,* 25 February 2005

In the town of Hit during October 2004, insurgents reduced the police station to rubble and beheaded a few locals that they deemed too close to U.S. forces. In February 2005, U.S. forces moved in to restore order. One month later, without the local police force being reconstituted, the Marines departed. More than a few residents indicated that the Marines should either come and stay or not come at all. They said there were no guarantees for their safely when the Americans left.[80]

The Rest of the Foe's 4GW Formula

Since the elections of January 2005, there has been no letup in the assault on Iraqi infrastructure and governing apparatus. By attacking all who assist in the occupation, the foe has undermined the democracy. By interrupting the flow of vital commodities (i.e., fuel) and basic services (i.e., security), he has gained popular support.

> Insurgent attacks to disrupt Baghdad's supplies of crude oil, gasoline, heating oil, water and electricity have reached a degree of coordination and sophistication not seen before, Iraqi and American officials say. The new pattern, they say, shows that the insurgents have a deep understanding of the complex network of pipelines, power cables and reservoirs feeding Baghdad, the Iraqi capital.[81]
>
> — *New York Times,* 21 February 2005

The Iraqi insurgents' way of fighting may appear amateurish, but something similar has already worked in places like Afghanistan, Chechnya, and Southern Lebanon. Because Western occupiers try hardest to minimize their own daily losses, they establish bases at the edge of cities, patrol by vehicle, and rely heavily on supporting arms. That leaves the individual neighborhoods relatively devoid of security. When local residents experience shortages of basic services and vital commodities, they are reminded of the Iraqi government's ineptitude and look elsewhere for help.

Throughout eastern Baghdad and most of the southern cities, al-Sadr and his Iranian affiliates have police, courts, clinics, and food/clothing distribution points.[82] It is through their "charities" that they do much of their military recruiting. Like *Hezbollah* in Lebanon and *Hamas* in Israel, the Mahdi Army has set up a parallel government that aspires to Shiite statehood. That government has its own social programs, religious courts, police patrols, and town councils.[83] In this way, al-Sadr and his followers build popular support.

Time to "Out-Guerrilla" the Insurgent

In post-election Iraq, the foe has continued to attack police stations. Within this—his favorite strategy—lies a golden opportunity. Any footballer knows what a goal line stand can do to an opponent's momentum. If the insurgents have reestablished control over the operational tempo, then the neighborhood equivalent of a U.S. goal line stand is in order.

To leverage the Iraqi election, U.S. and Iraqi forces must end their self-imposed isolation from the average city dweller. They must take back the neighborhoods. This may mean blanketing every city with tiny outposts and then patrolling on foot. By patrolling on foot, they lessen their need for resupply and evade IEDs. By entering every neighborhood and buying what they need, Coalition forces will jump start the average Iraqi's security and economy. The insurgents can be beaten at their own game—death by a thousand cuts. Then, there will less need for supporting arms and less collateral damage among the Iraqi civilian population.

In a world where unconventional warfare has become the state of the art, firepower no longer ensures victory. By alienating the local population, it provides a growing base of support for the guerrilla, terrorist, or 4th generation warrior.[84]

As of 30 January 2005, each frontline U.S. unit entered the 4th quarter of a vital, localized football game. The outcome of that game (and ultimately the war) will depend on how well that unit maintains the momentum within its respective Tactical Area of Responsibility (TAOR). Unfortunately—with the insurgent assaults on Iraqi police facilities continuing—the ball has already gone over to the enemy in many locales. To maintain the operational tempo nationwide, many contested neighborhoods will have to be secured at the same time. In each, the tactical equivalent of goal line stand will be required. There is a way to safely "out-guerrilla" the insurgent in his own backyard and thereby facilitate the exit of U.S. forces.

To cover that many neighborhoods, Coalition forces will have to widely disperse their personnel. Thus, the focus is on squad tactics. Squad combat is like football. Each squad's success hinges on the tactical sophistication and situational adaptability of its plays. That takes practicing all tactical techniques under mock casualty assessment and expected conditions. As those techniques produce more surprise or fewer simulated losses, they become more tactically refined.

Unconventional Wars Must Be Fought Unconventionally

U.S. forces have been valiantly struggling with the Muslim militant's 4GW bag of tricks: IED planting, suicide bombing, hostage taking, and police/national guard intimidation. Instead of better defending against each threat, why not just limit that threat's applicability? For example, to curtail IED damage, U.S. forces could drastically reduce vehicular movement. If the roads are too dangerous for motorized patrols, why not just blanket the cities with foot patrol bases. If base occupants purchased most of what they needed locally, they would not need regular resupply. This is the easiest way to influence the most strategically important aspects of guerrilla war: (1) hearts-and-minds, (2) human intelligence, (3) infrastructure, and (4) local economy. Bombing of suspected safe houses would no longer be necessary. Neighborhood tips on guerrilla activity would increase. Local wells, sewers, and security would receive immediate, if not incremental, attention. Furthermore, the Iraqi economy would be infused with U.S. dollars.

While the Vietnam war may not have had a happy ending, it did produce some very effective ways to handle guerrilla activity. One of the most farsighted—and strictly of U.S. Marine Corps design and implementation—was the Combined Action Platoon (CAP). Lone Marine squads were stationed in scores of villages to help local residents organize their own defenses. There is an urban equivalent to the CAP concept that would work in a neighborhood setting. If the Muslim militant has widely dispersed throughout Iraqi society, must not the occupying force do likewise to beat him? Only necessary would be a few more easily learned individual, fire team, and squad techniques.[85]

The Urban Equivalent of CAP

Greater Baghdad covers a full 2,000 square miles. If the other Iraqi cities had a combined footprint that was roughly equivalent, the total area could be covered by 10,000 platoon-sized patrol bases at 1,000 meter intervals. If each base were manned by 12 Coalition troops, 12 Iraqi national guardsmen, and 12 Iraqi police, then only 120,000 Coalition troops would be needed. That would leave the other 50,000 to move around the satellite-monitored countryside by helicopter. With a little advanced infantry technique, every combat support and combat service support Marine or soldier could join in. While at a patrol base, each could help with that part of the local infrastructure/economy that best matched his or her occupational specialty. For example, engineers might work on water or sewage problems, bulk fuel men on a gas station, or typists on a local newspaper. The level of contribution would be less important than its underlying message. During the day, all patrol base members—whether Coalition or Iraqi—would provide basic services. After sunset, all would enforce a curfew.

To win in Iraq, the U.S. military must decentralize control. Active-duty Col. T.X. Hammes says it,[86] and 4GW expert William S. Lind says it.[87] Decentralization of control has been an integral part of Marine Corps' doctrine since 1986.[88] Only missing is a reason to take the additional risk that dispersion of personnel entails.

As most Iraqi police stations have been assaulted by better-than-average combatants, one can expect that most of those combatants are Baathist, *al-Qaeda,* Iranian Revolutionary Guard, or Lebanese *Hezbollah* recruiters/trainers. Thus, every successful defense of a patrol headquarters would make a strategic contribution to the war effort. The enemy's early warning apparatus is better than that of the Viet Cong. To find/remove the Muslim advisers/trainers, U.S. forces must lure them away from their familiar surroundings. They have already demonstrated an intention to overrun as many security headquarters as they can. Let us create headquarters that are too tempting to resist and engage their best with the following tactical technique.

The platoon headquarters will be only superficially conventional. It will have "safe rooms" at diagonally opposite corners. Hidden within the walls of the other rooms and hallways will be command-detonated claymore mines. When people are badly outnumbered, they fight with explosive devices to confound their adversary. To him, explosions mean mines or "incoming," not a human presence. Thus, Coalition squads will depend more on claymores and grenades than on small arms to enforce their curfew. Only inside the American headquarters building will small arms possibly play a role.

When the unsuspecting Baathist, *al-Qaeda, Sepah,* or *Hezbollah* assault force enters the building, its every movement will be monitored by safe-room occupants through electronic devices, tiny wall holes, or a series of mirror shards. To give the quarry enough time to fully enter the building, the safe rooms are prepared to repel attacks. Each has interior obstacles, bunker, communication, and escape route. That route will lead to another part of the block that is the American squad Area of Operations (AO). Once the claymores are blown, the insurgents may draw preplanned small-arms fire through interior walls (as facilitated by aiming stakes within the safe rooms). To withdraw, they must renegotiate Iraqi police and national guard cordons. Each would be comprised of two-man claymore/grenade ambushes.

The plan must preempt the preliminary car bomb. Spanning the streets at all four corners of the U.S. block will be portable cement barriers. Adjacent streets will have foot traffic only.

The Americans' nighttime role is only to defend their headquarters and its secret ways of egress. If the Iraqis are discretely inserted into their ambush sites, they will be safe as well. They can drop the two-man teams off the back of an impromptu patrol.

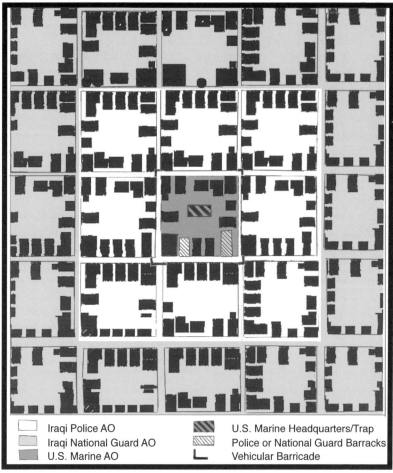

Iraqi Police AO		U.S. Marine Headquarters/Trap	
Iraqi National Guard AO		Police or National Guard Barracks	
U.S. Marine AO		Vehicular Barricade	

Figure 13.2: Combined-Action-Platoon TAOR

(Source: *The Last Hundred Yards*, Posterity Press, ©1994, p. 299)

To counter the threat of turncoats, all three squads need separate nighttime missions and AOs. Additionally, no Iraqi buddy team will know where any others are. Around the outer periphery of the kilometer-square TAOR will be the national guardsmen. With the most military training, they should be the first line of defense and

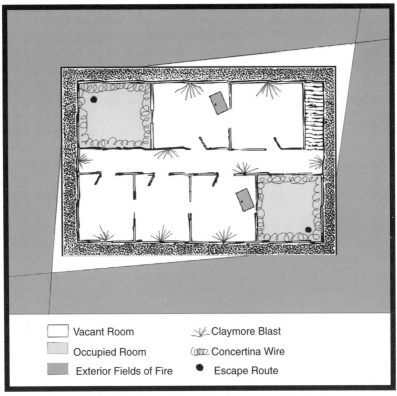

☐ Vacant Room	↘ Claymore Blast
▨ Occupied Room	⟳ Concertina Wire
▨ Exterior Fields of Fire	● Escape Route

Figure 13.3: The Headquarters Trap
(Source: *The Last Hundred Yards*, Posterity Press, ©1994, p. 336)

liaison with adjoining sectors. (See Figure 13.2.) The next concentric set of blocks will be manned by Iraqi police. With a little paramilitary training, they should be able to conduct a two-man ambush.

At the very center will be the U.S. block-sized AO. (See Figure 13.3.) It would not have barbed wire or look much different from any other block. But, at its center, is a very special building. During the day it functions as coordination center for all activities within the TAOR. At night, it becomes a trap. The Iraqi police and national guard barracks are within the same block, but separate. They are locked and empty at night, with everyone out on ambush.

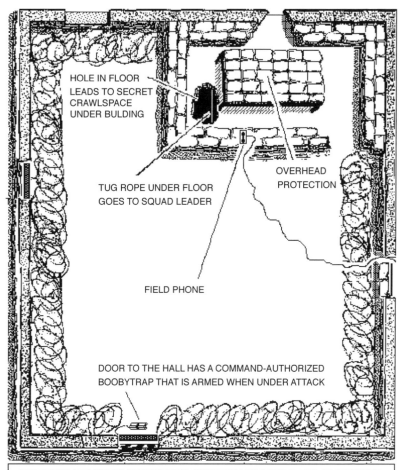

A PROPERLY DEFENDED ROOM POSES SOME REAL PROBLEMS FOR AN ATTACKER. THE FIGHTING POSITION AND ITS OBSTACLES ARE DESIGNED TO WITHSTAND THE INITIAL STAGES OF A WALL BREACH FROM ALMOST ANY DIRECTION. IT ALSO HAS TWO MEANS OF COMMUNICATION AND A HIDDEN ESCAPE ROUTE.

Figure 13.4: Safe-Room Design

(Source: *The Last Hundred Yards*, Posterity Press, ©1994, p. 310)

The American safe rooms are of special design. (See Figure 13.4.) Concertina wire lines their interior walls. In one corner will be a bunker and an escape tunnel for its two occupants through floor or wall. At the other end of this tunnel will be other U.S.

troops. Nearby will be a Viet Cong trick—the "underground hide facility." With a secret entrance, it allows the U.S. troops to completely vanish. Until such an excavation can be accomplished, the Americans can secretly exit their AO. While *al-Qaeda* elite used a tunnel in tribal Pakistan, the Americans need only a series of covered drainage ditches and shadowed gutters. With crawling and signals, they should be able to avoid ambush by their Iraqi counterparts. In 1968, a full North Vietnamese Army (NVA) division exfiltrated the U.S. cordon around the Hue City Citadel. It did so, one squad at a time.[89]

During the day, Americans, guardsmen, and police go out into the TAOR in whatever numbers are required to avoid harm. Shortly after dark, the guard and police barracks are locked and vacated. Then, six, four-man Iraqi patrols concurrently exit the U.S. AO along separate radial axes. Each deposits its two policemen at one ambush site and its two guardsmen at another. The police then slightly shift location. Of particular interest to both sets of ambushers will be the arterials leading toward the American Combat Operations Center (COC): streets, alleyways, and connected rooftops. All Iraqi ambushers are allowed to determine their own level of alertness until hearing a commotion at the U.S. COC. At dawn, all return by approximately the same routes to their barracks.

After dark, the Americans not manning the COC safe rooms deploy into two-man "fighting" outposts. As long as they use claymores and grenades only, the attackers have little chance of discovering their exact location. Two buddy teams guard the escape routes from the safe rooms. Another alternately ambushes the police and national guard barracks. The last functions initially as a "roving" listening post and then—after the COC is attacked—as an ambush. For all but the roving outpost, only one member of each team needs to be awake at any given time. When maneuver warfare is practiced at the platoon or squad level, the difference between defense and offense blurs.

As more outpost assaults go awry, the insurgents will commit more of their most seasoned soldiers—the recruiters/trainers/advisers—to the mission. As those recruiters/trainers/advisers go away, the insurgency will lose its most important strategic asset. No longer able to flood the battlefield with fledgling *jihadists,* the rebellion will fall apart.

Unless the insurgency is promptly defused, attacks on Iraqi infrastructure and governing apparatus may undermine and destabilize the fledgling democracy for many years to come. Insurgents are harder to beat than conventional forces. They are unfettered by doctrinal parameters and organizational inertia. The ones who survive develop excellent initiative and increasingly sophisticated tactical technique. Because Islamic insurgents often provide alternative basic services and infrastructure, they cannot be beaten by ground and aerial bombardment. They can only be bested by highly decentralized light infantry. While the literature contains little detail, the Cambodian Khmer Rouge were quickly suppressed by the NVA in 1979.[90]

The Less-Than-Acceptable Exit Strategy

Lebanon may appear to be a country, but it really isn't. It has a president and a parliament, but the real power is *Hezbollah*. The U.S. must not create another Iranian satellite in Iraq.

"I do not think we can stay in Iraq in the fashion we're in now," Brzezinski [President Jimmy Carter's national security adviser] said. "If it cannot be changed drastically, it should be terminated." He said it would take 500,000 troops, $500 billion and resumption of the military draft to ensure adequate security in Iraq.

The most optimistic outcome to expect, Brzezinski said, is that Iraq will become a Shiite-dominated theocracy, "not what we would normally call a democracy." [91]
— *The Washington Post,* 7 January 2005

While standing up the Iraqi police forces and army is important, it will not be enough to win according to the commander of the U.S. 1st Cavalry Division.[92] He says to defeat the insurgency, the underlying grievances about lack of basic services must be met. That means fixing the infrastructure—most notably water, sewage, trash, and electricity. With no more neighborhood security problem (thanks to the CAP platoons), a free and prosperous Iraq would emerge.

14 Things to Do for Afghanistan

- *Where did the Taliban go?*
- *Is the U.S. occupation being contested by anyone else?*

SMALLER PATROLS SURPRISE MORE PEOPLE

(Source: Courtesy of Sorman Info. & Media, illustration by Wolfgang Bartsch, from *SoldF: Soldaten i fält*, © 2001 Forsvarsmakten, Stockholm, p. 220)

Finding the Hidden Instigators in Afghanistan

Afghanistan lies between Iran and Pakistan. As was clearly demonstrated in Chapter 6, those two countries have been vying for its governmental system since the Soviets departed. As the Northern Alliance was decidedly pro-Iranian, Iran now has the edge in determining that system's particulars. Meanwhile, *Al-Qaeda*, the Taliban, and Hekmatyar's *HIG* all contest the occupier and ostensibly the new government.

Al-Qaeda is currently in a rebuilding phase. It functions more as an umbrella over other factions, than it did previously. It has no offensive militia, per se. Its only combat activities are defensive in nature. Its safe haven is probably now in the Kunar Region of Afghanistan or adjoining Chitral district of Pakistan. It may be receiving suicide bombers and special-operations teams from *MDI's* *LET* and *SSP's LJ.*

The Taliban do have an offensive militia. It is closely allied with *al-Qaeda,* but supported by *JUI/F* and thus—potentially—a Pakistani proxy. Its safe areas are near Quetta in Baluchistan. It may also have a small expeditionary force in the Khakrez mountains north of Kandahar.

Hekmatyar's *HIG* is also attack-oriented militia. It too is allied with *al-Qaeda,* but supported by *JI* and thus—potentially—an overt Pakistani proxy and covert Iranian proxy. Should an Iranian-inspired coup become necessary in Kabul, *HIG* could then—potentially—change sides to help out. Its safe areas are probably now between the other two—in the Waziristan regions of Pakistan.

All three of the above-mentioned safe-area regions are identical to those used by the *mujahideen* during the Soviet-Afghan War. Thus, Map 9 of Brigadier Yousaf's *Bear Trap* may disclose precise positions of still-operational base camps and way stations.[1] (See Map 14.1.) The current location of many *HUM (JUI/F), Hezb (JI), LET (MDI),* and *LJ (SSP)* camps have already been discussed in Chapter 6. Once the two sources of information are compared with satellite intelligence, U.S. forces should have much less trouble interdicting enemy raids and resupply.

The Afghan Resistance Has New Methods

The hidden instigator's grand strategy for Afghanistan would be the same as it was in the late 1980's, if not for two subsequent developments: (1) what can now be determined through electronic surveillance, and (2) what has worked for the Iraqi insurgent. His Afghan proxies have had to disperse and become much more secretive about what they do. To compensate for the decrease in martial activity, he has moved into the other 4GW arenas—politics/media, religion/psychology, and economy/infrastructure. To isolate the central government and non-Muslim occupier, he has encouraged a warlord society. And to fund their operations, he has permitted the widespread growing of opium. Once the occupier has been evicted and the central government either subverted or defeated, he plans

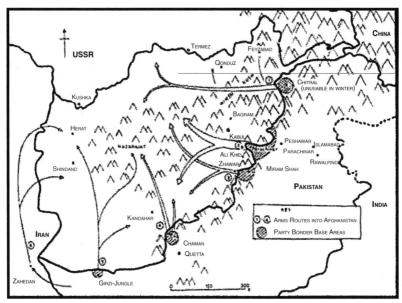

Map 14.1: Likely Safe-Area and Resupply Route Locations
(Source: *Bear Trap,* by Brigadier Mohammad Yousaf and Maj. Mark Adkin, © n.d. by Leo Cooper)

to bring the warlords together (by whatever means) and control the drug trade. At that point, his dream of a fundamentalist theocracy will again be possible.

While the instigator's battlefield objectives have remained about the same, his tactics haven't. As in Iraq, his objectives are shutting off basic commodities, defeating/undermining security forces, and limiting foreign intervention. To accomplish those objectives, he has already resorted to more hostage taking and IEDs than was used against the Russians.

259

The Counter-Initiative

The occupier's success will depend more on curtailing the opium trade and winning over the warlords, than on any battlefield exploit. Much will ride on the September 2005 parliamentary elections. If those on Karzai's list achieve a majority, and if the assembly can achieve a consensus, Afghanistan may become a Muslim state with democratic procedures. That so many of Karzai's immediate subordinates are decidedly pro-Iranian is still worrisome. There will be more enemy activity in Kabul and the other cities than there was with the Russians. It will involve hostage taking, IEDs, and suicide bombing. As in Iraq, the only way to counter the last two is to dismount the vehicles and deploy a CAP platoon in every neighborhood. *Al-Qaeda* has his reasons for doing more of its fighting in the cities: (1) to lift his people's morale while lowering that of the occupier; (2) more news coverage; (3) to punish the ruling government at its center; (4) to promote Allah and Mohammed; (5) to discredit the ruling government's ability to provide security; (6) to affect the economy; (7) to give the new *mujahideen* political experience; (8) to study and analyze mistakes; (9) to prepare the nation and new *mujahideen* for future battles; (10) to gain support from successful operations; and (11) to force the government to change its policies.[2]

Urban-Target Priorities

Al-Qaeda has three types of targets in the city: faith, economic, and human. In order of priority, here are their components to each type. Inferred by the list is *al-Qaeda's* shift to more of a 4GW format than was used against the Russians. *Al-Qaeda* learned much of that format from Iranian *Sepah* and Lebanese *Hezbollah* in the Iraqi theater.

For faith targets, it is as follows: (1) missionaries who are trying to convert Muslims to Christianity; (2) Muslim religious scholars who cooperate with the enemy; (3) Christian pastors who discredit Islam; and (4) any Jew or Christian who provides financial, military, or moral support against Muslims.

For economic targets, the list is a little longer: (1) Jewish and crusader investments in a Muslim land; (2) international companies; (3) international economic consultants and experts; and (4) investments from enemy countries (by military method or boycott); (5) stolen natural resources (as in tankers or pipelines); and (6) Jewish businessmen and those who, after being warned, still cooperate with them.

For human targets, the priority is chilling in its complexity: (1) Jews (American and Israeli first); (2) Christians (American and British first); and (3) renegades. Among the Christians, there is also an order of precedence: (1) businessmen, bankers, and economists; (2) diplomats, politicians, scholars, analysts, and diplomatic missions; (3) scientists, associates, and experts; (4) military commanders and soldiers; and (5) tourists, entertainers, or anyone warned not to enter a Muslim country. Among the renegades, there is also an order: (1) any Muslim leader who has close ties to a Jewish or Christian government; (2) seculars and those who spread evil between believers and those who mock the faith; and (3) intelligence agents and detectives.[3]

The Battlefield Solution

In the 1980's, the strategy of Pakistan's ISI was to defeat the Soviets with 1,000 cuts. If the Taliban and *HIG* now have a similar strategy, then the occupier must be capable of resisting each cut individually. That can only be done by the forces present at the time of the cut, regardless of size. As U.S. squads are never allowed to call or adjust their own supporting arms, they cannot save themselves with firepower. Their only chance for survival is a high level of light-infantry skill.

Unbeknownst to most Americans, such skill does not presently exist in the U.S. military. It should first be imparted to the U.S. forces in country. Then, they, in turn, can enhance what quasi-light-infantry skill already exists in their Afghan proteges. Only then will those proteges develop the requisite initiative to stand alone against the Taliban and *HIG*. Afghans are, by nature, mountain men. They should need less training than a city dweller.

If, on the other hand, the U.S. military were to try to create a mirror image of itself (as it did in Korea and Vietnam), then the Afghan army would have less of a chance. Then, whenever outnumbered or without air cover, it would have major problems.

Figure 14.1: Obscure Defense
(Source: MCO P1500.44B, p. 12-63)

The Difference between Offense and Defense Must Blur

To control a region as rugged and remote as Afghanistan, its new army will have to widely disperse. Then, without special abilities, each separate contingent will be in great danger. For true

Figure 14.2: Obscure Offense

(Source: Courtesy of Sorman Info. & Media, illustration by Wolfgang Bartsch, from *SoldF: Soldaten i fält,* © 2001 Forsvarsmakten, Stockholm, p. 274)

light infantrymen, there is little distinction between attacking and defending. (See Figures 14.1 and 14.2.) If their defenses are about to be overrun, they fight until dark and exfiltrate the enemy's cordon. If they partially lose the element of surprise while attacking, they hold their ground until it can be restored through deception.

Countering Enemy Ambush

After the *mujahideen* had attacked a convoy, the Soviets would insert ambush teams by helicopter along their likely escape routes.[4]

Figure 14.3: Fire-Team-Sized Hunter/Killer Groups
(Source: Courtesy of Sorman Info. & Media, illustration by Wolfgang Bartsch, from *SoldF: Soldaten i falt,* © 2001 Forsvarsmakten, Stockholm, p. 27)

As the enemy routinely guards his routes of egress, a similar U.S. ambush team would have to be inserted somewhere else and then walk a while.

Ambushing Enemy Supply Conduits

During the former occupation of Afghanistan, the Soviets used small teams armed with night vision devices and silenced sniper rifles to attack *mujahideen* supply "trains."[5] Not knowing where the shots were coming from, the quarry could not return accurate fire. The only real problem with this technique is that one might lose quite a few refugees this way. A command-detonated claymore permits a closer look at the quarry and better conceals the presence of its user. To the enemy, it seems like a mine.

The Soviets laid 2,131 minefields in Afghanistan and then left in a hurry. While fully charted, some of their contents may still be there. The Soviets also dropped thousands of antipersonnel mines by aircraft over *mujahideen* trails. Those *mujahideen,* in turn, set in countless numbers of other mines supplied by the U.S. and China. As their locations were never mapped, most were never retrieved. By some estimates, there may still be as many as three million mines of various descriptions across the length and breadth of Afghanistan.[6] Thus, "ambush" would be the last thing expected after an explosion at night. When a Muslim militant acquires a large, albeit silent, torso penetration, it can mean only one thing—that there are U.S. troops to encircle within rifle range.

Without tiny hunter/killer teams, the British could never have defeated the Communist insurgency in Malaysia. Those teams would track and then ambush their quarry. Of course, it's easier to hide in the jungle than in the desert. In sparsely vegetated Afghanistan, such teams would have to travel mostly at night. (Refer back to Figure 14.3.)

15 ___ Averting a Wider Conflict

- What do the Islamic militants want over the long term?
- Can they be stopped with firepower and technology?

IT TAKES LIGHT INFANTRY TO BEAT INSURGENTS

(Source: Courtesy of Sorman Info. & Media, illustration by Wolfgang Bartsch, from *SoldF: Soldaten i fält*, © 2001 Forsvarsmakten, Stockholm, p. 280)

Time for a Different Perspective on the Problem

It's clear that America's hopes for Iraq have yet to be realized. It is less obvious (but equally supportable) that its hopes for Afghanistan are in jeopardy. Who (if anyone) in the U.S. government is to blame is unimportant as long as enough of the deployed personnel find a solution. Iraq and Afghanistan are not America's first encounter with Eastern guerrillas. Its hopes for Vietnam were not realized for one simple reason—too few of its military and intelligence personnel learned to think like Asians. Herein lies the answer to the current dilemma.

Asians have always had a fascination with opposites. It springs from their *yin/yang* orientation (something's *yin* is like its reflection—embedded yet opposite). Thus, they believe that apparent opposites can serve identical ends,[1] just as heaven and earth both nourish life.

The Dual Method through Which Afghanistan Was Contested

Throughout Afghanistan's recent history, both of its neighbors have had proxies on both sides of the conflict. In other words, Iran has simultaneously supported opposing forces, and Pakistan has done likewise. Though their respective proxies occasionally fight each other, both nations generally cooperate to evict a non-Muslim occupier. Before examining such a confusing string of paradoxes, one must imagine their purpose. First and foremost, they make no sense to a Western strategist. Second, one needs a readily available backup when using a proxy to fight his battles. Third, one needs less sophisticated tactics when the opposition has already been infiltrated. In March 1990, Pakistani and Saudi intelligence agencies tried unsuccessfully to combine a coup of Afghanistan's provisional government with attacks from Hekmatyar.[2]

During the Soviet-Afghan War, Pakistan's proxy was Hekmatyar's forces. They were supplied/advised by ISI and manned by *JI*.[3] With an Afghan chapter (started by Rabbani in 1974), *JI* played the lead role in Pakistan's Afghan adventure.[4] (Through *JI* sponsorship, Hekmatyar's *Hezb-e-Islami* would later become the Pakistani *Hezb* of Kashmir fame.[5]) During the Afghan Civil War (after Hekmatyar failed to capture Kabul and instead joined the provisional government of Rabbani and Massoud),[6] Pakistan launched a second proxy—the Taliban. Taliban forces were supplied/advised by Pakistan's Interior Ministry (Frontier Constabulary Corps augmented by *Sibi Scouts* of the Pakistan Army) and manned by *JUI*.[7] Between Spin Buldak and Kandahar, the second proxy fought the first.[8] At that point, the ISI was forced to "co-opt for the Taliban"— augmenting the Taliban's Pakistani Army "advisers" with some of its own.[9]

Now that the U.S. occupation is being contested by both Hekmatyar and the Taliban, one suspects a slight variation on the previous theme. That variation would be starting off with two proxies. If one were to fail, the other could take over immediately. The two could also take turns attacking—a core concept in all Asian tactics. Did not al-Sadr and al-Zarqawi "tag-team" the Iraqi Coalition forces in 2004? And so, interest shifts back to Iran's role in Afghanistan. During the Soviet-Afghan War, Iran supported the *mujahideen* factions in the west and north. Around 1993, a provisional government was formed by pro-Iranian *mujahideen* commanders Rabbani, Massoud, and Hekmatyar.[10] The subsequent Taliban invasion was first contested by Hekmatyar's forces, then Khan's "western wing" of the Northern Alliance, and finally by the "main wing" of the Northern Alliance. Since the U.S. invasion, that main wing has occupied all of the central and eastern cities, Ismail Khan has regained control of the Herat region, and several pro-Iranian *mujahideen* have been chairing key committees of the *Loya Jirga*.[11] All the while, pro-Iranian Hekmatyar is ostensibly helping the Taliban to contest the new government. In 1992, he went so far as to ally himself with *Hezb-e-Wahdat,* Afghanistan's pro-Iranian political party.[12]

Thus, Iran is now represented on both sides of the conflict. On one side, its interests are being quietly appeased by the interim government. On the other, they are being actively pursued by Hekmatyar. The most obvious conclusion is that Pakistan and Iran have been working in concert. That their respective proxies periodically fight does not rule out their collusion. To weaken a powerful occupier, both rely on an initial "free-for-all." If the occupier leaves or a proxy forgets its purpose, they simply help the favored proxy to assert itself (by force if necessary). In other words, neither worries too much about the fate of its proxies. If Iran is running the same kind of deception in Iraq, America must do something about it.

Similarities Only in Strategy between Instigators

"In Afghanistan as well as Kashmir, Pakistan's intelligence agencies . . . realized the efficacy of covert warfare as a potent method of bleeding a stronger adversary while keeping the element of plausible deniability."[13] To wage those wars, the ISI relied (for trained militiamen) on Pakistan's fundamentalist religious parties. Before the U.S. invasion of Afghanistan, it supported both Hekmatyar and the Taliban.

A covert war now rages in Iraq. Its ultimate source is still being hotly debated. *Sepah* and Lebanese *Hezbollah* staff the training sections of the opposition's manpower pipeline.[14] *Sepah* recruits anti-U.S. martyrs inside Iran.[15] The Shiite Mahdi Army fought Coalition forces for a while and still (with the Badr Brigade) enforces *sharia* in the neighborhoods. So who is the hidden instigator of the trouble?

Competing Trails of Evidence

As the U.S. military operates from the top down, most Americans assume an overall manager of worldwide *jihad*. *Al-Qaeda* gets most of the media attention, so it is generally thought to be that manager. Unfortunately, the Eastern world has been perfecting— for the better part of a century—the concept of a "bottom-up" organization. Thus, one must consider the possibility that *al-Qaeda* has been actively courting the media to draw attention away from others. With little organizational structure, *al-Qaeda* cannot be dismembered.

The other candidates for the title of "global *jihad* coordinator" range from China or Iran on one hand to the Muslim Brotherhood or Pakistani equivalents on the other. That coordinator could secretly consolidate the activities of any number of terrorist groups in much the same way as the Pakistani ISI guided the seven *mujahideen* factions during the Soviet-Afghan War. The ISI simply provided mission-consistent wherewithal to the most cooperative group. Also possible, of course, would be a loose conglomerate of Islamic entities with similar goals and no one in charge. By networking, they could bring tremendous pressure to bear on a mutual adversary. As this type of arrangement is almost impossible to stop, the "hidden-instigator" theory must be pursued.

China
China needs Middle Eastern oil and a diversion to take back Taiwan. Large numbers of its personnel frequent Sudan—the location of choice for terrorist conferences and training.

Iran
Iran is ideologically committed to revolution throughout the region. *Sepah* is the catalyst of that revolution. Lebanese *Hezbollah*

is an offshoot of *Sepah*. There are Iranian supported *"Hizbullahs"* in Shiite communities throughout the Middle East and beyond. The most famous is in Lebanon. It was "a Saudi wing of *Hezbollah"*— possibly in conjunction with *al-Qaeda*—that conducted the 1995 and 1996 bombings of U.S. installations in Saudi Arabia.[16] There is evidence linking Iran to the Khobar Towers incident.[17] In Pakistan, Lebanese *Hezbollah* provides assistance to *Sipah-e Mohammed*.[18] In Sudan, several thousand *Sepah* members continue to run the old *al-Qaeda* training camps.[19]

Muslim Brotherhood
The Muslim Brotherhood has been an avowed enemy of Western "decadence" since before WWII. Its Sudanese headquarters organized the INF conferences of the early 1990's that were attended by the leaders of ISI, *al-Qaeda,* and *Hezbollah*.[20] With Azzam and al-Zawahiri, the Muslim Brotherhood spawned *al-Qaeda*. It influences Saudi Arabian politics through some *Wahhabis,* and Pakistani politics through *MDI (Jamaat ul-Dawa)*.[21]

Pakistan's Jamiat Ulema-i-Islam (JUI)
The *JUI* party has heavily influenced the affairs of Pakistan since the early 1970's. Its Fazlur Rehman Jalili faction *(JUI/F)* fathered several of the most active *jihadist* organizations—e.g., *Harakat ul-Mujahideen (HUM)*. Under President Zia's regime, Islamic fundamentalism was encouraged throughout the Pakistani government,[22] to include its ISI. Since then, a symbiotic relationship has existed between Pakistan's security agencies and religious extremists.[23] For over 20 years, their militant wings have waged its *de facto* wars in Afghanistan and Kashmir.[24] The ISI has become virtually autonomous—"a state within a state" or "invisible government."[25] Both *JUI/F* and ISI facilitated the birth of *al-Qaeda,* and both later supported the Taliban. When *al-Qaeda* and the Taliban fell from favor, the ISI turned to *LET*—the military wing of *MDI (Jamaat ul-Dawa)*.[26]

Al-Qaeda
While *al-Qaeda* thrives on attention, the other candidates for "terrorist coordinator" work hard to maintain their deniability. They do so through charities, authorized political parties, unlikely religious liaisons, and military proxies. Iran's on-call expeditionary force is Lebanese *Hezbollah*. In Palestine, *Hezbollah* has its own

subproxies—*Hamas* and the *Palestinian Islamic Jihad (PIJ)*. Both are Sunni. In 2002, the ISI encouraged Pakistani religious sects to enter Afghanistan and help the Taliban to defeat the Northern Alliance. Those sects were *Sipah-e-Sahaba (SSP), Lashkar-e-Jhangvi (LJ), Lashkar-e-Toiba (LET),* and *Harakat ul-Mujahideen (HUM).*[27] *HUM* went to Afghanistan in 2001 to resist the American invasion and still does so from just across the border.[28] In 2003, President Musharraf banned most of the *jihadi* factions associated with *al-Qaeda*. Despite the official ban, the leaders of *JEM, LET, HUM,* and *HMA* continued to enjoy full freedom of movement and speech into 2004.[29] *LET* was banned in 2002, but not rebanned in 2003. Instead, it was moved to Pakistan's "watch list."[30] That it was still active in 2004 leads to speculation that it may still play a role in Afghanistan.[31] That role would be to recruit/train suicide bombers for *al-Qaeda* or foot soldiers for the Taliban and Hekmatyar's *HIG.* Just like *Hezbollah* within Lebanon, *LET* has established its own infrastructure within semi-autonomous parts of Pakistan. In those regions, it has its own schools, hospitals, and other facilities.[32] It already has in training a large suicide-squad contingent for Iraq.[33]

Much of *al-Qaeda's* Support Has Come from Iran

Both al-Zawahiri and bin Laden are followers of the Salafi strand of Islam associated with Wahhabism. This allowed them to forge links with fundamentalist Shiite factions.[34] After the truck-bombing of the World Trade Center failed in 1993, *al-Qaeda* sent a contingent to Lebanon to learn more about the demolition of big buildings. Soon thereafter *al-Qaeda* received explosives from Iran that were used in bombing the East African targets.[35]

"Iran received nearly 10% of Osama's outgoing calls from Afghanistan from 1996 to 1998, suggesting that Iran was maintaining a relationship with al-Qaeda even after he developed close ties with the Taliban in Afghanistan, a regime unfriendly toward Tehran."[36]

According to a high-level *Sepah* defector, Mughniyeh (Iran's *jihadist* coordinator) delivered a written request from al-Zawahiri to the leaders of Iran asking for help in attacking the "Great Satan." He inferred that the request had been submitted (and rejected) before 9/11.[37]

The 9/11 Commission disclosed that Khalid Sheikh Mohammed—9/11 mastermind—had an "allegiance" with Abdul Rasul Sayyaf. Sayyaf's faction was part of the Northern Alliance and thus pro-Iranian.[38] This is the same Adbul Rasul Sayyaf who—at the start of 2004—was heading up one of the constitution-writing committees in Karzai's *Loya Jirga*.[39]

Shades of "Iran-Contra"

It has been over 20 years since 241 U.S. peacekeepers lost their lives in a single terrifying instant at the Marine Barracks in Beirut. In international affairs, such things must eventually be forgiven.

But evidence that Iran's Revolutionary Guard *(Sepah)* was responsible still troubles Americans,[40] not because of any desire for revenge but because *Sepah* and its Lebanese descendant have since destabilized other parts of the region.

From August 1985 to November 1986, the U.S. was involved in a clandestine negotiation with Iran in which weapons were traded for hostages and a cessation of hostage taking. Shortly thereafter, Iran's battlefield proxy—Lebanese *Hezbollah*—was firing TOW missiles at Israeli tanks and again taking Western hostages.[41] In January 1987, it captured four Americans, a Frenchman, and a Briton. A year later, it seized, tortured, and hung U.N. peacekeeper Lt.Col. William "Rich" Higgins USMC. In November 1989, the U.S. released $567 million of frozen Iranian assets. After five months, two of its last three hostages were freed.[42] Thus began a strange litany of French, U.S., and Israeli peace initiatives with people who view the bargaining process as an extension of battlefield deception.

Since that time, *Hezbollah* has been implicated (either directly or indirectly) in any number of highjackings, kidnappings, and suicide bombings. The West has responded with exchanges of prisoners and invitations to the political process.

Now, it appears that *Hezbollah* and its expansionist parent have been more deeply involved in the Iraqi insurgency than has been officially acknowledged. In fact, there is every indication that Iran has been orchestrating a 4th-generation war in which *Hezbollah* provides advisers/trainers/recruiters and most of the true suicide bombers. While barely holding their own in the martial arena, the insurgents have scored major victories in those of politics/media, religion/psychology, and economics/infrastructure. All the while,

273

they have led the U.S. administration and media to believe that the insurgency was Sunni inspired. The official U.S. position on that subject has not changed, despite repeated evidence that Chalabi was an Iranian confidant,[43] that al-Sadr's militia was being funded and trained by *Sepah*,[44] and that Iranian men were being recruited for (and participating in) the Sunni-Triangle fighting.[45]

Yes, *al-Qaeda* and the Baathists were involved, but only to the extent that they routinely diverted attention from the best finishers in a free-for-all—*Sepah*. Has *al-Qaeda* or the Baath party gone to the trouble of creating a quasi-state? It is the Shiites who have established an alternate network of basic services for the general population.

Why Take an Enemy News Release at Face Value?

On 14 September 2005, *"al-Qaeda* in Iraq" announced that it had bombed Shiite targets in retaliation for the joint Iraqi-U.S. operation against Tal Afar. It went on to say that it had declared all-out war on the country's Shiite majority.[46]

The enemy in Iraq is highly deceptive. He is practicing 4GW. That makes every news release double-talk with a hidden intent. Someone needs to start deciphering those news releases. Here is what this one really says. A fictitiously named Iranian proxy wants to discourage Iraqi Shiites from joining the Iraqi Army and the Coalition from bothering its Lebanese-*Hezbollah*-run manpower pipeline. It further wants to draw attention away from the recent proof of police department subversion in southern Iraq.

Things Were Not Going As Well As the Media Purported

While the mostly Shiite government watched and the Sunni-Triangle diversions continued, the Mahdi Army,[47] Badr Brigade, and *Hizbullah in Iraq* had been quietly consolidating the whole southern half of Iraq. Where al-Sadr's Mahdi Army goes, Iranian *Sepah* and Lebanese *Hezbollah* are not far behind.

Iraqi security forces in the south have largely fallen under the authority of [Shiite] militias.[48]
— Associated Press, 23 September 2005

Most heavily targeted had been the big-city police departments. Within the Basra statistics lay a hint of conspiracy. That takeover looked less like a power struggle between supposedly rival Shiite factions, and more like well-engineered cooperation. This came as no surprise to those who had seen the reports of "Karbala being infiltrated at every level of power by Iran's Ministry of Intelligence and Security."[49]

> Officials . . . said at least 60 percent of the [Basra] police force is made up of Shiite militiamen from . . . the Mahdi Army; the Badr Brigade . . . ; and Hezbollah in Iraq.[50]
> — Associated Press, 22 September 2005

SCIRI's greatly expanded military wing (the Badr Brigade) is closely affiliated with Iraq's ruling party (the UIA). The head of the UIA used to lead SCIRI,[51] and an Iraqi vice president is from SCIRI as well.[52] Thus, any Badr Brigade collusion with a confirmed Iranian proxy (the Mahdi Army) is very troubling.

On the 19th of September, a British unit had been forced to storm a Basra province prison to save two of its undercover commandos.[53] Once inside, they discovered that the Mahdi Army had been allowed to move those commandos to a "safe-house." No fools, the British then stormed that as well.[54]

Such momentous disclosures should have sparked an intense reassessment of all U.S. policies, strategies, and tactics. They not only challenged the viability of current regime and draft constitution, but also of Coalition-free neighborhood policing. Much would depend on America's ability to finally solve the Muslim militants' so-far-successful formula. Unfortunately, most of its top leaders had yet to realize that a firepower-dependent army can appear to win every battle and still lose a 4th-generation war.

The Inescapable Truth

Though "losing" most firefights, the Iraqi insurgents were nevertheless taking over the country. They had all but curtailed infrastructure repair and were costing the U.S. military far more than Congress would be willing to spend over the long term. To defeat those insurgents, the U.S. administration would have to endure the political embarrassment of drastically altering its policies, strategies, and tactics. While its Service Branches had been so fiercely defending their images and budgets, the Eastern world had almost perfected an alternative way of war. That "way" had evolved to the point that religious revolutionaries could challenge a superpower. However, America's new adversaries were overconfident and thus vulnerable.

The Muslim militant is hard, but not impossible, to "beat." He draws most of his strength from three sources: (1) the illegitimate raising of funds, (2) a gross misinterpretation of the Koran, and (3) and the bureaucratic ineptitude of his Western opposition. To beat him, a fledgling regime or occupying nation has only to shut off his money, facilitate moderate mullahs, and force its own military to decentralize control. If its army is predisposed (through casualty avoidance) to standoff bombardment, then it must refrain from using its "high-tech" heavy weaponry to preclude adverse media coverage. In this type of war, firepower is a poor substitute for light-infantry skill. If the Muslim militant likes to fight at close range, then that is where he must be defeated. As Iraqi and Afghan security forces become further infiltrated by *Sepah* and its proxy militias,[55] the tiny contingents with which they like to control every neighborhood will flourish.[56] Their so-far-successful takeover bid can only be arrested with a "bottom-up," counter-*Sepah* methodology. The U.S. Marine Corps' CAP platoon concept qualifies. It worked in the "villes" of Vietnam, and its Chapter 13 variation would work in the neighborhoods of Southwest Asia. In urban terrain, the American nucleus of this CAP platoon need not be professional infantrymen. With a little free help from Posterity Enterprises, U.S. support personnel could quickly acquire enough light-infantry skill.

The Consequences of Ignoring this Truth

More is at stake here than what happens in Iraq and Afghanistan. Until the Pentagon realizes the need to decentralize control, the enemy's method will continue to work. Until U.S. forces change how they train and operate, the Muslim militant will keep on coming. He will simply shift the location of his *jihad*. All of Northeast Africa, the Arabian Peninsula, the former Soviet Union, Afghanistan, and Southeast Asia are at risk. He already claims that all Muslims north of the equator in Africa are under Western attack.

The Radical Shiite/Sunni Alliance

The United States has not precipitated a Sunni insurgency in Iraq or Afghanistan. It has fanned the coals of a anti-Western uprising that was begun in 1928 by the Muslim Brotherhood and is most actively pursued by the Shiite Iranians. That fundamentalist Sunnis and fundamentalist Shiites don't particularly get along is immaterial. Theirs is a style of warfare that embraces chaos. With a mutual invader, both encourage every disruption from any source. By so doing, they simultaneously accomplish two things—one strategic and one tactical. Their mayhem not only discredits the invader's ability to provide basic services, but it also diverts his attention from attacks of import. Once he is expelled, the various factions will work out their differences. This is the way wars are fought in this region, and this is what U.S. planners must come to realize.

Al-Qaeda and *Hezbollah* have had very little difficulty finding a place to meet. Many of *al-Qaeda's* leaders now live in Iran and others in Lebanon. Former *Hezbollah* director of operations, Mughniyeh, easily coordinates the efforts of both organizations. When in Iraq, he is responsible for giving the insurgency a Sunni appearance.[57]

Sudan's Role in the Uprising

In the early 1990's, Osama bin Laden used Sudan as a base. Then he was evicted. On 29 March 2005, it was reported that *al-Qaeda* cells were again entering the country. Sudanese, authorities blamed al-Zarqawi.[58] That they are Iranian puppets would explain the double-talk. Lebanese *Hezbollah* has run terrorist training camps there for years.

Bin Laden Shares the First Part of His Grand Design

On 16 December 2004, bin Laden called for attacks on oil facilities by every militant cell in the Middle East.[59] From the trends in Iraq, one can guess the other parts of his strategy. Bin Laden's statement set another ominous precedent. It gave the initial guidance for extending the conflict into Saudi Arabia. What many U.S. leaders have yet to realize is that wars can be more effectively fought by armies with less organizational structure.

The captured *Al-Qaeda Training Manual* makes clear that *al-Qaeda* prefers to fight in the mountains or the city. It further provides for the falsification of its fighters' documents.[60] Thus the Afghan revolution may start shifting to the cities. Its participants may not come from where their papers stipulate. That manual makes "tourists," "prisons," "places of amusement," "economic centers," and "bridges" into vital targets.[61]

Other Parts of the Joint Strategy

By early 2004, the Iraqi militants' overall strategy had become clearly obvious: (1) curtail the flow of oil, (2) eliminate government-supplied social services, (3) isolate occupying forces, and (4) discredit/subvert local security forces. The first was done during commando raids. The second was accomplished with sabotage, assassination, and hostage taking. The third was achieved by using IEDs to limit the flow of supplies and tie occupying forces to their vehicles or bunkers. The fourth was performed through repeatedly corrupting or killing police and army personnel.

Something similar drove the Israelis out of Southern Lebanon and the Russians out of Afghanistan. Until someone finds a solution, this strategy will stalk the Third World.

Within Its Scale Lies the Answer

If the militants' strategy is to defeat America with hundreds of tiny incidents, then America must be capable of winning each incident as it happens. That can only be accomplished by a commensurate number of tiny U.S. units. It must be done tactically, because firepower alienates the people and damages the infrastructure. At present, most U.S. battalions lack the individual and small-unit skill to win hundreds of tiny engagements simultaneously. To do so, their squads, fire teams, buddy teams, and riflemen will need the equivalent of Eastern "light-infantry" techniques.

Until the U.S. military decentralizes control over its training and operations, it will have little chance of developing such techniques. To evolve tactically, its rifle companies will need more leeway and a well-tested experimental method.

"Shock and Awe" Is a Thing of the Past

In essence, the technologically deficient and financially strapped East has developed a style of warfare that requires no tanks or planes. It depends instead on surprise. That surprise is almost entirely based on the West's preoccupation with firepower. To penetrate a Western base, the Easterner creates the impression of an indirect-fire attack. To blow up something within that base, he pretends to score a lucky mortar hit. The Muslim militant has taken this analogy one step farther. With the suicide bomber, he has created a precision munition.

Because of the accuracy of hand-delivered munitions, the Russians may soon replace much of their artillery with "Shmel" thermobaric rounds from hand-held rocket launchers.[62] To escape bombardment, guerrillas, terrorists, and 4GW warriors will all "hug" a Western opponent. To decisively defeat them at short range, U.S. forces must develop more small-unit skill. Semi-autonomous small units get routinely cut off from their parent unit. Thus—for U.S. squads, fire teams, buddy teams, and riflemen—being able to outshoot their enemy counterpart will no longer be good enough. What happened to the U.S. Rangers in Mogadishu will happen to them. Theirs must be a higher level of infantry expertise. Without the help of supporting arms, they must be able to escape an encirclement by many times their number. That U.S. enlisted personnel can't do this is largely the doing of the arms manufacturers. Line infantrymen from East Asia and Germany have been doing it since WWI. All it takes is better hiding and movement technique.

What It Will Take to Shut Down the Iraqi Insurgency

Iraq's initial elections are over, but its insurgency isn't. Iran and Lebanese Hezbollah are more deeply involved than has been reported. North Korea has been educating the Iranians on psychological warfare and subterranean defense.[63] If that education ever extends to light-infantry subjects, the Iraqi war will get a lot harder.

Counterinsurgency is like peacekeeping or police work, it demands the prudent use of force—where surprise takes precedence over firepower. By defeating each enemy cell tactically, one keeps from harming/alienating the population. Sadly, that cell can only be surprised by a comparably sized, dismounted unit. Thus, counterinsurgency squad members are—because of their mission—at more risk than their conventional-warfare counterparts. Those without world-class light-infantry skills get hurt. Below is a brief discussion of how U.S. troops might be expected to fare in a Mao-like insurgency.

Maoist insurgents have been beaten. In Cambodia in 1979, North Vietnamese Army (NVA) foot soldiers easily swept the Chinese-supported Khmer Rouge up against the Thai border.[64] They could not have done so without equivalent "woods' smarts." North Vietnam may still have the world's best light infantry, but the 100,000-man North Korean Light Infantry Training Guidance Bureau is nothing to be scoffed at.[65]

Eastern light infantrymen can do the following: (1) traverse a battlefield undetected, (2) use supporting arms only as a deception, and (3) exfiltrate an encirclement.[66] Did not ten Chinese divisions reach the North Korean Chosin Reservoir undetected in 1950, and an NVA division exfiltrate the Hue City Citadel in 1968?[67] Only soldiers trained in both conventional and unconventional warfare skills can accomplish such a feat. One minute they are running a state-of-the-art squad-sized assault on a prepared enemy position; the next, they are fading away like guerrillas. By hitting and running, they can take on 10 times their number.

The Ongoing Shortfall in Tactical Evolution

Of the two U.S. infantry organizations, the United States Marine Corps has the best chance of evolving into light infantry. With a Maoist "gung ho" tradition that dates back to Carlson's Raiders, it has always prided itself on its Tactics, Techniques, and Procedures (TTP's). Through "tactics," its small-unit leaders theoretically determine which techniques and procedures to use. They are what the Corps has learned about squad combat. They are what the new lieutenant's troops will already know when he joins them. They are what his squads, fire teams, buddy teams, and riflemen will use to execute his every tactical decision. Such assumptions might be reasonable if the Corps had not changed doctrine in the mid-1980's.

The rewritten manuals no longer advise a 3 to 1 edge in the assault, but many of the enlisted handbooks and courses of instruction still assume it. As a result, Marines are not shown how to take on many times their number. Their Eastern counterparts (to include those from Iran) are. They spend their mornings in battledrill competitions and afternoons in combat free play. Their approach to training has nothing to do with their revolutionary governments, it has to do with their cultural predisposition toward collective thinking and field experimentation. The WWII Germans and Japanese were not Communist, yet they followed this same method. In the East, more time is dedicated to small-unit training.

The Marine Corps has always had excellent shooting techniques and procedures. Only missing are the ways to exercise discreet force at close range. Its movement methods are far less comprehensive. Those for walking point, stalking, tracking, and short-range infiltration are rarely practiced. They get their inspiration from microterrain appreciation, night familiarity, and obscurity intention. These are not attitudes to which "high-tech," well-armed, and motorized "heavy infantry" aspire. The Corps' communication methods are better, but its nonelectronic backups need work. They too must be "guarded"—silent and devoid of motion signature.

For the sake of discussion, look at the standard U.S. assault and its composite parts. The procedures for squad, fire team, buddy team, and individual are the same—everyone moves deliberately forward on line while firing all weapons at their maximum sustained rate. (See Figure 15.1.) For the squad and center fire team, the guide is toward the center. For the flank fire teams, the guide is toward whichever side is closest to that center. Individual riflemen maintain some spacing, remain upright, and hold their weapons in the elevated "eye-muzzle-target" stance. While none of these procedures seem worthy of rehearsal, several are. Infantrymen who do not regularly practice maintaining their interval while moving forward on line tend to converge toward the center and risk fratricide. Those who do not regularly practice moving on line through heavy vegetation have trouble guiding toward either center or flank. They forget to stay behind their buddy on that side.

While the above procedure may seem uncharacteristically weak, the real problem is in how enlisted men are trained. From the time they memorize their general orders, they "live and die" by the book. Whether the book is well written is never at issue. They (and their instructors) believe it to be their doctrinal edict. Unfortunately,

Figure 15.1: U.S. Assault Procedure
(Source: *The Last Hundred Yards*, Posterity Press, ©1994, p. 3)

most tactics manuals were never intended to be strictly followed. They contain guidelines to be situationally adapted. As control over enlisted training is centralized, this "live-and-die-by-the-book" syndrome is exacerbated. By decentralizing control, Eastern armies encourage initiative.

Eastern armies have had (and frequently used) the maneuver warfare option since WWI. Thus, they have more "basics" than Americans do. The U.S. triad of "shoot," "move," and "communicate" is only sufficient for attrition warfare. Their list includes "sensory awareness," "passive defense," and "individual deception." Their nonrates have procedures with which to better see, hear, smell, taste, and feel. They also have ways to protect themselves in static situations—like taking cover, hiding, and escaping. Lastly, they have methods with which to deceive their immediate adversary. An example of the first is enhancing peripheral vision by repeatedly defocusing one's eyes on a finger. Examples of the second are dropping to the ground during an ambush, digging a spider hole, and doubling back on one's own tracks. An example of the third is mimicking a cat after inadvertently kicking a can in the city. The assault most widely used in the East is a variation of the "stormtrooper" method. In 1918, lone German squads could successfully attack any number of Doughboys. They did so by covering the sound of their bangalores with precision artillery and assaulting with bayonets and concussion grenades when the bombardment shifted.[68] That way, the majority of defenders never realized they were under ground attack. The only difference in the North Vietnamese Army (NVA) version was following 82mm mortar rounds with satchel charges, or 61mm mortar rounds with thin-skinned "potato mashers." If the nine-man NVA squad remained undetected coming through the wire, it stayed in column with an RPG man in the lead.[69] (See Figure 15.2.) He could eliminate minor opposition without giving away the indirect-fire deception. His companions would then drop fragmentation grenades into bunker apertures.

If they were fired upon, they could shoot to the side and downward without endangering each other or sister squads. If the squad encountered light resistance coming through the wire, the first of its three-man fire teams or "cells" would deploy on line inside the breach.[70] Cell members with AK-47's fired in the semi-automatic mode.[71] When the entire squad was required on line, the RPD light machinegunner would only fire under the most dire of circumstances. Normally, he carried his weapon by the handle. Those on line maintained several yards of distance between themselves, moved forward at a slow trot, and shot from the waist or extended "combat-glide" stance.[72] Most notably different from the Marine assault is the greater degree of surprise in the NVA's composite technique.

Until the Marine Corps decentralizes control over training and operations, it may have difficulty improving its tactical techniques. Standardization does little to refine existing skills or develop new ones. Like the Stormtrooper leaders of WWI, each company commander must be allowed to identify and fix his own deficiencies. (Only required should be the expert way in which he does so.) His training must take the form of an ongoing experiment. He must allow his junior NCOs to collectively arrive at promising techniques and then ensure that enlisted instructors statistically track simulated casualties and surprise indicators (speed, stealth, and deception).[73] To accelerate the process, he and his platoon leaders can shed some light on applicable technique from world history.

Too Little Too Late

The "Iraqi-deployment" packages at Forts Irwin and Polk (for the Army), and March Air Force Base (for the Marines) may now simulate U.S. casualties. But, they still provide procedural practice instead of technique development. All require large units to deal with many variables at once without first allowing them to work on each variable individually. And all fail to build a firm foundation of individual, then buddy team, then fire team, and finally squad movement techniques.

Figure 15.2: North Vietnamese RPG Man

(Source: *The Tiger's Way*, Posterity Press, ©2003, p. 101)

There is no such thing as platoon tactical technique. That's why football teams are so small. The average U.S. soldier or Marine emerges from the canned unit training little better able to survive the first urban bullet. He has been introduced to many new circumstances, but not to each individually, and not to its appropriate action. Within both U.S. infantry branches, classroom instruction has been grossly overrated.

A Better Solution

Enlisted men learn best by doing. Unfortunately, neither branch has ever had a way to capture what they learn collectively in combat. That is largely why the manuals contain such simplistic tactical procedures. Most procedures are too devoid of surprise to qualify as technique. Until the U.S. infantry changes how it trains at the squad level and below, it will have no choice but to keep the enemy at standoff range with supporting arms. One cannot win hearts and minds with high explosives.

For every category of enemy encounter, U.S. soldiers and Marines can no longer replicate the single, outdated, and totally predictable squad choreography in their manuals. They must be allowed to exercise limited initiative while running the most situationally consistent of several locally developed, continually updated, and heavily practiced "tactical techniques." For an American rifle company to hold its own at short range against its Eastern counterpart, its tactical technique training for the squad and below must change. Instead of doctrinally driven from the top down, it must now be experimentally driven from the bottom up. Until the U.S. military decentralizes control over infantry training and operations, it may have trouble defeating any guerrilla, terrorist, or 4GW threat. All three adversaries fight at short range to evade bombardment.

Consider some other U.S. procedures. For as long as anyone can remember, Marine squads have been taught to immediately assault through any ambush that is less than 50 yards away. Instructors halfheartedly explain that this is the best way to protect those already wounded. Against anyone aware of this practice, such a procedure would be nothing short of disastrous. A piece about squad technique in Fallujah recently circulated in a military internet circle. Purportedly written by a Sgt., Cpl., and two L.Cpls., it proposed: (1) breaking every serious contact to allow for supporting arms, (2) frontally assaulting buildings from the bottom up to facilitate casualty removal, and (3) staying in a tight stack throughout an urban penetration.[74] The Marines' accomplishments in Fallujah are noteworthy, and their lessons refreshing, but the state of the art in urban assault remains the "blooming lotus," [75] or inside-out approach. It was applied to cities in Hue and Saigon, and to a building in the famous Peruvian hostage rescue. More consistent with this approach is the traditional "top-down" assault in which some dispersion is allowed and withdrawal is discouraged. It takes special ordnance and technique to safely move upwards in a building. (See Figure 15.3.) Rumor has it that half of all Marine casualties in Fallujah occurred in "stacks" (columns) that were too large or tightly grouped. As such a stack prepared to move through building's front entrance, someone would extend an AK-47 from an upstairs window.[76]

To understand the true significance of individual or small-unit tactical technique, one must go back to his days as a hunter, ROTC squad member, or football player. What Marines lack is *surprise-oriented* individual and small-unit movement memory. Their existing "Immediate Action" drills unnecessarily expose them and blatantly telegraph intentions. So, instead of reacting instinctively to enemy contact, the Marines must stop to discuss things and then do what has never been rehearsed. The enemy is now ready, and the Marines get their feet (and assignments) tangled up.

There is a better way to train enlisted Marines that has been already successfully tried in several battalions. It allows the NCOs of each company to collectively develop three ways to handle each category of combat situation and then requires all to routinely practice them. When the enemy shows up, every subordinate element then has three tactical options instead of the predictable standard. To use this method, one must have 20 or more NCOs, get three-fourths to agree, and test their solution against three-second sight pictures. Once the techniques are refined a little, they are rehearsed during squad physical fitness (PT). Armed with rubber rifles, the squad members run Indian file until their leader directs an appropriate "battledrill."[77] As the terrain and drills are varied, the squad becomes more adept at its mission.

The Muslim militant has proven quite flexible to changing circumstances. To handle such adaptive opposition, Marine squads

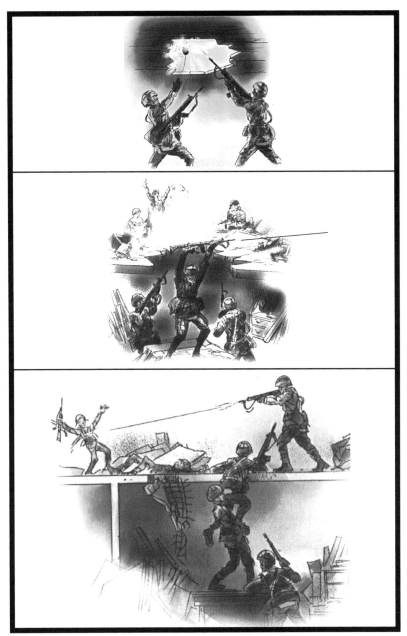

Figure 15.3: Safer Way to Clear a Building from the Bottom Up

(Source: Courtesy of Sorman Info. & Media, illustration by Wolfgang Bartsch, from *SoldF: Soldaten i fält*, © 2001 Forsvarsmakten, Stockholm, p. 301)

will need world-class light infantry tactical techniques. The U.S. military needs to change how it trains at the squad and below before the "War on Terror" gets any larger.

What Effective Urban Training Would Look Like

The urban offense is the most dangerous type of combat for two simple reasons. In a built-up area, movement is almost impossible to conceal. It is also almost impossible to cover by fire.

Unable to camouflage himself, the urban attacker is plainly visible in all but the darkest of corners. He is automatically silhouetted every time he moves through or across any opening. He can sometimes be seen and killed through several coincidently aligned openings. He also runs a greater chance of creating a movement signature, reflection, or unnatural shadow.

There is no way to fully cover by fire an urban attacker. While moving along a street, he can be shot from front, back, above, or below. He can be killed from 100 obvious places and any number of camouflaged ones. If his opponent fires through a curtain, his buddies won't see a muzzle flash. If that opponent fires from an elevated, interior location with a narrow sector of fire, they won't be able to hurt him at all. While outdoors, the urban attacker must defeat the first bullet himself—through how he moves. When he goes indoors, his problems magnify. There, he is more canalized than before and highly susceptible to ambush. He can be killed through walls, floors, ceilings, or through a window from 1,000 meters away. His buddies can only help by covering the hallways and stairwells.

So, it would appear that the key to preparing someone for urban offense is teaching him how to move individually. For the best results, the instructor works on each threat separately and then gradually combines them. Every student has different motivation and athletic ability. Thus, the instructor must put the onus on each to improve himself. By giving him back-to-back chances to move up on an aggressor counting simulated hits, the instructor gives him the required feedback. Then, how ever the majority of students avoid the threat becomes the working solution. To accelerate the learning curve, that working solution becomes the technique taught until a better one is found. (See Figure 15.4.)

Figure 15.4: Urban 4GW Takes Refined Movement Techniques

(Source: Courtesy of Sorman Info. & Media, illustration by Wolfgang Bartsch, from *SoldF: Soldaten i fält,* © 2001 Forsvarsmakten, Stockholm, p. 289)

As the students will now be responsible their own progress, they must first be reminded of all the ways to get shot in the street or between the buildings:

(1) By bullets deflected along walls
(2) By a machinegun at either end of the street
(3) From upper stories to the front or rear
(4) From spaces between buildings
(5) From windows, open doors, and tiny apertures (like air vents)
(6) Through closed doors or thin walls

Then the instructor finds a deserted city street that looks like one in the war zone. He splits the student body in half and issues rubber rifles. The two columns wait on opposite corners at the same end of the street. He sends four aggressors with rubber rifles to the other end of the street. Two sit in the middle to simulate long-range machinegun or sniper fire. Two separate and stand next to their respective building fronts to simulate the bullets that follow walls. Each will try to repeatedly "kill" the advancing man from his respective column. He will record a "kill" every time he acquires a three-second sight picture of an upright human being. He then debriefs each victim.

Then, the instructor sends one student from each column up the street. Their only instruction will be to move as fast as they can while avoiding the two threats. After learning the score, the runner takes the place of one aggressor, and that aggressor moves by alternate route to the starting point. When the next runner replaces the second aggressor, he too enters the rotation. By constantly switching roles, the participant can more quickly grasp the essence of his error. As soon as everyone has had a chance, the instructor repeats the drill and asks students to better their previous scores.

Then the instructor secretly repositions the aggressors to provide the third and fourth threats. He sends the troops, two at a time, up opposite sides of the street to work on fire from between the buildings and from above the street. After all have had one chance, he repeats the drill and asks students to beat their previous scores.

Next, the instructor secretly repositions the aggressors to provide the fifth and sixth threats. He sends the troops, two at a time, up opposite sides of the street to elude fire from apertures, closed doors, and thin walls. When all have tried, he allows them to better their scores.

Finally, as time permits, the instructor deploys more aggressors and works on four threats at once, and finally all six threats concurrently. Only two people can be trained every five minutes with this drill, so each column should be no larger than eight people. For more students, the command must set up identical courses on additional streets or on each block of the same street. Similar training packages would then be needed for street-crossing and interior-movement. (See Figure 15.5.)

Figure 15.5: Street Crossings Are by Fire Team Columns
(Source: Courtesy of Sorman Info. & Media, illustration by Wolfgang Bartsch, from *SoldF: Soldaten i fält,* © 2001 Forsvarsmakten, Stockholm, pp. 22, 23)

There Are Only Little Solutions to Some Very Big Problems

Might the U.S. have fallen behind at short-range combat, simply because it was trying too hard to excel at standoff range? A deficit at close combat equates to insufficient maneuver technique at the squad level and below. In effect, the squads, fire teams, buddy teams, and riflemen are unable to generate enough surprise to secretly close with their enemy counterpart. Most U.S. military headquarters only exacerbate the problem: (1) by concentrating on large-unit exercises, VIP visits, and bureaucratic procedures; (2) by allocating little, if any, "platoon sergeant's time" on training schedules; and (3) by giving squad leaders no chance to work—with an intact squad—on maneuvers. (The latter occurs when too many of the riflemen are otherwise occupied by working parties, bureaucratic processing, or authorized absence.) Close combat is—by definition—dependent on little things. It can only be enhanced by allowing each company's NCOs to collectively identify and fix their own deficiencies. Until that is accomplished, every U.S. company will continue to operate the same way at short range, making them and their subordinate elements almost totally predictable in combat.

Where in the *Bible, U.S. Constitution,* or *Uniform Code of Military Justice* does it say that small-unit training has to be standardized and simplistic? This is a concept that was applied to the U.S. military in the 1940's to facilitate the training of thousands of people in a hurry. While it was hoped that it would provide a framework around which U.S. units could exercise initiative, it hasn't turned out that way. It's time to change. To change quickly, the "top-down" military bureaucracy has to now tap into and trust the collective wisdom of its lowest ranks. It is they who perform short-range combat, and it is only they who know most about it. Until the control of training and operations is decentralized, the U.S. will have to depend almost entirely on its firepower to win. In a guerrilla or 4GW war (where the hearts and minds of the people are the deciding factor), firepower will not get the job done. That is what happened in Vietnam, and that is what is currently occurring in Iraq and Afghanistan.

"Asymmetric warfare" is not a new term for "chaos," "anarchy," "mob-rule," "Third-World barbarity," or "diabolical behavior." It is simply what happens when a "bottom-up" Eastern army comes to fully understand its "top-down" Western counterpart. Whether most U.S. military personnel realize it or not, they have become accustomed to thinking within certain established parameters. They were first introduced to those parameters at boot camp, Fort Benning, or Quantico. They have since been reprimanded or ostracized every time they ignored them. That's why Gen. Smedley Butler appeared—to active-duty Marines—as if he had lost his mind when, after retirement, he took the U.S. military-industrial complex to task. He didn't lose his mind; he just started to see the world as it really was. The East Asian soldier and now the Muslim militant have discovered these limits to Western military thought and make every effort to work just outside them. Every time they do on a strategic initiative, that initiative will be so hard for a Western foe to imagine that it may go unopposed. That again is what happened in Vietnam, and is now occurring in Iraq and Afghanistan.

The U.S. military commander has a choice. He can succumb to the seductive lure of bureaucratic inertia, or he can decentralize control over training and operations. He must choose the latter to have any chance at all against an unconventional foe. While the status quo was being so fiercely defended in America, "unconventional warfare" became the world norm. There will never again be a set-piece battle between mechanized forces. Future conflicts will look like those in Iraq and Afghanistan (be characterized by urban small-unit action). If the U.S. military cannot successfully conclude these 4th-generation wars, it can expect an endless string of others throughout Southwest Asia and North Africa. With "5th-generation" tactical aspects, they will be fought, and can only be won, from the bottom up.[78] The term "bottom up" will apply not only to the method of control, but also to the type of terrain. Thousands of tiny maneuver elements will receive only the broadest of strategic guidance from above. Then, to escape electronic surveillance, they will operate from roofed or tunneled areas.

To stop the spread of Muslim militancy or win the next world war, the U.S. Marine Corps and U.S. Army must now change. They must shift from a weapons-oriented, standoff way of war to a tactics-oriented, short-range format. Future battles will be fought on a scale at which U.S. forces are almost totally predictable and only partially responsive. This is the scale of the single, tiny encounter—each "cut" of the thousands promised. During this encounter, the enemy fighters may not be very good "shots," but they will be deceptive and opportunistic. If they are further allowed to anticipate the U.S. contingent's every action, some will score strategic victories before running away. To deny them that chance, each

───────────────────────────

U.S. rifle company will need its own unique portfolio of squad, fire team, buddy team, and individual techniques. Those techniques must deal with things other than just shooting; they must cover concealed movement, in-place hiding, and surprise assault. To respond quickly enough to the enemy's trickery, each enlisted American will also need the leeway, confidence, and skill to make his or her own tactical decisions. The U.S. Marine Corps and U.S. Army can achieve both capabilities at once by simply advancing from the headquarters-driven (standardized) way of training infantry squads to the more productive NCO-generated (experimental) approach. As in East Asia, each rifle company's junior NCOs best determine—through collective opinion and field experimentation—what each of that company's squads should be able to do at short range.

Notes

SOURCE NOTES

Illustrations

Pictures on pages 3, 16, 91, 96, 228, 242, 253, 258, 259, 261, 278, 280, and 282 reproduced with permission of Sorman Information and Media and the Swedish Armed Forces, from *SOLDF: SOLDATEN I FALT,* by Forsvarsmakten, with illustrations by Wolfgang Bartsch. These pictures appear on pages 293, 253, 219, 30, 287, 306, 220, 274, 27, 280, 301, 289, and 22/23 of the Swedish publication, respectively. Copyright © 2001 by Forsvarsmakten, Stockholm. All rights reserved.

Maps on pages 4 and 88 reprinted after written assurance from *GENERAL LIBRARIES OF THE UNIVERSITY OF TEXAS AT AUSTIN* that they are in the public domain.

Picture on page 80 reproduced with permission of *The New York Times* and the artist, from "Switched Off in Basra," by Steven Vincent, with illustration by M.K. Perker. Copyright © 2005 M.K. Perker. All rights reserved.

Map on page 112 reproduced with permission of *KHYBER GATEWAY* at www.khyber.org. This map had Khyber designator "nwfpmap01.gif." Copyright © n.d. by Khyber Gateway. All rights reserved.

Map on page 119 reproduced with permission of *PAKISTAN & THE KARAKORAM HIGHWAY, LONELY PLANET,* and *KHYBER GATEWAY.* This map had Khyber Gateway designator "chitraldistrict.gif." Copyright © 2005 by Lonely Planet Publications. All rights reserved.

Picture on page 199 reproduced with permission of Bates Creative Group, Silver Spring, MD, from *MARINES MAGAZINE,* January-March 2005, cover art by Seth Sirbaugh. Copyright © 2005 by Bates Creative Group. All rights reserved.

Map on page 259 reproduced after asking permission of Pen & Sword Books Ltd., South Yorkshire, UK, from *BEAR TRAP: AFGHANISTAN'S UNTOLD STORY* by Brigadier Mohammad Yousaf and Major Mark Adkin. It is from Map 9 of the Pen & Sword publication. Copyright © n.d. by Leo Cooper. All rights reserved.

Text

Reprinted with permission of the *NEW YORK TIMES,* from the following articles: (1) "The Conflict in Iraq," by James Glanz, 21 February 2005; (2) "Switched Off in Basra," by Steven Vincent, 31 July 2005; and (3) "Some Bombs in Iraq Are Made in Iran, U.S. Says," by Jeffrey Imm, 6 August 2005. Copyright © 2005 by New York Times Company. All rights reserved.

Reprinted with permission of *DEBKAFILE,* Israel, from two articles: (1) "New Warfront Opens in Iraq Three Months before Handover," by Art Theyson, 5 April 2004; and (2) "Shiite Radicals Join with Sunni Insurgents in Ramadi," 7 April 2004. Copyright © 2004 by DEBKAfile. All rights reserved.

Reprinted with permission of Vintage Books, a Division of Random House, from *SOLDIERS OF GOD: WITH ISLAMIC WARRIORS IN AFGHANISTAN AND PAKISTAN,* by Robert D. Kaplan. Copyrights © 1990, 2000, and 2001 by Robert D. Kaplan. All rights reserved.

Reprinted with permission of *TIME MAGAZINE,* from "Inside Iran's Secret War for Iraq," by Michael Ware, 22 August 2005. Copyright © 2005 by Time, Inc. All rights reserved.

Reprinted with permission of *AGENCE FRANCE-PRESSE,* from "Iraq Shiite Leaders Demand Islam Be the Source of Law," 6 February 2005. Copyright © 2005 by Agence France-Presse. All rights reserved.

Reprinted with permission of Alfred A. Knopf, Inc., a Division of Random House, from *CROSSING THE THRESHOLD OF HOPE,* by His Holiness John Paul II. Copyright © 1995. All rights reserved.

Reprinted with permission of the *ST. LOUIS DISPATCH,* from "Hell in Hilla," 1 March 2005. Copyright © 2005 by St. Louis Dispatch. All rights reserved.

299

ENDNOTES

Preface

1. H. John Poole, *Phantom Soldier: The Enemy's Answer to U.S. Firepower* (Emerald Isle, NC: Posterity Press, 2001), chap. 7.
2. H. John Poole, *The Tiger's Way: A U.S. Private's Best Chance for Survival* (Emerald Isle, NC: Posterity Press, 2003), pp. 114, 115.
3. Neamatollah Nojumi, *The Rise of the Taliban in Afghanistan: Mass Mobilization, Civil War, and the Future of the Region* (New York: Palgrave, 2002), p. 227.
4. Stephen E. Hughes, *Warring on Terrorism: A Comprehensive Dispatch Briefing,* Part I (internet piece, Soda Springs, ID, 2005), p. 17.
5. *Patterns of Global Terrorism, 2003 Report (Washington*, D.C.: U.S. Dept. of State, April 2004). (This work will henceforth be cited as *Patterns of Global Terrorism, 2003.)*
6. Aaron Mannes, *Profiles in Terror: Guide to Middle East Terror Organizations* (Lanham, MD: Rowman & Littlefield, 2004), p. 42; Amir Mir, *The True Face of Jihadis* (Lahore: Mashal Books, 2004), p. 328.
7. Rohan Gunaratna, *Inside al-Qaeda: Global Network of Terror* (Lahore: Vanguard, 2002), p. 82.
8. Al-Zawahiri, as quoted in "Al Qaeda to West: It's about Policies," by Dan Murphy, *Christian Science Monitor,* 5 August 2005, pp. 1, 10.
9. Hamza Hendawi, AP, "Iraq Still in Turmoil after Regaining Sovereignty," *Jacksonville (NC) Daily News,* 26 June 2005, p. 5A.
10. ABC's Nightly News, 28 June 2005.
11. *Catechism of the Catholic Church* (New York: Doubleday, 1994), par. 2309.
12. His Holiness John Paul II, *Crossing the Threshold of Hope* (New York: Alfred A. Knopf, 1995), pp. 205, 206.
13. *The Battle of Dien Bien Phu,* Visions of War Series, vol. 10 (New Star Video, 1988), 50 min., videocassette #4010.
14. Poole, *The Tiger's Way,* p. xxiv.
15. Poole, *Phantom Soldier,* p. 28.
16. Bill Gertz, "Notes from the Pentagon," *Washington Times,* 5 March 2004; "Top Iranian Defector On Iran's Collaboration with Iraq, North Korea, Al-Qa'ida, and Hizbullah," Special Dispatch No. 473, 21 February 2003, Iran Jihad and Terrorism Studies, from Middle East Media Research Inst.

Chapter 1: *The Deteriorating Situation in Iraq*

1. Scott Peterson, "Iraqi Christians Struggle to Stay," *Christian Science Monitor,* 18 October 2004, pp. 6, 7.

2. Robert H. Reid, AP, "Hostage Aide Chief Pleading for Her Life," *Jacksonville (NC) Daily News,* 23 October 2004, pp. 1A, 5A.

3. "Despite Having Agreed to a Truce," World News in Brief, *Christian Science Monitor,* 11 June 2004.

4. Todd Pitman, AP, "Jets Target Rebels," *Jacksonville (NC) Daily News,* 1 July 2004, p. 6A.

5. Todd Pitman, AP, "U.S. Warplanes Bomb Suspected Terror Den," *Jacksonville (NC) Daily News,* 2 July 2004, pp. 1A, 4A.

6. Fisnik Abrashi, AP, "Militant Cleric Vows to Keep Fighting in Iraq," *AOL News,* 5 July 2004.

7. Abdul Hussein Al-Obeidi, AP, "Mosque Turnover Disputed," *Jacksonville (NC) Daily News,* 21 August 2004, p. 6A; ABC's Nightly News, 22 August 2004.

8. ABC's Nightly News, 26 August 2004.

9. Scott Peterson, "Economic Fallout of $50 a Barrel," *Christian Science Monitor,* 27 August 2004, p. 6.

10. Scott Baldauf, "Standoff Bolstered Sadr's Support," *Christian Science Monitor,* 30 August 2004, p. 4.

11. ABC's Nightly News, 8 October 2004.

12. "Followers of . . . al-Sadr Trickled into Police Stations," World News in Brief, *Christian Science Monitor,* 12 October 2004, p. 20.

13. Scott Peterson, "Signs of Progress amid Turmoil in Iraq," *Christian Science Monitor,* 15 October 2004, pp. 1, 5; ABC's Morning News, 20 October 2004.

14. Jason Burke, *Al Qaeda: The True Story of Radical Islam* (London: Penguin Books, 2003), pp. 18, 270-271.

15. Rod Nordland and Christopher Dickey, "Hunting Zarqawi," *Newsweek,* 1 November 2004, pp. 32, 34.

16. Mannes, *Profiles in Terror,* p. 163.

17. Jim Krane, AP, "U.S. Split on Foreign Involvement in Iraq," *Jacksonville (NC) Daily News,* 5 March 2004, p. 4A.

18. Dan Murphy, "In Iraq, a Clear-Cut bin Laden-Zarqawi Alliance," *Christian Science Monitor,* 30 December 2004, pp. 1, 10.

19. Robert H. Reid, AP, "Marines Continue Assault," *Jacksonville (NC) Daily News,* 16 October 2004, pp. 1A, 6A.

20. Abdul Hussein Al-Obeidi, AP, "U.S. Increases Pressure on Najaf," *Jacksonville (NC) Daily News,* 24 August 2004, p. 3A.

21. Scott Peterson, "Fallujans Flee from US, Zarqawi Fight," *Christian Science Monitor,* 19 October 2004, pp. 1, 7.

22. "Iraqi Campaigning Has Begun," from AP, *Jacksonville (NC) Daily News,* 16 December 2004, p. 4A.

23. Peter Ford, "A Suspect Emerges As Key Link in Terror Chain," *Christian Science Monitor,* 23 January 2004, pp. 1, 7.

24. ABC's Morning News, 28 December 2004.

25. Bassem Mroue and Abdul-Qader Saadi, AP, "Marines Capture Militants," *Jacksonville (NC) Daily News,* 26 December 2004, pp. 1A, 9A.

26. Howard Lafranchi, "Anti-Iran Sentiment Hardening Fast," *Christian Science Monitor,* 22 July 2002, pp. 1, 10.

27. Annia Ciezadlo, "Fragmented Leadership of the Iraqi Insurgency," *Christian Science Monitor,* 21 December 2004, pp. 1, 10.

28. Scott Peterson, "For Iraq's Insurgents, What Next," *Christian Science Monitor,* 1 February 2005.

29. Louis Meixler, AP, "Extremists Send Recruits into Iraq via Iranian Border," *Jacksonville (NC) Daily News,* 8 November 2004, p. 4A.

30. Tom Masland, "Jihad without Borders," *Newsweek,* 8 November 2004, p. 30.

31. Babak Denghanpisheh, "'This Ain't Over Yet'," *Newsweek,* 22 November 2004, pp. 40, 41.

32. "The Ayn Tzahab Training Camp in Syria," Israel News Agency, 5 October 2003.

33. "A Troublemaker Surrounded," *The Economist,* 2 October 2004, p. 47.

34. Ibid.

35. Robert H. Reid, AP, "Insurgents Kill 50 Iraqi Troops in Bold Ambush," *Jacksonville (NC) Daily News,* 25 October 2004, p. 1A.

36. Robert H. Reid, AP, "Rebels Spread Attacks," *Jacksonville (NC) Daily News,* 7 November 2004, pp. 1A, 8A.

37. ABC's Morning News, 9 November 2004.

38. ABC's Morning News, 12 November 2004.

39. FOX's News, 11 November 2004.

40. ABC's Morning News, 12 November 2004.

41. Tini Tran, AP, "Insurgents Hit Mosul Police Stations," *Jacksonville (NC) Daily News,* 15 November 2004, p. 1A.

42. Katarina Kratovac, AP, "U.S., Iraqi Units Take Back Police Stations," *Jacksonville (NC) Daily News,* 17 November 2004, p. 1A.

43. Jim Krane, AP, "Occupied, Not Subdued," *Jacksonville (NC) Daily News,* 14 November 2004, pp. 1A, 9A.

44. Krane, "Occupied, Not Subdued," pp. 1A, 9A.

45. Robert H. Reid, AP, "Rebels Cornered in City," *Jacksonville (NC) Daily News,* 13 November 2004, pp. 1A, 4A.

46. Robert H. Reid, AP, "Insurgent Violence Sweeps across Baghdad," *Jacksonville (NC) Daily News,* 21 November 2004, pp. 1A, 4A; Krane, "Occupied, Not Subdued," pp. 1A, 9A.

47. Tran, "Insurgents Hit Mosul Police Stations," p. 1A.

48. Tini Tran, AP, "Car Bomber, Troop Clashes Kill 27 in Iraq," *Jacksonville (NC) Daily News,* 18 November 2004, pp. 1A, 4A.

49. Robert H. Reid, AP, "Bombings Target Troops," *Jacksonville (NC) Daily News,* 16 November 2004, pp. 1A, 4A.

50. Ibid.
51. Maggie Michael, AP, "Iraq Sets Date for Election," *Jacksonville (NC) Daily News,* 22 November 2004, pp. 1A, 2A; CBS's Nightly News, 21 November 2004.
52. Maggie Michael, AP, "U.S. Raid Finds Links to Terrorist," *Jacksonville (NC) Daily News,* 19 November 2004, pp. 1A, 6A.
53. ABC's Noon News, 15 Nov. 2004.
54. Reid, "Insurgent Violence Sweeps across Baghdad," pp. 1A, 4A.
55. Ibid.
56. Tran, "Car Bomber, Troop Clashes Kill 27 in Iraq," pp. 1A, 4A.
57. Reid, "Bombings Target Troops," pp. 1A, 4A.
58. Michael, "U.S. Raid Finds Links to Terrorist," pp. 1A, 6A.
59. Michael, "Iraq Sets Date for Election," pp. 1A, 2A.
60. ABC's Noon News, 15 November 2004; Reid, "Bombings Target Troops," pp. 1A, 4A.
61. Michael, "U.S. Raid Finds Links to Terrorist," pp. 1A, 6A.
62. Scott Peterson, "Marine, Insurgent Tactics Evolve," *Christian Science Monitor,* 17 November 2004, p. 6.
63. "Iraqi Rebels Not Giving Up," from AP, *Jacksonville (NC) Daily News,* 19 November 2004, p. 6A.
64. Reid, "Insurgent Violence Sweeps across Baghdad," pp. 1A, 4A.
65. Ibid.
66. Michael, "Iraq Sets Date for Election," pp. 1A, 2A.
67. Tini Tran, AP, "Tape Targets Clerics," *Jacksonville (NC) Daily News,* 25 November 2004, pp. 1A, 4A.
68. Maggie Michael, AP, "Al-Zarqawi Cell Owns Up to Killings," *Jacksonville (NC) Daily News,* 29 November 2004, pp. 1A, 6A.
69. Marion Fam, AP, "Iraq's Sunni President Backs January Elections," *Jacksonville (NC) Daily News,* 2 December 2004, p. 4A.
70. Nick Wadhams, AP, "Rebels Drop Mortar Shells on Baghdad," *Jacksonville (NC) Daily News,* 3 December 2004.
71. Slobodan Lekic, AP, "Attacks Pick Up in Iraq," *Jacksonville (NC) Daily News,* 4 December 2004, p. 1A; ABC's Nightly News, 3 December 2004.
72. Slobodan Lekic, AP, "Attacks Target Troops, Police," *Jacksonville (NC) Daily News,* 12 December 2004, pp. 1A, 7A.
73. ABC's Nightly News, 24 December 2004.
74. Dusan Stojanovic, AP, "Rebels Spread Attacks," *Jacksonville (NC) Daily News,* 29 December 2004, pp. 1A, 8A.
75. ABC's Nightly News, 20 November 2004.
76. Stojanovic, "Rebels Spread Attacks," pp. 1A, 8A.
77. Dusan Stojanovic, AP, "Car Bombings Kill 25 in Iraq," *Jacksonville (NC) Daily News,* 6 January 2005, p. 4A.
78. Tini Tran, AP, "Marines, Iraqis Launch Offensive," *Jacksonville (NC) Daily News,* 24 November 2004, pp. 1A, 2A.

79. Robert H. Reid, AP, "Deadly Month inside Iraq," *Jacksonville (NC) Daily News,* 30 November 2004, pp. 1A, 2A.
80. Fam, "Iraq's Sunni President Backs January Elections," p. 4A.
81. Nick Wadhams, AP, "Insurgents Blow Up Police Station," *Jacksonville (NC) Daily News,* 9 December 2004, p. 4A.
82. Stojanovic, "Rebels Spread Attacks," pp. 1A, 8A.
83. Nick Wadhams, AP, "Iraqi Forces Hit Hard," *Jacksonville (NC) Daily News,* 3 January 2005, pp. 1A, 2A.
84. Stojanovic, "Rebels Spread Attacks," pp. 1A, 8A; ABC's Nightly News, 24 December 2004.
85. Ibid.
86. Robert H. Reid, AP, "Officials Rejecting Vote Delay for Iraqis." *Jacksonville (NC) Daily News,* 28 November 2004, pp. 1A, 2A.
87. Fam, "Iraq's Sunni President Backs January Elections," p. 4A.
88. Reid, "Insurgent Violence Sweeps across Baghdad," pp. 1A, 4A.
89. ABC's Nightly News, 5 December 2004.
90. Robert Bryce, "Gas Pains," *Atlantic Monthly,* vol. 295, no. 4, May 2005.
91. Robert Bryce, "Running Out of Gas in Iraq," 23 December 2004, in e-mail from robert@robertbryce.com.
92. Scott Peterson, "Rebels Return to 'Cleared' Areas," *Christian Science Monitor,* 3 December 2004, p. 6.
93. "Terrorists in Iraq Killed At Least 68 More People," World News in Brief, *Christian Science Monitor,* 6 December 2004, p. 20.
94. ABC's Nightly News, 14 December 2004.
95. Paul Garwood, AP, "7 Marines Are Killed in Anbar," *Jacksonville (NC) Daily News,* 13 December 2004, pp. 1A, 6A.
96. Peterson, "Rebels Return to 'Cleared' Areas," p. 6.
97. Nick Wadhams, AP, "Fallujah Fighting Is Heavy," *Jacksonville (NC) Daily News,* 24 December 2004, pp. 1A, 4A.
98. Lee Keath, AP, "Chaos Grips Iraq," *Jacksonville (NC) Daily News,* 10 April 2004, p. 1A; Bassem Mroue and Abdul-Qader Saadi, AP, "Fighting Spreads in Iraq," *Jacksonville (NC) Daily News,* 8 April 2004, p. 6A; Hamza Hendawi, "Najaf Battle Grows," *Jacksonville (NC) Daily News,* 15 May 2004, p. 7A.
99. Dan Murphy, "High Stakes of Taking Fallujah," *Christian Science Monitor,* 8 November 2004, pp. 1, 10.
100. Tran, "Car Bomber, Troop Clashes Kill 27 in Iraq," p. 1A.
101. ABC's Nightly News, 22 Nov. 2005.
102. Tran, "Marines, Iraqis Launch Offensive," pp. 1A, 2A.
103. Reid, "Officials Rejecting Vote Delay for Iraqis," pp. 1A, 2A.
104. Tran, "Marines, Iraqis Launch Offensive," pp. 1A, 2A.
105. Tran, "Tape Targets Clerics," pp. 1A, 4A.
106. Michael, "Al-Zarqawi Cell Owns Up to Killings," pp. 1A, 6A.

107. Scott Peterson, "U.S. Heading into Major Urban Assault," *Christian Science Monitor,* 8 November 2004. pp. 1, 7.

108. Reid, "Rebels Cornered in City," pp. 1A, 4A.

109. Scott Peterson, "U.S. Forces Pour into Iraqi City," *Christian Science Monitor,* 10 November 2004, pp. 1, 10.

110. Edward Harris, AP, "Rebels Try to Escape Fallujah," *Jacksonville (NC) Daily News,* 12 November 2004, pp. 1A, 2A.

111. "In an Anti-Bush World, Key Backers." Global Views, *Christian Science Monitor,* 1 November 2004, p. 1; "Iranian Government Gives Backing to Bush," World Briefs Wire Reports (AP), *Jacksonville (NC) Daily News,* 20 October 2004, p. 10A.

112. Richard Clarke (former U.S. antiterrorism czar), interview by Peter Jennings, ABC's election day coverage, 2 November 2004.

113. ABC's Nightly News, 29 November 2004.

114. Reid, "Officials Rejecting Vote Delay for Iraqis," pp. 1A, 2A.

115. Kenneth Katzman, *Warriors of Islam: Iran's Revolutionary Guard* (Boulder, CO: Westview Press, 1993), p. 99.

116. Juan Cole, "The United States and Shi'ite Religious Factions in Post-Ba'thist Iraq," *Middle East Journal,* vol. 57, no. 4, autumn 2003, p. 554.

117. Dan Murphy, "Second Front in Iraq: Shiite Revolt," *Christian Science Monitor,* 6 April 2004, p. 10.

118. Dan Murphy, "No Wide Shiite Rally to Sadr's Forces," *Christian Science Monitor,* 7 April 2004, p. 4

119. Krane, "Occupied, Not Subdued," pp. 1A, 9A.

120. Peter Grier and Faye Bowers, "After the Fallujah Fight, Then What," *Christian Science Monitor,* 10 November 2004, pp. 1, 10.

121. Rick McDowell and Mary Trotochaud, "Humanitarian Aid Is a Casualty of Iraq," *Christian Science Monitor,* 23 November 2004, p. 7.

122. Lekic, "Attacks Pick Up in Iraq," p. 1A.

123. ABC's Nightly News, 6 January 2005.

124. Alexandra Zavis, AP, "Bombers Penetrate Security," *Jacksonville (NC) Daily News,* 15 October 2004, pp. 1A, 4A.

125. Barry Schweid, AP, "Explosions Pierce U.S. Safeguards in Baghdad," *Jacksonville (NC) Daily News,* 15 October 2004, p. 6A.

126. Maggie Michael, AP, "Iraq Sets Date for Election," *Jacksonville (NC) Daily News,* 22 November 2004, pp. 1A, 2A; ABC's Morning News, 25 November 2004.

127. Sameer N. Yacoub, AP, "Car Bombs in Baghdad, Mosul Kill 14," *Jacksonville (NC) Daily News,* 5 December 2004, pp. 1A, 2A.

128. NPR's Morning News, 14 December 2004.

129. Robin Wright and Peter Baker, "Iraq, Jordan See Threat To Election from Iran," *Washington Post,* 8 December 2004, p. A01.

130. Ibid.

131. Nick Wadhams, AP, "Cleric Leads List of Shi'ite Candidates, *Washington Times,* 11 December 2004.

132. "Iraqi Campaigning Has Begun," from AP, *Jacksonville (NC) Daily News,* 16 December 2004, p. 4A.

133. Ibid.

134. Annia Ciezadlo, "Intrigue, Power Plays as Iraq Campaign Season Starts," *Christian Science Monitor,* 16 December 2004.

135. Hala Jaber, "Go Home Yanks, Says PM In Waiting," *London Sunday Times,* 23 January 2004.

136. Bassem Mroue, AP, "Shi'ite Faction Eyes Prime Minister's Post," *Washington Times,* 3 February 2005.

137. NPR's Morning News, 14 December 2004.

138. Lekic, "Attacks Target Troops, Police," pp. 1A, 7A.

139. "Allawi: Insurgents Want Iraq Split by Civil War," from AP, *USA Today,* 21 December 2004, p. 7A.

140. Wadhams, "Iraqi Forces Hit Hard," pp. 1A, 2A.

141. Stojanovic, "Car Bombings Kill 25 in Iraq," p. 4A.

142. Ibid.

143. Dan Murphy, "Iraqi Police Take Brunt of Attacks," *Christian Science Monitor,* 11 January 2005, pp. 1, 7.

144. Ibid.

145. ABC's Nightly News, 28 January 2005.

146. ABC's Nightly News, 31 January 2005.

147. ABC's Nightly News, 29 January 2005.

148. Abdul Hussein Al-Obeidi, AP, "Car Bombs Hit Najaf, Karbala," *Jacksonville (NC) Daily News,* 20 December 2004, pp. 1A, 6A.

149. Dan Murphy, "Will Shiites Hold Their Fire," *Christian Science Monitor,* 22 December 2004, pp. 1, 10.

150. Dusan Stojanovic, AP, "Allawi: Sunni Insurgents Trying to Foment Civil War," *Jacksonville (NC) Daily News,* 21 December 2004, p. 4A.

151. Ibid.

152. "Allawi: Insurgents Want Iraq Split by Civil War," from AP, p. 7A; Cole, "The United States and Shi'ite Religious Factions in Post-Ba'thist Iraq," p. 554.

153. "Iraq's Most Feared Terror Chief Declared a Fierce War on Democracy," World News in Brief, *Christian Science Monitor,* 24 January 2005, p. 20.

154. Marion Fam, AP, "Terror Leader's Tape Sees Insurgent Victory," *Jacksonville (NC) Daily News,* 21 January 2005, pp. 1A, 6A.

155. Rod Nordland and Christopher Dickey, "Tribe Versus Tribe," *Newsweek,* 24 January 2005, pp. 44, 45.

156. "U.S. Iraq Say They're Closing on al-Zarqawi," from AP, *Jacksonville (NC) Daily News,* 7 May 2005, p. 4A.

157. Slobodan Lekic, AP, "15 Killed in Blast, Key Shiite Survives Assassination Try," *Jacksonville (NC) Daily News,* 28 December 2004, p. 6A.

158. Babak Dehghanpisheh, Melinda Liu, and Rod Nordland, "We Are Your Martyrs," *Newsweek,* 19 April 2004, pp. 39-41.

159. Ibid., p. 39.

160. "Terrorists Struck Close to Iraq's Highest Ranking Muslim Cleric," World News in Brief, *Christian Science Monitor,* 14 January 2005, p. 20.

161. Sameer N. Yacoub, AP, "Suicide Bomber Hits Shiite Party Offices," *Jacksonville (NC) Daily News,* 19 January 2005, pp. 1A, 2A.

162. Hamza Hendawi, AP, "Iraqis Begin Voting," *Jacksonville (NC) Daily News,* 30 January 2005, pp. 1A, 8A; ABC's Nightly, 3 February 2005.

163. ABC's Nightly News, 2 February 2005.

164. Scott Peterson, "Iraqis Crowd the Polls," *Christian Science Monitor,* 31 January 2005, pp. 1, 10.

165. "How Iraq's Election Will Work," Briefing, *Christian Science Monitor,* 28 January 2005, p. 10.

166. Hendawi, "Iraqis Begin Voting," pp. 1A, 8A.

167. ABC's Nightly News, 2 February 2005.

168. Bassem Mroue, AP, "Insurgents Launch Wave of Attacks," *Jacksonville (NC) Daily News,* 4 February 2005, pp. 1A, 7A.

169. Marion Fam, AP, "Kurdish Ticket Pulls into Second," *Jacksonville (NC) Daily News,* 8 February 2004, p. 3A.

170. Jamie Tarabay, AP, "Insurgents Use Human Bombs," *Jacksonville (NC) Daily News,* 9 February 2005, p. 1A.

171. Marion Fam, AP, "Violence Claims More Than 40 Lives in Iraq," *Jacksonville (NC) Daily News,* 11 February 2005, p. 5A.

172. Ali Al-Fatlawi, AP, "At Least 115 Die in Worst Attack Yet," *Jacksonville (NC) Daily News,* 1 March 2005.

173. Patrick Quinn, AP, "Iraqi Legislators Are Sworn In," *Jacksonville (NC) Daily News,* 17 March 2005, p. 1A.

174. "Insurgent Attacks Continue 2 Years after the U.S. Invasion," *Los Angeles Times,* 20 March 2005.

175. Rawya Rageh, AP, "Bloodshed Goes On As Iraq War Enters 3rd Year," *Jacksonville (NC) Daily News,* 21 March 2004, p. 2A.

176. "Suicide Bomber Kills 5 in Iraq," from AP, *Jacksonville (NC) Daily News,* 1 April 2005, p. 6A.

177. Marion Fam, AP, "Two Years Later, Protests Set for Baghdad Square," *Jacksonville (NC) Daily News,* 9 April 2005, p. 5A; NPR's Morning News, 11 April 2005.

178. "Tens of Thousands of Supporters of Militant Shiite Cleric," World News in Brief, *Christian Science Monitor,* 11 April 2005, p. 20.

179. Jaber, "Go Home Yanks, Says PM In Waiting."

180. Abdul Hussein al-Obeidi, AP, "Iraqi Shiites Stage Anti-American Rallies," *Jacksonville (NC) Daily News,* 21 May 2005, p. 4A.

181. "Tens of Thousands of Supporters of Militant Shiite Cleric," p. 20.

182. Tracy Carl, AP, "Iraqi Parliament Prepares to Pick President," *Jacksonville (NC) Daily News,* 6 April 2005, p. 4A.

183. Thomas Wagner, AP, "Iraq Insurgents Launch Series of Bombings," *Jacksonville (NC) Daily News,* 30 April 2005, p. 4A.

184. Thomas Wagner, AP, "Iraqi Leaders Try for an 11th Hour Political Deal," *Jacksonville (NC) Daily News,* 3 May 2005, p. 4A.

185. Alexandra Zavis, AP, "Another Day of Bombings, Firefights in Iraq," *Jacksonville (NC) Daily News,* 12 May 2005, p. 4A.

186. Patrick Quinn, AP, "Insurgents Kill 5 Marines in Western Iraq," *Jacksonville (NC) Daily News,* 11 June 2005, p. 4A.

187. Robert H. Reid, AP, "At Least 26 Die in Iraqi Suicide Bombings," *Jacksonville (NC) Daily News,* 3 July 2005, p. 4A.

188. Robert H. Reid, AP, "Bomb Kills 54 in Iraq," *Jacksonville (NC) Daily News,* 17 July 2005, pp. 1A, 7A.

189. Janaki Kremmer, AP, "Australia Dips Toe Back into Afghan Effort," *Christian Science Monitor,* 22 July 2005, p. 4.

190. Bassem Mroue, AP, "Amid Violence, Iraqi Democracy Nears Impasse," *Jacksonville (NC) Daily News,* 31 July 2005, p. 4A; ABC's Morning News, 7 September 2005.

191. Murtada Faraj, AP, "Car Bombs Kill 18 on Baghdad Street," *Jacksonville (NC) Daily News,* 15 April 2005, p. 6A.

192. NPR's Morning News, 27 April 2005.

193. Scott Peterson, "Iraq's Religious Factions Make Calls for Restraint," *Christian Science Monitor,* 23 May 2005, pp. 1, 10; NPR's Morning News, 28 April 2005.

194. Alexandra Zavis, AP, "Iraqi Leaders Have Formed Government," *Jacksonville (NC) Daily News,* 29 April 2005, p. 4A.

195. ABC's Nightly News, 29 April 2005.

196. ABC's Nightly News, 11 May 2005.

197. Alexandra Zavis, AP, "Suicide Bombers Strike in Central Baghdad," *Jacksonville (NC) Daily News,* 8 May 2005, p. 4A; Thomas Wagner, AP, "Insurgent Attacks Kill 7 American Troops in Iraq," *Jacksonville (NC) Daily News,* 9 May 2005, p. 4A.

198. NBC's Nightly News, 15 May 2005.

199. Scott Peterson, "Iraq Starts Battle over Constitution," *Christian Science Monitor,* 16 May 2005, pp. 1, 10.

200. Scott Peterson, "Iran Flexes Its 'Soft Power' in Iraq," *Christian Science Monitor,* 20 May 2005, p. 6.

201. Jacob Silberberg, AP "Iraqi, U.S. Troops Hit Insurgent Stronghold," *Jacksonville (NC) Daily News,* 11 September 2005, p. 7A.

202. Jacob Silberberg, AP, "Militants Flee Tal Afar in Wake of U.S.-Iraqi Offensive," *Jacksonville (NC) Daily News,* 12 September 2005, p. 3A.
203. Antonio Castaneda, AP, "Marines Capture Weapons in Iraq," *Jacksonville (NC) Daily News,* 5 June 2005, p. 1A.
204. Tom Lasseter, Knight Ridder, "Iraqi Forces May Need Years of Preparation," *Jacksonville (NC) Daily News,* 28 August 2005, p. 5A.
205. Steven Vincent, "Shiites Bring Rigid Piety to Iraq's South," *Christian Science Monitor,* 13 July 2005; Steven Vincent, "Switched Off in Basra," *New York Times,* 31 July 2005.

Chapter 2: *The Iraqi Insurgents' Tactical Methods*

1. Patrick Quinn, AP, "Iraqi Leader Wants to Keep Job," *Jacksonville (NC) Daily News,* 24 February 2005, p. 4A.
2. ABC's Nightly News, 24 November 2004.
3. NPR's Morning News, 15 November 2004.
4. Katarina Kratovac, AP, "Marines Say Clearing Fallujah of Arms Hinders Civilian Return," *Jacksonville (NC) Daily News,* 25 November 2004, p. 4A; ABC's Nightly News, 24 November 2004.
5. ABC's Morning News, 23 November 2004.
6. Krane, "Occupied, Not Subdued," pp. 1A, 9A.
7. Tran, "Insurgents Hit Mosul Police Stations," p. 1A.
8. NPR's Morning News, 15 November 2004.
9. Peterson, "Marine, Insurgent Tactics Evolve," p. 6.
10. ABC's Nightly News, 4 December 2004.
11. "Four Israeli Soldiers Die in Explosion," World Briefs Wire Reports (AP), *Jacksonville (NC) Daily News,* 13 December 2004, p. 5A.
12. "Militants Target Israeli Army Outpost," from AP, *USA Today,* 27 June 2004.
13. "Hundreds of Russians Guarding Bushehr Reactor," *Geostrategy-Direct,* week of 8 March 2005.
14. Edward Harris, AP, "U.S. Military Guards Discover Escape Attempt at Camp Bucca," *AOL News,* 26 March 2005.
15. Joseph C. Goulden, *Korea: The Untold Story of the War* (New York: Times Books, 1982), p. 295.
16. Scott Peterson, "New Rebel Tactics Emerge in Fallujah," *Christian Science Monitor,* 12 November 2004, pp. 1, 10.
17. Dan Murphy, "In Iraq with 'Reservists That Fight'," *Christian Science Monitor,* 24 March 2005, p. 4.
18. Peterson, "Marine, Insurgent Tactics Evolve," p. 6.
19. Kratovac, "Marines Say Clearing Fallujah of Arms Hinders Civilian Return," p. 4A.
20. ABC's Nightly News, 7 October 2005.

21. Murphy, "In Iraq with 'Reservists That Fight'," p. 4.
22. Peterson, "Marine, Insurgent Tactics Evolve," pp. 1, 6.
23. Ibid.
24. Ibid.
25. Peterson, "Rebels Return to 'Cleared' Areas," p. 6.
26. E-mail from wilsongi@aol.com in December 2004.
27. Peterson, "Rebels Return to 'Cleared' Areas," p. 6.
28. Ibid.
29. Ibid.
30. "A Sgt., a Cpl., and Two L.Cpl.'s Eye View of the Fallujah Battle," purported excerpt from 3d Bn., 5th Marines "Lessons-Learned," as sent to internet circle MILINET by majusmcret@aol.com on 8 March 2005. (This work will henceforth be cited as "A Sgt., a Cpl., and Two L.Cpl.'s Eye View.")
31. Ibid.
32. ABC's Nightly News, 14 December 2004.
33. Scott Peterson, "U.S. Smooths Way in Fallujah for Muslim Relief Agency," *Christian Science Monitor,* 29 November 2004, p. 7.
34. Antonio Castenada, AP, "Marines on Offensive," *Jacksonville (NC) Daily News*, 11 May 2005, pp. 1A, 2A.
35. ABC's Nightly News, 29 December 2004, 6 January 2005.
36. Thomas Cristi, "Insurgents In Iraq Using Armor-Piercing Bombs," *Washington Times,* 8 January 2005.
37. Nick Wadhams, AP, "Iraq Insurgents Increase Explosives' Power," through access@g2-forward.org on 10 January 2005.
38. Robert H. Reid and Jim Krane, AP, "Bombs Biggest Killer for U.S. in Iraq," *Jacksonville (NC) Daily News*, 7 August 2005, pp. 1A, 4A; ABC's Nightly News, 3 August 2005.
39. Lester Grau, "For All Seasons: The Old But Effective RPG-7 Promises to Haunt the Battlefields of Tomorrow" (Fort Leavenworth, KS: Foreign Military Studies Office, n.d.).
40. Maj.Gen. Pete Chiarelli, CG, 1st Cavalry Div., comments at Ft. Hood AUSA dinner, as recorded by John Bell, Research Analysis and Maintenance Inc., on 14 March 2005.
41. Peterson, "Marine, Insurgent Tactics Evolve," p. 6.
42. Reid, "Rebels Spread Attacks," pp. 1A, 8A.
43. Tran, "Car Bomber, Troop Clashes Kill 27 in Iraq," p. 1A.
44. Fam, "Iraq's Sunni President Backs January Elections," p. 4A; "Nobody Lingers in 'RPG Alley'," from AP, *Jacksonville (NC) Daily News,* 2 December 2004, p. 4A.
45. ABC's Noon News, 15 February 2005.
46. "Top Five Most Deadly Tactics, Techniques, and Procedures (TTP's)" (Fort Leavenworth, KS: ADCSINT, TRADOC, 1 April 2005).
47. Ibid.

48. John J. Lumpkin, AP, "U.S. Official: Iraqi Forces Infiltrated," *Jacksonville (NC) Daily News,* 22 October 2004, p. 4A.

49. Wadhams, "Iraqi Forces Hit Hard," pp. 1A, 2A.

50. NPR's Morning News, 3 December 2004.

51. Eric Steinkopff, "MEU Goes After Weapons," *Jacksonville (NC) Daily News,* 8 December 2004, pp. 1A, 2A.

52. Al-Manar TV, 21 November 2003.

53. Christian Chaise, "Attack on U.S. Embassy Jeddah: How Done," from Middle East Media Research Inst., December 2004.

54. Faiza Saleh Ambah, AP, "Islamic Militants Hit U.S. Consulate," *Jacksonville (NC) Daily News,* 7 December 2004, pp. 1A, 4A; CBS's Nightly News, 6 December 2004.

55. Ibid.

56. Neil MacFarquhar, "Freed Captive Tells of Ordeal in Attack on Consulate in Jidda," *New York Times,* 8 December 2004.

57. CNN News, 7 December 2004.

58. ABC's Morning News, 6 December 2004; NPR's Morning News, 6 December 2004.

59. Faiza Saleh Ambah and Dan Murphy, "Attack Tests Saudi Security Strategy," *Christian Science Monitor,* 7 December 2004, pp. 1, 5.

60. NPR's Morning News, 3 April 2005.

61. ABC's Nightly News, 5 April 2005.

62. "Abu Ghraib Attack," official CENTCOM news release, 6 April 2005.

63. Marion Fam. AP, "Militants Again Strike at Abu Ghraib," *Jacksonville (NC) Daily News,* 5 April 2005, p. 6A.

64. Ibid.

65. "Bomb Attack," *USA Today,* 18 April 2005.

66. Cpl. Tom Sloan, "Marine Stops Enemy Attack, Saves Lives," *Camp Lejeune (NC) Globe,* 28 April 2005, p. 6A.

67. ABC's Nightly News, 26 December 2004.

68. Mark Mosher (U.S. serviceman in Iraq), in e-mail to author on 13 May 2005.

69. Ibid.

70. Mark Sexton (U.S. veteran of Iraq), in conversation with author on 24 May 2005; H. John Poole, *Tactics of the Crescent Moon: Militant Muslim Combat Methods* (Emerald Isle, NC: Posterity Press, 2004), pp. 36-39.

71. David H. Hackworth, "So-Called VIPs Jet-Setting at Taxpayer Expense," Liberty Sound Off, *Jacksonville (NC) Daily News,* 2 December 2004, p. 2C.

72. Lee Keath, AP, "Shiites Retreat in Najaf," *Jacksonville (NC) Daily News,* 13 April 2004, p. 2A.

73. Charles Crain, "U.S. Troops Battle al-Sadr Supporters in Najaf," *USA Today,* 13 August 2004, p. 6A.

74. Rawya Rageh, AP, "Iraqi Prime Minister Blames Coalition for Ambush," *Jacksonville (NC) Daily News,* 27 October 2004, pp. 1A, 6A.
75. Keath, "Shiites Retreat in Najaf," p. 2A.
76. Marion Fam, AP, "Complaints of Irregularities Emerge after Iraq's Election," *Jacksonville (NC) Daily News,* 6 February 2005.
77. ABC's Nightly News, 3 December 2004.
78. Patrick Quinn, AP, "Body of Reporter Found in Iraqi City," *Jacksonville (NC) Daily News,* 27 February 2005, p. 11A.
79. Awadh al-Taee and Steve Negus, "Cynicism Hits the Thirst for Iraq's Elections," *London Financial Times,* 22 January 2005.
80. Nick Wadhams, AP, "Insurgents Slay 17 Iraqi Civilians," *Jacksonville (NC) Daily News,* 6 December 2004, pp. 1A, 2A.
81. Howard Lafranchi, "Abductions in Iraq a Big Business." *Christian Science Monitor,* 15 September 2004.
82. Sameer N. Yacoub, AP, "Iraqi Leaders Try to End Impasse," *Jacksonville (NC) Daily News,* 26 April 2005, p. 3A.
83. "Shiite Radicals Join with Sunni Insurgents in Ramadi," *DEBKAfile* (Israel), 7 April 2004.
84. "Iran Role in the Recent Uprising in Iraq," Special Dispatch No. 692, 9 April 2004, from Middle East Media Research Inst.; Scott Peterson, "U.S. Pressure on Cleric Pushes Militants South," *Christian Science Monitor,* 10 May 2004, p. 4.
85. Cole, "The United States and Shi'ite Religious Factions in Post-Ba'thist Iraq," p. 543.
86. Art Theyson, "New Warfront Opens in Iraq Three Months before Handover," *DEBKAfile* (Israel), 5 April 2004.
87. Scott Peterson, "Shadows of Tehran over Iraq," *Christian Science Monitor,* 19 April 2004, pp. 1, 10.
88. Ann Scott Tyson, "Sadr's Militia Regrouping, Rearming," *Christian Science Monitor,* 15 July 2004, pp. 1, 7.
89. Abdul H. al-Obeidi, AP, "Holy City Najaf Fighting Worst Since Saddam Fell," *Jacksonville (NC) Daily News,* 7 August 2004, pp. 1A, 4A.
90. Dan Murphy, "Sadr Army Owns City Streets," *Christian Science Monitor,* 4 August 2004, pp. 1, 7, 10.
91. Memo for the record by H. J. Poole.
92. Peter Grier, "The Rising Economic Cost of the Iraqi War," *Christian Science Monitor,* 19 May 2004, pp. 1, 10.
93. Waleed Ibrahim and Mussab Khairallah, Reuters, "Suicide Policeman Hits Iraq's Wolf Brigade HQ," *Yahoo! News,* 11 June 2005.
94. Scott Johnson and Melinda Liu, "The Enemy Spies," *Newsweek,* 27 June 2005, pp. 24-29.
95. Yahya Barzanji, AP, "Marines Wrap Up Operation Spear," *Jacksonville (NC) Daily News,* 21 June 2005, p. 1A.
96. ABC's Nightly News, 16 June 2005.
97. ABC's Nightly News, 14 July 2005.

98. Neil MacDonald, "After Iraq Attacks, Calls for Militias Grow," *Christian Science Monitor,* 18 July 2005, pp. 6, 7.

Chapter 3: *The Iraqi Militants' Point of Origin*

1. Steven Stalinsky, "Arab and Muslim Fighters in Iraq," an excerpt from *Al-Nahar* (Lebanon) of 1 April 2003, in No. 19, 27 July 2003, by Middle East Media Research Inst.

2. "Syrian Agents Trained Iraqi-Bound Insurgents in Asymmetrical Warfare," *Geostrategy-Direct,* week of 8 March 2005.

3. Rod Nordland, Tom Masland, and Christopher Dickey, "Unmasking the Insurgents," *Newsweek,* 7 February 2005, pp. 24, 25.

4. Ibid.

5. ExO or CO of 2d Battalion, 7th Marines, in conversation with author during training evolution of 14, 15 January 2005.

6. "Iraqi Intelligence Service Chief Interviewed on Terrorism, Related Issues," *Al-Sharq Al-Awsat* (London), 5 January 2005, telephone interview of Maj.Gen. Muhammad Abdallah al-Shahwani, Dir. of Iraq's Nat. Intell. Service, by Mu'idd Fayyad on 4 January 2005.

7. "Hundreds of Russians Guarding Bushehr Reactor."

8. Michael Ware, "Inside Iran's Secret War for Iraq," *Time,* 22 August 2005.

9. Nicholas Blanford, "Hizbullah Reelects Its Leader," *Christian Science Monitor,* 19 August 2004, p. 6; Baer, *See No Evil,* in *Warring on Terrorism,* by Hughes, p. 35; Faye Bowers, "A Collaboration between al-Qaeda and Hizbullah . . . ," *Christian Science Monitor,* n.d., in *Warring on Terrorism,* by Hughes, p. 35.

10. C.J. Chivers, "Threats and Responses . . . ," *New York Times,* 13 January 2003, and "Here Is the Kurdish Al-Qaeda," *Financial Times Information,* 7 January 2003, in "Iraqi Wahabbi Factions Affiliated with Abu Musaab al Zarqawi," by Deanna Linder, Rachael Levy, and Yael Shahar, Internat. Policy Inst. for Counter-Terrorism, November 2004; Michael Rubin, "Ansar al-Sunna: Iraq's New Terrorist Threat," *Middle East Intelligence Bulletin,* vol. 6, no. 5, May 2004; "Translation of Ansar al-Sunna Army's 'Banners of Truth' Video," TIDES World Press Reports, in "Ansar al-Sunna," by Rubin; "Hizbullah Suspected of Joining Sunni Insurgents," *Iraqi News,* 17 February 2005, from www.iraqinews.com; "Top Iranian Defector On Iran's Collaboration with Iraq, North Korea, Al-Qa'ida, and Hizbullah," from Middle East Media Research Inst.

11. "Profile: Tawhid and Jihad Group," BBC News, 8 October 2004, in "Iraqi Wahabbi Factions Affiliated with Abu Musaab al Zarqawi," by Deanna Linder, Rachael Levy, and Yael Shahar, Internat. Policy Inst. for Counter-Terrorism, November 2004; Lafranchi, "Anti-Iran Sentiment Hardening Fast," pp. 1, 10.

12. "Shiite Radicals Join with Sunni Insurgents in Ramadi."

13. Faiza Saleh Ambah, AP, "Iraq: Spinning Off Arab Terrorists," *Christian Science Monitor,* 8 February 2005, p. 6.

14. "An Analysis of Foreign "Martyrs," in Iraq," from Terrorism Research Center, Inc., *Terror Web Watch Report,* 20 May 2005, item 1.

15. "Group Says Thousands Ready for Suicide Raids," Across the Region, *Daily Star* (Lebanon), 7 June 2004.

16. Ali Akbar Dareini, AP, "Iranian Organization Seeks Suicide Bombers," *Jacksonville (NC) Daily News,* 29 November 2004, pp. 1A, 2A; NPR's Morning News, 30 November 2004.

17. Dareini, "Iranian Organization Seeks Suicide Bombers," pp. 1A, 2A.

18. Romesh Ratnesar, "Can This War Be Won?" *Time,* 4 October 2004, pp. 35-37.

19. NPR's Morning News, 13 December 2004.

20. Kaveh L. Afrasiabi, "How Iran Will Fight Back," *Asia Times Online,* 16 December 2004.

21. "Annan: Syria Hasn't Departed Lebanon," World Briefs Wire Reports (AP), *Jacksonville (NC) Daily News,* 2 October 2004, p. 8A.

22. "Shiites March throughout Middle East," from AP, *Jacksonville (NC) Daily News,* 22 May 2004, p. 10A; "Hizbullah Offers to Pay Up to Five Times More for Suicide Attacks," Middle East Report, *Geostrategy-Direct,* week of 22 February 2005.

23. Rachel Ehrenfield, *Funding Evil: How Terrorism is Financed and How to Stop It* (Chicago: Bonus Books, 2005), in *Warring on Terrorism,* by Hughes, pp. 24-26.

24. Jason Keyser, AP, "Israel Bombs Syria," *Jacksonville (NC) Daily News,* 6 October 2003.

25. Ali Nouri Zadeh, *Al-Sharq Al-Awsat* correspondent, as quoted in "Iran Increases Funding and Training for Suicide Bombings . . . ," Special Dispatch Series, No. 387, 11 June 2002, Middle East Media Research Inst.

26. Zeina Karam, AP, "Lebanon Says It Has Arrested Country's Top Al-Qaida Operative in Bombing Plot," *Jacksonville (NC) Daily News,* 23 September 2004, p. 4A.

27. Nicholas Blanford, "Sealing Syria's Desolate Border," *Christian Science Monitor,* 21 December 2004, p. 6.

28. NBC's Nightly News, 6 December 2004.

29. ABC's Nightly News, 27 December 2004.

30. Nordland et al, "Unmasking the Insurgents," pp. 20-29.

31. American general on ABC's Nightly News, 19 June 2005; Patrick Quinn, AP, "AP Study: Iraqi Car Bombings Have Risen in Last Two Months," *Jacksonville (NC) Daily News,* 24 June 2005, p. 6A.

32. Antonio Castaneda, AP, "Funeral Blast Adds to Toll of Recent Days," *Jacksonville (NC) Daily News,* 2 May 2005, pp. 1A, 2A.

33. Ron Harris, St. Louis Post-Dispatch, "Marines Return to Violent City," *Jacksonville (NC) Daily News,* 19 April 2004, p. 5A.

34. Ron Harris, St. Louis Post-Dispatch, "5 Marines, Scores of Iraqis Die in Battle," *Jacksonville (NC) Daily News,* 18 April 2004, p. 4A; company commander in 3d Battalion, 7th Marines, in conversation with author during training evolution of 15, 16 January 2005.

35. Ibid.

36. Poole, *Phantom Soldier,* pp. 119, 120; Poole, *The Tiger's Way,* pp. 81-85.

37. Ambah, "Iraq: Spinning Off Arab Terrorists," p. 6.

38. Luke McIlveen, "Bounty Hunters Target Diggers," *Sydney Sunday Telegraph,* 12 December 2004.

39. George Jahn, "Iran May Be Stock-Piling High Tech Small Arms," from AP, 25 March 2005; Curt Anderson, AP, "Iranians Arrested in Bid to Buy Night Vision Gear, *Jacksonville (NC) Daily News,* 5 December 2004, p. 4A.

40. Mannes, *Profiles in Terror,* p. 160.

41. Nicholas Blanford, "More Signs of Syria Turn Up in Iraq," *Christian Science Monitor,* 23 December 2004, pp. 1, 10.

42. Robin Wright and Peter Baker, "Iraq, Jordan See Threat To Election from Iran," *Washington Post,* 8 December 2004, p. AO1; Rod Nordland, Tom Masland, and Christopher Dickey, "Unmasking the Insurgents," p. 24.

43. Dan Murphy, "Iraq's Critical Sistani Factor," *Christian Science Monitor,* 20 January 2005, pp. 1, 10.

44. Rod Nordland and Babak Dehghanpisheh, "What Sistani Wants," *Newsweek,* 14 February 2005, pp. 26, 27; Rod Nordland, "Free to Be Angry," *Newsweek,* 31 January 2005, p. 27.

45. "Captured Commander Says Iran [and] Syria Provided Funds [and] Equipment," *World Tribune,* Middle East Newsline, week of January 18, 2005.

46. Memo for the record by H.J. Poole.

47. Scott Peterson, "Hostile in Public, Iran Seeks Quiet Discourse with U.S," *Christian Science Monitor,* 25 September 2003, p. 7.

48. Faye Bowers, "Iran Shows New Willingness to Deal with U.S.," *Christian Science Monitor,* 24 October 2003, p. 3.

49. Dr. Robert Perry Bosshart (longtime resident of SE Asia and recent contract employee in Afghanistan), in e-mail to author of 28 December 2004.

50. Bowers, "Iran Shows New Willingness to Deal with U.S.," p. 3.

51. "Top Iranian Defector On Iran's Collaboration with Iraq, North Korea, Al-Qa'ida, and Hizbullah," from Middle East Media Research Inst.

52. Ibid.

53. Ibid.

54. Theyson, "New Warfront Opens in Iraq Three Months before Handover."

55. "Iran Role in the Recent Uprising in Iraq," from Middle East Media Research Inst.

56. "Iraq Shiite Leaders Demand Islam Be the Source of Law," Agence France-Presse (AFP), 6 February 2005.

57. Dan Murphy, "View Emerging of Shiite-Ruled Iraq," *Christian Science Monitor,* 7 February 2005, pp. 1, 10.

58. Dan Murphy, "Shiite Islamists to Shape the New Iraq," *Christian Science Monitor,* 14 February 2005, pp. 1, 10; photograph, Khamenei.jpg 177x236 pixels-8k, en.wikipedia.org/ wiki/Ali_Khamenei.

59. Maggie Michael, AP, "Likely Leader Vows Moderation," *Jacksonville (NC) Daily News,* 16 February 2005, pp. 1A, 5A.

60. Maggie Michael, AP, "Shiites to Vote on Chief," *Jacksonville (NC) Daily News,* 17 February 2005, pp. 1A, 6A.

61. Jamie Tarabay, AP, "Blast Kills Dozens in Iraq," *Jacksonville (NC) Daily News,* 19 February 2005, pp. 1A, 8A.

62. Dan Murphy and Jill Carroll, "A 'Pragmatic' Islamist for Iraq," *Christian Science Monitor,* 17 February 2005, p. 6.

63. Mahan Abedin, "The Supreme Council for the Islamic Revolution in Iraq (SCIRI)," *Middle East Intelligence Bulletin,* autumn 2003.

64. ABC's Nightly News, 27 February 2005.

65. Abedin, "The Supreme Council for the Islamic Revolution in Iraq (SCIRI)."

66. Babak Dehghanpisheh, Eve Conant, and Rod Nordland, "Iraq's Hidden War," *Newsweek,* 7 March 2005, pp. 24, 25.

67. Jalal Muhammad, "Hizb al-Khatf," Al-Majalla, 20 April 1988, from "Islamism in Lebanon: A Guide," by A. Nizar Hamzeh, in *Middle East Quarterly,* vol. 1, no. 3, September 1997.

68. Gary C. Gambill and Ziad K. Abdelnour, "Hezbollah between Tehran and Damascus," *Middle East Intelligence Bulletin,* vol. 4, no. 2., February 2002.

69. Sindbad Ahmed, AP, "Suicide Bombing Kills 47 People in Iraqi City," *Jacksonville (NC) Daily News,* 11 March 2005, p. 5A.

70. NPR's Morning News, 16 March 2005.

71. Quinn, "Iraqi Legislators Are Sworn In," p. 2A.

72. Marion Fam, AP, "Iraqi Parliament Elects Kurd as President," *Jacksonville (NC) Daily News,* 7 April 2005, p. 4A.

73. Dan Murphy and Jill Carroll, "Thorny Issues for Iraq Leaders," *Christian Science Monitor,* 8 April 2005, p. 6.

74. "Intel. Estimates on Size of Insurgency Are All Over the Map," Focus on Counter-Insurgency, *Geostrategy-Direct,* week of 1 March 2005.

75. Nordland and Dehghanpisheh, "What Sistani Wants," p. 30.

76. Christopher Dickey, Mark Hosenball, and Michael Hirsh, "Looking for a Few Good Spies," *Newsweek,* 14 February 2005, p. 30.

77. ABC's Nightly News, 17 April 2005.

78. Khalid Mohammed, AP, "Residents: Hostage-Taking a Hoax," *Jacksonville (NC) Daily News,* 18 April 2005, p. 2A; Hadi Mizban, AP, "Iraqi Forces Seek Insurgents in 'Triangle of Death'," *Jacksonville (NC) Daily News,* 19 April 2005, p. 3A.

79. Rod Nordland, "Just a Little Longer," *Newsweek,* 2 May 2005, p. 34.

80. ABC's Morning News, 21 April 2005.

81. Jill Carrol, "Iraq's Rising Industry: Domestic Kidnapping," *Christian Science Monitor,* 22 April 2005, p. 6.

82. Nordland, "Just a Little Longer," p. 34.

83. Ibid., p. 32.

84. ABC's Nightly News, 1 May 2005.

85. Abdul-Zahra, AP, "Iraq's Prime Minister Compiles Cabinet List," *Jacksonville (NC) Daily News,* 28 April 2005, p. 5A.

86. Ibid.

87. NPR's Morning News, 2-7 May 2005; Zavis, "Suicide Bombers Strike in Central Baghdad," p. 4A.

88. NPR's Morning News, 29 April 2005.

89. Castaneda, "Funeral Blast Adds to Toll of Recent Days," p. 1A; ABC's Morning News, 4 May 2005.

90. Wagner, "Iraqi Leaders Try for an 11th Hour Political Deal," p. 4A.

91. Neil MacDonald, "Could Bigger Sunni Role Stop Attacks," *Christian Science Monitor,* 6 May 2005, p. 1; NPR's Morning News, 8 May 2005.

92. Zavis, "Another Day of Bombings, Firefights in Iraq," p. 4A; ABC's Morning News, 13 May 2005.

93. Castenada, "Marines on Offensive," pp. 1A, 2A.

94. Sameer N. Yacoub, AP, "Suicide Car Bomber Kills at Least 22 People," *Jacksonville (NC) Daily News,* 25 July 2005, p. 4A.

95. Qassim Abdul-Zahra, AP, "Sunnis Say U.S., Shiites Making Constitution Deals," *Jacksonville (NC) Daily News,* 21 August 2005, p. 7A.

96. Scott Peterson, "Familiar Face Emerges in Iran Vote," *Christian Science Monitor,* 26 April 2005, p. 6.

97. Scott Peterson, "Iran Votes Hard-Liner into Runoff," *Christian Science Monitor,* 20 June 2005, pp. 1, 4; "Pragmatist Throws His Hat in the Ring," from Reuters, *Christian Science Monitor,* 11 May 2005, p. 4; Brian Murphy, AP, "Tehran Mayor Wins Spot in Presidential Runoff," *Jacksonville (NC) Daily News,* 19 June 2005, p. 5A; "Hardliner Wins Iranian Vote in Landslide," World Briefs Wire Reports (AP), *Jacksonville (NC) Daily News,* 25 June 2005, p. 6A; ABC's Nightly News, 27 June 2005; Babak Dehghanpisheh, "The Mullahs Win Again," *Newsweek,* 4 July 2005, p. 26; Peterson, "Familiar Face Emerges in Iran Vote," p. 6.

98. Vincent, "Shiites Bring Rigid Piety to Iraq's South," 13 July 2005.

99. Bassem Mroue, AP, "Iraqis Ready to Control Some Cities," *Jacksonville (NC) Daily News,* 13 July 2005, p. 6A.

100. Abbas Fayadh, AP, "U.S. Reporter Critical of Basra Police Is Abducted and Killed," *Jacksonville (NC) Daily News,* 4 August 2005, p. 4A.

101. Vincent, "Switched Off in Basra," *New York Times,* 31 July 2005.

102. Kremmer, "Australia Dips Toe Back into Afghan Effort," p. 4.

103. "Iran's Intelligence Service Occupies Key Iraqi City," *Iran Watch,* 4 September 2005; Dan Murphy, "Iraqis Thirst for Water and Power," *Christian Science Monitor,* 11 August 2005, pp. 1, 10.

104. Bassem Mroue, AP, "Iraqis Miss Third Constitution Deadline," *Jacksonville (NC) Daily News,* 26 August 2005, p. 4A.

105. Ibid.

106. Jill Carroll, "Iraq's Shiites Split Violently," *Christian Science Monitor,* 26 August 2005, pp. 1, 4; ABC's Nightly News, 26 August 2005.

107. Lawrence Pintak, *Seeds of Hate: How America's Flawed Middle East Policy Ignited the Jihad* (London: Pluto Press, 2003), pp. 313-314.

108. *Warfare in Lebanon, Warfare in Lebanon,* ed. Kenneth J. Alnwick and Thomas A. Fabyanic (Washington, D.C.: Nat. Defense Univ., 1988), pp. 71, 72.

109. Ibid., p. 71.

110. Ibid., p. 54.

111. Sepehr Zabih, *The Iranian Military in Revolution and War* (London: Routledge, 1988), pp. 210-212.

112. "Giving Thanks" photograph caption from AP, *Jacksonville (NC) Daily News,* 26 August 2005, p. 5A.

113. Lawrence Pintak, *Seeds of Hate,* p. 184.

114. Mannes, *Profiles in Terror,* pp. 127, 128.

115. Ibid., pp. 195, 329.

116. Blanford, "Hizbullah Reelects Its Leader," p. 6.

117. Peterson, "Shadows of Tehran over Iraq," pp. 1, 10.

118. "Hundreds of Russians Guarding Bushehr Reactor."

119. Mohammed Barakat, "U.S. Wraps Up Offensive Near Syrian Border," *Jacksonville (NC) Daily News,* 15 May 2005, p. 4A.

120. Poole, *Phantom Soldier,* pp. 114, 115, 144, 145; Poole, *The Tiger's Way,* pp. 119-124.

121. "In One of the Worst 24-Hour Periods for Terrorists in Iraq to Date," World News in Brief, *Christian Science Monitor,* 24 March 2005, p. 20; ABC's Nightly News, 21-23 March 2005.

122. Jacob Silberberg, AP, "Troops Press Fight," *Jacksonville (NC) Daily News,* 19 June 2005, pp. 1A, 2A.

123. Michael Rubin, "Ansar al-Sunna: Iraq's New Terrorist Threat," *Middle East Intelligence Bulletin,* vol. 6, no. 5, May 2004.

124. Deanna Linder, Rachael Levy, and Yael Shahar, "Iraqi Wahabbi Factions Affiliated with Abu Musaab al Zarqawi," Internat. Policy Inst. for Counter-Terrorism, November 2004.

125. Abedin, "The Supreme Council for the Islamic Revolution in Iraq (SCIRI)."

126. Lt.Col. (Ret., IDF) David Eshel, "Counterguerrilla Warfare in South Lebanon," *Marine Corps Gazette,* July 1997, p. 41.

127. Pintak, *Seeds of Hate,* pp. 113, 184.

128. Anthony H. Cordesman and Arleigh A. Burke Chair, "Iran's Developing Military Capabilities," working draft (Washington, D.C.: Center Strategic Internat. Studies, 14 December 2004), pp. 35-38.

129. ExO or CO, 2/7 conversation.

130. Eshel, "Counterguerrilla Warfare in South Lebanon," p. 41; Mannes, *Profiles in Terror,* p. 161.

131. Poole, *The Tiger's Way,* pp. 52-54; Dr. Ramadan Shalah, IRNA article, 22 May 2002, as quoted in *Warring on Terrorism,* by Hughes, p. 17.

132. Mannes, *Profiles in Terror,* p. 164.

133. Ibid., pp. 165, 330.

134. Ibid., p. 327.

135. Gunaratna, *Inside al-Qaeda,* p. 147.

136. Ehrenfield, *Funding Evil,* in *Warring on Terrorism,* by Hughes, p. 26.

137. "Report Al Qaeda members in Lebanon, " from AP, from Middle East Media Research Inst., September 2002.

138. Mannes, *Profiles in Terror,* p. 42.

139. Thomas E. Ricks, "U.S. Iraq Rebels Aided by Sources in Syria," *Washington Post,* 8 December 2004.

140. Matthew Levitt, "Sponsoring Terrorism Syria and Islamic Jihad," (Washington, D.C.: The Washington Inst. for Near East Policy, n.d.), as it appeared in *Middle East Intelligence Bulletin,* November-December 2003; Gary C. Gambill, "The Military-Intelligence Shakeup in Syria," and "Sponsoring Terrorism Syria and the PFLP-GC," *Middle East Intelligence Bulletin,* vol. 4, no. 2, February 2002.

141. Mannes, *Profiles in Terror,* p. 330.

142. Col. Mirri Eisen IDF, as quoted in "Sponsoring Terrorism Syria and Islamic Jihad," by Levitt.

143. Hughes, *Warring on Terrorism,* pp. 20-23.

144. Keyser, "Israel Bombs Syria"; "The Ayn Tzahab Training Camp in Syria."

145. Rowan Scarborough, "Israeli Warns of Terrorist Training Nov 03," *Washington Times,* 14 November 2003.

146. Mannes, *Profiles in Terror*, p. 330; Gary C. Gambill, "The Military-Intelligence Shakeup in Syria," *Middle East Intelligence Bulletin,* vol. 4, no. 2, February 2002.

147. "Iran Shifting Its Attention . . . ," *New York Times,* 13 December 1991, p. A7.

148. Mannes, *Profiles in Terror*, p. 21.

149. Interview, U.S. intelligence community, February 2000, in *Inside al-Qaeda,* by Gunaratna, p. 158.

150. Gunaratna, *Inside al-Qaeda,* p. 158.

151. Ibid., pp. 154, 158.

152. Ibid., p. 159.

153. Amir Mir, *The True Face of Jihadis* (Lahore: Maktaba Jadeed Press, 2004), p. 105.

154. Bill Gertz, "Yemen Hosts 4000 'Suspicious' Madrassahs Run by Extremists," *Geostrategy-Direct,* week of 22 February 2005.

155. "Top Iranian Defector On Iran's Collaboration with Iraq, North Korea, Al-Qa'ida, and Hizbullah," from Middle East Media Research Inst.

Chapter 4: *Developments in Afghanistan*

1. Barbara Slavin, "Iran Helped Overthrow Taliban, Candidate Says," *USA Today,* 10 June 2005, p. 14A.

2. "Iran Report," *Radio Free Europe/Radio Liberty,* vol. 5, no. 3, 28 January 2002; Halima Kasem, "Brewing Power Struggle in Kabul," *Christian Science Monitor,* 17 October 2003, p. 6; Pepe Escobar, "The Roving Eye," *Asia Times Online,* 15 November 2001.

3. Rahimullah Samander and Rahim Gul Sarwan, "Concern That Jihad Chieftains Will Set Political Agenda," Inst. for War and Peace Reporting, ARR No. 88, 18 December 2003.

4. Brigadier Mohammad Yousaf and Mark Adkin, *Bear Trap: Afghanistan's Untold Story* (South Yorkshire, UK: Leo Cooper, n.d.); John L. Esposito, *Unholy War: Terror in the Name of Islam* (London: Oxford Univ. Press, 2002), pp. 50, 51, 84.

5. Ibid.

6. Ali Jalali and Lester W. Grau, *Afghan Guerrilla Warfare: In the Words of the Mujahideen Fighters* (St. Paul, MN: MBI Publishing, 2001), first published as *The Other Side of the Mountain* (Quantico, VA: Marine Corps Combat Development Cmd., 1995), p. 295; Ibrahim, as quoted in *Afghan Guerrilla,* id., pp. 286-289.

7. "Iran Report," *Radio Free Europe.*

8. Jalali and Grau, *Afghan Guerrilla,* pp. 401, 409; Topkhana, as quoted in *Afghan Guerrilla,* id., p. 301.

9. Pepe Escobar, "The Roving Eye," *Asia Times Online,* 15 November 2001.

10. Stephen Graham, AP, "U.S. Says 2000 Insurgents Threaten Afghan Election," *Jacksonville (NC) Daily News,* 1 October 2004, p. 7A.

11. Scott Baldauf and Owais Tohid, "Aid Workers Increasingly a Target in Combat Zones," *Christian Science Monitor,* 5 November 2004, p. 7.

12. Pamela Constable, "Assignment Afghanistan," *Smithsonian,* February 2005, p. 123.

13. "Militants Hold Off Killing Hostages," World Briefs Wire Reports (AP), *Jacksonville (NC) Daily News,* 8 November 2004, p. 4A.

14. Baldauf and Tohid, "Aid Workers Increasingly a Target in Combat Zones," pp. 7, 11.

15. Kaplan, *Soldiers of God,* p. 18.

16. "Three Aid Workers Slain in Southern Afghanistan," News Brief Wire Reports, *Jacksonville (NC) Daily News,* 29 November 2004, p. 6A.

17. Lane Harthill, "Sifting Intelligence Tips from Vendettas in Afghanistan," *Christian Science Monitor,* 26 January 2005, p. 7.

18. Ibid.

19. Susanna Loof, "Report: Drugs Threaten Afghanistan, Iraq," from AP, 2 March 2005.

20. Constable, "Assignment Afghanistan," p. 121.

21. Jahn, "Iran May Be Stock-Piling High-Tech Small Arms."

22. Stephen Graham, AP, "U.S. Military Boosts Number of Troops Embedded in Afghan Military," *Jacksonville (NC) Daily News,* 21 February 2005, pp. 1A, 2A.

23. Scott Baldauf, "Afghanistan's New Jihad Targets Poppy Production," *Christian Science Monitor,* 16 May 2005, p. 7.

24. ABC's Nightly News, 16 March 2005.

25. Scott Wallace, "The Many Faces of Moslem Countries," *Christian Science Monitor,* 17 March 2005, p. 14.

26. Graham, "U.S. Military Boosts Number of Troops Embedded in Afghan Military," pp. 1A, 2A.

27. ABC's Morning News, 6 April 2005.

28. Stephen Graham, AP, "Americans Aboard Afghanistan Copter Crash," *Jacksonville (NC) Daily News,* 7 April 2005, pp. 1A, 2A.

29. ABC's Nightly News, 28 January 2005.

30. ABC's Nightly News, 3 May 2005.

31. Stephen Graham, AP, "Afghan Rebels Killed in Firefight," *Jacksonville (NC) Daily News,* 22 April 2005, p. 5A.

32. Scott Baldauf, "Taliban Coming In from Cold," *Christian Science Monitor,* 28 April 2005, pp. 1, 5.

33. Stephen Graham, AP, "4 Militants, 1 Afghan Soldier Killed in Border Clashes," *Jacksonville (NC) Daily News,* 25 April 2005, p. 8A.

34. ABC's Morning News, 4 May 2005.

35. "At Least 20 Militants Killed in Afghan Fighting," from AP, *Jacksonville (NC) Daily News,* 5 May 2005, p. 5A.

36. Ibid.

37. ABC's Morning News, 8 May 2005.

38. Yousaf and Adkin, *Bear Trap.*

39. ABC's Noon News, 4 May 2005.

40. Paul Haven, AP, "Being No. 3 Leader in al-Qaida Is a Risky Job," *AOL News,* 6 May 2005.

41. NPR's Morning News, 5 May 2005.

42. Robert Burns, AP, "Afghan Progress Is Cited," *Jacksonville (NC) Daily News,* 22 May 2005, pp. 1A, 7A.

43. Daniel Cooney, AP, "U.S. Kills 12 Insurgents in Afghanistan," *Jacksonville (NC) Daily News,* 23 May 2005, p. 4A.

44. "Two Insurgents Killed in Afghanistan Fight," World Briefs Wire Reports (AP), *Jacksonville (NC) Daily News,* 25 May 2005, p. 10A.

45. BBC News, 29 May 2005.

46. Daniel Cooney, AP, "Rocket Attacks Kills 2 Americans at Base in Afghanistan," *Jacksonville (NC) Daily News,* 9 June 2005, p. 4A.

47. "U.S. Soldier, 7 Militants Die in Afghan Firefight," World Briefs Wire Reports (AP), *Jacksonville (NC) Daily News,* 11 June 2005, p. 5A.

48. Cooney, AP, "Rocket Attacks Kills 2 Americans at Base in Afghanistan," p. 4A.

49. Noor Khan, AP, "Four American Soldiers Hurt in Afghanistan Blast," *Jacksonville (NC) Daily News,* 14 June 2005, p. 4A.

50. Noor Khan, AP, "Seven Medical Center Workers Killed in Afghan Violence," *Jacksonville (NC) Daily News,* 16 June 2005, p. 4A.

51. Pakistani TV News, 31 May 2005.

52. Noor Khan, AP, "Afghan Cops Abducted by Taliban," *Jacksonville (NC) Daily News,* 19 June 2004, p. 4A.

53. "76 Militants Die in Afghan Battles," World Brief Wire Reports (AP), *Jacksonville (NC) Daily News,* 23 June 2004. p. 5A.

54. Daniel Cooney, AP, "Violence Spikes in Afghanistan," *Jacksonville (NC) Daily News,* 26 July 2005, p. 6A.

55. "Suicide Bomber Kills Peacekeeper, Civilian in Afghan Capital," World Briefs Wire Reports (AP), *Jacksonville (NC) Daily News,* 28 January 2004.

56. "Suicide Bomber Kills 20 in Afghan Mosque Attack," World Briefs Wire Reports (AP), *Jacksonville (NC) Daily News,* 2 June 2005, p. 4A.

57. Amir Shah, AP, "Afghans Stone U.S. Base Gate," *Jacksonville (NC) Daily News,* 27 July 2005, p. 4A.

58. ABC's Morning News, 25 September 2005.

59. Scott Baldauf and Ashraf Khan, "New Guns, New Drive for the Taliban," *Christian Science Monitor,* 26 September 2005, pp. 1, 4.

60. Jeffrey Imm, "Some Bombs in Iraq Are Made in Iran, U.S. Says," *New York Times,* 6 August 2005.

61. Baldauf and Khan, "New Guns, New Drive for the Taliban," pp. 1, 4.

Chapter 5: *The Afghan Guerrillas' Tactical Trends*

1. Edgar O'Ballance, *Afghan Wars: Battles in a Hostile Land, 1839 to Present* (Karachi: Oxford Univ. Press, 2002), pp. 139, 160, 186.

2. "Afghan Drug Kingpin Arrested in New York," National Brief Wire Reports (AP) , *Jacksonville (NC) Daily News,* 26 April 2005, p. 5A; NPR's Morning News, 26 April 2005.

3. Musadeq Sadeq, AP, "Angry Afghans Riot . . . ," *Jacksonville (NC) Daily News,* 12 May 2005, p. 4A.

4. "The Indian Mutiny," by Sir Richard Temple, chap. 1 of *The World's Great Events,* vol. VII (1857-1904) (New York: P.F. Collier & Son Corp. 1944), pp. 1-7.

5. Scott Baldauf and Faye Bowers, "Afghanistan Riddled with Drug Ties," *Christian Science Monitor,* 13 May 2004, pp. 1, 11.

6. Ibid.

7. "Militants Kill Five Afghans Involved in Opium Project," World News Wire Reports (AP), *Jacksonville (NC) Daily News,* 19 May 2005, p. 5A.

8. "Six Afghans Die in Rebel Ambush," World News Wire Reports (AP), *Jacksonville (NC) Daily News,* 20 May 2005, p. 4A.

9. Ibid.

10. Neamatollah Nojumi, *The Rise of the Taliban in Afghanistan: Mass Mobilization, Civil War, and the Future of the Region* (New York: Palgrave, 2002), pp. 135, 136.

11. David Rohde and C.J. Chivers, "Al Qaeda's Grocery Lists and Manuals of Killing," the Jihad Files, *New York Times,* 17 March 2002.

12. Ibid.

13. H. John Poole, *Tactics of the Crescent Moon: Militant Muslim Combat Methods* (Emerald Isle, NC: Posterity Press, 2004), chap. 9.

14. Poole, *The Tigers Way,* chaps. 12, 19.

15. ABC's Nightly News, 28 June, 10 July 2005; ABC's Morning News, 29, 30 June 2005; Daniel Cooney, AP, "Military Reveals Details of Crash," *Jacksonville (NC) Daily News,* 7 July 2005, p. 4A.

16. Memo for the record by H.J. Poole.

17. "NATO Force Could Patrol Afghanistan," from AP, *Jacksonville (NC) Daily News,* 5 August 2005, p. 4A.

18. ABC's Morning News, 17 August 2005.

19. O'Ballance, *Afghan Wars,* p. 162.

20. Yousaf and Adkin, *Bear Trap.*
21. O'Ballance, *Afghan Wars,* p. 183.
22. Ibid., p. 164.
23. Ibid. p. 190.
24. Grau, "For All Seasons," pp. 1-8.
25. Ibid.
26. Aleksandr Sykholesshiy, "Artilleriya partisan," *Soldatudachi,* February 1996, p. 43, in "For All Seasons," by Grau, p. 2.
27. "Two Insurgents Killed in Afghanistan Firefight," p. 10A.
28. Memo for the record by H.J. Poole.
29. Cooney, "Rocket Attacks Kills 2 Americans at Base in Afghanistan," p. 4A.
30. Ibid.
31. O'Ballance, *Afghan Wars,* p. 145.
32. "Afghan Soldiers Fail to Assassinate Defense Minister," World Briefs Wire Reports (AP), *Jacksonville (NC) Daily News,* 11 September 2005, p. 7A.
33. O'Ballance, *Afghan Wars,* p. 124.
34. Noor Khan, AP, "10 Afghan Soldiers Beheaded by Taliban," *Jacksonville (NC) Daily News,* 11 July 2005, p. 3A.
35. Robin Batty and David Hoffman, "Afghanistan: Crisis of Impunity," *Human Rights Watch,* vol. 13, no. 3(c), July 2001, p. 25.
36. "NATO Force Could Patrol Afghanistan," from AP.
37. ABC's Morning News, 18 August 2005.
38. ABC's Nightly News, 21 August 2005.
39. Daniel Cooney, AP, "U.S., Afghan Forces Kill Dozens of Militants," *Jacksonville (NC) Daily News,* 23 August 2005, p. 3A.
40. Amir Shah, AP, "Bombing Kills 9 Afghan Soldiers," *Jacksonville (NC) Daily News,* 29 September 2005, p. 5A.

Chapter 6: *The Afghan Rebels' Base of Support*

1. O'Ballance, *Afghan Wars,* pp. 16, 131.
2. Ibid., p. 116.
3. Nojumi, *The Rise of the Taliban in Afghanistan,* p. 84.
4. Fr. Patrick Gaffney (recognized authority on the Middle East), in a letter to author on 29 August 2004; Brigadier Mohammad Yousaf, *The Silent Soldier: The Man behind the Afghan Jehad* (South Yorkshire, UK: Leo Cooper, n.d.
5. Nojumi, *The Rise of the Taliban in Afghanistan,* p. 85.
6. Yousaf and Adkin, *Bear Trap.*
7. O'Ballance, *Afghan Wars,* p. 116; Nojumi, *The Rise of the Taliban in Afghanistan,* p. 222; Gunaratna, *Inside al-Qaeda,* p. 17.
8. Gunaratna, *Inside al-Qaeda,* p. 17.

9. Yousaf and Adkin, *Bear Trap.*
10. Nojumi, *The Rise of the Taliban in Afghanistan,* p. 95.
11. Batty and Hoffman, "Afghanistan: Crisis of Impunity," p. 38, editorial footnote 171.
12. Ibid., pp. 35, 36.
13. O'Ballance, *Afghan Wars,* p. 159.
14. Ibid., pp. 234, 235.
15. Nojumi, *The Rise of the Taliban in Afghanistan,* p. 96.
16. O'Ballance, *Afghan Wars,* p. 214.
17. Ibid., p. 241; Nojumi, *The Rise of the Taliban in Afghanistan,* p. 115.
18. O'Ballance, *Afghan Wars,* p. 238.
19. Nojumi, *The Rise of the Taliban in Afghanistan,* p. 23.
20. O'Ballance, *Afghan Wars,* p. 242.
21. Ibid., pp. 242, 243.
22. Mir, *The True Face of Jihadis,* p. 130.
23. Nojumi, *The Rise of the Taliban in Afghanistan,* p. 179; Batty and Hoffman, "Afghanistan: Crisis of Impunity," p. 26.
24. Interviews with Western observers and a Taliban official in Kabul during 1999 and 2000, in "Afghanistan: Crisis of Impunity," by Batty and Hoffman, p. 23.
25. Batty and Hoffman, "Afghanistan: Crisis of Impunity," p. 35.
26. Interviews with a Taliban official in Kabul and diplomatic sources in Kabul, Islamabad and Washington, D.C., in late 2000; Ahmed Rashid, "Sanctions Will Hurt Pakistan More than Taliban," *The Nation* (Lahore), 23 November 2000; Robin Wright, "Taliban's Gains in Afghanistan Worry U.S.," *Los Angeles Times,* 2 October 2000; all in "Afghanistan: Crisis of Impunity," by Batty and Hoffman, p. 26.
27. Interview with senior Pakistani military officer at Lahore during June 1999, in "Afghanistan: Crisis of Impunity," by Batty and Hoffman, p. 28.
28. Interviews with Pakistani religious party recruits and Taliban prisoners during 1999, in "Afghanistan: Crisis of Impunity," by Batty and Hoffman, p. 29.
29. Ibid, pp. 29, 30.
30. Anwar-ul Haq Ahady, "Saudi Arabia, Iran, and the Conflict in Afghanistan," p. 125, from *Fundamentalism Reborn,* ed. Maley; Barnett R. Rubin, *The Search for Peace in Afghanistan* (New Haven: Yale Univ. Press, 1995), pp. 130, 172; "Massacres of Hazaras in Afghanistan," from *Human Rights Watch;* all in "Afghanistan: Crisis of Impunity," by Batty and Hoffman, pp. 36, 37.
31. E-mail with author of "How the Taliban Became a Military Force" during March 1999, and interview with a Tashkent based journalist during June 1999, and two U.N. reports of 1997, in "Afghanistan: Crisis of Impunity," by Batty and Hoffman, p. 38.

32. Batty and Hoffman, "Afghanistan: Crisis of Impunity," p. 37.

33. Ibid., pp. 39, 40.

34. O'Ballance, *Afghan Wars,* p. 252.

35. Ibid., p. 256.

36. Ibid., p. 253.

37. Ibid., p. 256.

38. Memo for the record from H.J. Poole.

39. NPR's Morning News, 16 November 2004.

40. "Pakistani Visa Instructions," as acquired at the Embassy of Pakistan in Washington, D.C. on October 2004.

41. Musharraf, "Speech at OIC Conference," *World Report,* CNN, 31 May 2005.

42. *Pakistan Country Study,* Area Handbook Series (Washington, D.C.: Library of Congress, 2003), pp. xxxv-xxxvii; Mir, *The True Face of Jihadis,* p. 43.

43. Mir, *The True Face of Jihadis,* p. 23.

44. Scott Peterson, "As Reformer Exits, Who Will Lead Iran," *Christian Science Monitor,* 17 June 2005, pp. 1, 7; *Pakistan Country Study.*

45. Musharraf, "Speech at OIC Conference."

46. Ibid.; Makhdoom Babar, "President Envisages Vibrant OIC to Face New Challenges," *Daily Mail* (Islamabad), 30 May 2005, pp. 1, 5.

47. Gretchen Peters and Aleem Agha, "Weary Taliban Coming In from the Cold," *Christian Science Monitor,* 14 December 2004, pp. 1, 7.

48. Gunaratna, *Inside al-Qaeda,* p. 206.

49. Ibid., pp. 40, 206; Ahmed Rashid, "Taliban Ready for 'Decisive' Push, *Daily Telegraph* (London), 22 July 1999, in "Afghanistan: Crisis of Impunity," by Batty and Hoffman, p. 32.

50. Sami Yousafzai and Ron Moreau, "Rumors of bin Laden's Lair," *Newsweek,* 8 September 2003, pp. 24-27; Nojumi, *The Rise of the Taliban in Afghanistan,* p. 226.

51. ABC's Nightly News, 17 June 2005; Escobar, "The Roving Eye."

52. "Domel Nisar," *Explore Pakistan,* from ContactPakistan.com; O'Ballance, *Afghan Wars,* p. 147.

53. Escobar, "The Roving Eye."

54. Mir, *The True Face of Jihadis,* pp. 21, 138.

55. Daniel Cooney, AP, "Top Taliban Commanders May Be with Afghan Rebels," *Jacksonville (NC) Daily News,* 24 June 2005, p. 8A; Gunaratna, *Inside al-Qaeda,* p. 40; Nojumi, *The Rise of the Taliban in Afghanistan,* pp. 117, 118.

56. Matthew Pennington, AP, "Pakistan Unsure If Target Is al-Zawahri," *Jacksonville (NC) Daily News,* 21 March 2004, p. 5A.

57. O'Ballance, *Afghan Wars,* p. 158; "DoD News Briefing—ASD PA Clarke and Rear Adm. Stufflebeem," 14 January 2002.

58. Jalali and Grau, *Afghan Guerrilla Warfare*, p. 409; Topkhana, as quoted in *Afghan Guerrilla*, id., p. 301.
59. Batty and Hoffman, "Afghanistan: Crisis of Impunity," p. 13.
60. Mir, *The True Face of Jihadis*, p. 138.
61. "Iran Report," *Radio Free Europe*.
62. Mannes, *Profiles in Terror*, p. 67.
63. *Patterns of Global Terrorism, 2003*.
64. Mir, *The True Face of Jihadis*, pp. 95, 96, 103.
65. Mariane Pearl, *A Mighty Heart: The Inside Story of the Al Qaeda Kidnapping of Danny Pearl* (New York: Scribner, 2003), pp. 72-74.
66. *Patterns of Global Terrorism, 2003*.
67. Mir, *The True Face of Jihadis*, p. 31.
68. Ibid., pp. 68, 104.
69. Gunaratna, *Inside al-Qaeda*, p. 40.
70. Mir, *The True Face of Jihadis*, p. 129.
71. Yousaf and Adkin, *Bear Trap*.
72. Brigadier Mohammad Yousaf, *The Silent Soldier: The Man behind the Afghan Jehad* (South Yorkshire, UK: Leo Cooper, n.d.
73. Yousaf and Adkin, *Bear Trap;* Jalali and Grau, *Afghan Guerrilla*, p. 409.
74. Yousaf and Adkin, *Bear Trap*.
75. Gunaratna, *Inside al-Qaeda*, p. 40.
76. Pearl, *A Mighty Heart*, p. 28.
77. "Al-Qaeda's New Front," *Frontline*, NC Public TV, 25 January 2005.
78. Mannes, *Profiles in Terror*, p. 22.
79. Robert D. Kaplan, *Soldiers of God: With Islamic Warriors in Afghanistan and Pakistan* (New York: Vintage Books, 1990), pp. 234, 235.
80. Jason Burke, "Waiting for a Last Battle with the Taliban," *The Observer* (UK), 27 June 1999.
81. Ahmed Rashid, "Pakistan, the Taliban and the US," Feature Story, *The Nation* (Lahore), 8 October 2001.
82. Gunaratna, *Inside al-Qaeda*, p. 167.
83. Ami Ayalon, ed., *Middle East Contemporary Survey* (Boulder, CO: Westview Press, 1991), p. 184.
84. Stephen Graham, AP, "Latest Assault Leaves 2 Brits, Afghan Interpreter Dead," *Jacksonville (NC) Daily News*, 6 May 2004, p. 8A.
85. Jalali and Grau, *Afghan Guerrilla Warfare*, p. 409.
86. "Taliban Blamed for Deadly Afghan Resistance," World Briefs Wire Reports (AP), *Jacksonville (NC) Daily News*, 24 September 2003.
87. Pearl, *A Mighty Heart*, p. 72.
88. Jalali and Grau, *Afghan Guerrilla Warfare*, p. 409.

89. "Harakat ul-Mujahidin Reference Page," from www.military.com, 5 July 2004.

90. "Harakat ul-Mujahidin," *Patterns of Global Terrorism, 2002 Report* (Washington, D.C.: U.S. Dept. of State, April 2003).

91. Pearl, *A Mighty Heart,* p. 73.

92. "Redesignation of Foreign Terrorist Organizations," Public Notice 4561 (Washington, D.C.: U.S. Dept. of State, 2003), from www.fas.org. (This work will henceforth be cited as "Redesignation of Foreign Terrorist Organizations.")

93. "CIA Factbook 19 Oct 2004 for Pakistan," from *Patterns of Global Terrorism, 2003.* (This work will henceforth be cited as "CIA Factbook.")

94. Pearl, *A Mighty Heart,* pp. 72, 73.

95. Ibid., pp. 73, 74.

96. Mannes, *Profiles in Terror,* p. 18.

97. *Pakistan Country Study,* sec. 7. of 64.

98. Yousaf, *The Silent Soldier;* Gaffney letter; Mannes, *Profiles in Terror,* p. 18.

99. John L. Esposito, *Unholy War: Terror in the Name of Islam* (London: Oxford Univ. Press, 2002), pp. 50, 51, 84.

100. Yousaf and Adkin, *Bear Trap.*

101. Mir, *The True Face of Jihadis,* p. 282.

102. Nojumi, *The Rise of the Taliban in Afghanistan,* p. 119.

103. *Pakistan Country Study;* Tran, "Tape Targets Clerics," pp. 1A, 4A.

104. *Pakistan Country Study,* sec. 7 of 64.

105. Nojumi, *The Rise of the Taliban in Afghanistan,* pp. 101, 189.

106. Esposito, *Unholy War,* pp. 15-17.

107. Graham, "Latest Assault Leaves 2 Brits, Afghan Interpreter Dead," p. 8A.

108. Pennington, "Pakistan Unsure If Target Is al-Zawahri," p. 5A.

109. Mir, *The True Face of Jihadis,* pp. 341-344.

110. Jalali and Grau, *Afghan Guerrilla Warfare,* p. 410.

111. *Pakistan Country Study,* sec. 1 of 64, 5 of 64.

112. Mannes, *Profiles in Terror,* p. 24.

113. Ibid., p. 66.

114. *Patterns of Global Terrorism, 2003.*

115. Ibid.

116. Ibid.

117. Carlotta Gall, "Pakistan Allows Taliban to Train, a Detained Fighter Says." *New York Times,* 4 August 2004.

118. Mannes, *Profiles in Terror,* p. 66.

119. *Patterns of Global Terrorism, 2003.*

120. "Jaish, Harkat Change Names: Report," from PTI (Pakistan), as posted at www.rediff.com on 12 March 2003.
121. *Patterns of Global Terrorism, 2003.*
122. *Jaish e-Mohammed* profile, *Global Security News & Reports,* Overseas Security Advisor Council, from its website, www.ds-osac.org; Danny Pearl, as quoted in *A Mighty Heart,* by Mariane Pearl, p. 75; Pearl, *A Mighty Heart,* p. 74.
123. Wadhams, "Insurgents Slay 17 Iraqi Civilians," pp. 1A, 2A.
124. Mir, *The True Face of Jihadis,* p. 218.
125. "Crackdown against Banned Groups Underway in Pakistan," from IRNA, as posted at www.globalsecurity.org on 21 November 2003; *Jaish e-Mohammed* profile, *Global Security News & Reports.*
126. Pearl, *A Mighty Heart,* p. 26.
127. "Harakat ul-Jihad-I-Islami (HUJI) entry," from Federation of American Scientists website, www.fas.org.
128. *Patterns of Global Terrorism, 2003;* "Iran Report," *Radio Free Europe.*
129. "Harakat-ul Mujahideen Al Alami (HMA) entry," Memorial Inst. for the Prevention of Terrorism (MIPT) Knowledge Base, U.S. Dept. of Homeland Security, 24 July 2005. (This work will henceforth be cited as HMA entry, MIPT.)
130. Mir, *The True Face of Jihadis,* p. 31.
131. HMA entry, MIPT.
132. Mannes, *Profiles in Terror,* p. 67.
133. Mir, *The True Face of Jihadis,* p. 105.
134. *Patterns of Global Terrorism, 2003.*
135. K.J.M. Varma, "PoK Also Banns Jihadi Outfits," from PTI (Pakistan), as posted at www.rediff.com on 5 December 2003.
136. Mir, *The True Face of Jihadis,* pp. 103, 104.
137. Ibid., pp. 183, 184.
138. *Patterns of Global Terrorism, 2003.*
139. Mir, *The True Face of Jihadis,* pp. 123-135; Nojumi, *The Rise of the Taliban in Afghanistan,* p. 128.
140. "Crackdown against Banned Groups Underway in Pakistan," from IRNA; Tariq Mahmood, AFP, "Hizbul Tahreer shout anti-US slogans," picture caption, as posted at uk.news.yahoo.com on 29 October 2004.
141. Mir, *The True Face of Jihadis,* p. 328.
142. Syed Saleem Shahzad, "The Remaking of al-Qaeda," *Asia Times Online,* 25 February 2005.
143. "CIA Factbook."
144. "Redesignation of Foreign Terrorist Organizations."
145. *Patterns of Global Terrorism, 2003.*
146. Ashraf Khan, "Voters Reverse Islamists' Rise in Pakistani Politics," *Christian Science Monitor,* 6 September 2005, p. 4.

147. "Harkat-ul Mujahideen Reincarnates as Jamiat-ul Ansar," as posted at pakistan-facts.com on 21 March 2003.

148. "Redesignation of Foreign Terrorist Organizations."

149. Owais Tohid, "Baloch Nationalism Rises As Pakistan Fights War on Terror," *Christian Science Monitor,* 26 January 2005, p. 7.

150. Ibid.

151. Owais Tohid, "'Talibanization' Fears in Pakistan," *Christian Science Monitor,* 13 April 2005, p. 6; Mir, *The True Face of Jihadis,* p. 184.

152. Zulfiqar Ahmad, "Intra-MMA Friction Swells over NSC," *Daily Mail* (Islamabad), 30 May 2005, pp. 1, 5; Mir, *The True Face of Jihadis,* p. 95; Ben Arnoldy and Owais Tohid, "Why Koran Is Such a Hot Button," *Christian Science Monitor,* 16 May 2005, pp. 6, 7.

153. Burke, "Waiting for a Last Battle with the Taliban"; Mir, *The True Face of Jihadis,* p. 29.

154. Cordesman and Chair, "Iran's Developing Military Capabilities," pp. 35-38.

155. Slavin, "Iran Helped Overthrow Taliban, Candidate Says," p. 14A.

156. "Iran Report," *Radio Free Europe.*

157. Carlotta Gall, "Afghan-Iranian Road Opens," *New York Times,* 28 January 2005.

158. Nojumi, *The Rise of the Taliban in Afghanistan,* pp. 176, 189, 198-201, 223.

159. ABC's Nightly News, 12 July 2005.

160. Mannes, *Profiles in Terror,* p. 163.

161. O'Ballance, *Afghan Wars,* pp. 253, 230.

162. Mir, *The True Face of Jihadis,* p. 20.

163. Ibid., p. 23.

164. Ibid., p. 129.

165. Ibid., p. 24.

166. *Patterns of Global Terrorism, 2003.*

167. Mir, *The True Face of Jihadis,* p. 118.

168. Owais Tohid, "Next Wave of Al Qaeda Leadership," *Christian Science Monitor,* 5 October 2004, pp. 1, 4.

169. Mir, *The True Face of Jihadis,* p. 33.

170. Mannes, *Profiles in Terror,* p. 19; Gunaratna, *Inside al-Qaeda,* pp. 19, 23.

171. O'Ballance, *Afghan Wars,* p. 172.

172. Gunaratna, *Inside al-Qaeda,* p. 19.

173. Ibid., pp. 31, 56.

174. Ibid., p. 42.

175. Ibid., p. 151.

176. Ibid., p. 22.

177. John K. Cooley, *Unholy Wars: Afghanistan, America, and International Terrorism* (n.p., n.d.), in *Pakistan: Behind the Ideological Mask*, by Khaled Ahmed (Lahore: Vanguard, 2004), p. 225.

178. Gunaratna, *Inside al-Qaeda*, pp. 23, 42.

179. O'Ballance, *Afghan Wars*, p. 158.

180. "DoD News Briefing—ASD PA Clarke and Rear Adm. Stufflebeem," 14 January 2002.

181. Bruce B. Auster, "The Recruiter for Hate," *U.S. News & World Report*, 31 August 1998, p. 49, from *Inside al-Qaeda*, by Gunaratna, p. 20.

182. Gunaratna, *Inside al-Qaeda*, p. 58; O'Ballance, *Afghan Wars*, p. 253.

183. Gunaratna, *Inside al-Qaeda*, p. 60.

184. Mir, *The True Face of Jihadis*, p. 95.

185. Gunaratna, *Inside al-Qaeda*, p. 207.

186. *Human Rights Watch* interviews with Pakistani volunteers and Taliban soldiers, in "Afghanistan: Crisis of Impunity," by Batty and Hoffman, p. 28.

187. Gunaratna, *Inside al-Qaeda*, pp. 207-215.

188. Mir, *The True Face of Jihadis*, pp. 24, 105.

189. Ibid., p. 96.

190. Ibid., p. 97.

191. Ibid., p. 101.

192. Ibid., p. 237.

193. Ibid., pp. 195-198.

194. Nojumi, *The Rise of the Taliban in Afghanistan*, p. 122.

195. Mir, *The True Face of Jihadis*, p. 21; Nojumi, *The Rise of the Taliban in Afghanistan*, p. 124.

196. Mark Rice-Oxley and Owais Tohid, "British Keep a Wary Eye on Pakistan," *Christian Science Monitor,* 27 July 2005, pp. 1, 4.

197. Batty and Hoffman, "Afghanistan: Crisis of Impunity," editorial footnote 24, p. 11.

198. Gunaratna, *Inside al-Qaeda*, p. 41.

199. Khaled Ahmed, *Pakistan: Behind the Ideological Mask* (Lahore: Vanguard, 2004), p. 223; Mir, *The True Face of Jihadis*, p. 21.

200. Nojumi, *The Rise of the Taliban in Afghanistan*, p. 228.

201. Sayyid A.S. Pirzada, *The Politics of the Jamiat Ulema-i-Islam Pakistan 1971-77* (Lahore: Oxford, 2000), p. 231.

202. Ahmed, *Pakistan*, pp. 223, 226.

203. Jalali and Grau, *Afghan Guerrilla Warfare*, p. 410; Gunaratna, *Inside al-Qaeda*, p. 40.

204. Nojumi, *The Rise of the Taliban in Afghanistan*, p. 122.

205. Ibid., p. 120.

206. Andrew North, "Stung in an Afghan 'Hornets' Nest," BBC News, July 2005.

207. Varma, "PoK Also Banns Jihadi Outfits."
208. Rice-Oxley and Tohid, "British Keep a Wary Eye on Pakistan," p. 4.
209. "Harkat-ul Mujahideen Reincarnates as Jamiat-ul Ansar."
210. Ahmed, *Pakistan,* p. 223.

Chapter 7: *Stratagems When in a Superior Position*

1. Poole, *Phantom Soldier,* chap. 3.
2. *The Wiles of War,* comp. and trans. Sun Haichen (Beijing: Foreign Languages Press, 1991), pp. 1, 2. (This work will henceforth be cited as *The Wiles of War.)*
3. Ibid., p. 1.
4. *The Wiles of War,* pp. 1, 2.
5. *36 Stratagems: Secret Art of War,* trans. Koh Kok Kiang and Liu Yi (Singapore, Asiapac Books, 1992), p. 7. (This work will henceforth be cited as *36 Stratagems.)*
6. Stefan H. Verstappen, *The Thirty-Six Strategies of Ancient China* (San Francisco: China Books & Periodicals, 1999), p. 3.
7. Ibid, p. 9.
8. *The Wiles of War,* p. 10.
9. *The Wiles of War,* p. 10.
10. Sun Zi, quoted in *The Thirty-Six Strategies of Ancient China,* by Verstappen, p. 9.
11. *36 Stratagems,* pp. 25, 26.
12. Bing Fa Bai Yan, "Borrow," from *A Hundred War Maxims* (n.p., n.d.), quoted in *The Wiles of War,* p. 26.
13. S.L.A. Marshall, *The Soldier's Load and the Mobility of a Nation* (n.p., n.d.).
14. "A Sgt., a Cpl., and Two L.Cpl.'s Eye View."
15. Verstappen, *The Thirty-Six Strategies of Ancient China*, p. 15.
16. *An Introduction to Saudi Arabia*, as produced by McDonnel Douglas Services, Inc. (n.p., n.d.). (This work will henceforth be cited as *An Introduction to Saudi Arabia.)*
17. *36 Stratagems,* p. 20.
18. Ibid., p. 27.
19. Ibid., p. 33.
20. *The Wiles of War,* p. 35.
21. Sun Zi Bing Fa, *Art of War,* chap. 6 (n.p., n.d.), quoted in *The Wiles of War,* p. 38.
22. *36 Stratagems,* pp. 39, 40.
23. Ibid., p. 34.
24. Verstappen, *The Thirty-Six Strategies of Ancient China*, p. 23.

25. Sun Zi Bing Fa, *Art of War,* chap. 4 (n.p., n.d.), quoted in *The Wiles of War,* p. 45.
26. *36 Stratagems,* trans. Koh Kok Kiang and Liu Yi, p. 41.
27. Ibid., p. 47.

Chapter 8: *Stratagems for Confrontation*

1. Verstappen, *The Thirty-Six Strategies of Ancient China*, p. 34.
2. *36 Stratagems,* p. 50.
3. "A Company of Soldiers," *Frontline,* NC Public TV, 5 April 2005.
4. *The Wiles of War,* p. 60.
5. Slobodan Lekic, AP, "Truck Bomb Hits Italians at Iraq Base," *Jacksonville (NC) Daily News,* 13 November 2003, p. 1A.
6. Charles J. Hanley, AP, "Dozens Killed in Wave of Blasts," *Jacksonville (NC) Daily News,* 28 October 2003, p. 1A.
7. Charles J. Hanley, AP, "Attackers Burn, Loot Army Supply Train in Iraq," *Jacksonville (NC) Daily News,* 1 November 2003, p. 7A.
8. *The Wiles of War,* pp. 55, 56.
9. ExO or CO, 2/7 conversation.
10. Verstappen, *The Thirty-Six Strategies of Ancient China*, p. 31.
11. Fam, "Militants Again Strike at Abu Ghraib," p. 6A.
12. Tang Tai Zong Li Jing Wen Dui, *Li Jing's Reply to Emperor Taizong of Tang,* tome one (n.p., n.d.), quoted in *The Wiles of War,* p. 61.
13. *The Wiles of War,* p. 68.
14. *36 Stratagems,* p. 57.
15. Verstappen, *The Thirty-Six Strategies of Ancient China*, p. 35.
16. Sun Zi, quoted in *The Thirty-Six Strategies of Ancient China,* by Verstappen, p. 41.
17. *The Wiles of War,* pp. 77, 78.
18. Bing Fa Bai Yan, "Wait," from *A Hundred War Maxims* (n.p., n.d.), quoted in *The Wiles of War,* p. 78.
19. *36 Stratagems,* p. 70.
20. "Allawi: Insurgents Want Iraq Split by Civil War," from AP, p. 7A; Cole, "The United States and Shi'ite Religious Factions in Post-Ba'thist Iraq," p. 554.
21. Peterson, "Shadows of Tehran over Iraq," pp. 1, 10.
22. Baldauf, "Standoff Bolstered Sadr's Support," p. 4.
23. Verstappen, *The Thirty-Six Strategies of Ancient China*, p. 42.
24. *36 Stratagems,* p. 71.
25. *The Wiles of War,* p. 88.
26. *The Six Secret Teachings of Tai Gong* (n.p., n.d.), quoted in *The Thirty-Six Strategies of Ancient China*, by Verstappen, p. 45.

27. Bai Zhan Qui Fa, "Battle of Pride," from *A Hundred Marvelous Battle Plans* (n.p., n.d.), quoted in *The Wiles of War,* p. 89.

28. Verstappen, *The Thirty-Six Strategies of Ancient China*, p. 49.

29. *36 Stratagems,* pp. 80-82.

30. Lao Zi, quoted in *The Thirty-Six Strategies of Ancient China,* by Verstappen, p. 49.

31. Li Su, Tang Dynasty general, quoted in *The Wiles of War,* p. 97.

32. *36 Stratagems,* p. 83.

33. *The Wiles of War,* p. 106.

34. Jiang Yan, "Grasp Opportunity," from *The Art of Generalship* (n.p., n.d), quoted in *The Wiles of War,* pp. 106, 107.

35. *36 Stratagems,* p. 84.

36. Sun Zi, quoted in *The Thirty-Six Strategies of Ancient China,* by Verstappen, p. 53.

Chapter 9: *Stratagems for Attack*

1. Verstappen, *The Thirty-Six Strategies of Ancient China*, p. 59.

2. *36 Stratagems,* p. 90.

3. Qassim Abdul-Zahra, AP, "Troops Repel Insurgent Attacks," *Jacksonville (NC) Daily News,* 7 August 2005, p. 5A.

4. Sima Fa, *Law of Master Sima,* chap. 5 (n.p., n.d.), quoted in *The Wiles of War,* pp. 116, 117.

5. Wu Bei Ji Yao, *An Abstract of Military Works* (n.p., n.d.), quoted in *The Wiles of War,* p. 117.

6. *Mao Tse-tung: An Anthology of His Writings,* ed. Anne Fremantle (New York: Mentor, 1962), p. 71.

7. Michael Fabey, "Flying and Surviving the Unfriendly Skies," *Savannah Morning News,* 7 February 2005, p. 1A.

8. Verstappen, *The Thirty-Six Strategies of Ancient China*, p. 65.

9. Ibid., pp. 96, 97.

10. Ibid., p. 101.

11. Tou Bi Fu Tan, *A Scholar's Dilettante Remarks on War,* chap. 1 (n.p., n.d.), quoted in *The Wiles of War,* pp. 126, 127.

12. Sun Zi, quoted in *The Thirty-Six Strategies of Ancient China,* by Verstappen, p. 71.

13. Verstappen, *The Thirty-Six Strategies of Ancient China,* p. 71.

14. *36 Stratagems,* p. 102.

15. Bai Zhan Qi Fa, "Battle of Contest," from *A Hundred Marvelous Battle Plans* (n.p., n.d.), quoted in *The Wiles of War,* p. 134.

16. Jaber, "Go Home Yanks, Says PM In Waiting"; Tarabay, "Blast Kills Dozens in Iraq," pp. 1A, 8A.

17. Verstappen, *The Thirty-Six Strategies of Ancient China*, p. 76.

18. Sun Zi, quoted in *The Thirty-Six Strategies of Ancient China*, by Verstappen, p. 75.
19. *36 Stratagems*, p. 107.
20. Bai Zhan Qi Fa, "Battle of Extremity," from *A Hundred Marvelous Battle Plans* (n.p., n.d.), quoted in *The Wiles of War*, p. 143.
21. *36 Stratagems*, p. 111.
22. Ibid., p. 114.
23. *The Wiles of War*, comp. and trans. Sun Haichen, p. 151.
24. Ibid.
25. Bing Fa Bai Yan, "Abandon," from *A Hundred War Maxims* (n.p., n.d.), quoted in *The Wiles of War*, p. 153.
26. Verstappen, *The Thirty-Six Strategies of Ancient China*, p. 81.
27. Sun Zi, quoted in *The Thirty-Six Strategies of Ancient China*, by Verstappen, p. 81.
28. Sun Zi Bing Fa, *Art of War*, chap. 5 (n.p., n.d.), quoted in *The Wiles of War*, pp. 153, 154.
29. *36 Stratagems*, trans. Koh Kok Kiang and Liu Yi, p. 119.
30. Bai Zhan Qi Fa, "Battle of Necessity," from *A Hundred Marvelous Battle Plans* (n.p., n.d.), quoted in *The Wiles of War*, pp. 159, 160.
31. Hu Qian Jing, *Canon of the General* (n.p., n.d.), quoted in *The Wiles of War*, p. 160.
32. Verstappen, *The Thirty-Six Strategies of Ancient China*, p. 85.
33. Sun Zi Bing Fa, *Art of War*, chap. 11 (n.p., n.d.), quoted in *The Wiles of War*, p. 160.

Chapter 10: *Stratagems for Confused Cases*

1. *The Wiles of War*, p. 170.
2. *36 Stratagems,* p. 126.
3. ExO or CO, 2/7 conversation.
4. *36 Stratagems,* pp. 128-130.
5. Verstappen, *The Thirty-Six Strategies of Ancient China*, p. 91.
6. Wei Liao Zi, *Book of Master Wei Liao,* chap. 4 (n.p., n.d.), quoted in *The Wiles of War*, p. 172.
7. Verstappen, *The Thirty-Six Strategies of Ancient China*, p. 97.
8. *36 Stratagems,* p. 130.
9. *The Six Secret Teachings of the Tai Gong* (n.p., n.d.), quoted in *The Thirty-Six Strategies of Ancient China*, by Verstappen, p. 97.
10. Tou Bi Fu Tan, *A Scholar's Dilettante Remarks on War,* chap. 8 (n.p., n.d.), quoted in *The Wiles of War*, p. 179.
11. *36 Stratagems*, p. 132.
12. Verstappen, *The Thirty-Six Strategies of Ancient China*, p. 103.
13. *36 Stratagems*, p. 136.

14. *The Wiles of War,* p. 190.
15. *36 Stratagems,* p. 140.
16. *The Wiles of War,* p. 189.
17. *36 Stratagems,* p. 141.
18. Mushashi Miyamoto, Book *of Five Rings* (n.p., n.d.), quoted in *The Thirty-Six Strategies of Ancient China,* by Verstappen, p. 109.
19. ABC's Nightly News, 29 December 2004.
20. *The Wiles of War,* p. 196.
21. *36 Stratagems,* p. 148.
22. Verstappen, *The Thirty-Six Strategies of Ancient China,* p. 113.
23. *The Wiles of War,* comp. and trans. Sun Haichen, p. 206.
24. Ibid., p. 205.
25. ABC's Nightly News, 28 April 2005.
26. Verstappen, *The Thirty-Six Strategies of Ancient China,* p. 117.
27. *36 Stratagems,* p. 153.
28. Ibid., p. 159.

Chapter 11: *Stratagems for Gaining Ground*

1. Tom Lasseter, Knight Ridder, "Marines Hunt Insurgents," *Jacksonville (NC) Daily News,* 6 August 200, pp. 1A, 2A.
2. Verstappen, *The Thirty-Six Strategies of Ancient China,* p. 123.
3. *The Wiles of War,* p. 220.
4. *36 Stratagems,* p. 162.
5. *The Wiles of War,* p. 220; *36 Stratagems,* p. 163.
6. Guilherme "Bill" Pereira (DoD contract employee in Iraq), in telephone conversation with author on 28 June 2004.
7. *36 Stratagems,* p. 166
8. Scott Peterson, "U.S. Smooths Way in Fallujah for Muslim Relief Agency," *Christian Science Monitor,* 29 November 2004, p. 7.
9. Mosher e-mail.
10. Verstappen, *The Thirty-Six Strategies of Ancient China,* p. 129.
11. *36 Stratagems,* p. 171.
12. Ibid., p. 172.
13. Ibid., p. 178.
14. *The Wiles of War,* p. 242.
15. Bing Lei, *Essentials of War,* chap. 9 (n.p., n.d.), quoted in *The Wiles of War,* p. 243.
16. Verstappen, *The Thirty-Six Strategies of Ancient China,* p. 135.
17. Ibid., p. 141.
18. *The Wiles of War,* p. 251.
19. Sun Zi, quoted in *The Thirty-Six Strategies of Ancient China,* by Verstappen, p. 141.
20. Poole, *Tactics of the Crescent Moon,* pp. 119-121.

21. *36 Stratagems,* p. 179.
22. Ibid., pp. 180, 181.
23. *The Wiles of War,* p. 252.
24. *36 Stratagems,* p. 184.
25. Ibid., p. 188.
26. Ford, "A Suspect Emerges As Key Link in Terror Chain,"
pp. 1, 7.
27. John J. Lumpkin, AP, "Source: Top Terrorist Suspect Eluded
U.S. Military," *Jacksonville (NC) Daily News,* 27 April 2005, p. 7A.
28. Verstappen, *The Thirty-Six Strategies of Ancient China*, p. 147.
29. Bing Fa Bai Yan, "Display," from *A Hundred War Maxims*
(n.p., n.d.), quoted in *The Wiles of War,* p. 262.
30. Tou Bi Fu Tan, *A Scholar's Dilettante Remarks on War,*
chap. 10 (n.p., n.d.), quoted in *The Wiles of War,* pp. 262-264.
31. Ibid.
32. Bing Lei, *Essentials of War,* chap. 19 (n.p., n.d.), quoted in *The
Wiles of War,* p. 262.
33. *36 Stratagems,* trans. Koh Kok Kiang and Liu Yi, p. 195.
34. Verstappen, *The Thirty-Six Strategies of Ancient China*, p. 153.
35. *The Wiles of War,* p. 274.
36. *36 Stratagems,* p. 189.
37. Lao Zi, quoted in *The Thirty-Six Strategies of Ancient China*,
by Verstappen, p. 153.

Chapter 12: *Stratagems for Desperate Times*

1. *36 Stratagems,* p. 198.
2. Ibid., p. 199.
3. *The Wiles of War,* p. 285.
4. Sima Fa, *Seven Military Classics* (n.p., n.d.), quoted in
The Thirty-Six Strategies of Ancient China, by Verstappen, p. 161.
5. Verstappen, *The Thirty-Six Strategies of Ancient China*, p. 169.
6. Sun Zi, quoted in *The Thirty-Six Strategies of Ancient China*,
by Verstappen, p. 169.
7. Reid, "Rebels Spread Attacks," pp. 1A, 8A.
8. *The Wiles of War,* p. 296.
9. Reid, "Insurgents Kill 50 Iraqi Troops in Bold Ambush," p. 1A.
10. Rageh, "Iraqi Prime Minister Blames Coalition for Ambush,"
pp. 1A, 6A.
11. Sun Zi, quoted in *The Thirty-Six Strategies of Ancient China*,
by Verstappen, p. 173.
12. Verstappen, *The Thirty-Six Strategies of Ancient China*, p. 174.
13. ABC's Nightly News, 24 December 2004.
14. *36 Stratagems,* trans. Koh Kok Kiang and Liu Yi, p. 208.

15. Ibid., p. 212.
16. Ibid., p. 209.
17. ABC's Noon News, 10 November 2004.
18. Reid, "Insurgent Violence Sweeps across Baghdad," p. 1A.
19. *36 Stratagems,* p. 213.
20. *The Wiles of War,* p. 311.
21. Thomas Wagner, AP, "Iraq's Parliament Wants Apology," *Jacksonville (NC) Daily News,* 20 April 2005, pp. 1A, 3A.
22. *An Introduction to Saudi Arabia.*
23. *36 Stratagems,* p. 217.
24. *The Wiles of War,* p. 319.
25. Yagyu Munenori, *Family Book on the Art of War* (n.p., n.d.), quoted in *The Thirty-Six Strategies of Ancient China*, by Stefan H. Verstappen, p. 185.
26. Sun Zi, quoted in *The Thirty-Six Strategies of Ancient China*, by Stefan H. Verstappen, p. 185.
27. *The Wiles of War,* p. 319.
28. ABC's Nightly News, 7 October 2004.
29. *36 Stratagems,* p. 219.
30. Lekic, "Truck Bomb Hits Italians at Iraq Base," p. 1A.
31. *The Wiles of War,* pp. 319, 320.
32. Verstappen, *The Thirty-Six Strategies of Ancient China*, p. 186.
33. ABC's Nightly News, 26 August 2004.
34. Vincent, "Shiites Bring Rigid Piety to Iraq's South"; Vincent, "Switched Off in Basra."
35. Verstappen, *The Thirty-Six Strategies of Ancient China*, p. 193.
36. *Handbook on the Chinese Communist Army,* DA Pamphlet 30-51 (Washington, D.C.: Hdqts. Dept. of the Army, 7 December 1960), pp. 5-7.
37. Sun Zi, quoted in *The Thirty-Six Strategies of Ancient China*, by Verstappen, p. 193.

Chapter 13: *Ways to Turn the Tide in Iraq*

1. Wright and Baker, "Iraq, Jordan See Threat To Election from Iran," p. A01; Ciezadlo, "Intrigue, Power Plays as Iraq Campaign Season Starts"; "Iraq's Most Feared Terror Chief Declared a Fierce War on Democracy," p. 20.
2. Michael, "Likely Leader Vows Moderation," pp. 1A, 5A; Tarabay, "Blast Kills Dozens in Iraq," pp. 1A, 8A; Jaber, "Go Home Yanks, Says PM In Waiting."
3. ABC's Morning News, 14 February 2005.
4. ABC's Nightly News, 16 February 2005.

5. Murphy, "View Emerging of Shiite-Ruled Iraq," pp. 1, 10.

6. Dehghanpisheh et al, "Iraq's Hidden War," pp. 24, 25.

7. Ali Akbar Dareini, AP, "Iran Warns of More Instability If Nukes Issue Goes Before U.N," *Jacksonville (NC) Daily News,* 6 March 2005. p. 4A.

8. *Warfare in Lebanon,* ed. Alnwick and Fabyanic, pp. 71, 72.

9. *Iran Country Study,* DA PAM 550-68, Area Handbook Series (Washington, D.C.: Hdqts. Dept. of the Army, 1989), p. 267.

10. Bassem Mroue, AP, "Bomb Kills Former Lebanese Prime Minister, 10 Others," *Jacksonville (NC) Daily News,* 15 February 2005, p. 3A.

11. Gary C. Gambill and Ziad K. Abdelnour, "Hezbollah between Tehran and Damascus," *Middle East Intelligence Bulletin,* vol. 4, no. 2., February 2002.

12. Zeina Karam, AP, "Lebanese Take to the Streets; Pro-Syrian Government Quits," *Jacksonville (NC) Daily News,* 1 March 2005, p. 3A.

13. Nicholas Blanford, "Which Way Will Lebanon Go Next," *Christian Science Monitor,* 11 March 2005, p. 6.

14. Neil MacFarquahar, "Hezbollah Becomes Potent Anti-U.S. Force," *New York Times,* 24 December 2002.

15. "U.S. Rejects Pullback by Syria As Not Enough," World Briefs Wire Reports (AP), *Jacksonville (NC) Daily News,* 8 March 2005, p. 5A.

16. ABC's Morning News, 9 March 2005.

17. Tanalee Smith, AP, "Hezbollah Flexes Its Muscle in Syrian Protest, *Jacksonville (NC) Daily News,* 9 March 2005, p. 4A.

18. Nicholas Blanford, "Stark Choice for Militant Hizbullah," *Christian Science Monitor,* 7 March 2005, p. 5.

19. Ibid.

20. Smith, "Hezbollah Flexes Its Muscle in Syrian Protest, p. 4A.

21. "Hundreds of Thousands of People Turned Out for a Hizbullah Rally," World News in Brief, *Christian Science Monitor,* 14 March 2005, p. 20.

22. Zeina Karam, AP, "Momentum Swings toward Anti-Syrian Opposition," *Jacksonville (NC) Daily News,* 15 March 2005, p. 4A.

23. NPR's Morning News, 16 March 2005.

24. Nicholas Blanford, "Syrian Troops Move East, Not Out," *Christian Science Monitor,* 8 March 2005, p. 6.

25. Blanford, "Stark Choice for Militant Hizbullah," p. 5.

26. NPR's Morning News, 16 March 2005.

27. Blanford, "Which Way Will Lebanon Go Next," p. 6.

28. NPR's Morning News, 12 March 2005.

29. Nicholas Blanford, "Pro-Syria Voices Push Back," *Christian Science Monitor,* 9 March 2005, pp. 1, 10.

30. "Hezbollah to Take New Role in Politics," World Briefs Wire Reports (AP), *Jacksonville (NC) Daily News,* 12 March 2005, p. 10A.

31. Martin Kramer, "Hizbullah: The Calculus of Jihad," *Bulletin of the American Academy of Arts and Sciences,* May 1994, pp. 41, 42; and A. Nizar Hamzeh, "Lebanon's Hizbullah: From Islamic Revolution to Parliamentary Accommodation," *Third World Quarterly,* Spring 1993, pp. 327-329; in "Islamism in Lebanon: A Guide," by A. Nizar Hamzeh, *Middle East Quarterly,* vol. 1, no. 3, September 1997.

32. *An-Nahar al-'Arabi wa'd-Duwali,* 18-24 October 1989, p. 17, in "Islamism in Lebanon: A Guide," by A. Nizar Hamzeh, *Middle East Quarterly,* vol. 1, no. 3, September 1997.

33. Memo for the record by H.J. Poole.

34. NPR's Morning Radio, 4 April 2005.

35. Nicholas Blanford, "Blast Sharpens Memories of Lebanon's Civil War," *Christian Science Monitor,* 24 March 2005, p. 7.

36. Nicholas Blanford, "Victory for Lebanese Hungry for 'Truth'," *Christian Science Monitor,* 28 March 2005, pp. 6, 7.

37. "Najib Mikati Accepted an Appointment as Prime Minister," World News Wire Briefs, *Christian Science Monitor,* 19 April 2005, p. 20; Dan Murphy and Joshua Mitnick, "In Mideast Elections, Militants Gain," *Christian Science Monitor,* 8 June 2005, pp. 1, 10.

38. "Bush Leaves Opening for Hezbollah Move to Political Mainstream," National Briefs Wire Reports (AP), *Jacksonville (NC) Daily News,* 16 March 2005, p. 7A.

39. Poole, *Tactics of the Crescent Moon,* pp. 163-167.

40. "Hizballah," *Patterns of Global Terrorism, 2002 Report* (Washington, D.C.: U.S. Dept. of State, April 2003); "Hezbollah," *Encyclopedia,* www.nationmaster.com, 5 July 2004.

41. "Suicide Bombing Is A Crime against Humanity," Israel advocacy group, "StandwithUs." At its website, www.standwithus.com.

42. Ibid.

43. "Suicide Bomber Kills Peacekeeper, Civilian in Afghan Capital."

44. "Suicide Bombing Is A Crime against Humanity."

45. "The Supreme Council for the Islamic Revolution in Iraq (SCIRI)," by Abedin.

46. Abbas Fayadh, AP, "Suicide Attacks Kill At Least 68," *Jacksonville (NC) Daily News,* 22 April 2004, pp. 1A, 10A.

47. Nicholas Blanford, "Insurgent and Soldier: Two Views on Iraq Fight," *Christian Science Monitor,* 25 February 2004, p. 4.

48. Tarek Al-Issawi, AP, "Suicide Bombers Strike Almost at Will in Iraq," *Jacksonville (NC) Daily News,* 19 March 2004, p. 4A.

49. Lekic, "Truck Bomb Hits Italians at Iraq Base," p. 1A; Murphy, "Iraq Bombs Hit Kurdish Leaders," p. 11.

50. Dehghanpisheh et al, "We Are Your Martyrs," pp. 39-41.

51. ABC's Nightly News, 27 December 2003.

52. Dehghanpisheh et al, "We Are Your Martyrs," p. 39.

53. Scott Peterson, "U.S. Pressure on Cleric Pushes Militants South," *Christian Science Monitor,* 10 May 2004, p. 4.

54. Baldauf, "Standoff Bolstered Sadr's Support," p. 4.

55. Peter Grier and Faye Bowers, "Iraqi Militants Raise Pitch of Attacks," *Christian Science Monitor,* 22 April 2004, p. 10.

56. Nordland and Dehghanpisheh, "What Sistani Wants," p. 28.

57. Al-Fatlawi, "At Least 115 Die in Worst Attack Yet," p. 1A.

58. Abdul-Zahra, AP, "Iraqis Condemn Terrorism," *Jacksonville (NC) Daily News,* 2 March 2005, pp. 1A, 2A.

59. "Hell in Hilla," *St. Louis Post Dispatch,* 1 March 2005.

60. Ibid.

61. Ahmed, "Suicide Bombing Kills 47 People in Iraqi City," p. 5A.

62. Mixture of information from Yossef Bodansky books and (Israeli) Project for Research of Islamist Movements' articles (www.e-prism.org) in "The State Sponsorship of the Islamic Terrorist Network," by Stephen E. Hughes (unpublished study, Salt Lake City, UT, 2003).

63. Mannes, *Profiles in Terror,* p. 20; Gunaratna, *Inside al-Qaeda,* pp. 29, 21.

64. Esposito, *Unholy War,* pp. 18, 19.

65. Mannes, *Profiles in Terror,* p. 36.

66. Ibid.

67. Poole, *Tactics of the Crescent Moon,* chap. 10.

68. Mannes, *Profiles in Terror,* p. 162.

69. Poole, *Tactics of the Crescent Moon,* chap. 8.

70. U.S. Congressional Testimony, in "Iran Continues Support of Terrorism," *Iran News* (VOA), 17 February 2005.

71. "Shiite Radicals Join with Sunni Insurgents in Ramadi," from DEBKAfile.

72. CNN News, 6 August 2005.

73. UPI, 6 August 2005.

74. Imm, "Some Bombs in Iraq Are Made in Iran, U.S. Says."

75. Ware, "Inside Iran's Secret War for Iraq."

76. Fairweather, "Four out of 10 Desert New Security Force When Under Fire."

77. Donna Bryson, AP, "Bin Laden Message: Bleed U.S. Economically," *Jacksonville (NC) Daily News,* 2 November 2004, p. 4A; Lumpkin, "U.S. Official: Iraqi Forces Infiltrated," p. 4A; "A Troublemaker Surrounded," p. 47.

78. Dan Murphy, "Iraq's Neighborhood Councils Are Vanishing," *Christian Science Monitor,* 25 February 2005, pp. 1, 5.

79. Ibid.

80. Dan Murphy, "After Temporary Gains, Marines Leave Iraqi Cities," *Christian Science Monitor,* 3 March 2005.

81. James Glanz, "The Conflict in Iraq," *New York Times,* 21 February 2005.

82. "Iran Role in the Recent Uprising in Iraq," from Middle East Media Research Inst.

83. Scott Baldauf, "Sadr Loyalty Grows, Even as Sistani Returns," *Christian Science Monitor,* 26 August 2004, p. 6.

84. Poole, *Tactics of the Crescent Moon,* chap. 11.

85. Poole, *The Tiger's Way,* chaps. 4-21.

86. Hammes, T.X., excerpt from *The Sling and the Stone* (St. Paul, MN: MBI Publishing, 2004), in "Inside the Pentagon," 2 December 2004, p. 16.

87. William S. Lind, *Maneuver Warfare Handbook* (Boulder, CO: Westview Press, 1985.)

88. *Warfighting,* FMFM 1 (Washington, D.C.: Hdqts. U.S. Marine Corps, 1989).

89. Poole, *Phantom Soldier,* chap. 13.

90. Grant Evans and Kelvin Rowley, *Red Brotherhood at War* (London: Verso, 1984), p. 161.

91. Dana Priest and Robin Wright, "Scowcroft Skeptical Vote Will Stabilize Iraq," *Washington Post,* 7 January 2005, p. A12.

92. Maj.Gen. Pete Chiarelli, as quoted in "Twists Make Predictions a Dubious Bet in Iraq," by Bradley Graham, *Washington Post,* 20 March 2005.

Chapter 14: *Things to Do for Afghanistan*

1. Yousaf and Adkin, *Bear Trap,* map 9; Poole, *Tactics of the Crescent Moon,* map 6.2, p. 97.

2. *Al-Qaeda Targeting Guidance* (Alexandria, VA: IntellCenter/ Tempest Publishing, 1 April 2004).

3. Ibid.

4. O'Ballance, *Afghan Wars,* p. 146.

5. Ibid., p. 144.

6. Ibid., p. 181.

Chapter 15: *Averting a Wider Conflict*

1. Poole, *Phantom Soldier,* chap. 3.

2. Nojumi, *The Rise of the Taliban in Afghanistan,* p. 188.

3. Ibid., p. 153; Esposito, *Unholy War,* pp. 15-17.

4. Yousaf, *Silent Soldier.*

5. Mir, *The True Face of Jihadis,* pp. 123, 130, 138.

6. Nojumi, *The Rise of the Taliban in Afghanistan,* p. 223.

7. Ibid., pp. 120, 121, 132, 135, 226.
8. Ibid., pp. 117, 188.
9. Ibid., p. 132.
10. Ibid., p. 40.
11. Samander and Sarwan, "Concern That Jihad Chieftains Will Set Political Agenda;" Nojumi, *The Rise of the Taliban in Afghanistan,* p. 132.
12. Nojumi, *The Rise of the Taliban in Afghanistan,* p. 189.
13. Mir, *The True Face of Jihadis,* p. 25.
14. "Iran Shifting Its Attention . . . ," p. A7.
15. "Group Says Thousands Ready for Suicide Raids," 7 June 2004.
16. Katherine Shrader and John Solomon, AP, "Iran May Be Hiding Terrorist Figures," *Jacksonville (NC) Daily News,* 4 June 2005, p. 4A; Mannes, *Profiles in Terror,* p. 163.
17. Robert Baer, *See No Evil* (New York: Crown Publishers, 2003), in *Warring on Terrorism,* by Hughes, p. 34.
18. Mannes, *Profiles in Terror,* p. 163.
19. Stephen E. Hughes (researcher of Islamic militant groups), in e-mail on 8 June 2005.
20. "Al-Qaeda's New Front."
21. Mir, *The True Face of Jihadis,* p. 104.
22. Ibid., pp. 39, 43.
23. Ibid., p. 346.
24. Ibid., pp. 345-354.
25. Ibid., p. 23.
26. Ibid., p. 104.
27. Ibid., p. 282.
28. Ibid., p. 121; Dr. Sharad S. Chauhan, *The al-Qaeda Threat* (New Delhi: A.P.H. Publishing Corp., 2003), p. 236.
29. Mir, *The True Face of Jihadis,* p. 121.
30. Ibid., pp. 114, 283.
31. Ibid. p. 104.
32. Ibid., p. 103.
33. Ibid., p. 105.
34. Gunaratna, *Inside al-Qaeda,* p. 158.
35. Ibid., p. 147.
36. Ibid., p. 146.
37. "Top Iranian Defector On Iran's Collaboration with Iraq, North Korea, Al-Qa'ida, and Hizbullah," from Middle East Media Research Inst.
38. "The 9/11 Commission Report: The Terrorist Plot," *Los Angeles Times,* 23 July 2004, pp. A1, A15.
39. Samander and Sarwan, "Concern That Jihad Chieftains Will Set Political Agenda," from Inst. for War and Peace Reporting.
40. Poole, *Tactics of the Crescent Moon,* p. 184.

41. Mannes, *Profiles in Terror,* p. 149.
42. Ibid.
43. "How Iraq's Election Will Work," p. 10; Peterson, "Iran Flexes Its 'Soft Power' in Iraq," p. 6.
44. Peterson, "Shadows of Tehran over Iraq," pp. 1, 10.
45. Poole, *Tactics of the Crescent Moon,* pp. 163, 167; "Shiite Radicals Join with Sunni Insurgents in Ramadi," from DEBKAfile.
46. Slobodan Lekic, AP, "20 Bodies Found Dumped in the Tigris near Baghdad," *Jacksonville (NC) Daily News,* 19 September 2005, p. 4A.
47. Jill Carroll, "Sadr Militia's New Muscle in South," *Christian Science Monitor,* 21 September 2005, pp. 1, 10.
48. Tarek el-Tablawy, AP, "Top Shiite Cleric Backing Iraqi Constitution," *Jacksonville (NC) Daily News,* 23 September 2005, p. 4A.
49. "Iran's Intelligence Service Occupies Key Iraqi City," *Iran Watch,* 4 September 2005.
50. Thomas Wagner, AP, "Iraqis Rally against 'British Aggression'," *Jacksonville (NC) Daily News,* 22 September 2005, p. 4A.
51. Quinn, "Iraqi Legislators Are Sworn In," p. 2A.
52. Fam, "Iraqi Parliament Elects Kurd as President," p. 4A.
53. Abbas Fayadh, AP, "British Troops Free Comrades Held in Iraqi Jail," *Jacksonville (NC) Daily News,* 20 September 2005, p. 4A.
54. Wagner, "Iraqis Rally against 'British Aggression'," p. 4A.
55. Vincent, "Switched Off in Basra"; Vincent, "Shiites Bring Rigid Piety to Iraq's South"; "Iran's Intelligence Service Occupies Key Iraqi City," *Iran Watch,* 4 September 2005; Lasseter, "Iraqi Forces May Need Years of Preparation," p. 5A.
56. Katzman, *Warriors of Islam,* pp. 82-84.
57. "Shiite Radicals Join with Sunni Insurgents in Ramadi," from DEBKAfile.
58. "Sudan Claims Zarqawi behind Migration of Al Qaida Cells," Middle East Report, *Geostrategy-Direct,* week of 29 March 2005.
59. ABC's Nightly News, 16 December 2004.
60. Dr. Sharad S. Chauhan, *The al-Qaeda Threat* (New Delhi: A.P.H. Publishing Corp., 2003), p. 53.
61. Ibid., pp. 42, 43.
62. Arkady Shipunov and Gennady Filimonov, "Field Artillery to be Replaced with Shmel Infantry Flamethrower," *Military Parade* (Moscow), Issue 29, September 1998.
63. "Top Iranian Defector On Iran's Collaboration with Iraq, North Korea, Al-Qa'ida, and Hizbullah," from Middle East Media Research Inst.
64. Evans and Rowley, *Red Brotherhood at War,* chap. 7.

65. Joseph S. Bermudez, Jr., *North Korean Special Forces* (Annapolis: Naval Inst. Press, 1998), p. 147.

66. Poole, *Tactics of the Crescent Moon,* p. 230.

67. Poole, *Phantom Soldier,* chaps. 7, 13.

68. Bruce I. Gudmundsson, *Stormtroop Tactics—Innovation in the German Army 1914-1918* (New York: Praeger, 1989), pp. 146-149.

69. Nguyen Khac Can and Pham Viet Thuc, *The War 1858 - 1975 in Vietnam* (Hanoi: Nha Xuat Ban Van Hoa Dan Toc, n.d.), figs. 544, 510.

70. Ibid., fig. 557.

71. *NVA-VC Small-Unit Tactics and Techniques Study*, part I, UASARV, ed. Thomas Pike (Washington, D.C.: Archival Publishing, 1997), p. X-5.

72. Can and Thuc, *The War 1858 - 1975 in Vietnam,* fig. 565.

73. H. John Poole, *One More Bridge to Cross: Lowering the Cost of War* (Emerald Isle, NC: Posterity Press, 1999), chap. 13.

74. "A Sgt., a Cpl., and Two L.Cpl.'s Eye View."

75. Lt.Col. Robert W. Lamont, "'Urban Warrior'—A View from North Vietnam," *Marine Corps Gazette,* April 1999, p. 33.

76. L.Cpl. Fisher (Iraqi war veteran), in telephone conversation with author on 4 May 2005.

77. Poole, *The Tiger's Way,* appendix C.

78. Attributed to Robert D. Steele.

Glossary

ABC	American Broadcasting Company	U.S. TV network
AIM	Armed Islamic Movement	Sudan-based alliance of militant sects, may be same as INF
AK-47	Russian or Chinese acronym	Assault rifle
ANP	Awami National Party	Pakistani political organization
AO	Area of Operations	Zone of action
AP	Associated Press	U.S. news service
APC	Assault Personnel Carrier	Lightly armored tracked vehicle
AWOL	Absent without Leave	Unauthorized absence
C-130	U.S. military designator	Cargo plane
CAP	Combined Action Platoon	Unit with both U.S. and local forces
CARE	Cooperative for Assistance and Relief Everywhere	U.S. relief agency
CD	Computer Disk	Electronic record
CENTCOM	Central Command	Headquarters of U.S. military in Mid-East
CH-53	U.S. military designator	Heavy-lift helicopter

CIA	Central Intelligence Agency	U.S. spy organization
CNN	Cable News Network	U.S. TV network
COC	Combat Operations Center	Headquarters facility
CPA	Coalition Provisional Authority	Interim government in Iraq
DIA	Defense Intelligence Agency	U.S. government bureau
DMZ	Demilitarized Zone	Buffer area between North and South Vietnam
DoD	Department of Defense	U.S. agency
F-18	U.S. military designator	Fighter jet
FATA	Federally Administered Tribal Areas	Pakistani territory
4GW	4th-Generation Warfare	War in which martial and nonmartial strategies combine
GC	Governing Council	Iraqi-province administration group
GI	Government Issue	U.S. soldier
Hezb	*Hezbollah ul-Mujahidin*	Hekmatyar's militia in Kashmir, affiliated with *JI*
HI	*Hezb i-Islami*	Early Afghan resistance group
HIA	*Harakat i-Islami-yi Afghanistan*	Muhsini's Shiite *mujahideen* faction
HIG	*Hezb-i Islami Gulbuddin*	Hekmatyar's militia in 2005 Afghanistan

HIH	*Hezb-i Islami Hekmatyar*	Hekmatyar's militia in Soviet-Afghan War, supported by *JI*
HIK	*Hezb-i Islami Khalis*	Sister faction to *HIH*, supported by *JI*
HMA	*Harakat-ul Mujahideen Al Alami*	Pakistani militants, linked to *JUI/F*
HMMV	American acronym	Modern equivalent of U.S. jeep
HUA	*Harakat ul-Ansar*	Pakistani militants, affiliated with *JUI/F*
HUJI	*Harakat ul-Jihad-i-Islami*	Pakistani militants, affiliated with *JUI/F*
HUM	*Harakat-ul Mujahidin*	Pakistani militants, affiliated with *JUI/F*
IA	Islamic Association	Another name for Rabbani's *JIA*, affiliated with *JI*
ID	Identification	Card showing owner's identity
IED	Improvised Explosive Device	Remote-control bomb
IIF	International Islamic Front	Bin Laden's Afghan alliance of Pakistani religious party wings
IIFJ	International Islamic Front for the Jihad against Jews and Crusaders	Bin Laden's world terrorist coalition
IIS	*Itehar i-Islami Sayyaf*	Sayyaf's *mujahideen* faction, *JI* linked
INF	Islamic National Front	Sudan-based alliance of militant sects, may be same as AIM

IRGC	Iranian Revolutionary Guards Corps	Overseers of the Iranian revolution
IRMA	Islamic Revolutionary Movement	*Harakat-i Inqilab-i Islami,* pro-Iranian *mujahideen* faction
ISI	Inter-Services Intelligence	Pakistan's intelligence agency
IULA	Islamic Unity for Liberation	Alias of Sayyaf's *IIS*
JEM	*Jaish-e-Mohammed*	Pakistani militants, affiliated with *JUI/F*
JI	*Jamaat i-Islami*	Pakistani religious political party
JIA	*Jamaat i-Islami Pakistan*	Rabbani's *JI*-backed *mujahideen*
JUA	*Jamiat ul-Ansar*	Pakistani militants, affiliated with *JUI/F*
JUF	*Jamaat ul-Furqan*	Pakistani militants, affiliated with *JUI/F*
JUI	*Jamiat Ulema-i-Islam*	Pakistani religious political party (early)
JUI/F	*Jamiat Ulema-i-Islam Fazlur Rehman Jalili faction*	Pakistani religious political party (now)
KDP	Kurdish Democratic Party	Iraqi political party
KIA	Killed in Action	Friendly fatality
KUI	*Khuddam ul-Islam*	Pakistani militants, affiliated with *JUI/F*
LET	*Lashkar e-Toiba*	Pakistani militants, affiliated with *MDI*
LJ	*Lashkar-e-Jhangvi*	Pakistani militants, affiliated with *SSP*

LT	*Lashkar Toiba*	Same as LET
M-1	U.S. military designator	Main battle tank
M-14	Iraqi agency designator	Part of Iraq's former intelligence service
MDI	*Markaz-ud-Dawa-wal-Irshad*	Pakistani group of fundamentalists
MIRI	Mujahedin for Islamic Revolution in Iraq	Paramilitary outfit directed from Iran
MMA	*Mutahida Majlis Amal*	Pakistani religious political party alliance (includes both *JUI/F* and *JI*)
NAP	National Awami Party	Early version of ANP
NATO	North Atlantic Treaty Organization	European military alliance
NBC	National Broadcasting Company	U.S. TV network
NCO	Noncommissioned officer	Junior enlisted leader
NIF	National Islamic Front	Sudanese political party
NPR	National Public Radio	U.S. radio network
NVA	North Vietnamese Army	Vietnam War foe
NWFP	Northwest Frontier Province	Pakistani territory
OIC	Organization of Islamic Conference	Pakistan-inspired political alliance
PA	Public Address	Loudspeaker system
PA	Palestinian Authority	Self-Governing body, Occupied Palestine
PFC	Private First Class	Second enlisted rank

PFLP-GC	Popular Front for the Liberation of Palestine-General Command	Palestinian resistance group
PIJ	*Palestinian Islamic Jihad*	Palestinian resistance group
POW	Prisoner of War	Captured enemy
PT	Physical Training	Daily exercises
PUK	Patriotic Union of Kurdistan	Iraqi political party
ROTC	Reserve Officers Training Command	College preparation for commissioning
RPD	Russian or Chinese acronym	Light machinegun
RPG	Rocket-Propelled Grenade	Shoulder-fired grenade launcher
SAW	Squad Automatic Weapon	Light machinegun
SCIRI	Supreme Council of the Islamic Revolution in Iraq	Iraqi political party
SSP	*Sipah-e-Sahaba*	Pakistani group of fundamentalists
SUV	Sports Utility Vehicle	Preferred means of conveyance for Iraqi Coalition officials
T-72	Russian military designator	Tank
TAOR	Tactical Area of Responsibility	Unit's assigned zone of operations
TKI	*Tehrik Khuddam-ul Isla*	Pakistani militants, linked to *JUI/F*
TOW	American acronym	Wire-guided antitank missile
TTP	Tactics, Techniques, and Procedures	Individual and small-unit methods

354

TV	Television	Video medium
UIA	United Iraqi Alliance	Iraqi political party, *Dawa* affiliated
UN	United Nations	World peace organization
US	United States	America
USMC	United States Marine Corps	U.S. Service Branch
VBIED	Vehicle-Borne Improvised Explosive Device	Vehicular remote-control bomb
VC	Viet Cong	Local enemy militia in Vietnam
VIP	Very Important Person	Military slang for U.S. official
WIFJ	World Islamic Front for the Jihad (or Struggle) against Jews and Crusaders	Another name for bin Laden's *IIFJ*
WWI	World War One	First worldwide conflict
WWII	World War Two	Second worldwide conflict

Bibliography

U.S. Government Publications

Afghanistan Country Study. DA PAM 550-65. Area Handbook
   Series. Washington, D.C.: Hdqts. Dept. of the Army,
   1986.
"DoD News Briefing—ASD PA Clarke and Rear Adm. Stufflebeem,"
   14 January 2002. From the DoD website, www.defenselink.mil.
Grau, Lester. "For All Seasons: The Old But Effective RPG-7 Promises
   to Haunt the Battlefields of Tomorrow." Fort Leavenworth, KS:
   Foreign Military Studies Office, n.d.
Handbook on the Chinese Communist Army. DA Pamphlet 30-51.
   Washington, D.C.: Hdqts. Dept. of the Army, 7 December 1960.
Iran Country Study. DA PAM 550-68. Area Handbook Series.
   Washington, D.C.: Hdqts. Dept. of the Army, 1989.
"Iran Report." *Radio Free Europe / Radio Liberty.* Vol. 5, no. 3,
   28 January 2002. From its website www.rferl.org via
   www.globalsecurity.org.
Iraq Country Study. DA PAM 550-31. Area Handbook Series.
   Washington, D.C.: Hdqts. Dept. of the Army, n.d.
Jalali, Ali and Lester W. Grau. *Afghan Guerrilla Warfare: In the Words
   of the Mujahideen Fighters.* St. Paul, MN: MBI Publishing, 2001.
   First published as *The Other Side of the Mountain.* Quantico,
   VA: Marine Corps Combat Development Cmd., 1995.
NVA-VC Small-Unit Tactics and Techniques Study. Part I, UASARV.
   Edited by Thomas Pike. Washington, D.C.: Archival Publishing,
   1997.
Pakistan Country Study. Area Handbook Series. Washington, D.C.:
   Library of Congress, 2004.
Patterns of Global Terrorism, 2002 Report. Washington, D.C.: U.S.
   Dept. of State, April 2003. From its website.
Patterns of Global Terrorism, 2003 Report. Washington, D.C.: U.S.
   Dept. of State, April 2004. From its website.
"Redesignation of Foreign Terrorist Organizations." Public
   Notice 4561. Washington, D.C.: U.S. Dept. of State, 2003. From
   www.fas.org.

"A Sgt., a Cpl., and Two L.Cpl.'s Eye View of the Fallujah Battle." Purported excerpt from 3d Bn., 5th Marine "Lessons-Learned." As sent to internet circle MILINET by majusmcret@aol.com on 8 March 2005.

Sloan, Cpl. Tom. "Marine Stops Enemy Attack, Saves Lives." *Camp Lejeune (NC) Globe,* 28 April 2005.

"Top Five Most Deadly Tactics, Techniques, and Procedures (TTP's)." Fort Leavenworth, KS: ADCSINT, TRADOC, 1 April 2005.

Warfare in Lebanon. Edited by Kenneth J. Alnwick and Thomas A. Fabyanic. Washington, D.C.: Nat. Defense Univ., 1988.

Warfighting. FMFM 1. Washington, D.C.: Hdqts. U.S. Marine Corps, 1989.

Civilian Publications

Analytical Studies

Ahmed, Khaled. *Pakistan: Behind the Ideological Mask.* Lahore: Vanguard, 2004.

Al-Qaeda Targeting Guidance. Alexandria, VA: IntellCenter/Tempest Publishing, 1 April 2004. From its website, www.intelcenter.com.

Ayalon, Ami. Editor. *Middle East Contemporary Survey.* Boulder, CO: Westview Press, 1991.

Batty, Robin and David Hoffman. "Afghanistan: Crisis of Impunity." *Human Rights Watch,* vol. 13, no. 3(c), July 2001, footnote 24, p. 11. From its website, www.hrw.org.

Bermudez, Joseph S., Jr. *North Korean Special Forces.* Annapolis: Naval Inst. Press, 1998.

Burke, Jason. *Al Qaeda: The True Story of Radical Islam.* London: Penguin Books, 2003.

Can, Nguyen Khac and Pham Viet Thuc. *The War 1858 - 1975 in Vietnam.* Hanoi: Nha Xuat Ban Van Hoa Dan Toc, n.d.

Catechism of the Catholic Church. New York: Doubleday, 1994.

Chauhan, Dr. Sharad S. *The al-Qaeda Threat.* New Delhi: A.P.H. Publishing Corp., 2003.

Cordesman, Anthony H. and Arleigh A. Burke Chair. "Iran's Developing Military Capabilities." Working draft. Washington, D.C.: Center Strategic Internat. Studies, 14 December 2004.

Crossing the Threshold of Hope. By His Holiness John Paul II. New York: Alfred A. Knopf, 1995.

Esposito, John L. *Unholy War: Terror in the Name of Islam.* London: Oxford Univ. Press, 2002.

Evans, Grant and Kelvin Rowley. *Red Brotherhood at War.* London: Verso, 1984.

Gohari, M.J. *The Taliban: Ascent to Power.* Karachi: Oxford Univ. Press, 1999.

Goulden, Joseph C. *Korea: The Untold Story of the War.* New York: Times Books, 1982.

Gudmundsson, Bruce I. *Stormtroop Tactics—Innovation in the German Army 1914-1918.* New York: Praeger, 1989.

Gunaratna, Rohan. Inside al-Qaeda: Global Network of Terror. Lahore: Vanguard, 2002.

Hammes, T.X. Excerpt from *The Sling and the Stone.* St. Paul, MN: MBI Publishing, 2004. In "Inside the Pentagon," 2 December 2004.

Hughes, Stephen E. "The State Sponsorship of the Islamic Terrorist Network." Unpublished study. Salt Lake City, UT, 2003. From reload762308@hotmail.com.

Hughes, Stephen E. "Warring on Terrorism: A Comprehensive Dispatch Briefing." Internet piece. Soda Springs, ID, 2005. From reload762308@hotmail.com.

An Introduction to Saudi Arabia. As produced by McDonnel Douglas Services, Inc. N.p., n.d.

Kaplan, Robert D. *Soldiers of God: With Islamic Warriors in Afghanistan and Pakistan.* New York: Vintage Books, 1990.

Katzman, Kenneth. *Warriors of Islam: Iran's Revolutionary Guard.* Boulder, CO: Westview Press, 1993.

Lind, William. S. *Maneuver Warfare Handbook.* Boulder, CO: Westview Press, 1985.

Linder, Deanna and Rachael Levy and Yael Shahar. "Iraqi Wahhabi Factions Affiliated with Abu Musaab al Zarqawi." Internat. Policy Inst. for Counter-Terrorism, November 2004. From its website, www.ict.org.il.

Mannes, Aaron. *Profiles in Terror: The Guide to Middle East Terror Organizations.* Lanham, MD: Rowman & Littlefield Publishers, Inc., 2004.

Mao Tse-tung: An Anthology of His Writings. Edited by Anne Fremantle. New York: Mentor, 1962.

Mir, Amir. *The True Face of Jihadis.* Lahore: Mashal Books, 2004.

Nojumi, Neamatollah. *The Rise of the Taliban in Afghanistan: Mass Mobilization, Civil War, and the Future of the Region.* New York: Palgrave, 2002.

O'Ballance, Edgar. *Afghan Wars: Battles in a Hostile Land, 1839 to Present.* Karachi: Oxford Univ. Press, 2002.

Pearl, Mariane. *A Mighty Heart: The Inside Story of the Al Qaeda Kidnapping of Danny Pearl.* New York: Scribner, 2003.

Pintak, Lawrence. *Seeds of Hate: How America's Flawed Middle East Policy Ignited the Jihad.* London: Pluto Press, 2003.

Pirzada, Sayyid A.S. *The Politics of the Jamiat Ulema-i-Islam Pakistan, 1971-77.* Karachi: Oxford Univ. Press, 2000.

Poole, H. John. *One More Bridge to Cross: Lowering the Cost of War.* Emerald Isle, NC: Posterity Press, 1999.

Poole, H. John. *Phantom Soldier: The Enemy's Answer to U.S. Firepower.* Emerald Isle, NC: Posterity Press, 2001.

Poole, H. John. *Tactics of the Crescent Moon: Militant Muslim Combat Methods.* Emerald Isle, NC: Posterity Press, 2004.

Poole, H. John. *The Tiger's Way: A U.S. Private's Best Chance for Survival.* Emerald Isle, NC: Posterity Press, 2003.

36 Stratagems: Secret Art of War. Translated by Koh Kok Kiang and Liu Yi. Singapore, Asiapac Books, 1992.

Verstappen, Stefan H. *The Thirty-Six Strategies of Ancient China.* San Francisco: China Books & Periodicals, 1999.

The Wiles of War. Compiled and translated by Sun Haichen. Beijing: Foreign Languages Press, 1991.

The World's Great Events. Vol. VII (1857-1904). New York: P.F. Collier & Son Corp., 1944.

Yousaf, Brigadier Mohammad. *The Silent Soldier: The Man behind the Afghan Jehad.* South Yorkshire, UK: Leo Cooper, n.d. From www.afghanbooks.com.

Yousaf, Brigadier Mohammad and Maj. Mark Adkin. *Bear Trap: Afghanistan's Untold Story.* South Yorkshire, UK: Leo Cooper, n.d. From www.afghanbooks.com.

Zabih, Sepehr. *The Iranian Military in Revolution and War.* London: Routledge, 1988.

Photographs and Video Documentaries

"Giving Thanks," picture caption from Associated Press. *Jacksonville (NC) Daily News,* 26 August 2005.

The Battle of Dien Bien Phu. Visions of War Series. Vol. 10 (New Star Video, 1988), 50 min., videocassette #4010.

Letters, E-Mail, or Verbal Communications

Bosshart, Dr. Robert Perry (longtime resident of SE Asia and recent contractor in Afghanistan). In e-mail to author of 28 December 2004.

Robert Bryce, "Running Out of Gas in Iraq," 23 December 2004. In e-mail from robert@robertbryce.com to wilsongi@aol.com and then forwarded to author.

Chiarelli, Maj.Gen. Pete, CG, 1st Cavalry Div. Comments at Ft. Hood
AUSA dinner. As recorded by John Bell, Research Analysis and
Maintenance Inc., on 14 March 2005. Forwarded to author by
Lt.Col. Steve Holste, I MEF.

Company commander of 3d Battalion, 7th Marines. In conversation with
author during training evolution of 15, 16 January 2005.

ExO or CO of 2d Battalion, 7th Marines. In conversation with author
during training evolution of 14, 15 January 2005.

Fisher, L.Cpl. (Iraqi war veteran). In telephone conversation with
author on 4 May 2005.

Gaffney, Fr. Patrick (recognized authority on the Middle East). In a
letter to author on 29 August 2004.

Hughes, Stephen E. (researcher of Islamic militant groups). In e-mail
to author on 8 June 2004.

Mosher, Mark (U.S. serviceman in Iraq). In e-mails to author from May
to September 2005.

Pereira, Guilherme "Bill" (DoD contract employee in Iraq). In telephone
conversation with author on 28 June 2004.

Sexton, Mark (U.S. veteran of Iraq). In conversation with author on
24 May 2005.

Wilson, G.I. (retired Marine colonel who had been in Fallujah during the
fighting). In e-mails from wilsongi@aol.com to author in December
2004.

Newspaper, Magazine, or Website Articles

Abdul-Zahra, Qassim. Associated Press. "Iraqis Condemn Terrorism."
Jacksonville (NC) Daily News, 2 March 2005.

Abdul-Zahra, Qassim. Associated Press. "Iraq's Prime Minister
Compiles Cabinet List." *Jacksonville (NC) Daily News,* 28 April
2005.

Abdul-Zahra, Qassim. Associated Press. "Sunnis Say U.S., Shiites
Making Constitution Deals." *Jacksonville (NC) Daily News,*
21 August 2005.

Abdul-Zahra, Qassim. Associated Press. "Troops Repel Insurgent
Attacks." *Jacksonville (NC) Daily News,* 7 August 2005.

Abedin, Mahan. "The Supreme Council for the Islamic Revolution in
Iraq (SCIRI)." *Middle East Intelligence Bulletin,* autumn,
2003.
From its website, www.meib.org.

Abrashi, Fisnik. Associated Press. "Militant Cleric Vows to Keep
Fighting in Iraq." *AOL News,* 5 July 2004.

"Abu Ghraib Attack." Official CENTCOM news release. As retrieved
from www.mudvillegazette.com, 6 April 2005.

"Afghan Drug Kingpin Arrested in New York." News Brief Wire Reports (AP). *Jacksonville (NC) Daily News,* 26 April 2005.

"Afghan Soldiers Fail to Assassinate Defense Minister," World Briefs Wire Reports (AP). *Jacksonville (NC) Daily News,* 11 September 2005.

Afrasiabi, Kaveh L. "How Iran Will Fight Back." *Asia Times Online,* 16 December 2004.

Ahmad, Zulfiquar. "Intra-MMA Friction Swells over NSC." *Daily Mail* (Islamabad), 30 May 2005.

Ahmed, Sindbad. Associated Press. "Suicide Bombing Kills 47 People in Iraqi City. *Jacksonville (NC) Daily News,* 11 March 2005.

"Allawi: Insurgents Want Iraq Split by Civil War." From Associated Press. *USA Today,* 21 December 2004.

"Al-Qaeda's New Front." *Frontline.* NC Public TV, 25 January 2005.

Ambah, Faiza Saleh. Associated Press. "Iraq: Spinning Off Arab Terrorists." *Christian Science Monitor,* 8 February 2005.

Ambah, Faiza Saleh. Associated Press. "Islamic Militants Hit U.S. Consulate." *Jacksonville (NC) Daily News,* 7 December 2004.

Ambah, Faiza Saleh and Dan Murphy. "Attack Tests Saudi Security Strategy." *Christian Science Monitor,* 7 December 2004.

"An Analysis of Foreign "Martyrs" in Iraq." From Terrorism Research Center, Inc. *Terror Web Watch Report,* 20 May 2005.

Anderson, Curt. Associated Press. "Iranians Arrested in Bid to Buy Night Vision Gear." *Jacksonville (NC) Daily News,* 5 December 2004.

"Annan: Syria Hasn't Departed Lebanon." World Briefs Wire Reports (AP). *Jacksonville (NC) Daily News,* 2 October 2004.

Arnoldy, Ben and Owais Tohid. "Why Koran Is Such a Hot Button." *Christian Science Monitor,* 16 May 2005.

"At Least 20 Militants Killed in Afghan Fighting." From Associated Press. *Jacksonville (NC) Daily News,* 5 May 2005.

"The Ayn Tzahab Training Camp in Syria." Israel News Agency, 5 October 2003.

Babar, Makhdoom. "President Envisages Vibrant OIC to Face New Challenges." *Daily Mail* (Islamabad), 30 May 2005.

Baldauf, Scott. "Afghanistan's New Jihad Targets Poppy Production." *Christian Science Monitor,* 16 May 2005.

Baldauf, Scott. "Sadr Loyalty Grows, Even as Sistani Returns." *Christian Science Monitor,* 26 August 2004.

Baldauf, Scott. "Standoff Bolstered Sadr's Support." *Christian Science Monitor,* 30 August 2004.

Baldauf, Scott. "Taliban Coming In from Cold." *Christian Science Monitor,* 28 April 2005.

Baldauf, Scott and Faye Bowers. "Afghanistan Riddled with Drug Ties." *Christian Science Monitor,* 13 May 2004.

Baldauf, Scott and Ashraf Khan. "New Guns, New Drive for the Taliban." *Christian Science Monitor,* 26 September 2005.

Baldauf, Scott and Owais Tohid. "Aid Workers Increasingly a Target in Combat Zones." *Christian Science Monitor,* 5 November 2004.

Barakat, Mohammed. "U.S. Wraps Up Offensive Near Syrian Border." *Jacksonville (NC) Daily News,* 15 May 2005.

Blanford, Nicholas. "Blast Sharpens Memories of Lebanon's Civil War." *Christian Science Monitor,* 24 March 2005.

Blanford, Nicholas. "Hizbullah Reelects Its Leader." *Christian Science Monitor,* 19 August 2004.

Blanford, Nicholas. "Insurgent and Soldier: Two Views on Iraq Fight." *Christian Science Monitor,* 25 February 2004.

Blanford, Nicholas. "More Signs of Syria Turn Up in Iraq." *Christian Science Monitor,* 23 December 2004.

Blanford, Nicholas. "Pro-Syria Voices Push Back." *Christian Science Monitor,* 9 March 2005.

Blanford, Nicholas. "Sealing Syria's Desolate Border." *Christian Science Monitor,* 21 December 2004.

Blanford, Nicholas. "Syrian Troops Move East, Not Out." *Christian Science Monitor,* 8 March 2005.

Blanford, Nicholas. "Stark Choice for Militant Hizbullah." *Christian Science Monitor,* 7 March 2005.

Blanford, Nicholas. "Victory for Lebanese Hungry for 'Truth'." *Christian Science Monitor,* 28 March 2005.

Blanford, Nicholas. "Which Way Will Lebanon Go Next." *Christian Science Monitor,* 11 March 2005.

"Bomb Attack." *USA Today,* 18 April 2005. From its website.

Bowers, Faye. "Iran Shows New Willingness to Deal with U.S." *Christian Science Monitor,* 24 October 2003.

Bryce, Robert. "Gas Pains." *Atlantic Monthly,* vol. 295, no. 4, May 2005.

Bryson, Donna. Associated Press. "Bin Laden Message: Bleed U.S. Economically." *Jacksonville (NC) Daily News,* 2 November 2004.

Burke, Jason. "Waiting for a Last Battle with the Taliban." *The Observer* (UK), 27 June 1999.

Burns, Robert. Associated Press. "Afghan Progress Is Cited." *Jacksonville (NC) Daily News,* 22 May 2005.

"Bush Leaves Opening for Hezbollah Move to Political Mainstream." National Briefs Wire Reports (AP). *Jacksonville (NC) Daily News,* 16 March 2005.

"Captured Commander Says Iran [and] Syria Provided Funds [and] Equipment." *World Tribune.* Middle East Newsline, week of January 18, 2005. From its website at World Tribune.com.

Carl, Tracy. Associated Press. "Iraqi Parliament Prepares to Pick President." *Jacksonville (NC) Daily News,* 6 April 2005.

Carrol, Jill. "Iraq's Rising Industry: Domestic Kidnapping." *Christian Science Monitor,* 22 April 2005.

Carroll, Jill. "Iraq's Shiites Split Violently." *Christian Science Monitor,* 26 August 2005.

Carroll, Jill. "Sadr Militia's New Muscle in South." *Christian Science Monitor,* 21 September 2005.

Castaneda, Antonio. Associated Press. "Funeral Blast Adds to Toll of Recent Days." *Jacksonville (NC) Daily News,* 2 May 2005.

Castaneda, Antonio. Associated Press. "Marines Capture Weapons in Iraq." *Jacksonville (NC) Daily News,* 5 June 2005.

Castaneda, Antonio. Associated Press. "Marines on Offensive." *Jacksonville (NC) Daily News,* 11 May 2005.

Chaise, Christian. "Attack on U.S. Embassy Jeddah: How Done." From Middle East Media Research Inst., December 2004. At its website, www.memri.org.

Chiarelli, Maj.Gen. Pete. As quoted in "Twists Make Predictions a Dubious Bet in Iraq," by Bradley Graham. *Washington Post,* 20 March 2005.

Ciezadlo, Annia. "Fragmented Leadership of the Iraqi Insurgency." *Christian Science Monitor,* 21 December 2004.

Ciezadlo, Annia. "Intrigue, Power Plays as Iraq Campaign Season Starts." *Christian Science Monitor,* 16 December 2004. From its website.

Clarke, Richard (former U.S. antiterrorism czar). Interview by Peter Jennings, ABC's election day coverage, 2 November 2004.

Cole, Juan. "The United States and Shi'ite Religious Factions in Post-Ba'thist Iraq." *Middle East Journal,* vol. 57, no. 4, autumn 2003.

"A Company of Soldiers." *Frontline.* NC Public TV, 5 April 2005.

Constable, Pamela. "Assignment Afghanistan." *Smithsonian,* February 2005.

Cooney, Daniel. Associated Press. "Military Reveals Details of Crash." *Jacksonville (NC) Daily News,* 7 July 2005.

Cooney, Daniel. Associated Press. "Top Taliban Commanders May Be with Afghan Rebels." *Jacksonville (NC) Daily News,* 24 June 2005.

Cooney, Daniel. Associated Press. "U.S., Afghan Forces Kill Dozens of Militants." *Jacksonville (NC) Daily News,* 23 August 2005.

Cooney, Daniel. Associated Press. "U.S. Kills 12 Insurgents in Afghanistan." *Jacksonville (NC) Daily News,* 23 May 2005.

Cooney, Daniel. Associated Press. "Violence Spikes in Afghanistan." *Jacksonville (NC) Daily News,* 26 July 2005.

"Crackdown against Banned Groups Underway in Pakistan." From IRNA. As posted at www.globalsecurity.org on 21 Nov 2003.

Crain, Charles. "U.S. Troops Battle al-Sadr Supporters in Najaf." *USA Today,* 13 August 2004.

Cristi, Thomas. "Insurgents In Iraq Using Armor-Piercing Bombs." *Washington Times,* 8 January 2005. Through access@g2-forward.org.

Dareini, Ali Akbar. Associated Press. "Iran Warns of More Instability If Nukes Issue Goes Before U.N." *Jacksonville (NC) Daily News,* 6 March 2005.

Dareini, Ali Akbar. Associated Press. "Iranian Organization Seeks Suicide Bombers." *Jacksonville (NC) Daily News,* 29 November 2004.

Dehghanpisheh, Babak. "The Mullahs Win Again." *Newsweek,* 4 July 2005.

Denghanpisheh, Babak. "'This Ain't Over Yet.'" *Newsweek,* 22 November 2004.

Dehghanpisheh, Babak, Eve Conant, and Rod Nordland. "Iraq's Hidden War." *Newsweek,* 7 March 2005.

Dehghanpisheh, Babak, Melinda Liu, and Rod Nordland. "We Are Your Martyrs." *Newsweek,* 19 April 2004.

"Despite Having Agreed to a Truce." World News in Brief. *Christian Science Monitor,* 11 June 2004.

Dickey, Christopher, Mark Hosenball, and Michael Hirsh. "Looking for a Few Good Spies." *Newsweek,* 14 February 2005.

"Domel Nisar." *Explore Pakistan.* From ContactPakistan.com.

Escobar, Pepe. "The Roving Eye." *Asia Times Online,* 15 November 2001.

Eshel, Lt.Col. (Ret., IDF) David. "Counterguerrilla Warfare in South Lebanon." *Marine Corps Gazette,* July 1997.

Fabey, Michael. "Flying and Surviving the Unfriendly Skies." *Savannah Morning News,* 7 February 2005.

Fairweather, Jack. "Four out of 10 Desert New Security Force When Under Fire." *London Daily Telegraph,* 2 February 2005. From DoD Short Clips at its website, ebird.dodmedia.osd.mil.

Fam, Marion. Associated Press. "Complaints of Irregularities Emerge after Iraq's Election." *Jacksonville (NC) Daily News,* 6 February 2005.

Fam, Marion. Associated Press. "Iraqi Parliament Elects Kurd as President." *Jacksonville (NC) Daily News,* 7 April 2005.

Fam, Marion. Associated Press. "Iraq's Sunni President Backs January Elections." *Jacksonville (NC) Daily News,* 2 December 2004.

Fam, Marion. Associated Press. "Kurdish Ticket Pulls into Second." *Jacksonville (NC) Daily News,* 8 February 2004.

Fam, Marion. Associated Press. "Militants Again Strike at Abu Ghraib." *Jacksonville (NC) Daily News,* 5 April 2005.

Fam, Marion. Associated Press. "Terror Leader's Tape Sees Insurgent Victory." *Jacksonville (NC) Daily News,* 21 January 2005.

Fam, Marion. Associated Press. "Two Years Later, Protests Set for Baghdad Square." *Jacksonville (NC) Daily News,* 9 April 2005.

Fam, Marion. Associated Press. "Violence Claims More Than 40
    Lives in Iraq." *Jacksonville (NC) Daily News,* 11 February 2005.
Faraj, Murtada. Associated Press. "Car Bombs Kill 18 on Baghdad
    Street." *Jacksonville (NC) Daily News,* 15 April 2005.
Al-Fatlawi, Ali. Associated Press. "At Least 115 Die in Worst Attack
    Yet." *Jacksonville (NC) Daily News,* 1 March 2005.
Fayadh, Abbas. Associated Press. "British Troops Free Comrades Held
    in Iraqi Jail." *Jacksonville (NC) Daily News,* 20 September 2005.
Fayadh, Abbas. Associated Press. "Suicide Attacks Kill At Least 68."
    Jacksonville (NC) Daily News, 22 April 2004.
Fayadh, Abbas. Associated Press. "U.S. Reporter Critical of Basra Police
    Is Abducted and Killed." *Jacksonville (NC) Daily News,* 4 August
    2005.
"Followers of . . . al-Sadr Trickled into Police Stations." World News in
    Brief. *Christian Science Monitor,* 12 October 2004.
Ford, Peter. "A Suspect Emerges As Key Link in Terror Chain."
    Christian Science Monitor, 23 January 2004.
"Four Israeli Soldiers Die in Explosion." World Briefs Wire Reports (AP).
    Jacksonville (NC) Daily News, 13 December 2004.
Gall, Carlotta. "Afghan-Iranian Road Opens." *New York Times,*
    28 January 2005. From DoD Short Clips at ebird.dodmedia.osd.mil.
Gall, Carlotta. "Pakistan Allows Taliban to Train, a Detained Fighter
    Says." *New York Times,* 4 August 2004. As extracted from
    www.worldthreats.com.
Gambill, Gary C. and Ziad K. Abdelnour. "Hezbollah between Tehran
    and Damascus." *Middle East Intelligence Bulletin,* vol. 4, no. 2.,
    February 2002. From its website, www.meib.org.
Gambill, Gary C. "The Military-Intelligence Shakeup in Syria."
    Middle East Intelligence Bulletin, vol. 4, no. 2., February 2002.
    From its website, www.meib.org.
Gambill, Gary C. "Sponsoring Terrorism Syria and the PFLP-GC."
    Middle East Intelligence Bulletin, vol 4, no. 2, February 2002.
    From its website, www.meib.org.
Garwood, Paul. Associated Press. "7 Marines Are Killed in Anbar."
    Jacksonville (NC) Daily News, 13 December 2004.
Gertz, Bill. "Notes from the Pentagon." *Washington Times,* 5 March
    2004.
Gertz, Bill. "Yemen Hosts 4000 'Suspicious' Madrassahs Run by
    Extremists." *Geostrategy-Direct,* week of 22 February 2005.
Glanz, James. "The Conflict in Iraq." *New York Times,* 21 February
    2005.
Graham, Stephen. Associated Press. "Afghan Rebels Killed in Firefight."
    Jacksonville (NC) Daily News, 22 April 2005.
Graham, Stephen. Associated Press. "Afghans to Cast Votes Sept. 18
    for Parliament." *Jacksonville (NC) Daily News,* 21 March 2005.

Graham, Stephen. Associated Press. "Americans Aboard Afghanistan Copter Crash." *Jacksonville (NC) Daily News,* 7 April 2005.

Graham, Stephen. Associated Press. "4 Militants, 1 Afghan Soldier Killed in Border Clashes." *Jacksonville (NC) Daily News,* 25 April 2005.

Graham, Stephen. Associated Press. "Latest Assault Leaves 2 Brits, Afghan Interpreter Dead." *Jacksonville (NC) Daily News,* 6 May 2004.

Graham, Stephen. Associated Press. "U.S. Military Boosts Number of Troops Embedded in Afghan Military." *Jacksonville (NC) Daily News,* 21 February 2005.

Graham, Stephen. Associated Press. "U.S. Says 2000 Insurgents Threaten Afghan Election." *Jacksonville (NC) Daily News,* 1 October 2004.

Grier, Peter. "The Rising Economic Cost of the Iraqi War." *Christian Science Monitor,* 19 May 2004.

Grier, Peter and Faye Bowers. "After the Fallujah Fight, Then What." *Christian Science Monitor,* 10 November 2004.

Grier, Peter and Faye Bowers. "Iraqi Militants Raise Pitch of Attacks." *Christian Science Monitor,* 22 April 2004.

"Group Says Thousands Ready for Suicide Raids." Across the Region. *Daily Star* (Lebanon), 7 June 2004.

Hackworth, David H. "So-Called VIPs Jet-Setting at Taxpayer Expense." Liberty Sound Off. *Jacksonville (NC) Daily News,* 2 December 2004.

Hamzeh, A. Nizar. "Islamism in Lebanon: A Guide." *Middle East Quarterly,* vol. 1, no. 3, September 1997.

Hanley, Charles J. AP Special Correspondent. "Attackers Burn, Loot Army Supply Train in Iraq." *Jacksonville (NC) Daily News,* 1 November 2003.

Hanley, Charles J. AP Special Correspondent. "Dozens Killed in Wave of Blasts." *Jacksonville (NC) Daily News,* 28 October 2003.

"Harakat ul-Jihad-I-Islami (HUJI) entry." From Federation of American Scientists website, www.fas.org.

"Harakat-ul Mujahideen Al Alami (HMA) entry." Memorial Inst. for the Prevention of Terrorism (MIPT) Knowledge Base, U.S. Dept. of Homeland Security. From its website, www.tkb.org, 24 July 2005.

"Harakat ul-Mujahidin Reference Page." From www.military.com, 5 July 2004.

"Hardliner Wins Iranian Vote in Landslide." World Briefs Wire Reports (AP). *Jacksonville (NC) Daily News,* 25 June 2005.

"Harkat-ul Mujahideen Reincarnates as Jamiat-ul Ansar." As posted at pakistan-facts.com on 21 March 2003.

Harris, Edward. Associated Press. "Rebels Try to Escape Fallujah." *Jacksonville (NC) Daily News,* 12 November 2004.

Harris, Edward. Associated Press. "U.S. Military Guards Discover Escape Attempt at Camp Bucca." *AOL News,* 26 March 2005.

Harris, Ron. St. Louis Post-Dispatch. "5 Marines, Scores of Iraqis Die in Battle." *Jacksonville (NC) Daily News,* 18 April 2004.

Harris, Ron. St. Louis Post-Dispatch. "Marines Return to Violent City." *Jacksonville (NC) Daily News,* 19 April 2004.

Harthill, Lane. "Sifting Intelligence Tips from Vendettas in Afghanistan." *Christian Science Monitor,* 26 January 2005.

Haven, Paul. Associated Press. "Being No. 3 Leader in al-Qaida Is a Risky Job." *AOL News,* 6 May 2005.

"Hell in Hilla." *St. Louis Post Dispatch,* 1 March 2005.

Hendawi, Hamza. Associated Press. "Iraq Still in Turmoil after Regaining Sovereignty." *Jacksonville (NC) Daily News,* 26 June 2005.

Hendawi, Hamza. Associated Press. "Iraqis Begin Voting." *Jacksonville (NC) Daily News,* 30 January 2005.

Hendawi, Hamza. Associated Press. "Najaf Battle Grows." *Jacksonville (NC) Daily News,* 15 May 2004.

"Hezbollah." *Encyclopedia*, www.nationmaster.com, 5 July 2004.

"Hezbollah to Take New Role in Politics." World Briefs Wire Reports (AP). *Jacksonville (NC) Daily News,* 12 March 2005.

"Hizbullah Offers to Pay Up to Five Times More for Suicide Attacks." Middle East Report. *Geostrategy-Direct,* week of 22 February 2005. From its website.

"Hizbullah Suspected of Joining Sunni Insurgents." *Iraqi News,* 17 February 2005. From its website, www.iraqinews.com

"How Iraq's Election Will Work." Briefing. *Christian Science Monitor,* 28 January 2005.

"Hundreds of Russians Guarding Bushehr Reactor." *Geostrategy-Direct,* week of 8 March 2005. From its website.

"Hundreds of Thousands of People Turned Out for a Hizbullah Rally." World News in Brief. *Christian Science Monitor,* 14 March 2005.

Ibrahim, Waleed and Mussab Khairallah. Reuters. "Suicide Policeman Hits Iraq's Wolf Brigade HQ." *Yahoo! News,* 11 June 2005.

Imm, Jeffrey. "Some Bombs in Iraq Are Made in Iran, U.S. Says." *New York Times,* 6 August 2005.

Imran, Mohammed. "Jamaatul Furqan Leader Arrested. *Daily Times* (Pakistan), 20 October 2004. From its website, dailytimes.com.pk.

"In an Anti-Bush World, Key Backers." Global Views. *Christian Science Monitor,* 1 November 2004.

"In One of the Worst 24-Hour Periods for Terrorists in Iraq to Date." World News in Brief. *Christian Science Monitor,* 24 March 2005.

"Insurgent Attacks Continue 2 Years after the U.S. Invasion." *Los Angeles Times,* 20 March 2005.

"Intel. Estimates on Size of Insurgency Are All Over the Map." Focus on Counter-Insurgency. *Geostrategy-Direct,* week of 1 March 2005. From its website.

"Iran Increases Funding and Training for Suicide Bombings, Islamic Jihad Leader 2002." Special Dispatch Series. No. 387, 11 June 2002. Middle East Media Research Inst. From its website, www.memri.org.

"Iran Role in the Recent Uprising in Iraq." Special Dispatch No. 692, 9 April 2004. From Middle East Media Research Inst. Precise URL: http://www.memri.org/bin/opener_latest.cgi?ID=SD69204.

"Iran Shifting Its Attention . . . ." *New York Times,* 13 December 1991.

"Iranian Government Gives Backing to Bush." World Briefs Wire Reports (AP). *Jacksonville (NC) Daily News,* 20 October 2004.

"Iran's Intelligence Service Occupies Key Iraqi City." *Iran Watch,* 4 September 2005. From its website, with precise URL, www.iranfocus.com/modules/news/article.php?storyid=3600.

"Iraq Shiite Leaders Demand Islam Be the Source of Law." Agence France-Presse, 6 February 2005. From its website, afp.com.

"Iraqi Campaigning Has Begun." From Associated Press. *Jacksonville (NC) Daily News,* 16 December 2004.

"Iraqi Intelligence Service Chief Interviewed on Terrorism, Related Issues." *Al-Sharq Al-Awsat* (London), 5 January 2005. Telephone interview with Major General Muhammad Abdallah al-Shahwani, Director of Iraq's National Intelligence Service (in Baghdad), by Mu'idd Fayyad (in London) on 4 January 2005. FBIS translated text. "Iraqi Rebels Not Giving Up." From Associated Press. *Jacksonville (NC) Daily News,* 19 November 2004.

"Iraq's Most Feared Terror Chief Declared a Fierce War on Democracy." World News in Brief. *Christian Science Monitor,* 24 January 2005.

Al-Issawi, Tarek. Associated Press. "Suicide Bombers Strike Almost at Will in Iraq." *Jacksonville (NC) Daily News,* 19 March 2004.

Jaber, Hala. "Go Home Yanks, Says PM In Waiting." *London Sunday Times,* 23 January 2004. From DoD Short Clips at its website, ebird.dodmedia.osd.mil.

Jahn, George. "Iran May Be Stock-Piling High Tech Small Arms." From Associated Press, 25 March 2005. Through access@g2-forward.org.

"Jaish, Harkat Change Names: Report." From PTI (Pakistan). As posted at www.rediff.com on 12 March 2003.

Jaish e-Mohammed profile. *Global Security News & Reports.* Overseas Security Advisor Council. Fromits website, www.ds-osac.org.

Johnson, Scott and Melinda Liu. "The Enemy Spies." *Newsweek,* 27 June 2005.

Karam, Zeina. Associated Press. "Lebanese Take to the Streets; Pro-Syrian Government Quits." *Jacksonville (NC) Daily News,* 1 March 2005.

Karam, Zeina. Associated Press. "Lebanon Says It Has Arrested Country's Top Al-Qaida Operative in Bombing Plot." *Jacksonville (NC) Daily News,* 23 September 2004.

Karam, Zeina. Associated Press. "Momentum Swings toward Anti-Syrian Opposition." *Jacksonville (NC) Daily News,* 15 March 2005.

Kasem, Halima. "Brewing Power Struggle in Kabul." *Christian Science Monitor,* 17 October 2003.

Keath, Lee. Associated Press. "Chaos Grips Iraq." *Jacksonville (NC) Daily News,* 10 April 2004.

Keath, Lee. Associated Press. "Shiites Retreat in Najaf." *Jacksonville (NC) Daily News,* 13 April 2004.

Keyser, Jason. Associated Press. "Israel Bombs Syria." *Jacksonville (NC) Daily News,* 6 October 2003.

Khan, Ashraf. "Voters Reverse Islamists' Rise in Pakistani Politics." *Christian Science Monitor,* 6 September 2005.

Khan, Noor. Associated Press. "Afghan Cops Abducted by Taliban." *Jacksonville (NC) Daily News,* 19 June 2004.

Khan, Noor. Associated Press. "Four American Soldiers Hurt in Afghanistan Blast." *Jacksonville (NC) Daily News,* 14 June 2005.

Khan, Noor. Associated Press. "Seven Medical Center Workers Killed in Afghan Violence." *Jacksonville (NC) Daily News,* 16 June 2005.

Khan, Noor. Associated Press. "10 Afghan Soldiers Beheaded by Taliban." *Jacksonville (NC) Daily News,* 11 July 2005.

Krane, Jim. Associated Press. "Occupied, Not Subdued." *Jacksonville NC) Daily News,* 14 November 2004.

Krane, Jim. Associated Press. "U.S. Split on Foreign Involvement in Iraq." *Jacksonville (NC) Daily News,* 5 March 2004.

Kratovac, Katarina. Associated Press. "Marines Say Clearing Fallujah of Arms Hinders Civilian Return." *Jacksonville (NC) Daily News,* 25 November 2004.

Kratovac, Katarina. Associated Press. "U.S., Iraqi Units Take Back Police Stations." *Jacksonville (NC) Daily News,* 17 November 2004.

Kremmer, Janaki. Associated Press. "Australia Dips Toe Back into Afghan Effort." *Christian Science Monitor,* 22 July 2005.

Lafranchi, Howard. "Abductions in Iraq a Big Business." *Christian Science Monitor,* 15 September 2004.

Lafranchi, Howard. "Anti-Iran Sentiment Hardening Fast." *Christian Science Monitor,* 22 July 2002.

Lamont, Lt.Col. Robert W. "'Urban Warrior'—A View from North Vietnam." *Marine Corps Gazette,* April 1999.

Lasseter, Tom. Knight Ridder. "Iraqi Forces May Need Years of Preparation." *Jacksonville (NC) Daily News,* 28 August 2005.

Lasseter, Tom. Knight Ridder. "Marines Hunt Insurgents." *Jacksonville (NC) Daily News,* 6 August 2005.

Lekic, Slobodan. Associated Press. "Attacks Pick Up in Iraq."
    Jacksonville (NC) Daily News, 4 December 2004.
Lekic, Slobodan. Associated Press. "Attacks Target Troops, Police."
    Jacksonville (NC) Daily News, 12 December 2004.
Lekic, Slobodan. Associated Press. "15 Killed in Blast, Key Shiite
    Survives Assassination Try." *Jacksonville (NC) Daily News,*
    28 December 2004.
Lekic, Slobodan. Associated Press. "Truck Bomb Hits Italians at
    Iraq Base." *Jacksonville (NC) Daily News,* 13 November 2003.
Lekic, Slobodan. Associated Press. "20 Bodies Found Dumped in the
    Tigris near Baghdad." *Jacksonville (NC) Daily News,* 19 September
    2005.
Levitt, Matthew. "Sponsoring Terrorism Syria and Islamic Jihad."
    Washington, D.C.: The Washington Inst. for Near East Policy,
    n.d. As it appeared in *Middle East Intelligence Bulletin,* November-
    December 2003. From its website, www.meib.org.
Loof, Susanna. "Report: Drugs Threaten Afghanistan, Iraq." From
    Associated Press, 2 March 2005. Through access@g2-forward.org.
Lumpkin, John j. Associated Press. "Source: Top Terrorist Suspect
    Eluded U.S. Military." *Jacksonville (NC) Daily News,* 27 April 2005.
Lumpkin, John J. Associated Press. "U.S. Official: Iraqi Forces
    Infiltrated." *Jacksonville (NC) Daily News,* 22 October 2004.
MacDonald, Neil. "After Iraq Attacks, Calls for Militias Grow."
    Christian Science Monitor, 18 July 2005.
MacDonald, Neil. "Could Bigger Sunni Role Stop Attacks." *Christian
    Science Monitor,* 6 May 2005.
MacFarquhar, Neil. "Freed Captive Tells of Ordeal in Attack on
    Consulate in Jidda." *New York Times,* 8 December 2004. From
    its website.
MacFarquahar, Neil. "Hezbollah Becomes Potent Anti-U.S. Force."
    New York Times, 24 December 2002.
Mahmood, Tariq. AFP. "Hizbul Tahreer shout anti-US slogans." Picture
    caption. As posted at uk.news.yahoo.com on 29 October 2004.
Masland, Tom. "Jihad without Borders." *Newsweek,* 8 November 2004.
McDowell, Rick and Mary Trotochaud. "Humanitarian Aid Is a
    Casualty of Iraq." *Christian Science Monitor,* 23 November 2004.
McIlveen, Luke. "Bounty Hunters Target Diggers." *Sydney Sunday
    Telegraph,* 12 December 2004. Through access@g2-forward.org.
Meixler, Louis. Associated Press. "Extremists Send Recruits into Iraq
    via Iranian Border." *Jacksonville (NC) Daily News,* 8 November
    2004.
Michael, Maggie. Associated Press. "Al-Zarqawi Cell Owns Up to
    Killings." *Jacksonville (NC) Daily News,* 29 November 2004.
Michael, Maggie. Associated Press. "Iraq Sets Date for Election."
    Jacksonville (NC) Daily News, 22 November 2004.

Michael, Maggie. Associated Press. "Likely Leader Vows Moderation." *Jacksonville (NC) Daily News,* 16 February 2005.

Michael, Maggie. Associated Press. "Shiites to Vote on Chief." *Jacksonville (NC) Daily News,* 17 February 2005.

Michael, Maggie. Associated Press. "U.S. Raid Finds Links to Terrorist." *Jacksonville (NC) Daily News,* 19 November 2004.

"Militants Hold Off Killing Hostages." World Briefs Wire Reports (AP). *Jacksonville (NC) Daily News,* 8 November 2004.

"Militants Kill Five Afghans Involved in Opium Project." World News Wire Reports (AP). *Jacksonville (NC) Daily News,* 19 May 2005.

"Militants Target Israeli Army Outpost." From Associated Press. *USA Today,* 27 June 2004.

Mizban, Hadi. Associated Press. "Iraqi Forces Seek Insurgents in 'Triangle of Death'." *Jacksonville (NC) Daily News,* 19 April 2005.

Mohammed, Khalid. Associated Press. "Residents: Hostage-Taking a Hoax." *Jacksonville (NC) Daily News,* 18 April 2005.

Mroue, Bassem. Associated Press. "Amid Violence, Iraqi Democracy Nears Impasse." *Jacksonville (NC) Daily News,* 31 July 2005.

Mroue, Bassem. Associated Press. "Bomb Kills Former Lebanese Prime Minister, 10 Others." *Jacksonville (NC) Daily News,* 15 February 2005.

Mroue, Bassem. Associated Press. "Insurgents Launch Wave of Attacks." *Jacksonville (NC) Daily News,* 4 February 2005.

Mroue, Bassem. Associated Press. "Iraqis Ready to Control Some Cities." *Jacksonville (NC) Daily News,* 13 July 2005.

Mroue, Bassem. Associated Press. "Shi'ite Faction Eyes Prime Minister's Post." *Washington Times,* 3 February 2005. From DoD Short Clips at its website, ebird.dodmedia.osd.mil.

Mroue, Bassem and Abdul-Qader Saadi. Associated Press. "Fighting Spreads in Iraq." *Jacksonville (NC) Daily News,* 8 April 2004.

Mroue, Bassem and Abdul-Qader Saadi. Associated Press. "Marines Capture Militants." *Jacksonville (NC) Daily News,* 26 December 2004.

Murphy, Brian. Associated Press. "Tehran Mayor Wins Spot in Presidential Runoff." *Jacksonville (NC) Daily News,* 19 June 2005.

Murphy, Dan. "After Temporary Gains, Marines Leave Iraqi Cities." *Christian Science Monitor,* 3 March 2005.

Murphy, Dan. "High Stakes of Taking Fallujah." *Christian Science Monitor,* 8 November 2004.

Murphy, Dan. "In Iraq, a Clear-Cut bin Laden-Zarqawi Alliance." *Christian Science Monitor,* 30 December 2004.

Murphy, Dan. "In Iraq with 'Reservists That Fight'." *Christian Science Monitor,* 24 March 2005.

Murphy, Dan. "Iraq Bombs Hit Kurdish Leaders." *Christian Science Monitor,* 2 February 2004.

Murphy, Dan. "Iraqi Police Take Brunt of Attacks." *Christian Science Monitor,* 11 January 2005.

Murphy, Dan. "Iraqis Thirst for Water and Power." *Christian Science Monitor,* 11 August 2005.

Murphy, Dan. "Iraq's Critical Sistani Factor." *Christian Science Monitor,* 20 January 2005.

Murphy, Dan. "Iraq's Neighborhood Councils Are Vanishing." *Christian Science Monitor,* 25 February 2005.

Murphy, Dan. "No Wide Shiite Rally to Sadr's Forces." *Christian Science Monitor,* 7 April 2004.

Murphy, Dan. "Sadr Army Owns City Streets." *Christian Science Monitor,* 4 August 2004.

Murphy, Dan. "Second Front in Iraq: Shiite Revolt." *Christian Science Monitor,* 6 April 2004.

Murphy, Dan. "Shiite Islamists to Shape the New Iraq." *Christian Science Monitor,* 14 February 2005.

Murphy, Dan. "View Emerging of Shiite-Ruled Iraq." *Christian Science Monitor,* 7 February 2005.

Murphy, Dan. "Will Shiites Hold Their Fire." *Christian Science Monitor,* 22 December 2004.

Murphy, Dan and Jill Carroll. "A 'Pragmatic' Islamist for Iraq." *Christian Science Monitor,* 17 February 2005.

Murphy, Dan and Jill Carroll. "Thorny Issues for Iraq Leaders." *Christian Science Monitor,* 8 April 2005.

Murphy, Dan and Joshua Mitnick. "In Mideast Elections, Militants Gain." *Christian Science Monitor,* 8 June 2005.

Musharraf, President General. "Speech at OIC Conference." *World Report.* CNN, 31 May 2005.

"Najib Mikati Accepted an Appointment as Prime Minister." World News Wire Briefs. *Christian Science Monitor,* 19 April 2005.

"NATO Force Could Patrol Afghanistan." From Associated Press. *Jacksonville (NC) Daily News,* 5 August 2005.

"The 9/11 Commission Report: The Terrorist Plot." *Los Angeles Times,* 23 July 2004.

"Nobody Lingers in 'RPG Alley'." From Associated Press. *Jacksonville (NC) Daily News,* 2 December 2004.

Nordland, Rod. "Free to Be Angry." *Newsweek,* 31 January 2005.

Nordland, Rod. "Just a Little Longer." *Newsweek,* 2 May 2005.

Nordland, Rod and Babak Dehghanpisheh. "What Sistani Wants." *Newsweek,* 14 February 2005.

Nordland, Rod and Christopher Dickey. "Hunting Zarqawi." *Newsweek,* 1 November 2004.

Nordland, Rod and Christopher Dickey. "Tribe Versus Tribe." *Newsweek,* 24 January 2005.

Nordland, Rod, Tom Masland, and Christopher Dickey. "Unmasking the Insurgents." *Newsweek,* 7 February 2005.

North, Andrew. "Stung in an Afghan 'Hornets' Nest.'" BBC News, July 2005.

Al-Obeidi, Abdul Hussein. Associated Press. "Car Bombs Hit Najaf, Karbala." *Jacksonville (NC) Daily News,* 20 December 2004.

Al-Obeidi, Abdul Hussein. Associated Press. "Holy City Najaf Fighting Worst Since Saddam Fell." *Jacksonville (NC) Daily News,* 7 August 2004.

Al-Obeidi, Abdul Hussein. Associated Press. "Iraqi Shiites Stage Anti-American Rallies." *Jacksonville (NC) Daily News,* 21 May 2005.

Al-Obeidi, Abdul Hussein. Associated Press. "Mosque Turnover Disputed." *Jacksonville (NC) Daily News,* 21 August 2004.

Al-Obeidi, Abdul Hussein. Associated Press. "U.S. Increases Pressure on Najaf." *Jacksonville (NC) Daily News,* 24 August 2004.

"Pakistani Visa Instructions." As acquired at the Embassy of Pakistan in Washington, D.C., on October 2004. From its website, www.embassyofpakistan.org.

Pennington, Matthew. Associated Press. "Pakistan Unsure If Target Is al-Zawahri." *Jacksonville (NC) Daily News,* 21 March 2004.

Peters, Gretchen and Aleem Agha. "Weary Taliban Coming In from the Cold." *Christian Science Monitor,* 14 December 2004.

Peterson, Scott. "As Reformer Exits, Who Will Lead Iran?" *Christian Science Monitor,* 17 June 2005.

Peterson, Scott. "Economic Fallout of $50 a Barrel." *Christian Science Monitor,* 27 August 2004.

Peterson, Scott. "Fallujans Flee from US, Zarqawi Fight." *Christian Science Monitor,* 19 October 2004.

Peterson, Scott. "Familiar Face Emerges in Iran Vote." *Christian Science Monitor,* 26 April 2005.

Peterson, Scott. "For Iraq's Insurgents, What Next?" *Christian Science Monitor,* 1 February 2005. From its website, www.csmonitor.com.

Peterson, Scott. "Hostile in Public, Iran Seeks Quiet Discourse with U.S." *Christian Science Monitor,* 25 September 2003.

Peterson, Scott. "Iran Flexes Its 'Soft Power' in Iraq." *Christian Science Monitor,* 20 May 2005.

Peterson, Scott. "Iran Votes Hard-Liner into Runoff." *Christian Science Monitor,* 20 June 2005.

Peterson, Scott. "Iraq Starts Battle over Constitution." *Christian Science Monitor,* 16 May 2005.

Peterson, Scott. "Iraqi Christians Struggle to Stay." *Christian Science Monitor,* 18 October 2004.

Peterson, Scott. "Iraqis Crowd the Polls." *Christian Science Monitor,* 31 January 2005.

Peterson, Scott. "Iraq's Religious Factions Make Calls for Restraint." *Christian Science Monitor,* 23 May 2005.

Peterson, Scott. "Marine, Insurgent Tactics Evolve." *Christian Science Monitor,* 17 November 2004.

Peterson, Scott. "New Rebel Tactics Emerge in Fallujah." *Christian Science Monitor,* 12 November 2004.

Peterson, Scott. "Rebels Return to 'Cleared' Areas." *Christian Science Monitor,* 3 December 2004.

Peterson, Scott. "Shadows of Tehran over Iraq." *Christian Science Monitor,* 19 April 2004.

Peterson, Scott. "Signs of Progress amid Turmoil in Iraq." *Christian Science Monitor,* 15 October 2004.

Peterson, Scott. "U.S. Forces Pour into Iraqi City." *Christian Science Monitor,* 10 November 2004.

Peterson, Scott. "U.S. Heading into Major Urban Assault." *Christian Science Monitor,* 8 November 2004.

Peterson, Scott. "U.S. Pressure on Cleric Pushes Militants South." *Christian Science Monitor,* 10 May 2004.

Peterson, Scott. "U.S. Smooths Way in Fallujah for Muslim Relief Agency." *Christian Science Monitor,* 29 November 2004.

Pitman, Todd. Associated Press. "Jets Target Rebels." *Jacksonville (NC) Daily News,* 1 July 2004.

Pitman, Todd. Associated Press. "U.S. Warplanes Bomb Suspected Terror Den." *Jacksonville (NC) Daily News,* 2 July 2004.

"Pragmatist Throws His Hat in the Ring." From Reuters. *Christian Science Monitor,* 11 May 2005.

Priest, Dana and Robin Wright. "Scowcroft Skeptical Vote Will Stabilize Iraq." *Washington Post,* 7 January 2005. From its website.

Quinn, Patrick. Associated Press. "AP Study: Iraqi Car Bombings Have Risen in Last Two Months." *Jacksonville (NC) Daily News,* 24 June 2005.

Quinn, Patrick. Associated Press. "Body of Reporter Found in Iraqi City." *Jacksonville (NC) Daily News,* 27 February 2005.

Quinn, Patrick. Associated Press. "Insurgents Kill 5 Marines in Western Iraq." *Jacksonville (NC) Daily News,* 11 June 2005.

Quinn, Patrick. Associated Press. "Iraqi Leader Wants to Keep Job." *Jacksonville (NC) Daily News,* 24 February 2005.

Quinn, Patrick. Associated Press. "Iraqi Legislators Are Sworn In." *Jacksonville (NC) Daily News,* 17 March 2005.

Rageh, Rawya. Associated Press. "Bloodshed Goes On As Iraq War Enters 3rd Year." *Jacksonville (NC) Daily News,* 21 March 2004.

Rageh, Rawya. Associated Press. "Iraqi Prime Minister Blames Coalition for Ambush." *Jacksonville (NC) Daily News,* 27 October 2004.

Rana, Amir. "Taliban Will Rise Again, Says Cleric." *Daily Times* (Pakistan), 11 May 2003. From its website, dailytimes.com.pk.

Rashid, Ahmed. "Pakistan, the Taliban and the US." Feature Story. *The Nation* (Lahore), 8 October 2001.

Ratnesar, Romesh. "Can This War Be Won?" *Time*, 4 October 2004.

Reid, Robert H. Associated Press. "At Least 26 Die in Iraqi Suicide Bombings." *Jacksonville (NC) Daily News*, 3 July 2005.

Reid, Robert H. Associated Press. "Bomb Kills 54 in Iraq." *Jacksonville (NC) Daily News*, 17 July 2005.

Reid, Robert H. Associated Press. "Bombings Target Troops." *Jacksonville (NC) Daily News*, 16 November 2004.

Reid, Robert H. Associated Press. "Deadly Month inside Iraq." *Jacksonville (NC) Daily News*, 30 November 2004.

Reid, Robert H. Associated Press. "Hostage Aide Chief Pleading for Her Life." *Jacksonville (NC) Daily News*, 23 October 2004.

Reid, Robert H. Associated Press. "Insurgent Violence Sweeps across Baghdad." *Jacksonville (NC) Daily News*, 21 November 2004.

Reid, Robert H. Associated Press. "Insurgents Kill 50 Iraqi Troops in Bold Ambush." *Jacksonville (NC) Daily News*, 25 October 2004.

Reid, Robert H. Associated Press. "Marines Continue Assault." *Jacksonville (NC) Daily News*, 16 October 2004.

Reid, Robert H. Associated Press. "Officials Rejecting Vote Delay for Iraqis." *Jacksonville (NC) Daily News*, 28 November 2004.

Reid, Robert H. Associated Press. "Rebels Cornered in City." *Jacksonville (NC) Daily News*, 13 November 2004.

Reid, Robert H. Associated Press. "Rebels Spread Attacks." *Jacksonville (NC) Daily News*, 7 November 2004.

Reid, Robert H. and Jim Krane. Associated Press. "Bombs Biggest Killer for U.S. in Iraq." *Jacksonville (NC) Daily News*, 7 August 2005.

"Report Al Qaeda members in Lebanon." From Associated Press. As posted by Middle East Media Research Inst. in September 2002. At its website, www.memri.org.

Rice-Oxley, Mark and Owais Tohid. "British Keep a Wary Eye on Pakistan." *Christian Science Monitor*, 27 July 2005.

Ricks, Thomas E. "For Zinni, a War That Ignores the Facts." *Washington Post*, nat. weekly ed., 12-18 January 2004.

Ricks, Thomas E. "U.S. Iraq Rebels Aided by Sources in Syria." *Washington Post*, 8 December 2004.

Rohde, David and C.J. Chivers. "Al Qaeda's Grocery Lists and Manuals of Killing." The Jihad Files. *New York Times*, 17 March 2002.

Rubin, Michael. "Ansar al-Sunna: Iraq's New Terrorist Threat." *Middle East Intelligence Bulletin*, vol. 6, no. 5, May 2004. From its website, www.meib.org.

Sadeq, Musadeq. Associated Press. "Angry Afghans Riot Following Reports that Gitmo Interrogators Desecrated Quran." *Jacksonville (NC) Daily News,* 12 May 2005.

Samander, Rahimullah and Rahim Gul Sarwan. "Concern That Jihad Chieftains Will Set Political Agenda." Inst. for War and Peace Reporting. ARR No. 88, 18 December 2003. As extracted from www.geocities.com.

Scarborough, Rowan. "Israeli Warns of Terrorist Training Nov 03." *Washington Times,* 14 November 2003. From its website.

Schweid, Barry. Associated Press. "Explosions Pierce U.S. Safeguards in Baghdad." *Jacksonville (NC) Daily News,* 15 October 2004.

"76 Militants Die in Afghan Battles." World Brief Wire Reports (AP). *Jacksonville (NC) Daily News,* 23 June 2004.

Shah, Amir. Associated Press. "Afghans Stone U.S. Base Gate." *Jacksonville (NC) Daily News,* 27 July 2005.

Shah, Amir. Associated Press. "Bombing Kills 9 Afghan Soldiers." *Jacksonville (NC) Daily News,* 29 September 2005.

Shahzad, Syed Saleem. "The Remaking of al-Qaeda." *Asia Times Online,* 25 February 2005.

"Shiites March throughout Middle East." From Associated Press. *Jacksonville (NC) Daily News,* 22 May 2004.

"Shiite Radicals Join with Sunni Insurgents in Ramadi." *DEBKAfile* (Israel), 7 April 2004.

Shipunov, Arkady and Gennady Filimonov. "Field Artillery to be Replaced with Shmel Infantry Flamethrower." *Military Parade* (Moscow), Issue 29, September 1998. From its website, www.milparade.com/security.

Shrader, Katherine and John Solomon. Associated Press. "Iran May Be Hiding Terrorist Figures." *Jacksonville (NC) Daily News,* 4 June 2005.

Silberberg, Jacob. Associated Press. "Iraqi, U.S. Troops Hit Insurgent Stronghold." *Jacksonville (NC) Daily News,* 11 September 2005.

Silberberg, Jacob. Associated Press. "Militants Flee Tal Afar in Wake of U.S.-Iraqi Offensive." *Jacksonville (NC) Daily News,* 12 September 2005.

"Six Afghans Die in Rebel Ambush." World News Wire Reports (AP). *Jacksonville (NC) Daily News,* 20 May 2005.

Slavin, Barbara. "Iran Helped Overthrow Taliban, Candidate Says." *USA Today,* 10 June 2005.

Smith, Tanalee. Associated Press. "Hezbollah Flexes Its Muscle in Syrian Protest. *Jacksonville (NC) Daily News,* 9 March 2005.

Stalinsky, Steven. "Arab and Muslim Fighters in Iraq." An excerpt from *Al-Nahar* (Lebanon) of 1 April 2003. In No. 19, 27 July 2003. By Middle East Media Research Inst. At its website, www.memri.org.

Steinkopff, Eric. "MEU Goes After Weapons." *Jacksonville (NC) Daily News,* 8 December 2004.

Stojanovic, Dusan. Associated Press. "Allawi: Sunni Insurgents Trying to Foment Civil War." *Jacksonville (NC) Daily News,* 21 December 2004.

Stojanovic, Dusan. Associated Press. "Car Bombings Kill 25 in Iraq." *Jacksonville (NC) Daily News,* 6 January 2005.

Stojanovic, Dusan. Associated Press. "Rebels Spread Attacks." *Jacksonville (NC) Daily News,* 29 December 2004.

"Sudan Claims Zarqawi behind Migration of Al Qaida Cells." Middle East Report. *Geostrategy-Direct,* week of 29 March 2005. From its website.

"Suicide Bomber Kills 5 in Iraq." From Associated Press. *Jacksonville (NC) Daily News,* 1 April 2005.

"Suicide Bomber Kills Peacekeeper, Civilian in Afghan Capital." World Briefs Wire Reports (AP). *Jacksonville (NC) Daily News,* 28 January 2004.

"Suicide Bomber Kills 20 in Afghan Mosque Attack." World Briefs Wire Reports (AP). *Jacksonville (NC) Daily News,* 2 June 2005.

"Suicide Bombing Is A Crime against Humanity." Israel advocacy group, "StandwithUs." At its website, www.standwithus.com.

"Syrian Agents Trained Iraqi-Bound Insurgents in Asymmetrical Warfare." *Geostrategy-Direct,* week of 8 March 2005. From its website.

Al-Taee, Awadh and Steve Negus. "Cynicism Hits The Thirst For Iraq's Elections." *London Financial Times,* 22 January 2005. From DoD Short Clips at its website, ebird.dodmedia.osd.mil.

El-Tablawy, Tarik. Associated Press. "Top Shiite Cleric Backing Iraqi Constitution." *Jacksonville (NC) Daily News,* 23 September 2005.

"Taliban Blamed for Deadly Afghan Resistance." World Briefs Wire Reports (AP). *Jacksonville (NC) Daily News,* 24 September 2003.

Tarabay, Jamie. Associated Press. "Blast Kills Dozens in Iraq." *Jacksonville (NC) Daily News,* 19 February 2005.

Tarabay, Jamie. Associated Press. "Insurgents Use Human Bombs." *Jacksonville (NC) Daily News,* 9 February 2005.

"Tens of Thousands of Supporters of Militant Shiite Cleric . . ." World News in Brief. *Christian Science Monitor,* 11 April 2005.

"Terrorists in Iraq Killed At Least 68 More People." World News in Brief. *Christian Science Monitor,* 6 December 2004.

"Terrorists Struck Close to Iraq's Highest Ranking Muslim Cleric." World News in Brief. *Christian Science Monitor,* 14 January 2005.

Theyson, Art. "New Warfront Opens in Iraq Three Months before Handover." *DEBKAfile* (Israel), 5 April 2004.

"Three Aid Workers Slain in Southern Afghanistan." News Brief Wire Reports (AP). *Jacksonville (NC) Daily News,* 29 November 2004.

Tohid, Owais. "Baloch Nationalism Rises As Pakistan Fights War on Terror." *Christian Science Monitor,* 26 January 2005.

Tohid, Owais. "Next Wave of Al Qaeda Leadership." *Christian Science Monitor,* 5 October 2004.

Tohid, Owais. "'Talibanization' Fears in Pakistan." *Christian Science Monitor,* 13 April 2005.

"Top Iranian Defector On Iran's Collaboration with Iraq, North Korea, Al-Qa'ida, and Hizbullah." Special Dispatch No. 473, 21 February 2003. Iran Jihad and Terrorism Studies. From Middle East Media Research Inst. Precise URL: http://www.memri.org/bin/opener_latest.cgi?ID=SD47303

Tran, Tini. Associated Press. "Car Bomber, Troop Clashes Kill 27 in Iraq." *Jacksonville (NC) Daily News,* 18 November 2004.

Tran, Tini. Associated Press. "Insurgents Hit Mosul Police Stations." *Jacksonville (NC) Daily News,* 15 November 2004.

Tran, Tini. Associated Press. "Marines, Iraqis Launch Offensive." *Jacksonville (NC) Daily News,* 24 November 2004.

Tran, Tini. Associated Press. "Tape Targets Clerics." *Jacksonville (NC) Daily News,* 25 November 2004.

"A Troublemaker Surrounded." *The Economist,* 2 October 2004.

"Two Insurgents Killed in Afghanistan Fight." World Briefs Wire Reports (AP). *Jacksonville (NC) Daily News,* 25 May 2005.

Tyson, Ann Scott. "Sadr's Militia Regrouping, Rearming." *Christian Science Monitor,* 15 July 2004.

U.S. Congressional Testimony. In "Iran Continues Support of Terrorism." *Iran News* (VOA), 17 February 2005. Through access@g2-forward.org.

"U.S., Iraq Say They're Closing on al-Zarqawi." From Associated Press. *Jacksonville (NC) Daily News,* 7 May 2005.

"U.S. Rejects Pullback by Syria As Not Enough." World Briefs Wire Reports (AP). *Jacksonville (NC) Daily News,* 8 March 2005.

"U.S. Soldier, 7 Militants Die in Afghan Firefight." World Briefs Wire Reports (AP). *Jacksonville (NC) Daily News,* 11 June 2005.

Varma, K.J.M. "PoK Also Banns Jihadi Outfits." From PTI (Pakistan). As posted at www.rediff.com on 5 December 2003.

Vincent, Steven. "Shiites Bring Rigid Piety to Iraq's South." *Christian Science Monitor,* 13 July 2005.

Vincent, Steven. "Switched Off in Basra." *New York Times,* 31 July 2005.

Yacoub, Sameer N. Associated Press. "Iraqi Leaders Try to End Impasse." *Jacksonville (NC) Daily News,* 26 April 2005.

Yacoub, Sameer N. Associated Press. "Suicide Bomber Hits Shiite Party Offices." *Jacksonville (NC) Daily News,* 19 January 2005.

Wadhams, Nick. Associated Press. "Cleric Leads List of Shi'ite Candidates." *Washington Times,* 11 December 2004. Through access@g2-forward.org.

Wadhams, Nick. Associated Press. "Fallujah Fighting Is Heavy." *Jacksonville (NC) Daily News,* 24 December 2004.

Wadhams, Nick. Associated Press. "Insurgents Blow Up Police Station." *Jacksonville (NC) Daily News,* 9 December 2004.

Wadhams, Nick. Associated Press. "Insurgents Slay 17 Iraqi Civilians." *Jacksonville (NC) Daily News,* 6 December 2004.

Wadhams, Nick. Associated Press. "Iraq Insurgents Increase Explosives' Power." Through access@g2-forward.org on 10 January 2005.

Wadhams, Nick. Associated Press. "Iraqi Forces Hit Hard." *Jacksonville (NC) Daily News,* 3 January 2005.

Wadhams, Nick. Associated Press. "Rebels Drop Mortar Shells on Baghdad." *Jacksonville (NC) Daily News,* 3 December 2004.

Wagner, Thomas. Associated Press. "Insurgent Attacks Kill 7 American Troops in Iraq." *Jacksonville (NC) Daily News,* 9 May 2005.

Wagner, Thomas. Associated Press. "Iraq Insurgents Launch Series of Bombings." *Jacksonville (NC) Daily News,* 30 April 2005.

Wagner, Thomas. Associated Press. "Iraqi Leaders Try for an 11th Hour Political Deal." *Jacksonville (NC) Daily News,* 3 May 2005.

Wagner, Thomas. Associated Press. "Iraqis Rally against 'British Aggression'." *Jacksonville (NC) Daily News,* 22 September 2005.

Wagner, Thomas. Associated Press. "Iraq's Parliament Wants Apology." *Jacksonville (NC) Daily News,* 20 April 2005.

Wallace, Scott. "The Many Faces of Moslem Countries." *Christian Science Monitor,* 17 March 2005.

Ware, Michael. "Inside Iran's Secret War for Iraq." *Time,* 22 August 2005. From its website, www.time.com.

Wright, Robin and Peter Baker. "Iraq, Jordan See Threat To Election from Iran." *Washington Post,* 8 December 2004.

Yacoub, Sameer N. Associated Press. "Car Bombs in Baghdad, Mosul Kill 14." *Jacksonville (NC) Daily News,* 5 December 2004.

Yacoub, Sameer N. Associated Press. "Iraqi Leaders Try to End Impasse." *Jacksonville (NC) Daily News,* 26 April 2005.

Yacoub, Sameer N. Associated Press. "Suicide Car Bomber Kills at Least 22 People." *Jacksonville (NC) Daily News,* 25 July 2005.

Yacoub, Sameer N. Associated Press. "Suicide Bomber Hits Shiite Party Offices." *Jacksonville (NC) Daily News,* 19 January 2005.

Yousafzai, Sami and Ron Moreau. "Rumors of bin Laden's Lair." *Newsweek,* 8 September 2003.

Zavis, Alexandra. Associated Press. "Another Day of Bombings, Firefights in Iraq." *Jacksonville (NC) Daily News,* 12 May 2005.

Zavis, Alexandra. Associated Press. "Bombers Penetrate Security." *Jacksonville (NC) Daily News,* 15 October 2004.

Zavis, Alexandra. Associated Press. "Iraqi Leaders Have Formed Government." *Jacksonville (NC) Daily News,* 29 April 2005.

Zavis, Alexandra. Associated Press. "Suicide Bombers Strike in Central Baghdad." *Jacksonville (NC) Daily News,* 8 May 2005.

Al-Zawahiri. As quoted in "Al Qaeda to West: It's about Policies," by Dan Murphy. *Christian Science Monitor,* 5 August 2005.

About the Author

After almost 28 years of commissioned and noncommissioned infantry service, John Poole retired from the United States Marine Corps in April 1993. While on active duty, he studied small-unit tactics for nine years: (1) six months at the Basic School in Quantico (1966), (2) seven months as a rifle platoon commander in Vietnam (1966-67), (3) three months as a rifle company commander at Camp Pendleton (1967), (4) five months as a regimental headquarters company (and camp) commander in Vietnam (1968), (5) eight months as a rifle company commander in Vietnam (1968-69), (6) five and a half years as an instructor with the Advanced Infantry Training Company (AITC) at Camp Lejeune (1986-92), and (7) one year as the SNCOIC of the 3rd Marine Division Combat Squad Leaders Course (CSLC) on Okinawa (1992-93).

While at AITC, he developed, taught, and refined courses on maneuver warfare, land navigation, fire support coordination, call for fire, adjust fire, close air support, M203 grenade launcher, movement to contact, daylight attack, night attack, infiltration, defense, offensive Military Operations in Urban Terrain (MOUT), defensive MOUT, Nuclear/Biological/Chemical (NBC) defense, and leadership. While at CSLC, he further refined the same periods of instruction and developed others on patrolling.

He has completed all of the correspondence school requirements for the Marine Corps Command and Staff College, Naval War College (1,000-hour curriculum), and Marine Corps Warfighting Skills Program. He is a graduate of the Camp Lejeune Instructional Management Course, the 2nd Marine Division Skill Leaders in Advanced Marksmanship (SLAM) Course, and the East-Coast School of Infantry Platoon Sergeants' Course.

In the 12 years since retirement, John Poole has heavily researched the small-unit tactics of other nations and written five other books: (1) *The Last Hundred Yards: The NCO's Contribution to Warfare,* a squad combat study based on the consensus opinions of 1,200 NCOs and casualty statistics of AITC and CSLC field trials; (2) *One More Bridge to Cross: Lowering the Cost of War,* a treatise on enemy proficiency at short range and how to match it; (3) *Phantom Soldier: The Enemy's Answer to U.S. Firepower,* an in-depth look at the highly deceptive Asian style of war; (4) *The Tiger's Way: A U.S. Private's Best Chance of Survival,* a study of how Eastern fire teams and individual soldiers fight; and (5) *Tactics of the*

Crescent Moon: Militant Muslim Combat Methods, a comprehensive analysis of the insurgents' battlefield procedures in Palestine, Chechnya, Afghanistan, and Iraq.

As of September 2005, John Poole had conducted multiday training sessions (on how to practice 4th-generation warfare at the small-unit level) for 37 Marine battalions, nine Marine schools, and five Army or Navy special-operations units. He has been stationed twice each in South Vietnam and Okinawa. He has visited Japan, Taiwan, the Philippines, Indonesia, South Korea, Mainland China, Hong Kong, Macao, North Vietnam, Myanmar (Burma), Thailand, Cambodia, Malaysia, Singapore, Tibet, Nepal, Bangladesh, India, Pakistan, Russia, East Germany, West Germany, Morocco, Israel (to include the West Bank), Turkey, Iran, and Lebanon.

Name Index